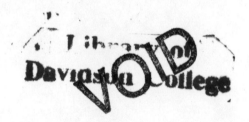

Library of
Davidson College

VOID

D1452939

Library of
Davidson College

A World Transformed

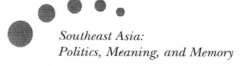

Southeast Asia:
Politics, Meaning, and Memory

Seeking to raise the visibility of Southeast Asia
in scholarly circles and among general readers, the
broad scope of this series covers history (memory) and
culture (meanings), especially when these topics also
elucidate issues of power (politics).

COEDITORS: DAVID CHANDLER AND RITA SMITH KIPP

KIM N. B. NINH
A World Transformed: The Politics of Culture in
Revolutionary Vietnam, 1945–1965

PETER ZINOMAN, EDITOR
Dumb Luck: A Novel by Vũ Trọng Phụng

M. CAMERON HAY
Remembering to Live: Illness at the Intersection of
Anxiety and Knowledge in Rural Indonesia

HEATHER L. CLAUSSEN
Unconventional Sisterhood: Feminist Catholic
Nuns in the Philippines

959.704
N714w

A World Transformed

The Politics of Culture in
Revolutionary Vietnam,
1945–1965

—•—

Kim N. B. Ninh

Ann Arbor

THE UNIVERSITY OF MICHIGAN PRESS

0492258821

Copyright © by the University of Michigan 2002
All rights reserved
Published in the United States of America by
The University of Michigan Press
Manufactured in the United States of America
♾ Printed on acid-free paper

2005   4 3 2

No part of this publication may be reproduced,
stored in a retrieval system, or transmitted in any form
or by any means, electronic, mechanical, or otherwise,
without the written permission of the publisher.

A CIP catalog record for this book is available from the British Library.

Library of Congress Cataloging-in-Publication Data

Ninh, Kim Ngoc Bao.
A world transformed : the politics of culture in revolutionary
Vietnam, 1945–1965 / Kim N.B. Ninh.
p.   cm.
Includes bibliographical references and index.
ISBN 0-472-09799-7 (cloth : alk. paper) —
ISBN 0-472-06799-0 (pbk. : alk. paper)
1. Vietnam—Politics and government—1945–1975.
2. Vietnam—Cultural policy.   I. Title.

DS556.8 .N56   2002
959.704'3—dc21   2002022501

To my parents,
Ninh Ngọc Hải and Nguyễn Kim Dung

As in other spheres, the task of construction in the cultural arena has to begin with destruction: for a new culture to develop, it needs a cleared piece of land that contains no vestiges of feudalism or colonialism. The first task, therefore, is to completely eradicate the poisonous venom of the feudalists and colonialists.

On one front, the government will resolutely suppress the disloyal culturalists and confiscate and nationalize the cultural organs belonging to the imperialists and the Vietnamese traitors.

On another front, the government will generate a great propaganda effort to disclose the terrible consequences of the degenerate feudalist and cruel imperialist cultural policies and also to support the new cultural policy of the independent Vietnamese government.

On yet another front, to the best of its ability, the government will immediately abolish the customs and habits that directly hinder the critical work of the construction of the nation-state.

Those decisive acts of destruction will naturally displease some people, especially those who are slaves to the old regime. They will raise their voices to criticize [us]: "There, those revolutionaries, those who destroy." But what we do will refute those slanders brilliantly because construction on the cultural revolution front will be much more important than destruction, as on other fronts of the revolution. No! Revolution is not only destruction. Revolution is also building, revolutionary primarily in the act of building, and building the grand plans that cannot materialize under antiprogress regimes.

Nguyễn Hữu Đang and Nguyễn Đình Thi
Một nền văn hóa mới (A new culture)
Hanoi, 25 November 1945

Contents

PART I
From the August Revolution to Điện Biên Phủ, 1945–54

PART II
The Construction of a Socialist State, 1954–65

Appendixes

Tables

Preface

The seed for this book was sown with my first visit to Vietnam in 1989. I did not have a concrete research topic in mind and in fact was not even sure that research was possible in Vietnam at that time. Fortunately I was spending a year at the Institute of Southeast Asian Studies in Singapore, which was interested in establishing a research component on Indochina and was making contacts with Vietnamese scholars and institutions. It was via this connection that I obtained the necessary invitation for a brief visit under the auspices of the Institute of Southeast Asian Studies in Hanoi.

It was a defining experience to be in the midst of a Hanoi that outwardly seemed to have stood still, singularly captured by its own quiet rhythm. The initial reservation of the people I met gave way, however, to passionate conversations in offices and homes about history, life, missed opportunities, and transformative experiences. I was overwhelmed by the sense that stories needed to be told, the frankness of the discussion, and the intensity of the intellectual exchange. There was so much going on underneath the surface that I could not comprehend and was not informed enough to even begin asking questions, although the sense of excitement was infectious. Young writers whose names I was hearing for the first time were making waves. Books and articles were read and discussed in detail. Scholars were keen to establish contacts with their peers regionally and internationally. It was the beginning of a period in which the intellectual community became very active in discussing a wide range of political, economic, and social issues as Vietnam turned toward a more open policy.

History, though, cast a long shadow, and I set out to return to Vietnam for an extended period to better understand the context in which these issues were first defined and how that, in turn, has affected the shape of the current intellectual discourse. The exciting intellectual environment that I discovered in 1989 was in full flower while I lived in Hanoi between 1991 and 1993. This book is the result of my interactions with many people in formal interviews and informal conversations, of the voracious consumption of a large number of Vietnamese-language books that became available during this period, and of archival research. I had the data, but I can honestly say that it took some time before they coalesced into some measure of coherence.

This book could not have been realized without the assistance of many individuals and institutions. In particular, James Scott has offered much needed intellectual and spiritual support over the years. New Haven was more bearable whenever he was around, though Kay Mansfield's warm presence provided the center toward which many of us gravitated. Chalmers Johnson, who first suggested that I focus on Vietnam, has been a steady source of encouragement since my Berkeley days. The list of those who have read all or parts of various drafts of this book is long, and they have contributed substantially to sharpening its content. I would like to thank James Scott, Chalmers Johnson, Ben Kiernan, Yitzhak Brudny, Ben Kerkvliet, David Marr, Terry Rambo, and Muthiah Alagappa. I am also grateful for the careful reading of and helpful comments on the manuscript by David P. Chandler, Rita Smith Kipp, and an anonymous reader for the University of Michigan Press.

Crucial financial support came from a number of sources. A preliminary field research grant was provided by the Yale Council on Southeast Asian Studies. Funding for the actual field research came from the Social Science Research Council, the Institute for the Study of World Politics, and the Yale Center for International and Area Studies. The writing phase was funded by a Yale University Dissertation Fellowship and a Pre-doctoral Fellowship from the East-West Center. Finally, I am grateful to have received a Luce Post-doctoral Fellowship at the Australian National University, which made possible the necessary revisions. Exposure to the wide-ranging research projects of many has certainly added depth to my own work. In particular, Ben Kerkvliet and David Marr have fostered a truly supportive intellectual environment, which was augmented immeasurably by the generous hospitality of Ben and Melinda Kerkvliet. A leave of absence graciously provided by the Asia Foundation is also happily acknowledged.

In Vietnam, the Center for Cooperative Research (Trung Tâm Hợp Tác Nghiên Cứu) of the University of Hanoi, under the capable leadership of Professor Phan Huy Lê, facilitated all the necessary logistics and paperwork while Nguyễn Văn Khánh efficiently arranged interviews for me. Members of the professional staff at the National Archives also went out of their way to help me find relevant documents. This book could never have been written, however, without the insights gained during the exhilarating hours spent in the company of those who generously shared with me their experiences and thoughts. With immense gratitude and affection, I thank especially *chú* Hoàng Cầm, *chú* Trần Độ, *anh* Lại Nguyễn Ân, *anh* Ngô Thảo and family, and *cô chú* Văn Tâm among many others. It is likely that they will not recognize in this book what they shared with me, and I take sole responsibility for its content.

Doing fieldwork in an environment in which one has relatives was both a curse and a blessing. They never quite understood my sorry excuse of being too busy with work to visit the most distant of relations or attend countless family gatherings. On the other hand, my relatives have added much to my understanding of life in Vietnam. I treasure the time spent not only with my uncle Lê Văn Chung and his family but the uproarious and yet gentle company of the regular clients of their small neighborhood café in Hanoi. A medal of valor goes to Nguyễn Kim Vân in Hồ Chí Minh City, who somehow miraculously manages to be both a doting aunt and a close friend.

The good friendship of many helped to sustain me throughout the life of this project, particularly that of Frederick Warner, Tai Ming Cheung, Lily Wu, Suriani Suratman, and Nguyễn-võ Thu Hương. Nguyễn Quí Đức, who graciously spent many hours on the cover for this book, deserves special mention. For giving me the space necessary to finish this book, I am grateful to my husband, Thắng Đỗ, for his love, faith, and understanding. Finally, blessed as I am with siblings and an ever enlarging circle of nieces and nephews who stand ready to remind me of the more concrete joys in life, I want to pay special tribute to my parents whose courage and sacrifice made possible a new horizon for their children. This book is dedicated to them and is in remembrance of my father, who sadly passed away when this book was in its final stage of production.

Abbreviations

BGD	Bộ Giáo Dục
BTCN	Bổ Túc Công Nông
BTVH	Bổ Túc Văn Hóa
BTVHCN	Bổ Túc Văn Hóa Công Nông
BVH	Bộ Văn Hóa
NVGP	Nhân Văn–Giai Phẩm
NXB	Nhà Xuất Bản
THCN	Trung Học Chuyên Nghiệp
VNQDĐ	Việt Nam Quốc Dân Đảng
WPCE	Worker-Peasant Complementary Education

Introduction

This book is about the politics of culture in socialist Vietnam between 1945 and 1965. In the broadest outline, I want to capture the complexities of ideas and motives of a particular time in which the Vietnamese communists managed to capture the nationalist discourse and took the leading role in the anticolonial struggle. The definition of history and culture embedded in the Vietnamese communists' formulation of cultural policies in those early years established a particular vision of the postrevolutionary nation-state. The content of cultural policies, the effort to construct new institutions designed to make concrete the communists' vision of state and society, and the multidimensional societal reactions to the institutionalization of such a vision, chiefly among the intellectual community, comprise the heart of the book. In short, it is about the evolution of the politics of culture under the leadership of the Vietnamese Communist Party as an integral component of the unfolding of the Vietnamese revolution.

The outcome of that revolution is well known and much discussed: it brought an end to French colonialism, succeeded in defeating the United States, reunited the two halves of the country, and established a socialist state in Vietnam. Bracketed by a brief moment of euphoria when Hồ Chí Minh and his followers declared Vietnamese independence from France on 2 September 1945 and by the communist takeover of Saigon on 30 April 1975, it took thirty years for the Vietnamese revolution to run its course. In between, a country called the Republic of Vietnam came into existence and disappeared, but its confrontation with the seemingly implacable trajectory of the revolution continues to reverberate both within and outside the country. The historic development of overseas Vietnamese communities in many parts of the world, for instance, is one consequence to which the current government still struggles to formulate appropriate responses. Domestically, after some twenty-five years of reunification, there is still much to be done in coming to terms with the legacy of the south and its incorporation into the larger national discourse.

As a process of radical transformation, therefore, a revolution cannot be so neatly bounded as its dates would suggest, offering us the comfort of order by providing a beginning and end to a series of events. In rare instances, when a revolution actually succeeds in making its political vision concrete, as in the case of Vietnam, it is crucial to examine the dynamics leading to the revolution to understand the shape it finally took as well as the enactment of the revolution itself to comprehend the structure of the new state, which continues to be redefined and contested. Indeed, that the Vietnamese revolution came to adopt a socialist character was not a narrative foretold. A number of works have shown that in the decades immediately preceding the revolution, Marxism was but one intellectual trend among many being discussed within various intellectual circles, with all participants earnestly searching for new ways to conceptualize the people and the nation under colonialism and in the modern world.[1] Nevertheless, the ultimate triumph of Marxism-Leninism in Vietnam and the Vietnamese Communist Party's ability to secure for itself the leading role in the nationalist struggle beg the question of how such a situation came about and, by extension, why a noncommunist nationalist discourse did not, or could not, prevail.

Many writers of early works on Vietnam therefore set out to understand the nature of the Vietnamese revolution and the rise of the Vietnamese Communist Party. In considerable measure, however, they were influenced by a particular time and political environment: many of the foreign scholars on Vietnam either had direct experience with the Vietnam War or had been involved in the antiwar movement.[2] Other views about the war existed, but a number of influential academic works were authored by those who came to believe that the U.S. involvement in Vietnam could not succeed because it took into account so little of the political, historical, and social impulses driving the Vietnamese. Their works therefore were also meant to address the lack of knowledge of Vietnam evident in the development of American policies.

Indeed, besides the colonial era scholarship and journalists' reports of the war in the 1950s and 1960s much research remained to be done. David Marr prefaced his 1971 work on Vietnamese anticolonialism from 1885 to 1925 with the comment that he was at "the barren starting point" of such an enterprise.[3] In his thought-provoking 1976 work on the Vietnamese revolution, Alexander Woodside stated rather mournfully that "Despite the two harrowing Indochina wars of the past three decades, and despite the fact that in population, resources, and cultural achievements it is the equal of many important European countries, Vietnam has never received much serious attention at universities in the Western world."[4] In different ways, this first generation of Vietnam scholars in the United States sought to restore history to Vietnam in order to counter distorted and patronizing assumptions embedded in the American approach to the war: Alexander Woodside reminded us that the country has more than twenty centuries of recorded history and that "Vietnam is and always has been one of the most intensely literary civilizations on the face of the planet"; Keith Taylor's work established the fact that Vietnamese society was sophisticatedly organized and had a cohesive sense of itself as early as the tenth century; and monographs by Truong Buu Lam and John Whitmore demonstrated that Vietnamese nationalism had been forged over a long period of time out of conflicts with its neighbors before the arrival of either the French or the Americans.[5] Moreover, American scholars' assertion that Vietnam is an independent subject worthy of inquiry was also meant to address the common view among Chinese historians and French sinologists that the country's history is simply a lesser version of Chinese history.

In the midst of the cold war, therefore, a different image of Vietnamese communists began to coalesce, not as orthodox adherents to Marxism-Leninism far removed from the general population but as rightful inheritors of the anticolonial tradition. In one of the few works to systematically compare the Vietnamese and Chinese revolutions, David Elliott argues that

> China's revolution was, in essence, a search for a political formula that could integrate its wide diversity while simultaneously pursuing a policy of social transformation that would increase its "wealth and power" and restore a position of international respect and prestige. Vietnam's goals were more modest, and its revolution aimed at re-integrating a society that had been disrupted by colonial occupation, and re-affirming the traditional ideals of the scholar-patriots who fought to maintain Vietnam's independence.[6]

By 1981, however, the evolution of the field was such that David Marr felt it necessary to comment on the pervasiveness of what he has called the continuity thesis or, in his words, "the tendency to argue that Vietnamese success in defeating first the French and then the Americans was due primarily to traditional strengths, for example, relative ethnic and linguistic homogeneity, ancient civilization, and a proud record of struggle against northern invaders."[7] These factors are important in the analysis of the Vietnamese revolution and the rise to power of the Vietnamese Communist Party, and these earlier works contributed enormously to the foundation of our understanding of Vietnam's recent history. Nevertheless, as Marr has suggested, "the cumulative effect of all these studies (in Vietnamese, English, and French) stressing the power of tradition has been to downgrade the historical significance of major transformations occurring during the colonial period in Vietnam (1859–1945)."[8]

Ironically, Marr himself contributed to the general acceptance of the continuity thesis. Through the Indochina Resource Center, which he and his colleagues founded in 1971 with the expressed intention of providing the public with access to alternative voices and interpretations of the war, Marr introduced the work of the Vietnamese Marxist Dr. Nguyễn Khắc Viện, whose views were already known in France, to an English-speaking audience. A well-respected Vietnamese communist intellectual who was trained in France, Dr. Viện maintained that the similarities between Confucianism and Marxism (e.g., a secular frame of reference and high moral standards) made it easy for the latter to be accepted by the Vietnamese revolutionaries, who were themselves, in Dr. Viện's words, "petty intellectuals."[9] It is certainly difficult to imagine a Chinese Communist Party theorist who would further argue that "it could even be said that Confucianism has left its mark on some aspects of Marxist thought" and offered by way of an example that "Revolutionary morality in Confucian countries often is more influential than notions of the law of historical development."[10] Dr. Viện's views were often quoted as exemplifying the uniqueness of Vietnamese Marxism's seemingly comfortable connection with the country's past.

For a number of different reasons, therefore, the themes of continuity and unity have pervaded Western works on Vietnam and coincided with Vietnamese communists' efforts to construct a natural teleology of Vietnamese anticolonialism and nationalism in which communism was the logical end.[11] One consequence of this development is a Confucian interpretation of the Vietnamese revolution. An early proponent of this was the colonial scholar Paul Mus, who emphasized the notion of a cosmology of Marxism and the "mandate of heaven" concept to explain Vietnamese peasants' acceptance of the communists.[12] Mus's views in turn heavily influenced Frances FitzGerald's popular and award-winning book *Fire in the Lake*.[13] One of the few works written on the Vietnam War at the time that paid much attention to the Vietnamese view of the conflict and sought to provide a rational explanation of Vietnamese nationalism in the context of the country's own history and political thought, FitzGerald's overarching use of the concept of the mandate of heaven essentially embalmed modern Vietnamese nationalism, leading one scholar to criticize her work for "denying the Vietnamese any social basis for their revolution."[14] When the Vietnamese communists managed to reunify the country in 1975, however, socialism must have seemed even more inevitable. In the words of historian John K. Whitmore:

> The [Vietnamese communists'] resolution of their dilemma took the form of successfully integrating traditional concerns and socialist dynamics. History and the past have a positive and unequivocal (though certainly not uncritical) meaning for the Vietnamese. There is no ambivalence in interpretation of cultural continuity, nor do the Vietnamese face any dilemma of historical discontinuity, as do the Chinese. The result has been formation of the SRV [Socialist Republic of Vietnam] over a united country after more than thirty years of struggle. The Vietnamese concerns have been less universal than local, their emphasis has been more voluntaristic than determinstic, and social harmony has a greater role than class contradiction. They accept the tenets of Marxist thought without feeling it necessary to insure that their past is completely in step with the universal flow. They are confident of their nation's place in the world.[15]

This is a peculiarly static view of Vietnamese nationalism, and the revolution itself is presented as largely devoid of drama. The logic of this view takes Vietnam out of the context of the international development of socialism, ascribing to the Vietnamese communists a unique ability to somehow overcome the tension between nationalism and international socialism that ran through the course of the Vietnamese Communist Party, particularly in its early years. In addition to downgrading the significance of major transformations during the colonial period, the continuity thesis also distorts our understanding of the construction of the socialist state in the north and blinds us to other political and intellectual discourses not sanctioned by the state. In this regard, intentionally or not, the emphasis on the inevitability of the socialist character of the Vietnamese revolution and the state can lead to neglect of the southern perspective. I am not interested here in the argument about the viability of South Vietnam as an independent nation; rather, I wish to emphasize that alternative views in Vietnam about nationalism and the state were in a sense kept alive during the existence of the Republic of Vietnam in the south and continue in Vietnam today. It is important, therefore, to understand those views—how they intersect with the official positions of the state and to what extent they resonate with other political and social currents in the country—for they may well constitute the boundaries of the effort to reconceptualize state and society in the foreseeable future.

The contemporary period, however, is beyond the scope of this book. My concern is that the pervasiveness of the continuity thesis has unwittingly engendered a static view of revolutionary politics in Vietnam, ignoring its radical and modern dimensions. Pioneering works have elucidated the chaotic but stimulating political and intellectual environment of the colonial period, and the ability to do fieldwork in Vietnam in recent years has broadened our knowledge of that era significantly.[16] The most significant gap in the scholarship, however, remains the period between 1945 and 1975.[17]

My intention is to go beyond 1945 to examine the dynamics of revolutionary politics *after* the Vietnamese communists had managed to capture the nationalist discourse and at the beginning of the process of constructing the socialist state. In his provocative work on nationalist thought and colonialism, Partha Chatterjee posits a three-stage development process of nationalist thought: (1) the "moment of departure," when nationalist consciousness first encounters the framework of post-Enlightenment rationalist thought; (2) the "moment of manoeuvre," a period of consolidation of a particular direction of nationalist thought that is fraught with many contradictory possibilities; and (3) the "moment of arrival," the beginning of the state-building process with its discourse of order and rational organization of power.[18] What I want to capture in this book is some measure of that very dramatic and complex movement from the moment of maneuver to the moment of arrival that defines revolutionary politics in the Vietnamese context. I take 1965 as the cutoff point, party because the escalation of the U.S. involvement in the Vietnam War constitutes a new period in the life of the Democratic Republic of Vietnam but also because by then the features of a socialist state have largely been institutionalized.

By revolutionary politics I mean both the ideology and the structure whose interaction gives shape to the postrevolutionary state or what Lynn Hunt has referred to as "the underlying patterns in political culture that made possible the emergence of distinctive policies and the appearance of new kinds of politicians, conflicts, and organizations."[19] First and foremost, far from the confident Vietnamese communists that the continuity thesis portrays, I aim to delineate the profound ambivalence, and at times the extreme hostility toward history and past intellectual achievements, at the heart of their views of politics and society, as these are evident in their definition of *culture* and the subsequent formulation of cultural policies. In this, communist theorists were participating in the larger intellectual milieu of the 1920s and 1930s, suffused as it was with painful attempts to formulate a distinct Vietnamese self from the heavy burden of the Chinese past and the recent experience of French colonialism. By the 1940s, however, their faith in Marxism-Leninism as both the guiding principle in interpreting Vietnam's historical conditions and the mode of organization that would bring about Vietnamese independence and the establishment of a new state armed Party theorists with what they perceived to be the scientific (and therefore incontrovertible) truth.

The modern faith in scientific progress and the radical impulse to create a whole new world upon the ashes of the old were what motivated the Vietnamese revolution under the communists and proved to be enormously appealing to many Vietnamese of diverse backgrounds and political persuasions. We would miss much of the extraordinary power of the revolution if we failed to recognize the impact of this radical dimension on the general population as well as on the politics of the new state in its earliest years of formation. One consequence of this radical view is the emphasis on organization as the concrete tool with which to realize the vision of new social, political, and economic relations that would define the new independent nation-state. The communists were the most organized of all anticolonial forces in Vietnam, and supreme organizational capability was key to the communist victory in the south. Alexander Woodside sees it, in the larger context of nationalist thought, as the search in the twentieth century for better collective organizations or communities in order to overcome both the fragmentation of the colonial period and the structural weaknesses of traditional Vietnamese society.[20] David Elliott has attributed the focus on organization to historical necessity and also as reflecting the rationalist attempt on the part of the communist leaders to impose order through complex organization and scientific management. In his view, over time this "predilection for organizational solutions" itself has become a development strategy for socialist Vietnam, one in which "institutional development provide both framework and stimulus for economic and social development."[21] In the context of this book, given the radicalism of the view that nothing much was worth saving from the hodgepodge of achievements that constituted Vietnamese history and culture, organization of both ideology and structure became key, for organization served the dual purpose of clearly establishing the path that society must follow and containing any inclination to stray from such a defined course.

Within the larger framework of the politics of culture in revolutionary Vietnam, therefore, the preoccupation with organization presents a theme that runs through this book, outlining a top-down transformative vision of state and society. The second theme probes instead the complex societal reactions against that vision in their different manifestations, from those of the intellectuals to those of the cadres in state institutions like the Ministry of Culture and Ministry of Education and among the general population. That there were signs of resistance early on testifies to the inherent gap between the theory and practice of revolutionary politics. Yet we would do well to remind ourselves of the faith many Vietnamese had in the Party and the revolution even as they struggled with the heavy weight of state structure. It is the painfully searching efforts to reconcile the self first with the needs of the revolution and then with the emerging shape of state and society that provide us with some understanding of the intensity of the revolutionary moment, unifying many in that heroic collective endeavor to preserve what was viewed as an extremely fragile nation and to forge the creation of a modern state in which to house it. In the end, the radical tendency was tempered because the escalation of the American presence in the south forced the Party to return to a more inclusive nationalist mode in order to mobilize popular support for the war effort but also because of the powerful legacy of the anticolonial struggle, which carried with it a different interpretation of what the postrevolutionary state should be.

In fleshing out the societal reactions to state policies in these early years, this book also addresses the role of intellectuals, the nature of dissent, and the definition of *civil society* in a socialist system. Intellectuals figure heavily because they were the target of the Party's earliest cultural pronouncements and they were cast firmly in the intermediate role of transmitting the Party's agenda to the larger public. As

Katherine Verdery has asserted in her work on socialist Romania, "For a political regime such as this, where discourse has a disproportionately productive role, and especially for one whose self proclaimed task is to change society, the producers of discourse *must* be incorporated within the regime."[22]

Much has been written and debated about what the term *intellectual* means. Here I offer only an operational definition in the context of my research on Vietnam. By intellectual I mean simply a person who participates in some significant way in literary, educational, and cultural activities. These creative intellectuals were the poets, novelists, critics, playwrights, and essayists, many of whom were prominent in the intellectual scenes of the 1930s and 1940s and played key roles in disseminating the Party's message during the revolution and helped to establish the foundation for the new art and literature, educational system, and culture in the socialist state. This study focuses on these creative intellectuals because they have been the most outspoken in promoting the Party's agenda as well as questioning it. This is partly because the country's low level of economic development did not provide the small number of scientific intellectuals much of a role but mostly because in Vietnam intellectual debates have always been the premise of creative intellectuals.

In this regard, literature is well within the political realm. The fact that Vietnamese intellectuals often view their world through the prism of literature or regard it as a solution to social issues testifies to the overwhelming importance of language and its perceived capabilities.[23] Unfortunate developments after 1954, in which research and teaching became polarized in institutes and universities, respectively, additionally undermined the power of social and political commentary that had previously existed in the educational system. Thus, post-1954 intellectual issues became even more concentrated within the creative intellectual circle. This study will also focus primarily on northern intellectuals since they were more influential in the intellectual discourse on nation and society in the years leading to the August Revolution and because they played such an important role in helping to create the Vietnamese socialist state.

Although intellectuals are variously defined as court jesters, mythmakers, and ideologists, the dominance of the totalitarian approach in the study of socialist systems has generally maintained that they cannot play an important and independent role given the regime's monopoly of power.[24] The pronouncements of the socialist states themselves testify to this view: intellectuals are thought of as merely workers or cultural cadres whose task is to be a means of communication between the leadership and the people. In response, studies of intellectuals in socialist states tend to share an implicit assumption that there is no autonomous space in which intellectuals can shape their own roles.[25] The interest, more often than not, is on dissent, and underground publications are viewed as being more revealing of intellectual situation than what the official press may have to say. One of the results of this tendency has been an overriding emphasis on individuals rather than the intellectual community as a whole. On the other hand, even when intellectual debates arise in the public sphere, this is labeled "permitted dissent."[26] The connotation is that the state is merely manipulating the situation for its own gains and holds the upper hand in the discussion from the outset. Intellectuals in socialist states are seen as being so wedded to the system that they have become "establishment intellectuals."[27]

The view adopted in this study departs from most of the writings on intellectuals in socialist states. Strict official parameters in socialist states do not mean that intellectuals become either victims or passive participants. As in any system, there is an arena in which policies are fought for, opinions are voiced, and issues discussed—even if the arena is much smaller than or different from intellectual freedom as it is known in the West. Far from the view that socialist intellectuals are essentially powerless (a view espoused by socialist intellectuals themselves, though I think they will be appalled at how much intellectual work goes unnoticed in the West in comparison), I see them as quite influential precisely because of the extraordinary demands made upon them by the state. Beyond the intellectual class, however, what this study suggests is that a broader definition of civil society is needed in examining socialist regimes like that of Vietnam. For all the overwhelming concentration of power in the Party and the extensive bureaucratization of all sectors of society, societal forces do find myriad ways to express discontent and resistance. The differentiation between the public and private that grows out of the experience of democratic political systems may blind us not only to the possibilities of dissent but to its locations within the very structures of the Party and the state.[28] The question of to what extent professionalism can play a role in transmitting norms and ethics that can transcend the state's imposed agenda is an interesting one to ponder.

In summary, this study covers the period from 1945 to 1965, from the Vietnamese communists' initial ascent to power to the beginning of the escalation of the American involvement in the country's conflict, by which time a full-fledged socialist state had been in place in North Vietnam for eleven years. There are two parts to the study. The first deals with the period from 1945 to 1954, when the nascent socialist state emerged during an anticolonialist struggle against the French. Chapter 1 examines the contemporary political and intellectual landscape in which Party theorists struggled to raise the banner of Marxism-Leninism. Examining in detail the Party's earliest cultural pronouncements, which continue to be regarded as the guiding principles of literary activities and cultural work in Vietnam today, I want to bring out that strand of radical modernism that shot through these attempts to define a new culture within the political platform that would bring the intellectuals to the side of the revolution. Chapter 2 explores the complex responses among intellectuals to the Party's cultural policies. Many were supportive of the Party's leadership role in the struggle for national independence but were already highly ambivalent about the inherent conflict between their desire to contribute to the heroic undertaking and what they perceived to be unnecessarily narrow and utilitarian definitions of the creative act. Chapter 3 describes the increasingly rigid orientation of the official intellectual policy as the Party began to emphasize its socialist agenda over the national front disposition. The opening of the northern border with China in 1950 reinforced orthodox tendencies in Vietnam, and the beginning of land reform coupled with the introduction of criticism and self-criticism heightened the issue of class. The chapter focuses also on the pivotal but little known 1949 Conference of Debates in Việt Bắc, which provides a fascinating glimpse of the Party's growing effort to capture the content and direction of the intellectual discourse. The shift from the intimate comradeship of the early days of the revolution to more hierarchical relations of authority is already discernible, underlined by the official emphasis on the need to organize the intellectuals as well as other sectors within society.

The second part of the book addresses the period from 1954 to 1965 and pays greater attention to the establishment of the structure that would institutionalize the ideological debate of the previous years. Chapter 4 examines the most significant instance of intellectual dissent in socialist Vietnam, which has come to be known as the Nhân Văn Giai Phẩm (NVGP) period, named after the two main publications airing the alternative views. Although NVGP dominated the discussion of intellectual activities during this period, what I want to show is that the dilemma inherent in state-intellectual relations affected the

whole of the intellectual community and not just those who participated in NVGP. As such, the way in which intellectuals came to be
organized was partly the state's effort to erect control mechanisms in
response to the widespread discontent exposed by NVGP. Moving
beyond the intellectual circle, chapter 5 examines the work of the Ministry of Culture, founded in September 1955 as the agency to promote
and safeguard the Party's cultural agenda from the cities down to the
villages. Here I explore the conflict within the ministry in the early
years as it struggled between competing goals, pitting professional
standards against political demands. Finally, chapter 6 analyzes the
educational system as the mechanism through which new generations
of socialist men and women were to emerge. The intense effort to
generate a new intellectual stratum composed of those from politically
pure class backgrounds attested to the commitment to the vision of a
socialist state. We see also here glimpses of the difficulties educators
had in reconciling the needs of the educational system with the political concerns of the time. In both the cultural and educational work,
what is remarkable is the extent to which state responses to NVGP also
affected these arenas in these early years. As such, NVGP's position as
a watershed moment of dissent in the history of socialist Vietnam
became firmly established, above and beyond what any of its initial
participants, faithful sons and daughters of the revolution, could ever
have imagined.

Material for this study comes from four sources. The first is the large
body of Vietnamese-language publications, literature in particular. Second, there are archival data, which have not been available until recently. All of my archival research was done at the National Archives in
Hanoi in 1992 and 1993.[29] Third, I have conducted a number of interviews, through both formal channels and private contacts, with officials and intellectuals. Fourth, the opportunity to simply observe the
intellectual community, mostly in Hanoi, over a period of a year and a
half has provided a background understanding of daily activities, con-
straints, and beliefs in a way that no amount of reading could provide.
Finally, unless otherwise noted, all translations are mine.

PART I

From the August Revolution
to Điện Biên Phủ, 1945–54

— 1 —

Constructing a Cultural Policy

Nowadays in poetry there should be iron
A poet must also know to charge ahead
—Hồ Chí Minh

Widely quoted, these two lines of poetry written by Hồ Chí Minh have become the official raison d'être for intellectuals and their labor in socialist Vietnam. They signify the intellectuals' commitment to action and a kind of distilled revolutionary determination required in their work that goes beyond abstract values and concepts. In effect, it is what the Vietnamese state would later define *art* and *literature* to be: a weapon in the struggle for national independence, unification, and socialist revolution.[1]

The process of defining the purpose of intellectual activity and the nature of intellectual responsibility, however, did not draw its inspiration simply from Hồ Chí Minh's poetry. What was subsequently enshrined as the state's prescient cultural policy was in the beginning an attempt to capture crucial support in urban areas during a particularly chaotic period in Vietnamese history. It was not achieved overnight, nor was it accomplished in isolation from contemporary social and political discussions. I want to emphasize that the Vietnamese communists' cultural and intellectual platform proved to be so appealing to many precisely because it tapped into strands of ideas that were already becoming dominant in the intellectual discourse, which increasingly focused on the fate of the bulk of the Vietnamese population and the need to place the modern individual within the larger community. Coinciding with the powerful reorientation on the part of many intellectuals themselves from the rebellious and brash 1930s to the more somber and introspective 1940s, the communists' cultural policy skillfully emphasized nationalist concerns within a coherent and systematic framework that provided a cogent critique of the contemporary intellectual environment, and offered an alternative view of what the new culture could be. It also helped to establish the communist-organized Việt Nam Độc Lập Đồng Minh Hội, or the Việt Minh as it came to be known, as the only agent capable of achieving national independence and a modern state. A clear and hopeful guide to action in times of upheaval has always been the draw of religious movements. Thus, it is not surprising that in referring to the Party's cultural work in these early years reminiscences were sprinkled with phrases like "the torch lighting the way" (*ngọn đuốc soi đường*) and "miraculous power" (*phép mầu*) along with the insistence that the basic tenets laid out then continue to be the guiding light today.[2]

That insistence on continuity deserves elaboration. First, the actual body of works that constituted the official cultural policy is quite small and focused on two particular documents, the succinct 1943 "Theses on Vietnamese Culture" (more commonly referred to as "Theses on Culture") and the longer, more sophisticated, 1948 "Marxism and the Issue of Vietnamese Culture" (more commonly known as "Marxism and Vietnamese Culture"). As Nam Mộc, one of the earliest Party members who did cultural work, remarked in 1985, "besides comrade Trường Chinh's book *Marxism and the Issue of Vietnamese Culture*, which was published in 1948, to date we still do not have a comprehensive theoretical work on culture."[3] In the early 1990s there were some discussion of new Theses on Culture, but there is no indication that this effort has amounted to anything concrete.[4] The lack of further development of the cultural policy in later years therefore means that certain tendencies of dilemmas contained in these early documents played a substantial role in shaping intellectual activities for the next thirty years.

Second, the name of one top Party leader constantly recurs in the discussion of Vietnam's cultural policy. Well known by his revolutionary name, Trường Chinh (1907–88) was probably the single most important Party theorist, particularly in the early years of the revolution.[5] He was also the leading Party theorist on cultural matters from the beginning of the Party's existence.[6] Holding at various times virtually all key Party and state positions, including the post of the Party's secretary general, he was, by many accounts, a well-read, meticulous, and disciplined person in his thinking and writing. All Party pronouncements on culture were cleared with the Politburo, but Trường Chinh is still seen as the key architect of these positions. He was also often the person who presented the Party's cultural platform to the public. His name is attached to the key documents under examination in this chapter, and his overwhelming influence in the early intellectual discourse is undeniable, although it would be misleading to assert that he alone constructed the intellectual policy or that only his writings are worth scrutinizing.

The Intellectual Setting

The literary critic Vũ Ngọc Phan recalled his entrance examination for the French high school level in 1923 as having been composed of two parts, written and oral. The written part covered mathematics, chemistry, physics, and/or biology and required an essay in French. After garnering a passing grade on the written section, the student would have an oral examination, which included in part singing, sculpting, and an expository essay on a given literary passage. In Phan's examination, he was given Alfred de Musset's poem "Le Pélican," which happened to be one of his favorites. He therefore received a high grade. For the music portion, Phan wisely chose to sing a French children's song on the advice of an older (and more musically talented) Vietnamese student. The examiner commented: "Vouz chantez comme un canard. Je vous donne par pitié 1."[7] Nevertheless, Phan gained enough points to pass. The success of such an examination would lead eventually to the achievement of the *brêvet d'enseignement primaire supérieur* (the equivalent of a high school diploma), the prerequisite to a job in the colonial administration or entrance into the university.

The end of the imperial examination system came in 1915 for the north and 1919 for the central part of Vietnam, where the vestiges of imperial rule remained, but Phan's interests indicated the far-reaching changes brought about by the 1920s by French colonial rule. The old imperial examination structure, with its attendant educational process, was replaced with the new colonial school system, topped by the University of Hanoi. Phan's generation became the first to be engaged in the new Franco-Vietnamese educational system.[8] Within the space of only a few decades, a clear demarcation emerged between *Hán học* (Chinese-style learning) and *tân học* (modern learning). A classical education had lost its value, not only because it seemed anachronistic in the colonial setting but because careers in the colonial government required the skills taught in the new Western-style schools.

With the nationalist movement virtually decimated by brutal French colonial authorities' reprisals at the end of 1930, the Vietnamese intellectual community was poised to shift the discussion of the country's problems to an arena other than those of political and armed struggles. If the nationalist effort hitherto had focused primarily on repelling foreign domination, the ensuing decade would see spirited discussions of social and cultural issues, which turned increasingly inward to find explanations for what was perceived to be the nation's debilitating weakness in confronting the challenges posed by the West.

Language became the battleground on which ideas of nation and culture were contested. The romanized alphabet, *quốc ngữ*, had been created in the seventeenth century by Catholic missionaries for pro-selytization purposes. French colonialists did not think much of *quốc ngữ*, preferring to turn all Vietnamese into French speakers. Such a colossal project was simply impossible, and in due course *quốc ngữ* came to be accepted as a bridge that would lead the Vietnamese from the sinic civilization to that of France.[9] Recognizing that *quốc ngữ* made widespread literacy a possibility (it had never existed previously given the difficulty of learning Sino-Vietnamese characters), a number of progressive mandarins seized upon the idea, conducting classes as early as 1907 to teach *quốc ngữ* to the people.[10] They began to painstakingly translate classical works into *quốc ngữ* as well as writing in the new form.[11]

Language is a primary component in the cohesiveness of a state, and it has been an issue of great debate in the emerging states since World War II. In Vietnam, the Việt Minh co-opted the issue of mass literacy early on and today *quốc ngữ* is the writing system in use. By the time of the August Revolution in 1945, *quốc ngữ* had become the main writing system in the country. The pace of the development of *quốc ngữ* into a national language with its own body of literature was astoundingly swift, taking only three decades or so to take root and spread from the beginning of the century. *Quốc ngữ's* eventual success also belied the incredible obstacles arrayed against it. Anticolonialist tracts were still being issued in Sino-Vietnamese characters well into the 1920s, and a substantial number of the new Western educated elites that dominated the intellectual discourse in the 1930s were disdainful of *quốc ngữ*. As late as 1936, the writer Hoàng Đạo could still comment thusly on what he saw as a rather rudimentary language: "Making six-year-old children study a few years of *quốc ngữ* is not the same as waiting another five years for them to grow up and then making them learn that language in two months."[12] Incredibly, in 1953 there was still a Vietnamese voice in the south denigrating the Vietnamese language in favor of French, even though he was roundly denounced by the public.[13]

The disdain for *quốc ngữ* was in fact disdain for Vietnamese culture. Even for its early champions, it was viewed mostly as an effective method for helping the common people overcome their ignorance and backwardness. Nguyễn Văn Vĩnh, who pioneered *quốc ngữ* journalism in the north, spent much of his time and ink exposing what he saw as the weakness and the stupidity of virtually all Vietnamese traditional practices and beliefs. For him, the ease with which *quốc ngữ* could be taught to the population primarily meant that ideas of social reform could reach more people. Nguyễn Văn Vĩnh himself always dressed in the Western manner, and his daily speech was French.[14] Even the sophisticated debates among Vietnamese intellectuals in urban cities like Hanoi and Saigon were dismissed by those who had received extensive training in Paris. Nguyễn Mạnh Tường, who in 1932 held two doctorates from Paris at the tender age of twenty-two, had this to say about the idealist versus materialist debate between the scholar Phan Khôi and the Marxist critic Hải Triều in 1933: "[Such a debate is futile] because all that is worth saying about the subject Frenchman have already said; [we] only need to open French books to see."[15]

However, language, and particularly this new Vietnamese form, became for many intellectuals, suffering as they were from a heightened inferiority complex about their own culture, a way to break away from the past and establish something new but nevertheless Vietnamese. Thus, hand in hand with the disdain for *quốc ngữ* there were also early champions from different political and social backgrounds who connected it explicitly to the existence of the nation and the indefinable national soul or spirit. What remained was the crucial need to generate a body of literature in this new language, a daunting prospect but also an opportunity, in the eyes of someone like Nguyễn Văn Vĩnh, to introduce new ideas into what he perceived to be a feudalistic and stagnant society. Nguyễn Văn Vĩnh himself became the foremost translator of many French works, particularly plays, into *quốc ngữ*.[16] In 1907 he proclaimed that "The future weakness or strength of our Vietnamese nation will depend on *quốc ngữ*."[17] The conservative mandarin-scholar Phạm Quỳnh, the antithesis of the ultra-Westernized Nguyễn Văn Vĩnh, believed that "A nation exists by means of language; when language exists, the nation cannot disappear."[18] More specifically, Phạm Quỳnh judged that "Whatever idea cannot be expressed in our language cannot yet be our idea; it remains a borrowed one."[19]

The Self-Reliant Literary Group and New Poetry:
Modernity and the Generation of 1932

The explosive growth of journalism in the 1920s and 1930s was certainly crucial to the consolidation of *quốc ngữ* as the national language, but it also established a national platform for the introduction of new ideas and debates about them. Moreover, language here became an expression of resistance against the other, the act necessary to reclaim oneself. In the context of colonialism, the ability to perceive oneself as being against, and therefore outside, the cultural, racial, and political domination of the colonizing power was absolutely crucial. Language, rediscovered in the form of *quốc ngữ*, provided the fundamental and indigenous opportunity to make the conscious comparison that would break the hold of colonialism over Vietnamese society and allow it to come into its own. People not only read but learned from the early newspapers and journals, and in turn the growth of a substantial reading public in *quốc ngữ* was critical to further intellectual experimentation and development.

The period between 1930 and 1945, therefore, saw a significant burst of intellectual production, which also marked the height of the modernization of Vietnamese literature. This intellectual flowering, however, came at a time when the anticolonial struggle was facing its darkest hour. As a colony dependent on exports, Vietnam was devastated by the Great Depression of 1929–30. Unemployment skyrocketed, and much land changed hands due to foreclosure.[20] The economic chaos was accompanied by political and social upheavals. The Vietnamese Nationalist Party's attempted armed uprising against the French colonial government ended in a disaster at Yên Báy in 1930 from which it never fully recovered. The newly reorganized Indochina Communist Party also suffered heavy losses when it tried in the same year to lead the rural movements in Nghệ An and Hà Tĩnh collectively referred to since as the Nghệ Tĩnh Movement or the Soviet Nghệ Tĩnh. In retaliation, the colonial authorities embarked on a severe crackdown, jailing and executing many suspected political activists. By 1932, it was estimated that there were about ten thousand political prisoners in Vietnam.[21] With leading nationalists either dead, in jail, or abroad and the political parties virtually destroyed, the anticolonial cause in Vietnam seemed lost.

The devastating political failure of the anticolonial movement and harsh economic conditions heightened the intellectual search for models and concepts that would address what many saw as debilitating weaknesses inherent in Vietnamese identity and culture. Newspapers, journals, and publishing houses flourished in spite of rigorous colonial censorship, and Marxist thought was simply one strand among many as it struggled to make its point within the intellectual community. The dominant intellectual trend of the 1930s was embodied in the Self-Reliant Literary Group (Tự Lực Văn Đoàn), whose platform was explicitly urban and decidedly Western. In the chaotic intellectual atmosphere of the time, the Self-Reliant Literary Group stood out for the clarity of its ideology and for its organization. The only literary group with defined criteria for membership, it was firm on the necessity of becoming modern. Issued in 1936, the writer Hoàng Đạo's ten concepts for the new life, the first of which was "Following the new, completely and decisively following the new," came to be seen as the group's own proclamation, specifically defined as the need for Westernization.[22] There was no middle ground; Vietnamese should abandon the illusion of a possible synthesis between East and West that had been held by an older generation of intellectuals. In Hoàng Đạo's view, there was nothing worth keeping in the old culture, which had severely restricted the individual within the confines of the family and society.

> The old culture remains only in a few social practices and the minds of those who belong to the "neutral" group. This group is very popular in our country and very powerful. It proclaims the idea of synthesizing the old and new cultures with very serious arguments. There is nothing better than maintaining the best of Chinese culture as a base and add to it what is good of French culture; as such, we will soon have two cultures and will become more civilized than any other country in the world. But those ideas are only an illusion. Two cultures are like two streams running from the top of the mountain. One is running to the east and one to the west, which cannot be combined: French culture is active in the sense that it is always changing while the old Eastern culture is primarily still, staying in one place.[23]

Bringing the form of the novel to a new height in the history of modern Vietnamese literature, the Self-Reliant Literary Group made its mark with its emphasis on the struggle waged by a newly modern generation, particularly the modern individual, against the family and society's outmoded traditions.[24] Although the group also attacked autocratic village elders, its view of the peasantry and country life alternated between disparagement and a patronizing but romantic pastoralism. This was the response of a new generation of Vietnamese intellectuals, sophisticated and self-assured, who came of age in the Franco-Vietnamese educational system. Their credo was modernity, and they were ready to lead the "live happily, live youthfully" (sống vui, sống trẻ) movement that was spreading among urban youth in the early 1930s, a reaction against the old ways but also an escapist response to the somber mood that enveloped Vietnamese society after the failures of Yên Báy and Soviet Nghệ Tĩnh.[25]

The emergence of the Self-Reliant Literary Group and its influential journal Mores (Phong Hóa) in 1932 coincided with the other major intellectual development of the decade, the rise of a movement that is now known as New Poetry (Thơ Mới). The generation of intellectuals that became active during this period, therefore, has often been referred to as the generation of 1932.[26] The desire for newness was also reflected in New Poetry. The movement was seen as breaking new ground by dropping the classical, Chinese-inspired, metrical pattern for a freer rhythm, allowing the poet to be more expressive and creative with both old and new themes. French influence was undeniable since this group of young rebels was much more at home with Baudelaire and Mallarmé than Tang poetry. The "invasion of prose into poetry" also allowed Vietnamese to be much more vernacular with their use of language, coming closer to spoken rhythms than ever before and establishing this as a legitimate form.[27] If the Sino-Vietnamese script (nôm) was a Vietnamese elite response to Chinese cultural domination in imperial times, the developments in the 1930s allowed a much greater break with the Chinese past by popularizing the French-created quốc ngữ and developing new directions for creativity.

From the 1930s to the 1940s: Individualism and the Community

By the end of the 1930s, however, the romantic, bourgeois elitism of the Self-Reliant Literary Group was becoming less persuasive. After

Nazi Germany occupied France in 1940, the French authorities in Indochina entered into an alliance with Japan. Essentially under the colonial rule of two nations, the Vietnamese economy underwent even more serious dislocation as Japanese military demands increased. Realist writers like Vũ Trọng Phụng and Nguyễn Công Hoan became prominent with their unsentimental descriptions of the underclass in both urban and rural areas and the direct consequences of colonial rule. The swaggering claims of modernity of the early 1930s had mellowed by the end of the decade to a realization that what was important was the preservation of the Vietnamese soul in whatever new form. The Party's pronouncements have tended to emphasize the hopelessly escapist tendencies of intellectuals like the poet Vũ Hoàng Chương, with his emphasis on finding solace in all sorts of vices, whether it be alcohol, opium, or women, but the beginning of the 1940s also saw a great surge of interest in religion, philosophy, archaeology, and popular culture.

We can speak of the 1930s, therefore, as making that necessary and overt break with the traditional past in order to define the modern Vietnamese self, and the 1940s took up the next question: now what? In part, the intellectual community was striving to find a new balance. New Poetry began its life with a clear demarcation between itself and the old form; its supporters vilified poets in the old tradition. The targets of this devastating attack included the venerable Tản Đà, himself a transitional figure between the classical and more indigenous Vietnamese poetic forms. By the end of the 1930s, however, there was a reappraisal of old poetry. Tản Đà's death in 1939 brought him back into the fold of the literary community. By 1941, an astute observer of the movement has noted:

In reality, old poetry withdrew from the front line but never took off its armor and surrendered. It retreated to village towns and took shelter in those collections circulating among a few brothers that were being handed down to their children and grandchildren.[28]

Furthermore, Vietnamese poets now recognized that further development of poetry would have to erase the false division between old and new. Quách Tấn, a young poet who wrote mainly in traditional forms, pointedly titled his 1941 collection *Mùa cổ điển* (A classical season) and drew rave reviews from the new poets.[29] Old poets, though, thought that it was not classical enough.[30] Nevertheless, it showed that old forms could be creatively modernized and adapted to the new age.

Thus, after a period in which everything old and traditional was condemned by a younger and more Westernized generation, it became clear that there was a need to synthesize these two extremes if something quintessentially Vietnamese was to emerge into the modern world. This process of reevaluating the past was seen as a life or death matter by a contemporary critic, who noted the loss of hope that came with the emergence of the individual. To break away from the well-established values of the East Asian world was to find the true Vietnamese self, though it now stood bereft and uncertain of the new anchoring values. Hoài Thanh argued that as much as the concept of individuality had brought new poetry into being and allowed for the emergence of uniquely different poetic voices, it was achieved at the expense of the community.

> In general, the entire spirit of ancient times—or the old poetry—and the present time—or the new poetry—may be summed up in two words: "I" and "we.". . . When the word "I" (speaking of it in its fullest sense) appeared in the realm of Vietnamese poetry, many people viewed it with disfavor. . . .
>
> But, day by day, gradually it has ceased to be so startling. People have gotten used to it. They have even found it to be worthy of affection and compassion. And it is indeed a piteous thing! . . .
>
> Our lives now lie within the sphere of "I." Having lost breadth, we seek depth. But the deeper we go, the colder it gets. . . . Never before has Vietnamese poetry been so sad, nor so much in an uproar, as it is now. Along with our sense of superiority, we have lost even the peace of mind of previous times.
>
> In the old time, even a victim of injustice . . . could still rely on something permanent. Today the layer of prejudice covering the soul has disappeared along with the flowery layer covering literature. The West has returned our spirit to us. But we are bewildered because looking into it we see that one thing is lacking, one thing that is more essential than a hundred thousand other things: a full faith.[31]

Hoài Thanh described this dilemma of the modern self as a tragedy being played out in the souls of Vietnamese youths, a tragedy that they consigned to the Vietnamese language because it represented the heritage of centuries of Vietnamese patriotism. Thus, he saw the response to the conflicting consequences of individualism brought to its highest level as a return to the past in order to find something permanent and transcendental that could provide the foundation for change. Hoài Thanh, therefore, explicitly linked literature to change and the evolution of individualism in the Vietnamese context. The "I" now must make its connection with the community in order to be at peace or, in Hoài Thanh's own formulation, young intellectuals wanted to "borrow the public spirit to entrust private worries."[32] If the boundary between old and new poetry came to be seen as meaningless and divisive by the end of the 1930s, then the individual emerging in the early 1940s was one who had to find his or her place firmly in the community, not outside of it.

The emphasis on the people and the recovery of the past, therefore, underlined intellectual discussions as the new decade began. One journal founded in Hanoi in 1941 was called *Tri Tân* (To know the new), a title that David Marr has found "misleading, since wartime censorship ruled out any wide-ranging discussion of current events" and because of *Tri Tân*'s emphasis on Vietnamese history, culture, language, and literature with a tendency "to dramatize and to romanticize the past rather than to analyze it."[33] The Tri Tân group, however, was consciously recovering the past, even if it meant only to publicize some of the scholarly historical findings of the previous period, reflecting the abandonment of precisely this kind of classical research in the 1930s and the gap that was created.[34] Indeed, the name *Tri Tân* itself was taken from a classical Confucian phrase *ôn cổ nhi tri tân*, meaning "reviewing the old in order to know the new."[35] The goal was to forge some level of harmony out of the contemporary chaos, one that would bring the lessons of the past to bear upon the present and its future course.

The surge of interest in religion and philosophy, particularly in Buddhism and Confucianism, has already been noted, but other trends, while continuing to draw their inspirations from Western ideas, were also much more adamant in their call for a national culture. The work of a group called Xuân Thu Nhã Tập took the literary developments of the 1930s one step further by moving in a more abstract direction while maintaining that Tang poetry had a place next to Valéry in the new culture.[36] This new expression, however, emphasized the primacy of art and literature, and such concepts as beauty and intellect remained highly elitist. It was not surprising that the ideas of the Xuân Thu Nhã Tập group found support on the pages of another new journal during this period, *Thanh Nghị* (Clear counsel). *Thanh Nghị* was essentially the voice of the group of intellectuals (of the same name) nurtured in the Franco-Vietnamese school system, including many who had been trained in France. Unlike the many Westernized intellectuals in the 1930s who were disdainful of *quốc ngữ* and the culture and philosophy of the East in general, Thanh Nghị intellectuals pushed for "the construction of a nationalist culture, in the direction of Western capitalist culture, but which must have a 'Vietnamese disposition.'"[37] The group's elitist orientation was expressed in its name, Clear Counsel, also a classical phrase resonating the role of the mandarin-official, although the discussions in *Thanh Nghị* on economics, education, culture, and literature used mainly French sources.[38]

The issue of the day, therefore, was *dân tộc,* a term evolved from the well-established sense of "peoplehood," more connected with ethnic and cultural-linguistic factors than national and territorial ones.[39] The term is thus loaded with emotional value, and it continues to be used in Vietnam today to refer to both people and nation. There was, however, a myriad of opinions offered as to how to best define *dân tộc* and what should be done to secure its existence and development. However that "Vietnamese disposition" was perceived by different intellectuals, a more specific connection was increasingly being made between this spiritual essence and the larger population, bringing together the components of nation and people embodied in *dân tộc.* There were elitist attempts to look for answers to the country's problems in the past, but there were also efforts to find the solution in the present and among the masses. In the south, this period was marked by the rise of two religious movements, Cao Đài and Hòa Hảo.[40] A longtime Party member active then went so far as to claim that the southern branch of the party did not have much opportunity to discuss cultural issues mostly because it had to deal with the growing strength of religious movements.[41]

The 1943 "Theses on Culture"

In retrospect, the history of early Vietnamese communism is a powerful lesson of the triumph of perseverance over formidable obstacles. It was only in 1930 that the Vietnamese communist movement finally became united after years of destructive factionalism. However, the

French colonial government's brutal retaliation in the aftermath of the Soviet Nghệ Tĩnh uprising (1930–31) virtually decimated the Party's organization. Yet Party activities continued underground and were given a respite when the Popular Front came to power in France in 1936. Although many Party members were released from prison, this period of relative relaxation was short lived, as World War II broke out and Germany occupied France in 1940.

The Vichy government in France installed a new governor-general in Indochina. Japan's arrival in Indochina soon after led to a new power arrangement in which France accommodated the Japanese presence while both powers sought to increase their own influence over Vietnamese political, social, and cultural life. During 1939 and 1940, French colonial authorities harshly suppressed the communists' activities and many Party leaders were jailed. With Hồ Chí Minh's return to Vietnam in 1941, the Vietnamese communists made a historic change in policy to put the issues of class struggle and socialist revolution on the back burner and concentrate wholly on the question of national independence under a national front. In 1941, the Việt Minh was formed to generate a broad front to rally all Vietnamese to the independence movement regardless of class background or political persuasion. Mass organizing was undertaken to mobilize popular support, resulting in such groups as the Peasants' Association for National Salvation, the Students' Association for National Salvation, and the Women's Association for National Salvation.[42]

The Cultural Association for National Salvation, however, was not formed until 1943, the same year in which the "Theses on Culture" was written. By then, it was clear that in order to energize the Việt Minh front, the Party needed urban support and the abilities of intellectuals, especially writers and poets, to broadcast the revolutionary message. First and foremost, the Party needed to convince intellectuals of the correctness of its view regarding the future of Vietnam and Vietnamese culture. It must be stressed, however, that the "Theses" had very little impact on intellectuals at the time; in 1943 it was extremely difficult to be an active revolutionary in Vietnam. The "Theses" was circulated among a tiny number of Party members doing cultural work and a few intellectuals already sympathetic to the Việt Minh. It was only after the August Revolution that the "Theses" was broadly disseminated, but its ready existence certainly made it easier for the communists to convince the intellectuals that they had a serious cultural agenda. The "Theses" became influential then and it was the first building block in the construction of the official cultural policy.

Yet for all the influence that the "Theses on Culture" was supposed to have subsequently had on the cultural life of socialist Vietnam, it was remarkably brief and free of Marxist formulations. The relationship between culture, economics, and politics was covered in one sentence: "The basic economic foundation of a society and the economic regime built upon that foundation decides the culture of that society (the foundation decides the superstructure.)"[43] According to the "Theses," the cultural revolution must be under the leadership of a communist party because "a vanguard party must lead the vanguard culture" and "the methods to renovate culture put forth now are only intended to clear the way for the subsequent thorough revolution." But only a vague image of a socialist society was offered.[44] Throughout the document, there is no mention of class struggle and the words *worker* and *peasant* are notably absent.

The document laid out the dangers to Vietnamese culture posed by French colonialism and Japanese occupation and presented a stark choice: either Vietnamese culture would become even more backward if the fascist culture won or it would break free of its chains and catch up with the rest of the world after a victorious national revolution. Intellectuals therefore must struggle against both Eastern and Western philosophy, which had had pernicious effects upon Vietnamese culture (e.g., Confucianism, Descartes, Bergson, Kant, and Nietzsche), and against the various intellectual schools of the day (e.g., classicism, romanticism, naturalism, and symbolism). Dialectical materialism, historical materialism, and socialist realism must win out in the end. The core of the document, and the response to the dangerous situation it portrayed, was embodied in the introduction of the three principles guiding the new Vietnamese culture: *dân tộc hóa, đại chúng hóa*, and *khoa học hóa*, rendered by David Marr as "patriotism, mass consciousness, and scientific objectivity."[45]

The use of these three principles indicated clearly Trường Chinh's knowledge of Mao Tse-Tung's pronouncements in Yenan. In a 1940 article entitled "On New Democracy," Mao had argued that China was not yet ready to wage a socialist revolution leading to a state under the dictatorship of the proletariat and suggested that the current state system was a transitional one. This transitional system meant "the establishment of a new-democratic society under the joint dictatorship of all the revolutionary classes of China headed by the Chinese proletariat."[46] This new democratic society would be served by the new democratic culture, which "as a whole is not yet socialist" but contained "an element of socialism, and by no means a mere casual element but one with a decisive role."[47] China's new demo-cratic culture would be "a national, scientific and mass culture."[48]

In the Vietnamese context, however, the word *patriotism*, as David Marr has defined *dân tộc hóa*, is inadequate. As Marr himself has noted elsewhere, the term *dân tộc* is embedded in a web of ethnic and cultural-linguistic factors rather than national and territorial concerns.[49] That potent, indefinable, and yet so fundamentally felt sense of being Vietnamese has always been the crux of modern Vietnamese nationhood. The suffic *hóa* when attached to a noun, does more than elevate it to the level of a concept or ideology. It carries the sense of an act being done to achieve such a concept. In comparison with Mao's formulation of nationalism, there is a sense of great urgency and an edge of desperation in Trường Chinh's version of *dân tộc hóa*. The phrase thus means more than "people" or "nation" or even "patriotism." It demands an active return to what is uniquely Vietnamese, or, simply put, it asks for Vietnamization. The fact that the Vietnamese have always felt deeply about their spirit and yet could ask for a return to this Vietnameseness may seem contradictory, but it was a dilemma in which many intellectuals found themselves at the end of the 1930s, a period of unprecedented development in Vietnamese intellectual life.

If the intellectual discussion from the 1920s through to the 1940s in one way or another continually returned to the issue of *dân tộc, dân tộc hóa*, as formulated by the "Theses on Culture," brought the concern together with a specific emphasis on action. For want of a better term, I will define *dân tộc hóa* here as "nationalization." Given the changing international environment, which was chipping away at the colonial hold over Vietnam, many Vietnamese felt the need to act. The eccentric writer Nguyễn Tuân, whom the Việt Minh had found impossible to recruit into the Cultural Association for National Salvation in 1943, still could not escape the overwhelming sense of history.[50] Sensing vaguely the importance of the political maneuvering in Europe but distinctly aware of the Japanese presence in neighboring China, Nguyễn Tuân ruminated in 1939 upon finding himself unable to concentrate on writing:

Are people—especially Vietnamese people of the year 1939—only concerned with literature? And only with writing? I am one who wants to serve art and literature, but many other worries have stolen into the soul of an artist [given] the sickness of the time [and] the anxieties of the current situation. . . .

. . . I still could not break from the joy of hearing poetry recited or writing poetry. But in this solemn moment of the period, I want people to sit upon the saddle of a warhorse to cast a poetic verse and blend it into the sound of the drum urging the moon to fall upon the city.[51]

By 1943, Nguyễn Tuân the writer, although still unattached to any political party or intellectual platform, was moved to say "I want to reverse the comment by Oscar Wilde, which essentially advocates that 'life imitates art more than art follows life.'"[52] He did join the Việt Minh after the August Revolution, and one of the most inspiring images of the early years of the anti-French resistance was that of Nguyễn Tuân pounding upon a drum, urging Việt Minh soldiers to take a French military post in a battle in the summer of 1949.[53] He had literally become the drummer for the revolution.

Nationalism, the Masses, and a New Vietnamese Culture

The second principle prescribed by the "Theses on Culture" was *đại chúng hóa* or "popularization." While the search for national identity for many intellectuals remained primarily an ideological and elitist one the Vietnamese population began to be perceived and to appear in works in a markedly different way in the 1940s. The school of critical realists became dominant, eschewing the Self-Reliant Literary Group's romantically pastoral but ultimately patronizing view of the peasantry to present an unsentimental and gritty account of what life was truly like for the rural and urban underclass. These writers chose to examine the grim daily lives of the working class and the destitute: the uneasy transition from peasants to workers, how they tried to eke out a living, and how they found solace in such vices as gambling, women, and opium. From this perspective, the critical realists showed the extent to which many activities of such a class were direct responses to the structure of colonialism. A new category of women, for example, came into existence, those who were rich and powerful because of their marriages to Frenchmen. This was the subject of Vũ Trọng Phụng's 1936 *Kỹ nghệ lấy Tây* (The art of marrying Frenchmen). In such a system, exploitation is endemic. The French exploited the Vietnamese, the Vietnamese rich and powerful exploited the Vietnamese poor and weak, and those at the bottom of the hierarchy did all they could to exploit one another for the most meager of gains.

Thus, to emphasize *dân tộc* gradually also meant to focus on those who made up the majority of the population and their living and working conditions. But as even the critical realists themselves would comment later, their works presented the nature of the sickness without offering a cure. The darkness and hopelessness of their works were criticized by contemporary intellectuals. Regarding Vũ Trọng Phụng, one of the most prominent of the critical realists, another writer opined: "Reading Vũ Trọng Phụng's writing, I never saw a glimmer of hope or an optimistic thought. After reading it, we must imagine that the world is a hellish place and all around us are those who kill, prostitute themselves, [and] speak and behave in a vulgar manner."[54] To this charge, Vũ Trọng Phụng could only reply that he did see life this way: "Personally, I only see this society as vile: officials are corrupt, women depraved, men adulterous, a group of writers manipulative and cunning, and the luxurious entertainment of the rich is truly an insult to the society of the poor and exploited peasants and workers."[55]

The focus had shifted irrevocably. In the 1930s the individual, well-educated and modern, had waged a personal revolution against family and social conventions, most often for love. This was radical because unions based on love and outside of family considerations did not exist in traditional Vietnamese society, although this personal revolution also frequently failed, testifying to the enormous power against which the individual must struggle. This character, however, had been replaced in the 1940s with an individual deadened by life in colonial Vietnam, only one among a multitude whose lives were full of suffering and violence, both physical and spiritual. This shift reveals how dysfunctional the colonial structure had become for most Vietnamese. Even among those who respected his talent, Vũ Trọng Phụng's focus on sexual promiscuity in his characters was unsettling. It was sexual promiscuity, however, that highlighted the total lack of morals affecting the larger society. Right and wrong were no longer well defined. The individual had come to be driven by base instincts since social norms had ceased to fulfill their functions.

Haunted by the war in Europe and living in the psychological chaos that had been caused in no small part by the French and Japanese presence, the "live happily, live youthfully" movement championed by the Self-Reliant Literary Group raged on but with a crucial change in spirit: it was "no longer soft and romantic like before but was acquiring a depraved and licentious mood."[56] Sexually charged novels were very popular, providing escapist entertainment and catering to the deeply cynical atmosphere, which called for instant gratification since there was no guarantee of a tomorrow. Nhất Linh, the nominal leader of the Self-Reliant Literary Group, had abandoned literature for politics in 1939. The last novel, written in 1942, by Khái Hưng, the other leader of the group, revolves around the love a father (a rich businessman) and a son (a law school student) have for the same woman, who in turn loves the father for money and the son for youth. The literary historian Phạm Thế Ngũ has commented that with *Băn khoăn*

> love under Khái Hưng's pen became distant from the initial idealistic attitude [in his earlier works] and took on a more realist flavor: love wrongly, love dissolutely, especially physical love, and see all sacrifices and transcendence as absurd. After ten years of writing romantic novels, the maturity of the author only meant loss of faith in the pure and noble ideas of the spirit to fall in line with the young's indulgence in dissipation from 1935 onward in which no illusion could dispel the skepticism and weariness.[57]

In the words of a character in *Băn khoăn*, "In the old days there was a generation of Kiều youth; now is the time of the generation of Anatole France youth."[58] Kiều here refers to a seventeenth-century Vietnamese classic, the *Tale of Kiều*, whose Confucian morality of love and righteousness had long been extolled. By 1942, however, morality no longer had a place. Pure need and desire dominated, even for a writer like Khái Hưng, who began his career in 1932 with the novel *Hồn bướm mơ tiên*, a dreamy tale of love with all its ideals preserved under the kind watch of Buddhism. The novel has long been established as a classic, a testament to its power and pioneering position in modern Vietnamese literature. *Băn khoăn*, on the other hand, has faded into the woodwork of history.

The death of the spirit was also expressed in the death of the body. In 1943, on the pages of the journal *Thanh Nghị*, Đoàn Phú Tứ, a member of the Xuân Thu Nhã Tập group, published a play called *Ngã ba* (Three-way intersection). The play revolves around a small group of young, well-educated urbanites who have ceased to believe in the possibilities of life. It ends with the suicide of one of the main characters. When it was presented to the public in 1944, the iconoclastic writer Nguyễn Tuân played the role of the suicide. In Nguyễn Tuân's own writing in the days immediately prior to the August Revolution, images of suicide also appeared.[59] The desperate economic circumstances of many intellectuals, which did drive some to early deaths, certainly contributed to the darkness that seemed to envelop intellectual writing at this time.

Since the newfound individuality had led to extreme moral corruption and even self-destruction under some circumstances, hopelessness pervaded creative works from the end of the 1930s into the 1940s.[60] Nguyễn Công Hoan's 1938 novel *Bước đường cùng* (Dead end), Hoàng Đạo's 1938 *Bùn lầy nước đọng* (Mud and stagnant water), and Ngô Tất Tố's 1939 *Tắt đèn* (When the light is put out) all provided detailed depictions of the peasants in all their desperation and hopelessness.[61] Here was the mass portrayed and understood in ways previously unknown, but that knowledge only generated further dissatisfaction and anger without outlining possible solutions. It was not surprising then that the "Theses on Culture" would strike a chord by emphasizing *đại chúng hóa* as a second principle guiding the new culture but with a crucial difference. This "massism" was tied to the possibility, the eventuality even, of victory.

The third criterion, *khoa học hóa,* or "scientific orientation," was the least prominent, defined in the Theses only as being "against all that would make culture antiscience, antiprogress."[62] The term *khoa học,* or "science," was everywhere in the intellectual discourse of the 1930s and 1940s, however, and it is difficult to capture its exalted meaning. For Vietnamese intellectuals, science opened up a new vision of the world, one that could be explored by means of rational thought in an explicitly human realm rather than the traditional world of pure morals, feelings, and supernatural influences. Science also assumes the possibility that the work of a later generation can override that of a previous one, bypassing, as it were, the implacable Confucian norm of truth based on the inherited experience of age. Resistance against authority and independent thinking were closely connected.[63] For the creative community, science meant a more systematic discussion of history and literature, and it was with this emphasis on science that Marxism came to the attention of many Vietnamese intellectuals.

Khoa học hóa was an explicit rejection of traditional practices that still influenced the thoughts and behavior of most Vietnamese, but it also stressed progress and the hope inherent in it. A number of intellectuals were less concerned with the scientific nature of the concept of *khoa học hóa* than with the emotional appeal of progress. According to one writer, "I remember that at that time the slogan *khoa học hóa* was very difficult for us to understand" and that when he first heard about the three criteria, "I did not understand [them] at all. Perhaps in the beginning the "Theses" was absorbed and culture for national salvation drew us mainly because of emotions."[64] At any rate, the fatalistic tendency so prominent in the late 1930s and early 1940s was now deemed to be surmountable. A new Vietnamese culture was entirely possible in the context of a mass-based, rational, and progressive national identity, which could only be achieved under the guidance of the political party with the most viable organizational capability, the Vietnamese Communist Party and its attendant Việt Minh front.

The brief "Theses on Culture" could only set out the most basic of guidelines, however, given the difficult political environment and the Party's emphasis on a united front. This general prescription was further refined and applied to the current situation in subsequent writings by Trường Chinh. In an important 1944 article, Trường Chinh argued that the three sicknesses afflicting Vietnamese culture were the lack of an independent nationalist spirit; the low level of scientific knowledge, which was affecting even literature with unclear and ungrammatical sentences; and a culture removed from the bulk of the population, having been produced only for the enjoyment of the elite. In short, contemporary Vietnamese culture was negatively defined as being against the nation, against science, and against the people.

Trường Chinh went on to elaborate on the three principles and proceeded to tie them together in a cohesive relationship.

> These principles are the three links in a chain. They are of a continuous, uninterrupted nature. We cannot achieve the task of generating a new Vietnamese culture if we leave out one principle of the three. We also cannot follow one and at the same time go against the others. If we are not cognizant of that, then we certainly cannot fulfill the task of building a new culture for our people and may even fall into the trap of the big powers or be used by them.[65]

By describing these three principles as an unbroken chain, Trường Chinh had tightened the discussion. What began as a general guideline for viewing the country's cultural development and its current situation had turned into a more specific policy formulated to weed out contending ideas and insist on a particular view of Vietnamese culture past, present, and future. In the article, he proceeded to apply this concept of an unbroken chain of three principles to the most prominent groups of the day. The Tri Tân group was composed of "feudalist intellectuals" who were inclined toward nationalization, but because they looked to the past they were hostile to science and the masses. Those belonging to the group Thanh Nghị were labeled "nationalist bourgeoisie" who "did not fully carry out the three slogans because they did not completely recognize the sickness in Vietnamese culture."[66] Trường Chinh reserved his harshest words, however, for those who wrote for the Marxist Hàn Thuyên group, whom he called "petite bourgeoisie." He berated them for their claim to science in their use of the methods of historical and dialectical materialism because what they actually presented was only "mechanistic materialism." Trường Chinh further accused the group of trying to cause dissension among Vietnamese nationalists at a time when what the country needed above all was unity. He thundered:

> Why are they pointing the flame of the cultural struggle toward the nationalist intellectuals (Tri Tân, Thanh Nghị) while the life and death calculation of our people demands an amicable alliance with them in order to point the flame of the cultural struggle toward fascist Japan-France? Is not that mask of "new culture" of the publishing house Hàn Thuyên, where a number of Trotskyists are running wild, very suspicious?[67]

The irony of the charge must have been obvious to many intellectuals since in the same article Trường Chinh himself had been adamant that both the Tri Tân and Thanh Nghị intellectuals had failed to meet the needs of the people and therefore could not guide the new cultural movement. He was, in effect, doing exactly what he accused the Hàn Thuyên group of doing. Nevertheless, there were reasons why a large number of intellectuals did not accept certain works published by the Hàn Thuyên group. In particular, Nguyễn Tế Mỹ's revisionist historical study, *The Trưng Sisters' Uprising*, was difficult to accept.[68] Against the established view that the Trưng sisters' uprising against Chinese forces in A.D. 40 was representative of Vietnamese nationalist will, Mỹ contended that the failure of the uprising had led to direct Chinese rule over Vietnam, which should be seen as a social revolution benefiting Vietnam's eventual development given the superiority of Chinese civilization. Feeling as oppressed and violated as they were by the French and Japanese presence in the country in the

1940s, Vietnamese intellectuals were hardly in the mood to accept such an objective argument about Chinese influence upon the development of the Vietnamese state. In the works of the most prominent member of the Hàn Thuyên group, Nguyễn Bách Khoa, who was better known as Trương Tửu, the strength of the popular will (as reflected in folk songs and sayings) was emphasized to the point of denying Confucianism and the mandarin class any goodness or even influence, and the concept of class was used to dissect such literary classics as *The Tale of Kiều* and well-known historical personages like Nguyễn Công Trứ.[69] The radical approach of the Hàn Thuyên group to history, society, and literature went against not only the traditional outlook of the Tri Tân group but many others who needed to reaffirm their sense of Vietnameseness and connection to a larger vision of history rather than the Hàn Thuyên group's brutal and economically deterministic view.[70]

Capitalizing on this mood, Trường Chinh increased his criticism of the Hàn Thuyên group and its Marxist claims with a 1945 article attacking Nguyễn Tế Mỹ's book, pointedly entitled "A Devil under the Marxist Guise." Taking the book's argument one step further, Trường Chinh contended that "according to that reasoning, our people's current struggle against fascist Japan-France is also against the progress of society, so we will be defeated? Here, Nguyễn Tế Mỹ's doctrine of mechanistic materialism becomes the doctrine of surrender, of defeatism!"[71] All the works of the Hàn Thuyên group were soon referred to as representing "mechanistic materialism" or the "distortion of Marxism" and castigated for providing assistance—wittingly or unwittingly—to the enemy.[72] There could only be one leader of the nationalist struggle, and there could only be one interpretation of Marxism in Vietnam.

Revolutionary Romanticism and Its Appeal

By 1944, the Việt Minh had declared itself a contender in the cultural front with a specific cultural policy. At the very least, its various cultural pronouncements and articles announced to intellectuals that they did have a role to play within the Việt Minh front. It is also worth mentioning that, far from the image of hard-line revolutionaries, many Vietnamese Marxists were as idealistic and romantic as other intellectuals. The insistence upon a strength of will capable of overcoming any material obstacle and the inheritance of a culture steeped in romanticism, both of its own nature and under French influence, struck easily understood and deeply felt chords in many Vietnamese intellectuals. The Vietnamese communists themselves would later designate the time of the anti-French struggle as the period of *cách mạng lãng mạn*, or revolutionary romanticism.

It was this quality of revolutionary romanticism that drew many intellectuals into the Việt Minh fold and cast a unique glow upon that period of anti-French struggle. After all, Vietnamese are fond of recalling that Vietnamese communist leaders were also poets and writers. Any anthology of Vietnamese literature published since 1945 would have to include Hồ Chí Minh, Trường Chinh, and Tố Hữu (another high-ranking Party theorist who is considered to be Vietnam's preeminent revolutionary poet) among others. Vietnamese intellectuals, on the other hand, often joke nowadays that the country would have fared better if its political leaders did not always possess literary pretensions. Nevertheless, such pretensions serve to reiterate the importance of literature in the political context. The literary achievements of political leaders may be inflated, but their creative efforts were of a credible quality and did influence other intellectuals in a way that pure revolutionary exhortations might not have.

Furthermore, literary creativity also represented those revolutionaries' own particular ways of responding to the situation at hand. To them, it was just as natural to talk of the Party's leadership and the worker-peasant alliance as the poems that moved them. General Trần Độ, one of the earliest proselytizers of the "Theses," remarked on the occasion of its fortieth anniversary: "Today in researching the 'Theses on Vietnamese Culture' we need to tie it closely to the poem 'As a Poet,' with the article 'Some Major Principles of the New Culture Movement' . . . and with comrade Trường Chinh's work *Marxism and Vietnamese Culture*."[73] The poem "As a Poet" was written by Trường Chinh in 1942 to parody Xuân Diệu's famous 1938 credo of romanticism embodied in his poem "Feelings and Emotions."[74] Xuân Diệu's poet dreamed of clouds and wind, but Trường Chinh's would use his pen to change the system and each of his verses would be the "ammunition to destroy brute force." Trần Độ himself recalled that on a clandestine trip with Lê Quang Đạo to meet with intellectuals for the purpose of persuading them to join the Việt Minh, they recited and discussed a poem by Huy Cận, who was prominent in New Poetry.[75] Poetry, albeit a particular kind, was an integral part of the revolutionary process.

It should be noted that Trường Chinh himself took the poetic craft very seriously, writing under the pen name Sóng Hồng, or Red Wave. Collections of his poetry appeared in 1966 and 1974, and they were reissued in one volume in 1983 by the Literature Publishing House.[76] The name Trường Chinh is nowhere to be found in the collection, whether in the publisher's introduction or the poet's preface, even though a photograph of the poet leads the collection. Referring to himself as "a revolutionary cadre who writes poetry and is not a poet," Trường Chinh had this to say about poetry in general and his own in particular.

> We cannot separate poetry from the revolution. Of course, not every poem is revolutionary, but where the revolution exists, there is poetry. Is not all of the revolutionary work of our Party and of our people a heroic ode of the time? . . .
>
> Poetry is the grand reflection of people and of the age. Poetry speaks not only about the poet's own private feelings but expresses through such sentiments the hope of a nation and the dreams of the people, outlining the heartbeat of the masses and the general tendency of human history. . . . Poetry is one of the most amazing arts of the creative mind. As such, the poet's responsibility is heavy.
>
> This brief view of poetry has guided me in my writing. Unfortunately my poetry is not as I would have liked it to be. That is because my poetic talent and my work in refining the poetic art are inadequate.[77]

The poetic disposition of the Vietnamese revolution coupled with the fact that much of the cultural work at the time was highly personal succeeded in persuading prominent intellectuals well known for their eclecticism and recalcitrant nature to join the Việt Minh. As already discussed, the three principles put forth by the Việt Minh as the cornerstone of its intellectual policy were very much trends of the time. Their formulation into a coherent whole, however, was made even more persuasive after the August Revolution, when the Việt Minh took advantage of the big-power vacuum in the aftermath of World War II to come to power with a tremendous surge of popular support. The much discussed possibility of an independent Vietnam had proven to be real, and the acute sense of participation in the country's history was overwhelming. The writer Nguyễn Tuân, whose pre-revolution work was a model of individualistic and passive response to chaos and a retreat to the world of pure sensation and beauty, responded thus to the question of why he joined the Việt Minh after the August Revolution: "By that time it was different. One must believe in somebody in fighting against the French, so I decided to follow the communists." He noted that Việt Minh leaders were careful to arrange trips for him and money for his family without demanding anything in return. For Nguyễn Tuân, this highly personal approach was extremely effective: "Those are small details, but with me they became impressions. It was precisely Tố Hữu and Trần Huy Liệu's friendly and open attitudes that were the additional key factors making me follow the revolution decisively and changing my view [away from art for art's sake and] toward life."[78] One looks in vain for any discussion more specifically Marxist.

The 1948 "Marxism and Vietnamese Culture"

Those who cast their lot with the Việt Minh after the August Revolution had to accept the Việt Minh's cultural policy, which became much more Leninist as the anti-French struggle continued and underscored the Party's leadership. Intellectual support of the anti-French struggle was so clearly defined by nationalism that almost immediately questions arose over a number of issues concerning intellectual freedom, which forced the Party to enunciate guidelines to respond to questions and shape the debates. Once more it was Trường Chinh who presented the Party's new and expanded cultural policy in a report called "Marxism and Vietnamese Culture" at the Second National Conference on Culture in July 1948.

The importance of this report cannot be overstated. In retrospect, all the major elements of the development of Vietnamese intellectual activities, as well as cultural and educational work, for the next three decades made their appearance in the report. In that regard, it presented a coherent view of the Vietnamese communists' interpretation of their struggle and their vision of the new society. Solutions to the country's predicament were prescribed, but the path that had to be taken to achieve them also generated a dilemma with which Vietnamese intellectuals are still wrestling today.

In seven parts, the report sought to establish a firm Party line and address a number of contentious issues. It intended to lay down a theoretical framework in which to view not only the current struggle and future developments but the Vietnamese past. This theoretical framework, roughly detailed in previous Party pronouncements, was now explicitly presented as *lập trường văn hóa mác xít,* or the Marxist

LIBRARY OF DAVIDSON COLLEGE

cultural position. This revolutionary and scientific approach would uncover once and for all the myths and lies imposed upon the society by the ruling class and disclose to the working class its historical mission. Furthermore, Marxist culture, with its dialectical materialism, "will not only accurately depict why the old society must perish, but it will explain why the new society must certainly emerge and the general state of the new order."[79]

By returning to the old debate of the 1930s between art for art's sake and art for life, Trường Chinh made a deft connection between nationalist and socialist points of view. He contended that in a society divided by class no work of art was without social content. Marxist culture also reflected a certain social content but one that was invincible because it was fighting for justice and freedom. All progressive Vietnamese, he argued, must take its side.

Speaking from the nationalist point of view, Trường Chinh asked pointedly how any Vietnamese could think of a "neutral culture" when the only choice was between the resistance and colonial forces. Those who spoke of "being above politics," "absolute freedom," and an "objective attitude" were not only cowardly but reactionary because their position allowed the enemy to take advantage of the situation and them. Freedom and truth were not abstract concepts but existed in reality in the struggle for the rights of the people against colonialism and the ruling class's exploitation. One must therefore make a choice, and the only possible choice was to join the resistance. In this formulation, class was never excluded but the nation was constantly reiterated. The matter was straightforward: "Like other revolutionary classes in Vietnamese society, the working class recognizes that only when the nation is liberated will it experience the condition for complete liberation."[80]

The Chinese influence is palpable here. At the 1941 Eighth Plenum of the Indochinese Communist Party, which marked Hồ Chí Minh's return to lead the revolution and the reemphasis on the "national question," it was notable that the formative political experiences of all the Central Committee members present had been in Vietnam or southern China.[81] Many of the Moscow-trained Party leaders had been executed or had died in jail as a result of the colonial authorities' reprisals following the Party's Southern Committee's attempt at insurrection in 1940. Moreover, for all of Hồ Chí Minh's internationalist credentials and in spite of the fact that he had lived outside of Vietnam for some three decades, mostly in France and the Soviet Union, he seemed more comfortable in the Sino-Vietnamese cultural milieu.

He was certainly more than conversant with Vietnamese language and literature. Upon his return in 1941, he wrote poems with historical and national themes to galvanize the revolutionary spirit among cadres and peasants alike, using the Vietnamese "six-eight" poetic form or writing a new "five character classic" like those of old to be used in literacy classes.[82] Here is another interesting fact to ponder: when he returned to Vietnam, he brought with him a history book of Russian communism written not in Russian or even in French but in Chinese.[83]

The Chinese influence would grow with the success of the Chinese revolution in 1949. Trường Chinh himself was known for his admiration of it: his revolutionary name, Trường Chinh, means "Long March." According to one account, Trường Chinh was paying particular attention to cultural issues from 1941 on, and therefore he must have been well aware of Chinese writings on the subject.[84] I have already noted Mao's influence on the formulation of Trường Chinh's "Theses on Culture," but the more Marxist stance of "Marxism and Vietnamese Culture" also showed his familiarity with Mao's 1942 cultural pronouncement on literature and art in Yenan. There was really nothing comparable to Yenan in the Vietnamese experience; no place in Vietnam could exist so far removed from French military forces and become an autonomous territory. Nevertheless, the Chinese communists' experience with the united front and the move toward a more socialist standpoint provided valuable lessons to the Việt Minh. Mao's insistence on doing away with the notion of neutral politics, art, and literature and his focus on "whom to serve" and "how to serve" defined the approach that the Việt Minh would soon follow.[85] By 1948, the Việt Minh was ready to begin dismantling the united front, and Mao's rejection of "a love transcending classes, love in the abstract and also freedom in the abstract, truth in the abstract, human nature in the abstract, etc." pointed the way.[86] Regarding the intellectuals, Mao's emphasis on "the problems of the class stand of the writers and artists, their attitude, their audience, their work and their study" and on the need for them to "go among the masses of workers, peasants and soldiers . . . in order to observe, experience, study and analyse all the different kinds of people, . . . all the raw materials of literature and art" would also be Trường Chinh's assessments and prescriptions for Vietnamese intellectuals.[87]

At any rate, in the years immediately following the August Revolution, the new version of socialism still had class struggle at its center but the revolution remained inside the boundary of the nation. In

November 1945, the Indochinese Communist Party actually dissolved itself with a resolution, which states that "the essential condition for the completion of the great task of national liberation is the solidarity and unity of our entire people regardless of class or party" and that it was time "to put the interests of the nation above class interests and to sacrifice partisan interests for the sake of the common interests of the Nation."[88] The "bourgeois-democratic revolution" was put aside in order to focus on the "national liberation revolution," one in which the united front strategy was critical. The Vietnamese communists' emphasis on the national question was more than a tactical move to achieve power, however. In Trường Chinh's "Marxism and Vietnamese Culture," the dominant concern was that Vietnam should be considered distinct from and equal to France and other states rather than adopting a utopian view of international communism. As such, the nation would remain intact, yet Vietnamese communists could earnestly proclaim that "this nation and socialism are one."[89]

Having explicated this Marxist cultural position, Trường Chinh went on to propound the official view of Vietnamese culture past and present. Despite the fact that he praised prominent Vietnamese cultural achievements, the wealth of Vietnamese popular culture, and the persistence of the Vietnamese national identity, his view of Vietnamese culture was dark and pessimistic. He saw Vietnamese classical culture as having two major weaknesses: it was lacking in scientific progress and it was heavily sinicized. He dismissed modern Vietnamese culture as "complicated and disorganized in content, frenchified and sinicized in form."[90] He conceded that French culture had had a great influence upon the Vietnamese, but "nevertheless, in summarizing French cultural influence with regard to us, we see that the good things are few [while] the bad things are many; the good is only superficial . . . while the bad has permeated to the bone."[91]

This line of socialist nationalism allowed the Party to be flexible in response to changing circumstances. It is therefore entirely characteristic that Trường Chinh's tone in "Marxism and Vietnamese Culture" alternated effortlessly between that of a stern revolutionary leader with a definite message and a yielding preacher using any means at hand to persuade his congregation to come to church. In the same report that spoke of Marxism as defining the direction of the country's future and its culture, he emphatically stressed that anyone could join the Việt Minh's cultural front as long as he or she supported the goals of national independence and democratic freedom. He cautioned against confusing the three guiding principles of cultural work with the need to consolidate support for the goal of national liberation at that time. He formulated the situation in this way.

> Anyone who enthusiastically participates in the anticolonial resistance naturally stands behind the unifying cultural front. Whoever is active in the cultural arena but for one reason or another currently stands neutral, is sympathetic to or supportive of, but does not directly participate in the resistance can still be a friend of the unifying cultural front.[92]

But this was the general policy. For those who actually engaged in cultural work for the Việt Minh, the specific guidelines outlined by Trường Chinh left little room for independent thinking. Responding to the debate that arose in 1946 over the difference between a work of art and art as propaganda, Trường Chinh decided the issue once and for all by means of a disingenuous, circular argument. While agreeing that there were differences between true art and art as propaganda, he contended that "when propaganda achieves a certain level, it becomes art. When art reaches a particular level of effectiveness, it clearly has a propagandistic nature."[93] Thus, in his views a propagandist might not be a true artist, but a true artist could not claim to be entirely neutral and propaganda free. Art could only be considered true if it was in service of the truth, and that truth was the revolution. In this regard, propaganda in the service of the revolution was not always true art, but it certainly carried the possibility of becoming so.

This debate over propaganda and art was also a reaction against the growing emphasis on "timely art and literature" (*văn nghệ kịp thời*) and the Party's insistence on the audience being workers and peasants. The demand for timely art and literature was in effect the demand for propaganda work, and that work had to be tailored to the needs of the masses. How, then, could intellectuals find the time and creative space to produce works of lasting value on subjects other than the immediate needs of the revolution, and how could such works be accepted and understood by the public?

This conflict among intellectuals led to another rousing debate as to whether the public must be educated in the arts in order to critique them. More than just producing intellectual works for the masses and taking the masses to be the main audience, the logic of this position when pushed to the extreme also meant the critique of art by the masses, or at least by those who operated in the name of the masses. The sentiment among intellectuals, which will be further explored in the next chapter, was that they were quite willing to create in the service of the revolution and the people, but their sphere of expertise should not be violated. To create for the masses was one thing, but to have the worth of their works determined by whether the general public liked them or not, regardless of the opinions of their peers, was another issue. A creative work had to be created to fulfill some public need and constantly revised based on public opinion, and this was a particularly difficult point for the artists to accept. According to Trường Chinh, the public did not have to learn about art in order to evaluate it because

> the masses are the ultimate art connoisseurs since they have many ears, eyes, intelligent brains, and a responsive collective sentiment. No other critic compares to the masses in this regard. Perhaps a large number of people are not informed about some professional technique, but the masses include both experts and amateurs. What one does not ascertain, naturally another will.[94]

It would help intellectuals if they kept in mind that the method guiding their work was socialist realism. Trường Chinh defined this as a way to create realist works about society based on the objective law of development leading to socialism. He placed much emphasis, however, on the "model characteristics of the model situations."[95] Quoting Tolstoy, he stressed that the artist's responsibility was to highlight what was the core of the truth in images with which the public could identify immediately, "making them see the inevitable transformation of society and the objective tendency of progress."[96] There was a twist for Vietnamese intellectuals, however. Although the disposition of socialist realism was objective, Trường Chinh pointed out that there was objective truth that was useful to the revolution and objective truth that was not. Thus, a defeat in battle could be presented because it was an objective truth, but

> we must make the readers recognize how our soldiers coura- geously sacrificed themselves, why we lost, in that defeat which part was victorious, and, even if we were defeated, how our soldiers never hesitated because everyone was enthusiastically learning from the experience so as to prepare for victory in fu- ture battles.[97]

The final arbiter of that truth, in this argument, was not the artist but the needs of the revolution and the people, as these were delineated by the Party. How creative works would satisfy those needs and what were thought to be the views of the public, however, needed to be communicated to the intellectual community. This was where criticism came in. Trường Chinh saw it as necessary to constantly elevate the standard of creative work by pointing out and eliminating false tendencies as well as attacking the enemy's position. He emphasized that it was important to remember that the ideological struggle could not be separated from the political, military, and economic struggle, especially when the French colonial authorities and their Vietnamese collaborators continued to mesmerize the masses with their degenerate culture. In addition, "without criticism, without debates by the pen, our country's art and literary movement will be too calm, too reticent! It is no different than a horse taking steps one at a time, its head to the ground, lacking a critical whip to lash it and make it rear up."[98] Far from providing the inspiration for art and literature, Trường Chinh's prescription for criticism would define its work in later years as the guardian of whatever orthodox political line was dominant at the time.

— • —

Between the 1943 "Theses on Culture" and the 1948 "Marxism and Vietnamese Culture," the communists had established a cultural policy that had enormous consequences. Capturing both the main trends in the spirit of the time and striking out to construct a brave new world, there was a constant process of gathering support in the name of the nation and the people that went hand in hand with the process of reshaping that commitment ultimately in the Party's interest. At any point in time, the Party would assert that it was the greater good that demanded the smaller sacrifices. Intellectual responses indicated at first confusion and then full awareness of this strategy, but as long as the Party could continue to convince them of the worth of the greater good they had no choice but to comply, and for the most part they did so willingly.

Above all, the cultural policy indicated a powerful reaction against the past. It did seek to return to peoplehood, but one that would contain a pure Vietnamese national essence untainted by either Chinese or French influences. For all the communists' emphasis on the richness of Vietnamese popular culture, their rejection of the classical past and the modern present testified to a profound disdain for

Vietnamese culture, gaining more credence for the socialist idea of creating anew. As Trường Chinh asserted in "Marxism and Vietnamese Culture,"

> We only want to conclude after an objective evaluation that our country's scientific and technological level is low; our country's economy is basically feudal and semifeudal, with many archaic vestiges remaining; politically, our country is at times semicolonial and at times colonial; there was a long period of independence, but we were still dependent on or influenced by feudal China within a definite sphere; and now for close to a century we have been under French colonial rule so that the national essence has been held back and our country's culture has not fully developed its nature. Is recognizing this situation pessimistic? Definitely not! On the contrary, it is done so that we can bravely bear the responsibility.[99]

This deep ambivalence with the Vietnamese self made the view espoused in these cultural and intellectual pronouncements profoundly idealistic in spite of the communists' insistence on the laws of historical and dialectical materialism and the importance of action. The Việt Minh's cultural policy insisted on the primary importance of the ideological struggle and that in the Vietnamese case "revolutionary culture has thus preceded economic reality and exerted a powerful influence on society."[100] David Marr has also cogently pointed out that Hải Triều, the Party's main intellectual in the 1930s debate over the art for art's sake position, subsequently "endorsed voluntarism to the point where historical materialism seemed to lose almost all significance."[101]

Intellectual commitment was required, in turn, to generate and sustain this collective willpower. Art and literature, too, had to undergo a painful process of transformation. "Timely art and literature" and "art and literature in the service of the masses" were early demands for the complete reorientation of the nature of intellectual creation and freedom as the Vietnamese intellectuals had come to know them by the early 1940s. The definitions of *socialist realism* and the role of criticism further tightened the space for discussion, and new ground rules were established. Increasingly, the success of intellectual activities was becoming a matter of the intellectuals' commitment to socialist ideals. It was not the lack of education, for example, that rendered the people's judgment of a creative work worthless; it was because the work itself was not true to the people's needs and desires. Similarly, criticism was not divisive but constructive, and only those who had reactionary motives would misuse it. But who was to decide when a creative work was not true to the people's needs and desires and when criticism became reactionary? The answer was, of course, unnecessary since those who possessed the truth of socialist realism would already know.

E. J. Hobsbawm has found it necessary to remind us that the influence of Russia's October Revolution was enormous. It was

> the first proletarian revolution, the first regime in history to set about the construction of the socialist order, the proof both of the profundity of the contradictions of capitalism, which produced wars and slumps, and of the possibility—the *certainty*—that socialist revolution would succeed. It was the beginning of world revolution. It was the beginning of the new world.[102]

This certainty was also at the heart of the Vietnamese revolution, and the intellectuals, too, saw that they were living during the "great days" of history, a period in which "mass heroism is a daily matter."[103] The tremendous hardship endured by many intellectuals in the eight years of anti-French resistance and their firsthand witnessing of the suffering and endurance of the people testified to the faith in that certainty, one that the Party's pronouncements alone could not provide but did capture and offer as such.

— 2 —

Intellectuals and Their Responses, 1945–48

With the success of the August Revolution, the Việt Minh became the dominant contender in the battle to define the shape of the new political structure and society. Dominant but not yet fully in control of the nationalist movement, the Việt Minh emphasized the banner of national unity by offering seats in the transitional government to nationalists, intellectuals, and other prominent members of the elite from different political persuasions while maneuvering to gain the political upper hand and continuing to disseminate its agenda to the public. French insistence on regaining its colonial possessions in Indochina after World War II, however, made the prospect of a political route to Vietnamese independence a dim one, and the Việt Minh finally issued a call for a general uprising in December 1946. The military phase of the struggle was on.

The ambivalence of many intellectuals dissolved with this call for an all out military struggle against the French. The matter became a clear battle between Vietnamese nationalism and French colonialism, and the decision to join the Việt Minh was an easy one to make for many. Intellectuals who joined the Việt Minh between 1945 and 1948 clearly saw themselves as equal participants in the debate on national culture when the ideological space was not yet so restricted as to force the discussion in any single direction. Much of the writing at this time focused on the painful transformation that the petite bourgeoisie, the class to which the bulk of the intellectuals belonged, would have to undergo in order to participate in the new era. Workers and peasants had yet to appear as dominant types in literature, and discussion of the people and popular culture was hesitant even among ardent Việt Minh intellectuals, whose writings continued to be suffused with pessimism and disdain for past cultural achievements. In all of this, the Party's growing emphasis on intellectuals as voices of the people was ambivalently received, even though the themes of being one and how to be one with the masses ran through all the writings produced during this period, along with an insistence on radically transforming or even destroying the self. The loss of intellectual creativity and independence was difficult for many intellectuals to accept, even when they fully supported the Việt Minh's goal of national independence.

Thus, at the point at which support for the revolution among many intellectuals was at its most intense there was also much soul searching. It would not be until late 1948 and early 1949 that the Vietnamese communists became organized enough to force the intellectual discussion along the desired course.

The Sociology of the Intellectuals

The appearance of modern political organizations in Vietnam in the mid-1920s, such as Hồ Chí Minh's Thanh Niên (Youth) Association and Nguyễn Thái Học's Kuomintang-inspired Việt Nam Quốc Dân Đảng (Vietnamese Nationalist Party), forcefully called for youthful involvement. The emergence of the Self-Reliant Literary Group and the New Poetry movement in 1932 developed the youthful theme further in the cultural and literary arena, reflecting both the widespread desire for change and the ways in which such a message could be brought to a much larger audience. The members of the generation of 1932 not only were much more conscious of their differences with their elders but were more aware of themselves as belonging to a particular generation and sharing similar dilemmas and frustrations.

The crucial difference between the generation of 1932 and the one immediately preceding it is the fact that most of its members, a good number of whom had been educated or had traveled abroad, had received a Franco-Vietnamese education. By this time, a young Vietnamese child could be educated entirely within the Franco-Vietnamese system and an initial classical education was no longer common. Comprehensive knowledge of Chinese and Sino-Vietnamese characters was becoming rare.

A Franco-Vietnamese education was, however, fraught with ambiguity. One study of colonial education in Vietnam notes that "Internal structural differentiation characterized the schools at all levels and that differentiation proceeded along regional lines, and within regions along class boundaries."[1] In short, a colonial education did not contribute to national integration either horizontally or vertically. Nevertheless, being part of a more systematic school system and enduring similar racist abuses did help to solidify a national and anticolonial outlook among Vietnamese students, though certainly not a unified view of the alternatives to the colonial order.

There were student strikes all over Vietnam in the 1920s and 1930s. Memoirs of those who attended the Franco-Vietnamese schools during this period are replete with accounts of maltreatment at the hands of teachers. The writer Nguyễn Công Hoan also recalled numerous fights between Vietnamese and French students because of the latter's insolent attitude and privileges they enjoyed.[2] The curriculum focused on French history and literature, and Vietnamese cultural propensities were often portrayed as backward and primitive.[3] Nevertheless, the curriculum did include Vietnamese language, history, and literature, although how well these subjects were taught varied widely from school to school and region to region. Thus, Vietnamese memoirs also spoke affectionately of dedicated teachers, both French and Vietnamese, who taught well and conscientiously. The scholar and critic Đặng Thái Mai, an ardent Marxist in his time, recalled a Vietnamese teacher who instilled a sense of nationalism in his students simply by teaching Alphonse Daudet's short story "The Last Lesson."[4] The story of the last lesson taught in French to a French youngster after the loss of Alsace-Lorraine to Germany in 1870 led to an inevitable comparison with the Vietnamese situation.

Đặng Thái Mai also remembered that at the College of Pedagogy in Hanoi his history professor, a Frenchman, was a member of France's socialist party. His discussion of Western philosophy was clearly Marxism in orientation, and he "did not hesitate to attack capitalist and conservative ideologies."[5] His professor of literature, a certain Milon, also received high praise for teaching him the basics of how to understand a work of literature and conduct research. In particular, according to Đặng Thái Mai, he was taught to examine a work's artistic values as well as its historical characteristics. The connection between a work's literary worth and contemporary events would prove to be the first step in his understanding and acceptance of the Marxist view, foretelling his involvement with the Hàn Thuyên group and later commitment to the Việt Minh's agenda. Nevertheless, it is worth reiterating that this first exposure to a Marxist, or at least a more materialist reading of history and literature, came by way of a Franco-Vietnamese education in the late 1920s, before the existence of the

Việt Minh. Such an education was also fairly comprehensive, and Đặng Thái Mai's experience could not have been unique.

> I gained a general knowledge about the thoughts of master phi-losophers from Socrates, Aristotle, and Plato to Descartes and Hegel and from Confucius and Mencius to Chu, Trinh, and Kháng Lương. I also read Tagore and Gandhi and glanced at the teachings of Buddhism, Mohammed, and even Jesus![6]

The generation of Vietnamese literati preceding Nguyễn Công Hoan and Đặng Thái Mai was the last to be entrenched in the court and classical education. Nguyễn Công Hoan and Đặng Thái Mai be-longed to a transitional generation. They both received a classical education in their childhood and were directed toward a Western education in their early teens. They straddled two different views of literary work. The intellectual generation of their fathers, according to the literary historian Thanh Lãng, "was composed mostly of scholars, of ideologists, those who focused on theory: their activities therefore mostly involved a translation or treatise of some kind."[7] On the other hand, by the time Nguyễn Công Hoan and Đặng Thái Mai entered the literary community in the late 1920s, and certainly by the early 1930s, the new generation armed with their Franco-Vietnamese educations focused on the creative aspects of literary activity, not didactic moraliz-ing aimed at instilling correct social behavior but the inner psychologi-cal struggle of the individual. This was to become the dominant mode of literary creation of the generation of 1932. The explosive growth of journalism, the publishing industry, and the reading public finally allowed for the emergence of intellectual professionals capable of mak-ing a living solely from writing.[8]

If the content and form of intellectual activities had changed dra-matically from one generation to the next, the backgrounds of the intellectuals themselves remained stable. For one thing, education continued to be the prerogative of the elite in the period between 1918 and 1938. Enrollment actually declined during the colonial period as the various indigenous educational systems were dismantled, and at the elementary level basic literacy was denied to more of the rural population than previously.[9]

Children of the Vietnamese elite, however, continued to have ac-cess to education at the higher levels, though this, too, varied from region to region. Many members of the southern elite, enjoying better access to French schooling since the south was under direct French rule, chose to send their children to French schools and then on to France. Thus, southern Franco-Vietnamese schools drew the majority of their students from what Gail Kelly has referred to as "Vietnamese *petites fonctionnaires*—low level civil service employees such as school teachers."[10] In the central region, the seat of the waning imperial government, the Franco-Vietnamese schools drew their students from midlevel civil service families and the traditional elite. The north was governed under French colonial authorities as a protectorate, and there the students of the Franco-Vietnamese schools came from the traditional and colonial elites.

Given that the south was only fully incorporated into Vietnam during the eighteenth century, mandarins came mostly from the central and the north. The vision of a village's son becoming a mandarin and returning to his village in glory was a powerful one in both the popular and elite traditions in the north and central regions but much less so in the south. In time, French colonial control undermined the imperial hold on power and intellectual life, and in Trinh Van Thao's study of three generations of modern Vietnamese intellectuals northerners came to the fore (see table 1). Thao's generation of 1925 would be comparable to what Thanh Lãng and others have referred to as the generation of 1932.[11]

The southern elite's access to a French education and French citizenship, with all the attending legal rights and cultural privileges, may provide one explanation as to why the number of southern intellectuals remained small in 1930; they had other channels through which to prosper and express themselves such as going to France or entering into commercial activities. Furthermore, since the Franco-Vietnamese system became the major educational route for the northern elite, northern intellectuals were much more active in dealing with questions relating to the development of Vietnamese language and culture in the face of Western hegemony in general and French colonialism in particular.

TABLE 1. Geographical Backgrounds of Intellectuals

Region	Generation of 1862 (%)	Generation of 1907 (%)	Generation of 1925 (%)
North	36	60	59
Central	45	27	20
South	18	13	21

Source: Trinh Van Thao, *Vietnam du Confucianisme au Communisme* (Paris: L'Harmattan, 1993), 61, 91, and 107.

Finally, as the University of Indochina, supposedly established to provide a university education for all residents of Indochina, was located in Hanoi, the majority of its students came from northern Vietnam.

As for the social background of the intellectuals, it has been noted that by the mid-1920s education was opened to a small group that included not only the traditional but also the colonial elite. The colonial elite in turn was composed of members of the traditional elite as well as others who were active in seizing the opportunity to gain wealth and power by providing the services and manpower required by the colonial administration. Again, the rise of the new intellectuals coming from classes other than the traditional elite seems to have existed mostly in the south.[12] On the whole, however, Trinh Van Thao's statistics indicate that the class compositions of the generations of 1862 and 1925 were virtually the same, with the majority coming from the scholar class.[13]

In short, the generation referred as 1925 by Trinh Van Thao and as 1932 by Thanh Lãng, the most Westernized and revolutionary, came from families that had always considered themselves to be among the cultural elite. Many members of the traditional elite turned their children toward a Western education while continuing to imbue them with Confucian ethics. Đặng Thái Mai's family, for example, was known to be anticolonial, but his elders were also searching for solutions to the country's dilemma through trips to China, Thailand, and Japan.[14] A Franco-Vietnamese education would lead to jobs in the colonial administration, but it was also a way in which Western learning, operating on very different standards than the classical tradition, could be gained.

While the social background of the intellectuals in the 1930s remained dominantly elitist, the content of their education and the environment in which they came of age were radically different than those of their elders. If someone like Đặng Thái Mai was straddling two worlds as he became active professionally in late 1920s and early 1930s, the next generation of intellectuals firmly and passionately proclaimed the power of modernity and called for a total break with the past. The category and concept of *văn nghệ sĩ* (creative intellectuals) became firmly entrenched, referring to a group of intellectuals who defined themselves more by their creative works rather than research or compilation. It foretold the importance of these intellectuals in shaping intellectual discussions. While *trí thức* is the broader term for intellectuals and includes all whose main occupation is the work of the mind (e.g., professors, scientists, lawyers, and doctors), it was mainly through the *văn nghệ sĩ* and their environment of newspapers, journals, and art exhibits that intellectuals as a whole came together to participate in the debates on society and culture. Finally, *văn nghệ* (literally, "literature and art") also carries a connotation of being carefree and unconventional. More often than not, a reference to someone as being very *văn nghệ* is praise as well as an explanation of eccentric behavior to be tolerated, a tacit acceptance of different standards for creative intellectuals because of the nature of their work.

The term *creative intellectual* contained something new for Vietnamese intellectuals in general, namely, the acceptance of a large measure of individualism unfettered by social conventions or traditions. Given that the category of *văn nghệ sĩ* only became viable between the 1920s and 1930s at the height of Westernization in Vietnam, it is not surprising that these intellectuals took on the bohemian air of Left Bank writers and poets, but it is important to note that this was how the general public had come to regard them as well. Their more fluid world, in comparison with the strictly elitist sphere of the scholar-official generation, was open to a wider constituency of men and women nurtured in the Franco-Vietnamese education system and the larger colonial society, with all their peculiar frustrations and promises. From late 1930s and early 1940s on, the writers and poets who were beginning to make a name for themselves came from more varied social backgrounds, and it was among these intellectuals that the Việt Minh found its first converts.[15]

The Cultural Association for National Salvation

For all that has been said about the importance of the "Theses on Vietnamese Culture" as a fundamental statement of the Việt Minh's cultural policy, the fact remains that the document itself affected only a few intellectuals. Written in 1943, it did not reach a number of key intellectuals sympathetic to the Việt Minh until a year later. More than anything else, it was written to clarify the Việt Minh's intellectual platform and justify an intellectual organization under Việt Minh leadership. Even this nascent intellectual organization, the Cultural Association for National Salvation (Hội Văn Hóa Cứu Quốc), founded in 1943, was barely in operation when the August Revolution swept the Việt Minh into power. Official histories would insist later that the "Theses" played a large role in influencing intellectuals to join the Việt Minh before the August Revolution, but the facts indicate otherwise. Reminiscences vary, but it would seem that even though the document was written in 1943, it did not reach key Party members and intellectuals until late 1944 and 1945. As Lê Quang Đạo recalled in his capacity as the secretary of Hanoi's Party committee, he presented the "Theses" to the first subgroup of the Cultural Association for National Salvation only in the summer of 1945, and even then he had only been briefed on it by Trường Chinh "a short time earlier."[16] It would not be impossible for the "Theses" to have reached a small number of people before that, but with the heavy-handed colonial restrictions and surveillance at the time it would have been impossible to spread the message further. Having a stranger sleeping in one's house was cause for arrest, and in fact key members of the Cultural Association for National Salvation were arrested at the end of 1944, although they were held for only a few weeks apparently because the French authorities did not want to bestow upon them the prestige of "political prisoners."[17] As one of the earliest members of the association commented,

> In terms of organization, we had done quite well: [we had] gathered or contacted a number of writers, poets, journalists, playwrights, painters, literacy campaigners. . . .
>
> But in terms of public activities, it must be said that [we] did not achieve much. Most notable was the volume of criticism *Văn Học Khái Luận* [An outline of literature] of comrade Đặng Thái Mai, which reflected fairly fully the Party's view on literature and art and the three slogans championing the new national culture [e.g., national, mass, and scientific]. We should also include Nguyễn Đình Thi's essay "Sức Sống của Dân Tộc Việt Nam qua Ca Dao" [The life of the Vietnamese people through folk sayings]. I don't remember if it was written before or after the "Theses on Culture," but [it was] quite in line with the slogan *"dân tộc hóa."*[18]

Even the supposed influence of the "Theses" on the works of Đặng Thái Mai and Nguyễn Đình Thi must be viewed with caution, however.[19] Overall, prior to the August Revolution the Việt Minh's cultural pronouncements did not have much real influence on the course of events and was not known to the majority of the intellectual community.[20]

The battle for intellectual support, therefore, became fierce only after the August Revolution. The Việt Minh came to enjoy a high level of popular and intellectual support, and the Marxist line was voiced openly in the Việt Minh's main publication at the time, the weekly newspaper *Tiên Phong* (Vanguard). The "Theses on Vietnamese Culture" was finally printed in *Tiên Phong*, and its main arguments were elaborated and defended by a number of Việt Minh intellectuals, particularly the critic Đặng Thái Mai. In a series of articles in 1946 whose tone grew increasingly strident, Đặng Thái Mai underlined the point of view that must be accepted by intellectuals: art and literature must be on the side of the working class and must be created to support the people's revolution.[21]

Even after the August Revolution, however, the Việt Minh was not completely free to broadcast its message. The vacuum among the big powers in the aftermath of World War II allowed the Việt Minh its moment of glory, but it was fragile. Popular support was high for an anticolonial and national solution, but it was not clear that a specifically Marxist option was the right choice. Other political and social ideas remained in contention even though the Việt Minh was the best organized group. There were still the Vietnamese Nationalist Party (VNQDĐ) and other smaller political parties, the religious movements of Cao Đài and Hòa Hảo in the south, and the possibility of a government under the last emperor, Bảo Đại. The uncertainty of the situation was great enough for the Việt Minh to emphasize unity, and the united front idea continued to be carried through to the establishment of various provisional governments between the August Revolution and the call for general uprising in December 1946, which included members of other political parties and prominent independent intellectuals. Nguyễn Tường Tam, better known as the writer Nhất Linh and the soul of the Self-Reliant Literary Group, was a member of the VNQDĐ by this time and even became the minister for foreign affairs in the coalition government.[22] The attempt by the Việt Minh to impose and control the united front was not only political but military. Engaging in an anticolonial struggle, the Việt Minh also fought against the VNQDĐ in the north and the Cao Đài and Hòa Hảo religious sects in the south.

Before the Revolution: National Heritage and the Self

The previous chapter explored the darker mood of Vietnamese society in the years prior to the August Revolution, with literature increasingly focused on physical and spiritual hunger, and throughout the country there was a surge of interest in philosophy and religion. Side by side with a call for a new Vietnam capable of functioning independently in the modern world was a devastating assault on what was considered to be the Vietnamese classical inheritance in all areas, particularly that of literature.

In retrospect, the repudiation of so much of the national past marked the emergence of a modern sensibility that reacted against the perceived debilitating weaknesses of a traditional society, which prohibited progress. At the moment of threat to the national existence, however, the instinct to preserve the past in order to safeguard the future competed against the desire to destroy the past in order to create a new future. The latter tendency placed little worth on past Vietnamese cultural achievements, seeing them as an uncreative derivative of Chinese accomplishments. Beginning in 1930, for example, there was already a fervent discussion as to whether Vietnam had ever had *quốc học,* or national culture.[23] Up to then, *quốc học* as a term referred to the imperial academy, but the debate in late 1930 focused on *quốc học* as national education or learning or national culture generally. The noted scholar Phạm Quỳnh (who was deemed a French collaborator and later executed by the Việt Minh) and the irascible Phan Khôi (who eventually joined the Việt Minh but fell out of favor in the late 1950s because of his independent views) both argued that Vietnamese scholars had never managed to formulate an ideological system that was specifically Vietnamese, unlike the Japanese, for example. The dissenting voice, that of a scholar named Lê Dư, presented a more syncretic definition of *national culture:* that which belonged to a nation or was borrowed from others but over time had become that nation's own. Based on this definition, he contended that there was indeed a Vietnamese culture embodied in the works of scholars written in *nôm,* the Sino-Vietnamese script, in Vietnamese customs and traditions, and in history and politics.[24]

It can easily be seen that Phan Khôi and Phạm Quỳnh defined *quốc học* as something greater, as national achievements of international stature rather than as the body of norms and traditions that nourished a society. Furthermore, to them that body of norms and traditions could not bring Vietnam into the global community as an equal partner of nations like France and Japan. Phan Khôi himself sparked another heated intellectual debate in 1933 when he argued against the well-accepted notion among Vietnamese intellectuals that Western civilization was materialistic while Eastern civilization was spiritual.

In fact, Phan Khôi asserted, the West had only achieved that level of material accomplishment because it was spiritually more powerful. Not surprisingly, he was passionately refuted by other intellectuals. Marxist critics also countered his point of view, bringing into the debate the categories of *duy vật* (materialism) and *duy tâm* (idealism), although Phan Khôi was faulted more for using the wrong methodology than for the actual content of his argument as it pertained to Vietnamese culture.[25] Phan Khôi himself, for all his ardent arguments about Vietnamese culture and society, never spelled out what must be done if Vietnam had never had a credible national culture or if the Eastern spirit was weak in contrast to that of the West.

If the self was liberated during the 1930s, it was at the expense of the traditional world. The first blows to the traditional culture, defined at the time primarily as classical and court culture, were dealt by those who considered themselves the immediate heirs of such a culture. Popular culture was barely noticed. Moreover, according to the composer Phạm Duy, in the period between 1930 and 1935,

> Ancient forms of music like *Hát Trống Quân, Hát Cò Lả, Hát Quan Họ* . . . disappeared in the cities. Even in the countryside, where these forms of traditional music has originated, the Vietnamese peasants living under colonial rule no longer truly sang in the traditional festivals. The traditional songs that I heard during the holidays, like the fourteenth of July celebrations organized by the French in France and the colonies to celebrate the downfall of the Bastille, for example, was the *hát xẩm* kind.[26]

Hát xẩm, the music sung by blind street singers in public places for money, generally consisted of bastardized versions of whatever musical influence was in existence. Phạm Duy suggests that even traditional music associated with the countryside was under threat in the 1930s. The intellectuals' reactions in the late 1920s and early 1930s remained elitist in that their concern was primarily with high rather than popular culture. Only in the late 1930s and early 1940s did popular culture come to be viewed as a legitimate repository of national values and traditions worthy enough to be examined systematically.[27]

The negative assessment of Vietnamese cultural past, therefore, was a latent impulse from the 1920s on. In one debate after another, aspects of traditional Vietnamese culture were condemned as worthless or inimical to progress, the prohibition on second marriage, for example. The past was increasingly seen as static and anachronistic.

The poet Lưu Trọng Lư lamented thus in 1933: "The Vietnamese youth today is anguished about [contemporary issues] while the Vietnamese poet can only sing of past sorrows."[28]

Throughout the 1930s the literary works of the Self-Reliant Literary Group and the group's influential journal, *Mores*, consistently defended the right of the individual to feel and act even if this placed him or her at odds with the family, the repository of traditional values and the enforcer of many of society's conventions. Overall, the works of the Self-Reliant Literary Group presented a powerful critique of many aspects of Vietnamese traditional culture, and the tenets of individualism were offered as a replacement. It was a distinctively Western notion of individualism in many respects, greatly inspired by French romanticism and interwar literature, which was suffused with cynicism, a deeply felt sense of the fragility of life and beauty, and a rebellious disregard for authority. Xuân Diệu, one of the New Poetry movement's brightest stars, could easily call on Verlaine and Rimbaud, as at home with these modern French poets as youthful Parisian poets would have been. At the height of New Poetry in 1935, a public debate between supporters of old and new poetry in Saigon could draw an audience of some eight hundred people.[29]

To claim that the nation's cultural past had no distinct value, however, meant that such worth had to be found elsewhere. In the 1930s, that answer had been individualism to a large extent. But by the end of the decade vigorous Westernization was no longer the attractive solution it had at first seemed. The poet Lưu Trọng Lư, that most fervent supporter of New Poetry, now pessimistically declared that "Before we were Chinese, recently we were westerners, and there was never a time when we were Vietnamese."[30]

These were harsh words, indeed, but even though individualism ceased to be the golden solution, it would seem that the negative view of the Vietnamese cultural past continued to pervade the thinking of many intellectuals. The works published by the Hàn Thuyên group continued to critically examine literary and social issues, but now specifically employing the methodology of dialectical materialism. The Marxist approach provided a new way to reassess the established past. Take *The Tale of Kiều*, the well-loved seventeenth-century verse story of the beautiful Kiều, who had to sell herself in order to save her father.[31] Reunited with her true love, who proclaimed that he loved her still, she yielded him to her sister since she herself, no longer pure, was unworthy of his affection. The tale had long been used as a moral lesson extolling female virtues and transcending life's dark situations. More than that, the tale was seen as containing nothing less than the Vietnamese national soul itself.[32] Although inspired by a minor Chinese work, the Vietnamese version was a masterful literary creation by the nineteenth-century poet Nguyễn Du, who gave *The Tale of Kiều* an autobiographical edge. During his lifetime, he saw the overthrow of the Lê dynasty by the Tây Sơn and the Tây Sơn by the Nguyễn. In the political chaos, he came to serve both the Lê and Nguyễn dynasties, violating the principle of dynastic loyalty. For the Vietnamese:

> Generations of poetry lovers, even illiterate ones, knew of Nguyen Du's personal dilemma, and saw in his verse-narrative more than the tragic story of a woman of beauty and talent of whom fate had been jealous. It was understood to be his *apologia pro vita sua* and a plea for compassion on behalf of all scholars trapped in the moral quicksands of political change.[33]

In 1945, Nguyễn Bách Khoa, the soul of the Hàn Thuyên group, launched a devastating attack against *The Tale of Kiều* in a work entitled *Văn chương Truyện Kiều* (The literature of *The Tale of Kiều*) and in the process, made crucial arguments about the role of intellectuals in society.[34] Reviewing the commentaries on Kiều, Nguyễn Bách Khoa noted three types that had developed over time. He argued that there was the feudal reaction to Kiều, which saw the tale as a moral lesson in Confucian terms in which literature was pedantically treated and the concept of literature as entertainment did not exist. From 1919 on, he contended that a new, Westernized elite had found Kiều appealing because of the notion of fate embodied in her life, reflecting a reaction against the lack of opportunity inherent in colonial life. The moral of the tale was essentially maintained, but *The Tale of Kiều* as a Vietnamese creation also became a source of national pride at a time when national insecurity was rampant. Finally, from about 1930 on, a new faction of petit bourgeois intellectuals emerged who lauded *The Tale of Kiều* not for its morality but for the beauty of the language and its broad view of human relations.

With forceful imagery and language, Nguyễn Bách Khoa derided the notion that art belonged to a transcendental and sacred realm and required a highly sensitive soul to understand it, a point of view espoused by the critic Hoài Thanh. Nguyễn Bách Khoa insisted on pinning artistic works to their earthly environment, making the Marxist argument that since the artist himself was created and conditioned by society it was "society [that] used artists as a tool to realize the momentum of its activities."[35] Regarding Kiều's long-extolled moral message, Nguyễn Bách Khoa characterized the classic work as permeated by a sense of failure, sadness, and hopelessness born of "a feudalist system at a point of crisis" and filled with "lives absolutely removed from the economic production process."[36] *The Tale of Kiều* was in his view an elite response to the decay of the feudalist order in which the dominant aesthetics was really that of the weak and defeated. The technical achievement of the work, the masterful use of the traditional Vietnamese six-eight couplet, in fact only signified the last stage before the downfall: "*The six-eight melody reaching perfection is a melody foreshadowing the end.*"[37]

The value of a work of art for Nguyễn Bách Khoa included both technical achievement and ideological content. He judged *The Tale of Kiều* to be antiprogress because it was suffused with romanticism, fantasies, pessimism, and sadness, whereas for him progressive works by nature were strong, angry, and practical.[38] In order to save the cherished elements of the past, it would be necessary to firmly break from elements of that past that were hostile to progress. Sadness and pessimism would have to be outlawed if the country was to move out of its torpor.

Đặng Thái Mai's work of literary theory, *Văn học khái luận* (An outline of literature), published by Hàn Thuyên in 1944, presented a more general discussion of intellectual activities in these new times. Harking back to the long running debate in the intellectual community between art for art's sake and art for life, he insisted that freedom was relative since no one could truly do as he or she pleased in society. No rigid rule ever prevented a genius from realizing his or her talent, but in the end a writer was restricted by the needs and desires of a society into which he or she was born. Staking his position unequivocally on the side of purpose, Đặng Thái Mai opined:

While a world, a regime, is still disintegrating, if we recognize [that] neutrality is only a meaningless term and [that] the freedom of an individual cannot not be disconnected from public life and [that] the meaning of art can only be realized within the community, within human society, then we also must realize that the new art and literature must flower in social reality, and it must be art and literature of the "socialist-realist" kind.[39]

The concern with the country's development underlined the emphasis on purpose and community. Đặng Thái Mai and Nguyễn Bách Khoa's works, however, remained elitist in their approach and in their appeal. Đặng Thái Mai's call for a socialist-realist culture did not contain any discussion of the involvement of the masses or even the suggestion that writers should write for the masses. Rather, it was a demand that intellectuals accept the inherent social responsibilities of their work instead of insisting on meaningless individual freedom. Đặng Thái Mai argued that a writer's greatest achievement would be to create characters that represented an age like those of Cervantes's Don Quixote, Lu Xun's AQ, and Balzac's old man Grandet while retaining their individual characteristics. The self-righteous Marxist concurred with the moralistic mandarin in Đặng Thái Mai's judgment that post–World War I European literature was "decadent" and "deformed" because of its lack of faith in humanity and society and its obsession with death, sexual gratification, and an anti-authoritarian message.[40] Such works did represent society but because they were "antisociety" and "inhuman" their values would not last.[41] The masses or the Party had yet to appear, but the inevitable question asserted itself: who, then, would judge which works were worthy and true to type?

The dual archetype-uniqueness demand on art and literature represented an idealist definition of *socialist realism*, which had been exemplified by Tolstoy in Lenin's assessment. According to Dave Laing, Lenin believed that the greatness of Tolstoy's work lay "in the fidelity with which it embodies the standpoint of the revolutionary peasantry, and thus the contradictions of rural Russia in the last part of the nineteenty century."[42] This was the highest level of achievement an artist could strive for, propelling history forward without losing oneself in the process. The allowance for individuality recognized that art was in the end the vision of an individual, but the demand that art had to be the embodiment of an age would eventually dominate. In Yenan in 1942, Mao commanded that writers and artists must now concentrate on "everyday phenomena, *typify* the contradictions and struggles within them and produce works which awaken the masses, fire them with enthusiasm and impel them to unite and struggle to transform their environment."[43] By 1948, Trường Chinh, too, would insist that the artist's responsibility was to bring the essence of truth to the public with the use of immediately recognizable images, "making them see the inevitable transformation of society and the objective tendency of progress."[44]

After the Revolution: National Heritage and the Self

It would be up to the Cultural Association for National Salvation to try to establish and elaborate the Party's cultural platform after the August Revolution. One of the first attempts to do so was a pamphlet written by Nguyễn Hữu Đang and Nguyễn Đình Thi entitled *Một nền văn hóa mới* (A new culture).⁴⁵ Written before the August Revolution, it came to be known more widely in print afterward.

The forty-five-page pamphlet was clearly designed to elaborate Trường Chinh's main points in the "Theses on Vietnamese Culture" in less politically dogmatic language. Following the line of argument made by Trường Chinh, the pamphlet attacked all other intellectual movements and groups and presented Trường Chinh's three main characteristics of the new culture, namely, scientific orientation (*khoa học hóa*), popularization (*đại chúng hóa*), and nationalization (*dân tộc hóa*). Again, the last characteristic, *dân tộc hóa*, was given the strongest emphasis. While stating that such a nationalist emphasis would not lead to either the unconditional acceptance of foreign influence nor fascism, the two writers had the confidence to claim that in order to build this new and unprecedented culture it would first be necessary to destroy the past.

> As in other spheres, the task of construction in the cultural arena has to begin with destruction: for a new culture to develop, it needs a cleared piece of land that contains no outdated or colonial vestiges. Therefore, the first task is to completely eradicate the poisonous venom of the feudalists and colonialists.⁴⁶

Such a view was accompanied by a plan of action. On the one hand, the government would take over and nationalize all the cultural organizations belonging to foreign powers and Vietnamese traitors. On the other, it would launch a massive propaganda campaign to expose the detrimental consequences of both feudal and imperialist cultural policies while bolstering the new one. The urgency and breadth of the plan were further underlined by the declaration that the government would immediately eliminate all the traditional customs and habits that were directly hindering the task of nation building. Far more emphatic than Trường Chinh had been in the "Theses on Vietnamese Culture" about what should be done, Nguyễn Hữu Đang and Nguyễn Đình Thi delineated a new national culture that would "not only construct a [body of] Vietnamese learning, but also a program to reform morals and customs and educate the people."[47] To really tackle popular change, the two authors concentrated on education that would first and foremost, eradicate illiteracy.

It is, however, the discussion of education for youth that is striking. While the eradication of illiteracy was a major concern for the Việt Minh, for Nguyễn Hữu Đang and Nguyễn Đình Thi there was a much stronger motive for a new education system in which children would be placed entirely outside the reach of the family and squarely within the confines of the community from the earliest phase of their lives. What underscored the firmness of such a vision was a distinct contempt for the Vietnamese youth and indeed, for Vietnamese culture overall.

This was what the authors thought of the contemporary Vietnamese youth: trapped within the narrow confines of his familial upbringing, he was spiritually and physically weak, overindulgent in his pleasure-seeking and entirely impractical in his education. The past which nurtured this weakling was so contemptible that it must be radically changed so that the new man could emerge into a utopian world as described at the end of the pamphlet.

> The persons who walk ahead will lead those behind, those with sight will lead the blind, [with] classes teaching *quốc ngữ* opening up everywhere; clubs and libraries for the masses growing like mushrooms; gymnasiums, information rooms, cinemas, and theaters attracting people; youth groups actively functioning; schools opening wide their doors to greet [students]; ships going to faraway destinations carrying loads of students [and consequently] new rays of light and new winds, . . . [all this will] surge forth, sweeping away fog and clouds, changing the sky, transforming the dark, backward, empty activities of yesterday into a bright, active, prosperous, and open life.[48]

This touching desire to reach for that new, bright and above all active life also meant eradicating the old, dark and, stagnant one. Erasing the past, however, was not entirely feasible since there still must be something Vietnamese, however it was to be defined, at the core of the new culture. If the East Asian world could no longer provide the overarching frame of reference for the critic Hoài Thanh in 1941,[49] then by 1945, for Nguyễn Hữu Đang and Nguyễn Đình Thi, the new frame of reference would be "the true and open national ideal."[50] This ideal would be embodied in the people and their culture, and it would be up to the same critic, Hoài Thanh, to ponder the entity called Vietnamese culture in 1946, this time as an ardent Việt Minh supporter.

In another pamphlet published by the Cultural Association for National Salvation, Hoài Thanh sought to delineate the special characteristics of Vietnamese culture. His uneasiness with the topic was palpable from the outset: the pamphlet itself was beseechingly entitled *Có một nền văn hóa Việt Nam* (There is a Vietnamese culture). He noted that not only French colonialists but many Vietnamese felt contempt for Vietnamese culture. The issue was important because, as he put it,

> All sincere Vietnamese are anxiously searching for faith in the race because only with such a faith can there come faith in themselves. Is it possible for the race to be weak and yet a Vietnamese can be strong? Once we see ourselves as weak, and believe that our ancestors have been weak these thousands of years, life cannot have any meaning![51]

He then proceeded to ask the question: "But is the truth that dismal? Are the Vietnamese people entirely impotent in terms of culture?"[52]

The truth was dismal indeed. Hoài Thanh dismissed outright Vietnamese classical achievements as mere repetitions of Chinese ideas, beliefs, and accomplishments. Having rejected much of high culture as a poor imitation, he then turned to popular culture as the body of folk sayings and poetry to find vestiges of a more authentic Vietnamese culture. Thus restricted, he brought forth two defining characteristics. He argued that the strength of Vietnamese culture was not a system of thought but feelings contained in the rhythm, sounds, and tones of language. As such, he deemed

> that psychology [to be] similar to the psychology of children. Children often sing but rarely pay attention to meaning. But we should not be embarrassed about it or think that our people are still juvenile, barbaric, or uncivilized, like the races in Africa. We are young, which means that we have a lot of energy and we can still go far.[53]

The second characteristic of Vietnamese culture as delineated by Hoài Thanh followed from this first point. Since Vietnamese cultural achievements were seen as resting primarily in folk art and literature, the nature of such achievements could not be regarded in terms of quantity but quality. Hence, "getting rid of the propensity toward the numerous and the grand, which is very illogical in matters of art and literature, [will lead people to] see that a folk saying or six-eight couplet can be more precious than hundreds of heavy volumes and a few simple artistic lines [can mean] more than a grand palace."[54]

To harp on the worth of Vietnamese culture and have to base it on so little is heartbreaking. If the past was an embarrassment for its slavish imitation of Chinese culture, then to have the national essence grounded in the people exposed a profound uneasiness. There is a vast difference here between Nguyễn Bách Khoa's insistence on the strength of the Vietnamese culture to the point of dismissing the considerable Confucian influence on society and Hoài Thanh's attempt to define his own view of Vietnamese popular culture.[55] Alexander Woodside was surely right in asserting that "The Vietnamese Communist movement's development of its remarkable historical vision, brimming with the feats of centuries-old mass movements, did not really begin until after 1940," but he saw the reason for the time lag to be the Vietnamese communists' orthodox adherence to Russian revolutionary precedents.[56] I want to emphasize here the internal impulse instead of the external one and that such a proud nationalist, populist, and historical vision was not enshrined even after the August Revolution. In Hoài Thanh's tentative formulation, Vietnamese culture was still the culture of children. It was rich only insofar as it concerned rhythm and sound rather than offering a unique system of indigenous ideology. Future growth was required, and intellectuals were entreated to become one with the masses as the only way to achieve a worthy career in the new Vietnam. The need to create anew went hand in hand with a life and death view of the anti-French struggle in which the survival of the self was entirely bound up with the survival of the larger community. The argument is circular.

> If we want to orient ourselves toward the masses then we must take the people's right to life as our own, struggle within the ranks of the masses, and become one with the masses. Saving the country means that at the same time the national culture will save us because we will have inherited the powerful and rich life of the people.[57]

Intellectuals as independent creative voices had disappeared entirely. Instead, intellectuals were exhorted to reach out and somehow absorb the people's energy in order to carry out their intellectual and creative tasks. Hoài Thanh, the one-time defender of the art for art's sake position, had made an uneasy transition to the Marxist stance: ambivalent about what constituted popular culture but, or perhaps because of it, ruthlessly abandoning intellectual creativity in order to serve and be saved.

In 1945–46, cultural issues were discussed widely on the pages of the journal *Tiên Phong* (Vanguard). Intellectuals were exhorted to focus on the people and write in the service of the revolution. The political aspect of the creative process was now deemed to be of primary importance.[58] Here, too, however, past cultural achievements continued to receive a harsh evaluation, and the contempt with which Việt Minh intellectuals viewed Vietnamese cultural capacity extended to recent accomplishments as well. Đặng Thái Mai certainly saw nothing of value in mainstream literature prior to the August Revolution, but he did not have kind words for the preevolution clandestine Marxist literature either: "Clandestine literature disclosed a bolder tendency, the revolutionary tendency with the goal of liberating the people. . . . [But it was] lacking in many things so that there was very little creative literature and nothing exceptional. Even the propaganda literature was superficial and not yet systematic."[59]

The harshness with which many intellectuals at the time judged Vietnamese culture even alarmed later communist commentators, who noted that "almost all of past Vietnamese literature was repudiated" due to a "rather simple class view" and conceded that "that mistaken viewpoint on the inherited literature must have generated some confusion in the creative community."[60] Hoài Thanh's discussion of Vietnamese culture was also later criticized for "placing more importance on form than content and not seeing the importance of the scientific orientation due to [his] emphasis on popularization [which] is still the art for art's sake position, even though the writer maintained that art must carry a national characteristic."[61]

United in the call for Vietnamese independence but pessimistic about the cultural past and uncertain about what a new culture should be, Việt Minh intellectuals were unequipped to respond vigorously to other intellectual currents. The Trotskyist Hàn Thuyên group, a congregation of like-minded writers rather than an active political organization, spoke out against the Việt Minh's emphasis on nationalization and called instead for a focus on socialist revolution.[62] Trương Tửu, the pseudonym for Nguyễn Bách Khoa of the Hàn Thuyên group, provoked the Việt Minh further by arguing: "What are art and literature if not the constant opposition against reality and the present?" On the role of intellectuals, Trương Tửu insisted on the absolute freedom of the creative act, which argued that intellectuals should not follow the directive of any one political party. Cooperative moments between intellectuals and the authorities, when they did happen, could "only occur occasionally."[63] A Marxist in ideology, Trương Tửu as an independent intellectual could not conceive of a situation in which intellectuals would be so firmly under state control.[64]

Other writers did not take kindly to the Việt Minh's didactic exhortations either. A character in a play entitled *Câu chuyện văn chương* (The conversation on literature), written by Khái Hưng, one of the most prominent members of the Self-Reliant Literary Group, spoke disdainfully of the Việt Minh's approach to intellectual activities.

> I am hesitant and reticent because I believe strongly in my view of art and literature. I always tell myself: up to now I have always written for myself, only to satisfy my own zealous soul, to satisfy the needs of a restless spirit in a society and under a regime inappropriate to it. . . . I could not help laughing when I heard not a writer but a revolutionary teaching me the three *hóa*s a few days after the general uprising.[65]

The Việt Minh's emphasis on nationalization was grating to these intellectuals because they perceived such a demand to be an encroachment on intellectual freedom and a bane on true creativity. If cultural insecurity was at the heart of the Việt Minh intellectuals' focus on national essence and how best to build up the meager national literary heritage, noncommunist intellectuals like Khái Hưng were bent on reaching the same goal by striving toward universalization. Countering virtually all the Việt Minh's prescriptions for intellectual creativity, Khái Hưng's protagonist proclaimed:

> Your dream of nationalizing literature is only a dream. On the contrary, in my opinion, if we want to raise the quality of our country's literature we must humanize it. We have to describe our people, our characters, not as Vietnamese but as human beings first.[66]

Living up to the Revolution: The Dilemma of the Petit Bourgeois Intellectual

The Việt Minh call for a general uprising against the French on 19 December 1946, however, quickly bonded the intellectual community.

The intensity of the moment forced the focus entirely on the national ideal, and many intellectuals felt motivated to disregard growing ideological differences to achieve much needed unity. The brief achievement of collective solidarity was touching to many who remembered the spirited intellectual environment in which they had participated prior to the revolution. Moreover, Việt Minh intellectuals were also coming to terms with the revolution, consciously aware of their petit bourgeois background but not yet fully driven by clear ideological considerations. In this context, the Việt Minh poet Nguyễn Đình Thi wrote a commentary that for most intellectuals captured the somber mood of the time. The piece, entitled "Nhận đường" (Recognizing the way), was later criticized for not being a definitive affirmation of the revolution's achievements and the intellectuals' participation. It did, however, enter collective history as representative of the intellectual atmosphere of this period.[67]

Written in 1947, "Recognizing the Way" is remarkable for its honest rendering of the painful process of transformation of the self: "I unsystematically record the often aching doubts of a shedding of the skin, the old body falling without fully separating, the newly grown young skin not yet strengthened, bleeding at the slightest touch."[68] As if to remind himself and assure his audience, the author insisted on the clarity of the mission at hand: everything was for the anti-French struggle and the people. At these moments, he spoke forcefully of the new life developing, with people from all backgrounds joining in the anti-French struggle. Intellectuals, too, had come to see the necessity of using their talents to promote the progressive force of the revolution beyond the present hardship. The problem for him was the writers' inability to create works that would be commensurate with that certainty of goal and the grandeur of the task at hand, and it was this tormented mood that suffused the piece.

> How wretched and hesitant we are. Looking at the works that have been achieved, we only see clumsy and feeble art, unable to generate the wind and storm of the struggle. Many of us want to throw our pens away in order to do something else more effective.[69]

What Nguyễn Đình Thi perceived as feeble in the works then being written was the unconvincing attempt to portray new characters such as soldiers, workers, and peasants. The course of the anti-French struggle thus far had highlighted the enormous sacrifices of ordinary people, whose capacity to endure and quiet heroism filled intellectuals like Nguyễn Đình Thi with wonder. In response, Thi demanded that the new literature achieve great things, "to change even the lives of the reader—*creating man,* pushing us toward a new life that formerly we could only stand observing from afar."[70] The intellectuals' inability to live up to this new charge in an authentic fashion was difficult to rationalize. Thi suggested that it was because intellectuals had yet to become fully open to the life that was going on around them, hence the notion of an incomplete shedding of the skin.

The solution to this problem would later become the mantra for all intellectuals throughout the life of socialist Vietnam: writers must constantly be on the go to accumulate the necessary "living experiences" (*vốn sống*) to be able to write authentically about the people. The turn of the phrase echoed Mao's Yenan speech on art and literature in which he deemed Chinese writers and artists to be lacking in knowledge. Toiling among the masses would be one way for them to "undergo a long and even painful process of tempering."[71] More than simply overcoming his petit bourgeois background so as to understand the people, however, Nguyễn Đình Thi reached toward a complete union with them.

How can we understand the spirit of the bulk of the population currently fighting? How can we erase the habits of the old life, which have become integral parts of our bodies? How can we become the people of another class in order to live their lives?[72]

Nguyễn Đình Thi's piece laid out the inner struggle with which intellectuals of the period were contending, and his prescription for what intellectuals must do would eventually be accepted as the norm. Written by authors who had honed their craft in the vibrant prerevolutionary intellectual atmosphere, most of whom at one point had strongly embraced the transcendental sacredness of art, short stories and plays of this period focused on the internal drama of people having to make difficult choices at a particularly demanding historical juncture rather than any simple demarcation of what was right and wrong. For all the talk of ordinary people as new characters in revolutionary literature, what concerned many intellectuals at this time was the transition between the old and the new, which seemed to be a much more profound change for petit bourgeois individuals like themselves and the people they knew than for the bulk of the population.

The short story "Đôi mắt" (Pair of eyes) by Nam Cao is an interesting example in this regard. As a writer Nam Cao had begun to make a name for himself before 1945, but the revolution was a turning point in his life. He became a fervent supporter of the revolution and in 1948 became a Party member. The writer Tô Hoài was present at the ceremony: "When he vowed to always sacrifice for the Party, I saw Nam Cao cry."[73] He died in 1951 while on a trip to his home village in Hà Nam, which was under French control. His early death and his strong belief in the revolution guaranteed his literary fame, and his small body of work is an integral part of the school curriculum in socialist Vietnam. He is better known for "Chí Phèo," a wonderful story that details the miserable life of the peasant Chí Phèo with a tone that is both brutal and sympathetic. "Chí Phèo," written in 1941, has often been upheld as a model for portraying peasants, though Nam Cao is also criticized for having "a pessimistic, dead-end view" that led his peasant characters to "either only bow their heads to endure or rebel blindly, recklessly, and hopelessly."[74]

Written in 1948, "Pair of Eyes," on the other hand, focused on the petite bourgeoisie, and this may explain why it was not as well publicized as "Chí Phèo" until fairly recently, when it garnered strong critical praise as being "a decisive refutation of his old self by the true intellectual who followed the revolution"[75] and "the collective declaration of the critical realist writers, marking the fundamental shift in their worldview in the process of . . . joining the revolution and the struggle."[76] A reading of the story itself, however, yields a much more complex impression.

"Pair of Eyes" recounts a visit by the narrator to an old friend named Hoàng who was a writer of some repute in Hanoi before the August Revolution. The war has forced Hoàng and his family to take refuge in his village, and his reaction to the rural experience forms the main theme of the story. The narrator is clearly disgusted with Hoàng's constant complaints about the peasants, which range from the closed-in nature of village life to the silliness of having illiterate peasants in charge, always ready to preach in revolutionary terms to city intellectuals like Hoàng and his wife. Hoàng's isolation from the village population is barely eased by his limited contact with other city folks such as "a retired provincial governor, a provincial education officer who was let go because he raped a student, [and] an old judge who used to make his living by helping others in lawsuits," who know nothing of art and literature and spend much of their time playing cards.[77] The situation as it is perceived by Hoàng and his wife leaves the couple mostly alone to entertain themselves, finding solace in the reading of the classical Chinese masterpiece *The Three Kingdoms.*

The narrator's critical stance dominates the story. In his view, Hoàng only sees the superficiality of rural life and not the "truly beautiful inner cause" of the revolution.[78] Hoàng's contempt for the "dregs of the elite and the intellectuals" only raises the question of why he does not join the struggle and engage himself in worthy activities that would give him a new lease on life. The narrator concludes early on that it is not worth speaking to Hoàng about what is truly on his mind because he "is used to seeing life and people in a particular way. . . . Still keeping that pair of eyes [with which] to view life, the more he travels and the more he observes he will only become more bitter and disheartened."[79] Yet Hoàng is not portrayed as a totally bad character. The complaints he makes about the changes in village life, such as the politicization of daily life to the point of mindless mimicry of stock revolutionary phrases and the elevation of poor peasants to positions of leadership, ring true in spite of the narrator's distaste for such politically incorrect views. There exists a level of underlying sympathy between the narrator and Hoàng, who come from the same intellectual circle and presumably a similar class background. The narrator tells Hoàng how his own view of the peasant has changed because of the revolution.

> No matter what, the peasants remain rather mysterious to us. I have spent much time with them. I was near complete hopelessness because I saw them as mostly uneducated, neglected, timid, and cowardly, enduring in a most pitiful way. . . . I still thought that the bulk of our country was [made up of] peasants, but our country's peasants would never take part in a revolution in ten thousand lifetimes. The eras of Lê Lợi and Quang Trung were perhaps truly dead, never to return.[80] But I was surprised when the general uprising came. It turned out that our country's peasants are still capable of waging a revolution and do so enthusiastically.[81]

If Hoàng and the narrator differ in their belief in the role of the peasantry in the country's future, Hoàng has yet to reach a totally pessimistic view regarding the revolution: he continues to believe in Hồ Chí Minh and the necessity of the anti-French struggle.[82] "Pair of Eyes" was written by a writer for himself and his peers to clarify his own position in the ideological struggle. Intellectuals who joined the revolution knew with certainty that it was a historic moment in the nation's history, but it was also a time when people like Hoàng could be seen critically and yet not be judged harshly. It was a time when miraculous change could occur to turn Nam Cao's illiterate peasants into heroic soldiers and traditionally wicked rural masters into sincere believers in the revolution.[83] Nam Cao, and no doubt many of his intellectual peers as well, truly believed in the possibility of national unity within a fervent faith in the Party as a nearly sacred entity. His early death, writers in Hanoi would often comment in personal conversations with me, effectively preserved the integrity of his literary achievements and saved him from disillusionment with later turns in the state's intellectual policy.

The Tô Ngọc Vân Debate: Art, Propaganda, and Who Would Define Them

The ambivalence between heartfelt support for the Việt Minh's goal of gaining national independence and the uneasiness with the Party's cultural direction came out in the open with the painter Tô Ngọc Vân. Vân, one of the first graduates of the famed Ecole de Beaux-Arts de l'Indochine (Indochinese College of Fine Arts), was a prominent prewar painter who had made a career out of painting middle-class women in their bourgeois surrounding. His paintings are considered to be classics, and a number of them can be viewed at the Museum of Fine Arts in Hanoi. He was an ardent proponent of bringing beauty to the Vietnamese environment, and before the August Revolution he, too, did not have anything kind to say about the state of Vietnamese art prior to the modern period.

> Before [the Indochinese College of Fine Arts] opened, there was no one in our nation who could be called an artist. The public had no aesthetic appreciation. The ugly houses, the tasteless furniture, the gaudy paintings of those times are emblems of complete confusion. But when the first graduates of the College of the Fine Arts began to appear, the situation began to change completely. The artistic displays and exhibitions made everyone aware of beauty in a more understanding manner. Art has even changed our way of life. We live in a beautiful environment. Our lives are more elegant than before.[84]

Along with many of his peers, Vân enthusiastically joined the revolution. The Việt Minh particularly needed painters, whose talents could be used in immediately effective ways. In this regard, painters understood intimately and intuitively the relationship between their work and the needs of the revolution. They were ready to accept their role as propagandists, and *"tuyên truyền"* (propaganda) during this period did not carry the negative connotation we have come to know. It was seen simply as the effort to broadcast the revolutionary message to the public through persuasion rather than brainwashing.

The move to define art in terms of the people's needs, however, was distressing to Vân, and he expressed his concern in a 1947 article entitled "Propaganda Art and Art." Intending to clear up what he perceived to be a misleading definition of art, Vân made a series of distinctions between propaganda art and true art. He argued that "propaganda art is not art because it expresses a political purpose, raises political slogans, delineates a political path for the people to follow, [and] displays situations that will generate in them a political attitude," while art was an expression of "an individual soul, an attitude of an individual toward things, telling his feelings more than philosophy about any issue." Furthermore, in Vân's opinion, "art has everlasting value while propaganda art has only temporary value." Vân was emphatic in his support of the revolution, stressing that "in our people's period of struggle today, this temporary value is bigger than the eternal value of the artistic treasures of mankind."[85] True and lasting artistic achievements, different from the propaganda art that was currently required by the resistance and occupied the artists, would have to wait for the end of the struggle. The lack of credible artistic works at the moment was therefore due to the current material hardships and the accepted needs of the revolution more than to any fundamental change in the ideology of the artist.

The clarity and forcefulness of Tô Ngọc Vân's view pushed the venerable scholar-critic Đặng Thái Mai to respond in January 1948.[86] Đặng Thái Mai asserted that an artist was invariably a propagandist for one ideology or another and that the work was only of value when it supported a "progressive" goal. Reacting further to the underlying concern expressed by many intellectuals that few of their achievements after the August Revolution could be judged as worthy, Mai contended that it was the intellectuals' lack of faith that had led to the creation of mediocre works.[87]

This simplistic view of the arts led Tô Ngọc Vân to speak out with unconcealed exasperation at what he saw as a complete misinterpretation of his views and, even more dangerous, of the nature of art itself. In a forceful article written in mid-1948, he countered Đặng Thái Mai's undifferentiated assumption about the arts by once more laying out what he perceived to be the fundamental differences between art created for propaganda purposes and that which was not. To Vân it was crucial not to conflate the two because in so doing, the erroneous conclusion that propaganda art could approach the level of true art would be reached. Furthermore, Vân insisted that it must be understood that art and propaganda art used different techniques to reach different goals. Paintings could only suggest meaning and reach the audience indirectly through some measure of emotional response, whereas propaganda paintings by nature spoke loudly and forcefully, capturing the audience's heart and mind by means of their direct messages.

Vân also protested against Đặng Thái Mai's prescription that true art and literature must exemplify the subtlety and uniqueness of individuality and the main characteristics of the ideal archetype, tenets of socialist realism that Mai had laid out earlier in his 1944 work *An Outline of Literature*. Vân argued that these demands were appropriate for art but not for the art of propaganda. Propaganda art, in Vân's words, would be "stumped, crushed by the [demand to be] 'unique,' making it difficult for people to understand and impossible to present to an audience only recently acquainted with the arts like the Vietnamese populace." In addition, requiring that propaganda be subtle was to Vân "an illogical invasion injurious to the art of propaganda, which by its nature must be plain and clear."[88]

Vân went to the heart of the matter, however, by objecting to the fundamental assumption underlying the discussion of the intellectual role in the national struggle, the commonly voiced and accepted notion that intellectuals had always been far removed from the lives of ordinary people.

It so happens that a few people do not understand a few paintings, and that led others to declare that artists want to be difficult, want to live away from the people, want to isolate themselves in "ivory towers" (*tháp ngà*). "Ivory towers"—is the Vietnamese language so poor that we have to use this clichéd image? The myth that artists live lives removed from the masses, one person tells it, two persons repeat it, and it has become almost a truth, to the point where people almost cannot think about it differently. Do people realize that in human society it is the artists who live

closest to the people? The Vietnamese artists knew and understood Việt Bắc long before the struggle. They have lived with the
minority tribes from Hòa Bình to Lạng Sơn and with people in
the delta in the remotest of villages stretching to the south of the
country. . . . The artists are close and sympathetic to the people,
so how can they be so isolated from them?[89]

Tô Ngọc Vân's reactions clearly showed his differences with the
basic assumptions made by Party intellectuals like Đặng Thái Mai. He
resolutely opposed the idea that all art should be viewed as propaganda. Moreover, speaking for many intellectuals, he argued that
Vietnamese artists were much more involved in the life of the nation
than the official characterization would have it. According to Vân, the
meager intellectual achievements since the August Revolution were
not due to a lack of faith, though he conceded that it might be due to
lack of talent. Like Nguyễn Đình Thi, Tô Ngọc Vân returned to the
dramatic changes generated by the revolution to which intellectuals
did not yet know how to respond.

It is because the struggle for independence has crumbled many
old ideological values. We want to change our blood. We want to
break with the artistic past, which fills us with embarrassment
even now when we think about it. This artistic change is so difficult; we feel it is as heavy as moving a mountain. The act is not as
easy as people think, as though it is [as simple as] turning over the
palm of one's hand or exchanging one label for another.[90]

Vân, too, as it turned out, was not exempt from the soul-searching
mood among intellectuals at the time, who sensed that life as they
knew it before the revolution was gone but what was to come was not
yet clear. Nevertheless, there is a measure of confidence in Vân's voice
that was lacking in that of Nguyễn Đình Thi. Revolution was difficult for anyone to come to terms with, and this revolution was
certainly necessary, but he did not exhibit self-destructive tendencies
that had given Thi's comments in "Recognizing the Way" such an
agonizing quality. Vân was simply much more anchored in his art,
and one senses his belief that he will ride out these hard times and
emerge a better person, changed but not radically transformed from
within. Vân's concerns exemplified the difficult position of intellectuals who came to believe in the nationalist cause and were willing
to do their part for the revolution but were troubled by the simplis-

tic, increasingly restrictive direction of intellectual discussion. Vân's comments in 1948 indicated substantial uneasiness with the official discourse. In a sense, he was trying to maintain a logical, sensible middle ground in which he, as an artist, could retain control over the creative sphere while accepting the requirements of the revolution. It was an untenable position, however, and his eventual acceptance of the priority of the revolution under the guidance of the Party would eventually overwhelm his efforts to participate as an equal in the dialogue.

The Party's Response

Vân's protests were in vain. Other articles, expressing the orthodox line, soon followed. Đặng Thái Mai wrote highlighting the needs of the resistance.[91] Not mentioning Tô Ngọc Vân and as if Vân had never raised his concerns, Đặng Thái Mai was firm on the orthodox purpose of literature, which had no room for individual creativity.

> [A writer] can write on anything as long as the people like and understand it. The size of the book is smaller. The literary style is getting close to the rural language. The circulation of urban dwellers in the countryside has brought many terms and images previously thought to be rustic into literature. In short, writing succinctly, clearly, and simply is the distinction of literature today. Literary genre and style both clearly exemplify the tendency toward the people and the nation.[92]

More than a required direction for intellectuals to follow, however, "the tendency toward the people and the nation" became elevated as revolutionary literature's central goal. Đặng Thái Mai, who had previously deemed revolutionary literature to be weak, now sought to assert that a resistance culture had been formed while betraying his own and others' insecurity with current intellectual achievements along with a distaste for those of the past.

> There are people who are worried about [the new culture] and afraid that it is only a low culture. But what is the "high" culture of the past? What does it look like? Why don't they accept that in the newly formed culture there exists a seed filled with life and prospects. . . .

A resistance culture has been formed. Its achievements cannot be assessed accurately right now because we cannot evaluate the cultural works of the past year and because if we want to discover all of the new culture's abilities in part we must give it more time.[93]

The seriousness of the discussion can be discerned by the fact that the Party leaders felt the need to respond beyond words. The Second National Congress on Culture was convened in mid-July 1948 in which Trường Chinh presented "Marxism and the Issue of Vietnamese Culture," better known as "Marxism and Vietnamese Culture," which I discussed at length in chapter 1. Part of the report was quickly reprinted in the journal Văn Nghệ (Literature and art), the organ of the Cultural Association for National Salvation.[94] The editorial staff of Văn Nghệ, a gathering of the most prominent intellectuals of the prerevolutionary years, chose a telling title for the excerpt, which reflected the uneasy mood: "Some Issues of Concern on Literature and Art."[95] The section chosen by Văn Nghệ had to do with art and propaganda, a key subject of a debate between Tô Ngọc Vân and Đặng Thái Mai, which had played out partly on the pages of Văn Nghệ earlier. This time, however, the matter was taken up by Trường Chinh, the Party's authority on culture.

Not naming the participants, Trường Chinh laid out the two positions argued by Tô Ngọc Vân and Đặng Thái Mai and proceeded to present his own formulation of the issue. While he rejected Đặng Thái Mai's declaration that art and propaganda were one and the same, he also dismissed Tô Ngọc Vân's argument that art and propaganda art were completely different. His definition, however, refined Đặng Thái Mai's orthodox view by presenting a circular argument in which the artist was grounded firmly in the political context.

When propaganda achieves a certain level, it becomes art. When art reaches a particular level of effectiveness, art clearly has a propagandistic nature. Thus, there may exist propagandists who are not or not yet artists, but it cannot be that there are artists who are not propagandists entirely.[96]

If art was defined by its effectiveness in serving a specific goal, that being the nation's independence, then all other concerns regarding the creative act became focused on the artist himself rather than any external complications. In effect, intellectuals could not take refuge in the excuses of lack of time or means. To Trường Chinh , "if the artists are realistic and faithful to the age then the [quality of the] art of their creations would rise and the meaning of the propaganda become more powerful."[97] The act of creation, therefore, no longer belonged to the intellectual, who would primarily be driven by the goal set forth by the Party, acting in the interest of the people. This was made clear by Trường Chinh's four steps defining the process of creation, a no nonsense response to the intellectuals' ambivalence, alluded to by Nguyễn Đình Thi, among others, over the difficulty of continuing to produce superior works, as before the revolution. Trường Chinh's succinct four steps were as follows.

1. Find the topic
2. Assess the audience
3. Gather the means to carry out the task
4. From the masses evaluate the creation[98]

Trường Chinh's prescriptions would have much more weight as the Party began the process of organizing intellectuals into associations both at the local level, in the military interzones (*liên khu*) where they lived and worked, and at the national level by establishing associations for different creative genres. This organizational effort and the heightened ideological struggle within the intellectual community are the subject of the next chapter.

The Second National Congress on Culture, with Trường Chinh's report "Marxism and the Issue of Vietnamese Culture," provided an official response to the intellectual debates. The firmer line was quickly adopted, with a number of intellectuals ready to dispel the anxious mood that had begun to pervade the atmosphere. That anxious, questioning mood was deemed weak and dangerous to the goal of the revolution. The ideological space was increasingly diminished, even though Trường Chinh had continued to emphasize national unity in his report. It was no longer enough to support the struggle. An intellectual must not lie to others or himself by stating that the revolutionary situation was temporary and that once national independence was achieved he could return to his transcendent, everlasting notion of high art and literature, a clear rejoinder to Tô Ngọc Vân's statement that artists could return to the production of better works once peace had finally arrived. In this the writer Hoài Thanh, one of the most earnest defenders of the art and art's sake position in the decade prior to the revolution, was emphatic. He denounced such a view as nothing less than desertion of the struggle. All acts ran the risk of being "indirectly" useful to the enemy.

> We go searching for peace. And while we think that we have found peace in some eternal world and some mysteriously magical hours, in effect we have found peace in the very common life of our class under French colonialism. That attitude has indirectly helped the colonialists. We must will ourselves never to return to the old way of life. We must be frank with ourselves in realizing that what is called a life of transcendence is a sham, or at least something very superficial.[99]

If the former champion of creative freedom had abandoned such a bourgeois platform, Nguyễn Đình Thi also took a more rigorous position. Gone were the concerns of a generation of intellectuals undergoing a soul-searching transition between the world as they knew it and the world that was to come, which Thi had so touchingly addressed in 1947. Thi instead focused on establishing the tenets of socialist realism as guidelines for creativity. Not straying far from the main lines set down by Trường Chinh, his effort was a more sophisticated attempt to chart a new course for intellectuals without forcing them to give up their creative rights.

A multitalented artist himself, who had achieved critical success with poetry, prose, and music, Thi dismissed the notion that tả thực (realism) simply meant to record real events like a camera: "If the creative works of the resistance period only record important events, then we will only place them in a museum as historical data in a few years."[100] Not emphasizing the demand that intellectuals must create for the masses, Thi appealed instead to their sense of a higher mission by defining *realism* as the ability to "make tomorrow appear in the midst of today. *Realist literature and art is that which exemplifies (by establishing models of) the social life that is growing.*"[101] The old idea that art and literature could forecast social changes and movements provided creative works and their creators with a measure of importance far beyond what Party leaders like Trường Chinh would have granted. But it was from this standpoint that Thi could see how effective art and literature could be for the Party and the revolution, that "literature and art are a kind of propaganda without propagandizing, and precisely because of this they are the most effective form of propaganda." A firmer political line was evident in Thi. The journal *Văn Nghệ* similarly underwent a transition from 1949 on, publishing articles and other writings that emphasized the heroic efforts of intellectuals and the people rather than the numerous intellectual concerns previously displayed on its pages.

— • —

The darkness of the views about the self and national culture enveloping the intellectual community is striking, not only before but also after the August Revolution, linking many of the intellectuals with the Party in the search for a more authentic national essence. The dismissal of national culture, which had long been defined largely as high culture, as an uncreative derivation of the Chinese model was a discernible theme from the 1930s onward. The turn toward popular culture, therefore, was an inevitable consequence that was heightened under the communists' emphasis on the people and popularization. The content and worth of popular culture, however, were discussed in extremely hesitant terms. The project to discover the national essence as embedded in popular culture was integral to the survival of the nation, and yet at the same time one can feel the underlying ambivalence about the existence of anything substantive enough to become the core of the new culture.

The destruction motif that runs through the writings of this period is notable in this regard, from self-destruction out of sheer hopelessness evident in the works produced in the days prior to the August Revolution to the more revolutionary call for destruction in order to create anew to the painful transformation of the petit bourgeois intellectual not quite ready to relinquish all of his or her prerevolutionary self. As socialist realism became increasingly established as *the* scientific methodology central to the creation of a new national culture, intellectual apprehensions broke into the open. Efforts by intellectuals like the painter Tô Ngọc Vân to maintain the necessary space for individual creativity while supporting the needs of the resistance were unacceptable to the leadership. The cornerstone of the Party's cultural policy, Trường Chinh's "Marxism and the Issue of Vietnamese Culture," was formulated precisely to firmly dispel any lingering doubts about the correctness of the Party's position on culture and the creative act.

Tô Ngọc Vân, however, continued to be less than fully persuaded by the arguments put forth by the Party and intellectual officials like Nguyễn Đình Thi and Hoài Thanh. Pointedly entitling his March 1949 article "Study or Not?", Vân objected specifically to Trường Chinh's assertion in his "Marxism and the Issue of Vietnamese Culture" that the masses did not need an education to judge and indeed, held the final judgment of creative works.[102] Up to a certain point, the meaning of art could not be understood by the public without a level of education in art because art itself was not simply a replication of life as it exists but as it exists in the mind of the artist. As such, Vân argued that "the masses must study art in order to appreciate art deeply, must study the vocabulary of image in order to understand the stories that the images are telling." For Vân, "without the practice of conforming to aesthetics, there is nothing to guarantee that those eyes and ears, those clever brains, and the sensibility [of the masses] can guide the professional artist on the creative road."[103] If Trường Chinh had demanded that intellectuals use their creative works to raise the people's standard of knowledge, for Vân what this entailed was not so much the tailoring of creative works to the people's level of understanding but the slow elevation of that understanding to the point at which the people themselves could fully participate in appreciating and criticizing creative works.

Vân's fundamental dilemma was his perception of two conflicting selves, that of the nationalist and that of the artist, which were now being pitted against one another. He saw with clarity that his capacity as a creative artist would be diminished, and substitution of a purer and stronger faith in the Party and the people could not assuage his torment. As he painfully noted,

> Here lies the principal point, the torment of my soul: how to make the self that serves the nation and the masses and the self that serves art—the artist of course cannot forget this responsibility—not to come into conflict or, even worse, betray one another.[104]

Đặng Thái Mai's contention that art and propaganda art are the same and Trường Chinh's insistence that art serving the people is indeed true art were unacceptable to Tô Ngọc Vân. Vân once more defended his right as an artist to control his acts of creation and remained committed to the vision of pure intellectual activity as beyond the realm of everyday politics. It would be his last moment of independent thought, for in 1949 the Party tightened its control by establishing more restrictive guidelines for intellectual creativity and imposing a more coherent organization. Vân and other intellectuals of a more contentious disposition were reined in, as the next chapter will show. Vân himself did not live to see the full development of state control over intellectual life. He died in 1954 in a French bombing raid, only a few months before the Việt Minh's victory at Điện Biên Phủ.

Toward a More
Socialist Viewpoint

I have noted the relatively free intellectual atmosphere of the early years following the August Revolution when the Việt Minh's strategy was to emphasize a united front. The fact that differences in opinion related to art and literature were voiced in public, even against high ranking Party members like Trường Chinh, indicated a level of communication in which intellectuals, for all their tormented questioning of their work, felt they had equal status. In particular, they emphasized their concern with losing control over the creative process.

Beginning with the Second National Congress of Culture in 1948, a series of organizations and reorganizations of the intellectual community was carried out in order to exploit more effectively the talents of the intellectuals for the resistance but also to establish control over their activities. The success of the Chinese revolution in 1949 provided tremendous inspiration to the Vietnamese communists and opened up the border area, which besides the military consequences also initiated a flow of Chinese ideas into Vietnam. In this heightened atmosphere, the Vietnamese prepared to launch their military struggle against the French as well as moving to establish the foundation of a new socialist state. This chapter will focus on this shift in the Party's approach to intellectuals after 1948, which aimed to shape and control the ideological content of the new society.

Organizing the Intellectual Community

The more fluid ideological and organizational situation of the period after the August Revolution began to change with the Second National Congress of Culture (16–20 July 1948). Determined to centralize and control the direction of intellectual activities, the Congress set in motion a process of organization that provided the foundation of the later structure of intellectual organization in the new socialist state. As Hồ Chí Minh stated in the letter he sent to the Congress,

> from now on, we need to construct a nation-building resistance culture that is realistic and broad in order to support the people's nation-building resistance effort. *To reach that goal, I believe that our intellectuals must be tightly organized and must go deeply among the people.* The responsibility of culture is not only to inspire the people's spirit and nation-building resistance forces but to clearly show the achievements of our great nation-building resistance to the world. Our intellectuals must have worthy works, not only to exemplify the current nation-building resistance endeavor but to pass on the heroic examples of nation-building resistance to future generations.[1]

The point is only a little less awkwardly expressed in Vietnamese. The term *kháng chiến kiến quốc*, which I have rendered here as "nation-building resistance," is used five times in four sentences. The reiteration of *kiến quốc*, or "nation-building," was done for a purpose; it underlined Hồ Chí Minh's emphasis on the resistance as being not only a momentary effort to repel French colonialism but a long-term enterprise intended to create an independent Vietnamese nation-state. Trường Chinh's report, "Marxism and Vietnamese Culture," discussed in chapter 1, was the keynote address of the congress, which served to further emphasize the socialist character of the new culture. Reprinted in numerous journals and newspapers after the congress, the report came to be considered "the fundamental document on the direction and theoretical aspect of art and literature."[2]

Immediately after the Second National Congress on Culture, a National Congress on Art and Literature (23–25 July 1948) was convened in which the Vietnamese Union of Art and Literature was founded, replacing the Cultural Association for National Salvation. The Vietnamese Association of Art and Literature was created as an umbrella organization, uniting all the professional organizations (e.g., the Writers' Association and the Artists' Association) to which all creative intellectuals belonged.

These organizational moves also established the revolutionary poet Tố Hữu as the Party figure directly overseeing matters related to art and literature. From this point on, as one Vietnamese work on the 1945–54 period has proclaimed, "the theorists of the Vietnamese revolutionary art and literature were Hồ Chí Minh, Trường Chinh, and Tố Hữu. That was a development that could be seen as representative of the Vietnamese situation: the leaders of the Party were all theorists of art and literature."[3] Control over intellectuals and their activities was therefore highly concentrated at the top of the Party structure. Tố Hữu himself acknowledged the aim to consolidate this control over the intellectual community in a contemporary article meant for circulation within the Party apparatus.

> Those two congresses mark a large, progressive step in our country's cultural movement. For the first time our Party has achieved the broad and sincere unity of the intellectuals, both inside and outside the country, and inspired them to serve the nation-building resistance. And it is also the first time that the Party's cultural policy was presented so clearly, generating more influence and prestige for the Party.[4]

For the intellectuals who had chosen to support the Việt Minh cause, the 1948 congress was remembered as the last gathering at which intellectuals were still very much free to discuss and debate the issues with their peers and Party cultural officials. As the writer Nguyễn Tuân recalled from the vantage point of 1987,

> The congress in Việt Bắc in 1948 was the happiest. A lot of hardship but happy, poor but good-natured, our writers were very poor then but very beautiful, full of love for one another. Hearts and minds were completely in support of the struggle to liberate [the country], for the independence and freedom of the people, which included ourselves. . . . At that time I had presented a discussion paper. In the middle [of the presentation] I stopped and asked the permission of the congress to tell a funny story. That "good-smelling fart, bad-smelling fart" story. Then I continued to read my paper. When I returned to my seat, a person . . . whispered in my ear: You sure have a big liver [i.e., courage]; the story you told is problematic. I did not pay any attention then to what a problem that could be, and, true enough, there was no problem. I still won [the seat of secretary general of the new Vietnamese Union of Art and Literature] with a high vote. But if I had spoken like that at the congress in 1958 I would have been in deep trouble, immediately problematic. And even more problematic now.[5]

This quotation provides a rare glimpse into the period from the intellectuals' point of view. As Nguyễn Hưng Quốc rightly notes, however, that open intellectual atmosphere did not come to an end in 1958 but much earlier, with the Conference of Debate of 1949.[6] Nevertheless, Nguyễn Tuân's recollections show us an era in which intellectuals were certainly functioning as the equals of the Party's cultural officials but also that on the whole many intellectuals were in substantial agreement with the Party's effort to organize the intellectual community.

Besides being structured along professional lines, wartime also forced the intellectuals to become grouped geographically. Since administratively the country was divided into zones (khu) and interzones (liên khu), the Vietnamese Association of Art and Literature also had offices in the interzones. There were six administrative and military interzones during the anti-French resistance. Interzone 1 covered Việt Bắc, the Việt Minh headquarters in the northeast section of northern Vietnam, which contained a substantial number of ethnic minority groups. Interzone 2 encompassed the western section of northern Vietnam, which also contained a large number of ethnic minority groups. Interzone 3 was the valley of the Red River, where the bulk of the ethnic Vietnamese population resided in the north. Interzone 4 was the northern half of central Vietnam, while Interzone 5 covered the southern half of central Vietnam. Indicative of the Việt Minh's strong hold on the north, all of the south was designated as only one interzone at this time, Interzone 6.[7] One of the few archival documents on intellectual activities during this period indicates that the Association of Art and Literature had offices in Interzones 1, 3, 4, 5, and 6.[8]

The interzones, created as an administrative and military system in wartime, went through numerous changes but continued throughout the life of North Vietnam in the war against the United States. For this reason, the zones came to have their own characteristics, which were closely aligned with the regions they encompassed. The memories of the people with whom I have spoken with are filled with references to moving in and out of interzones, what activity happened in which interzone, and commentaries about the nature of the people from a particular interzone. All of this was not strange to the history of Vietnam, in which regionalism played a large role, but what was different about the interzone system was its connection of a series of provinces into one interzone, a breaking down of the existing regionalism without moving entirely outside the nature of that regionalism.

Second, the interzones were intimately connected to the leaders in charge, who came to define the characteristic of an interzone as much as the people themselves. Interzone 4, for example, was the dominant locale in the memories of most intellectuals of the anti-French period in large part because it was under the leadership of Gen. Nguyễn Sơn. Gen. Nguyễn Sơn was a figure of mythic proportions even before the August Revolution because he was one of the few Vietnamese who had participated in the Long March with the Chinese Communist Party and managed to survive. He was also knowledgeable about art and literature and could speak with authority on Chinese theatre and therefore was very sympathetic to intellectual activities in his zone. As the composer Phạm Duy commented, "Nguyễn Sơn was perhaps the person who attracted almost all of the writers and artists of the lowland area into the resistance organizations" of Interzone 4.[9] Of course, it helped that Interzone 4 was fully under Việt Minh control and therefore living conditions there were much better than elsewhere, but intellectuals were drawn there also because of the vibrant intellectual atmosphere fostered under Nguyễn Sơn's leadership.

The scholar Đặng Thái Mai was the other dominant intellectual figure in Interzone 4. The list of activities that went on during the anti-French resistance years is breathtaking. There was a Trường Văn Hóa (School of Culture), which provided short-term courses in the arts and literature to budding writers and artists. Classes were taught by dominant names in the intellectual community, who in turn were organized into *làng văn*, or "literary villages," where they lived fairly comfortably. Nguyễn Xuân Sanh, the proponent of abstract poetry in the prewar literary group Xuân Thu Nhã Tập, taught poetry there. In prose, there was the writer Nguyễn Tuân among others. Đặng Thái Mai and Trương Tửu (the dominant writer of the Hàn Thuyên group) taught philosophy, while Nguyễn Đức Quỳnh (another member of the Hàn Thuyên group) taught history. Art was taught by Sỹ Ngọc and Nguyễn Văn Tý, shining names of that generation of artists trained at the Ecole de Beaux-Arts de l'Indochine in Hanoi. Theater was taught by Chu Ngọc and Bửu Tiến, and Phạm Sửu, among others, taught music.[10] There were a number of troupes performing various forms of traditional theatre such as *chèo, cải lương*, and *tuồng* as well as a modern theatre group that mounted many performances. Numerous debates were held with the participation of such diverse figures as Đặng Thái Mai and Trương Tửu, which indicated the existence of a spirited and open intellectual atmosphere. In Interzone 3, another locale where a large number of intellectuals congregated, art exhibits by prominent graduates of the Ecole de Beaux Arts de l'Indochine, plays, and *cải lương* theater performances were held.[11]

The intellectual environments of Interzones 3 and 4 were probably the most extraordinary of the period, and they clearly show the joy with which intellectuals of different political and artistic backgrounds came together. While the trend in 1948 was to structure the intellectuals into a more vertical, top-down arrangement through the development of professional creative organizations under a state umbrella, the interzone system generated a horizontal pull through which intellectuals of different disciplines and political persuasions could meet, create, and exchange ideas in a vibrant atmosphere. Although control was tightened over the intellectual sphere after the establishment of the socialist state in North Vietnam in 1954, the war against the United States effectively kept the interzone system in place until 1975.

The 1949 Conference of Debate in Việt Bắc

The Conference of Debate in Việt Bắc (Hội nghị tranh luận Việt Bắc), held on 25–28 September 1949, has not been discussed in detail in Western works on Vietnam of this period. Neither has it been discussed in Vietnamese works until recently, when references to this historic conference became more numerous, critical, and soul searching as a younger generation of Vietnamese intellectuals seeks to understand the proper genealogy of the state of intellectual activities in Vietnam today. The conference was convened by the Association of Art and Literature, and its title provides a glimpse into the intellectual climate of the time. Those were the days when differences of opinion were still acknowledged and discussed, even if we must assume that much of the tumultuous discussion was toned down for publication. Those were the days before unanimity became the cornerstone of public discourse.

The reasons for such a conference were numerous. The Party leadership found the tormented mood among intellectuals and growing debates on the different aspects of the intellectual policy and direction increasingly unacceptable, not only for the sake of the resistance movement but because the existence of conflicting views challenged the Party's own vision of the structure of postwar society. With the intellectual organizations having been recently formed, the conference provided the occasion for the Party to reshape the ideological component into something much more coherent and uniform than it had been thus far. This was crucial, as the Việt Minh was moving to start the fall-winter 1949 military campaign, which in turn would require further sacrifices from the population. Thus, the time had come to tighten control over intellectuals and their activities not only to rein in discussions that might get out of hand but to make sure that the tools were available to inspire the people to the level of sacrifice necessary for the resistance.

Thus, the conference, which ostensibly was to provide the diverse intellectuals with the occasion to voice their doubts and questions, was destined for a particular conclusion from the outset. As the secretary general of the Association of Art and Literature, the writer Nguyễn Tuân stated in his opening remarks to the conference: "The association saw the need to have a conference of debate in order to unify the ideological direction, the view on the issue of techniques, and more than that to unify the system of intellectual activities."[12] Thus, no fewer than three items were on the agenda: to specify ideological content, to decide on the different literary and cultural forms that would best guarantee the promotion of such ideological content, and, finally, to shape the structure of intellectual activities.

In some eleven sessions over four days, the conference addressed topics ranging from the people's culture to socialist realism to whether nonrhyming poetry was acceptable. A number of the sessions were designed to establish the ideological foundation through prepared speeches but also by answering questions from the intellectuals. The first session started off the conference with a talk by Tố Hữu on the matter of "The New Democratic Culture." Tố Hữu emphasized the "people's literature and art" (*văn nghệ nhân dân*), whereas previously much had been made of literature and art for the people and exploiting the treasure trove of popular culture and so on without making the people the absolute center of intellectual work. The Chinese model was acknowledged. Intellectuals, stated Tố Hữu in his address, should be prepared to "come in contact with the trends in literature and art in the new democratic countries, especially China."[13]

The appearance of the term *nhân dân* at this point in particular indicated a departure from earlier discussions of "the people." As I have noted, the intellectual discourse from the 1920s onward was increasingly concerned with *dân tộc*, a term that connotes both "people" and "nation." The term *nhân dân*, while it also means "people" (and only people), is distinct from *dân tộc*. According to the critic Văn Tâm, *nhân dân* recognizes a societal entity that is horizontal; one speaks here in terms of the people of a particular country or peoples of the world. *Dân tộc*, on the other hand, is vertical in the sense that it refers to a specific people in the context of geography, language, and culture connected through time. Therefore, for Văn Tâm, "The concept of *nhân dân* generates a comparison with *the ruler,* whereas the concept of *dân tộc* generates a comparison with *another people.*"[14]

In other words, there was an explicit political meaning of *nhân dân* that resonated with Hồ Chí Minh's emphasis on nation building or, more correctly, on state building. Moreover, *dân tộc*, with its viscerally emotional overtone, was especially effective for uniting people across the political divide, while the more benign *nhân dân* was necessary in the effort to channel the discourse along class lines. *Dân tộc* embraced all Vietnamese, whereas *nhân dân* referred to the bulk of the Vietnamese population that had endured much, first under feudalist and then petit bourgeois and capitalist Vietnamese. The politics of the revolution had begun to shift course. The political culture that drove the revolution thus far had been focused on the Vietnamese nation and its external enemies, but if the goal of revolutionary political action was to move toward socialism that political culture would also have to formulate fresh symbols and new language to construct the desired internal order. The Conference of Debate in Việt Bắc, concentrated as it was on the symbol makers, was an attempt to do just that.

The conference's slogan called on the intellectuals to change their petit bourgeois way of thinking through action: "revolutionize ideology, popularize activities" (*cách mạng hóa tư tưởng, quần chúng hóa sinh hoạt*). The second session of the conference was animated by questions from those intellectuals who were troubled by the emphasis on the people and more specifically on the leadership of the working class in art and literature and what that would mean to them and their work. The concern was therefore not only with the role that they would have to play but with the nature of control over the content of their work. Tố Hữu, who provided the definitive answers at the conference, was clear, even though he maintained some middle ground. All must realize, he said, that "besides the workers there cannot be any class that can correctly see the hope of the people and the development of the human race." The workers must lead, therefore, and other classes could participate by following the path charted by them. As for the petite bourgeoisie, they belonged to a "vacillating and static class," which meant that "they cannot have the correct ideology [or] a firm outlook on life, so they cannot see life clearly. Naturally, they cannot create works that can speak of the emotions of life." This dismissal of the petite bourgeoisie, in which he included the lot of writers and artists, was softened slightly: since Vietnam had always been under colonialism, this class had come to be closely attached with the work of liberating the people. Thus, for now those "who can only speak of their own revolutionary emotions have already done some good for the present." Only when they followed the prescription to "revolutionize ideology, popularize activities," however, would they truly exemplify the new life and the masses.[15]

The stage was set for the removal of the petit bourgeois person from the hearts and minds of the intellectuals and their works. The old self that they had been trying to reconcile with the revolution was now firmly defined as petit bourgeois (*tiểu tư sản*). For many intellectuals, it was easy to accept the Việt Minh victory in the August Revolution, but the demands of the long-term resistance and the establishment of the new society would require them to make fundamental changes in the way they viewed themselves and their creations. The poet Thế Lữ decried "the old way," "the old person," and "the old capital of knowledge." The writer Nguyễn Tuân confessed ornately that "I am not only petit bourgeois but also feudalist." The painter Nguyễn Đỗ Cung blamed everything on the "petit bourgeois string," which had caused him to stumble so many times in his career. He had reached a conclusion after a number of exhibitions he had held during the resistance: "We should simplify our art. Be among the masses, [have] simple feelings like the masses. Painting primitive people by rudimentary means I already have, I have made many people happy. I have come closer to art." But the clearest expression of the utilitarian view of intellectual creation came from the poetess Anh Thơ, who told the participants at the conference:

> Before I also used powder and perfume. I thought that revolutionaries must be more beautiful than others. Because of that many sisters distanced themselves from me. Learning from that experience, later I also wore brown clothes, and the sisters loved and respected me. Before I believed that writing must be sophisticated and difficult to understand. Practical work shows me that poetry and literature must be simple and easy to understand in order to be liked by the people. Living with the masses, it was hard to eat at first, but after being together with them I [have come to] love them and like living with them.[16]

Reading sentiments like these, one wonders on the one hand if the Party was not correct after all in sending dreamy writers such as Anh Thơ to the countryside to sample the lives of peasants and, on the other, whether she would ever really let go of the powder and perfume aspect of life in spite of her declarations. It is worth noting, however, that Anh Thơ's most notable literary achievement was a 1941 collection of poetry entitled *Bức tranh quê* (A rural portrait). Her previous poetic efforts had won her an encouragement prize from the Self-Reliant Literary Group in 1939. She was not a highly educated woman; her schooling consisted of a third-grade education completed when she was twelve years of age, which made it all the more remarkable to the critics Hoài Thanh and Hoài Chân that her poems about the country-side should "belong to the kind of poems [written by] educated indi-viduals."[17] By this they meant that she gave the long exploited rural themes a certain unexpected sophistication, but they also faulted her for being rather emotionally distant in her poetry.

Anh Thơ's own memoir presents a woman who grew up primarily in a small town between the countryside and the city, who was not well educated, and who came to literary fame by means of her gentle images of rural life.[18] Her poems reflected a literary mood dominant in Hanoi at the time: romantically dreamy with a touch of tragic nostalgia. The same thing could be said of her "powder and per-fume" touches, urban influences upon a rural soul. If her comments at the conference betrayed a sense that she would never really let go of the urban affectations noticeable in her outward appearance as well as her poetry, her background also shows that she was never really that far removed from life in the countryside.

One goes back once more to the indignant complaint of the painter Tô Ngọc Vân in 1948 that it had become a cliché to proclaim that Vietnamese intellectuals were living lives entirely removed from the countryside.[19] While it was true that many Vietnamese did manage to travel overseas or obtain some kind of education abroad in the 1930s, the bulk of Vietnamese intellectuals was schooled within the Franco-Vietnamese educational system. This system provided them with ac-cess to French literature and culture, but it could not obscure the village connections that had played a dominant role in their develop-ment. Many Vietnamese intellectuals became disconnected from the countryside but never to the same degree that some intellectuals would posit and the Party would insist. They were on the whole much more disconnected from a body of stable cultural values upon which they could build their creations with a sureness of touch.[20]

That Western facade and the ease with which they pursued the urban lifestyle in places like Hanoi and Saigon while the peasants were dying under the weight of colonialism, however, marked these intellectuals with great guilt. Over and over again at different sessions of the conference, the voice of guilt rang out, which made it easy for the intellectuals to condemn themselves and their past and accept the vision of a new society offered by the Party in which the workers and peasants presumably would lead.[21] Nevertheless, the divergence of concerns between the Party's view of intellectuals and their own anxiety made for a rather confused end. The disgust with which they viewed their Westernized past was sincere enough, but the effort to become one with the masses always seemed superficial. Exchanging powder and perfume for brown peasant garb, painting works that would cater to the people's happiness, writing simple poems that people could understand—these changes were deemed to be important if intellectuals were to begin the process of changing themselves on the inside. But the extent to which that internal composition should and must be changed would end up being highly contentious in the years to come.

Cultural and Literary Forms

The attempt to revolutionize thought, or content, went hand in hand with the effort to reconstruct form. The Conference of Debate focused much energy on discussing the various creative professions and their traditional forms. Some of the main sessions concentrated on criticism, art, music, and theatre. In the arena of literature, the session on "poems and prose of the soldiers" actually devoted part of its time to criticizing the writer Nguyễn Tuân, and another session was dedicated entirely to examining the poetry of the multitalented Nguyễn Đình Thi.

It should also be noted that the dominant character of this early period was not the peasant but the soldier. The peasant type was not emphasized until about 1950 onward, when the Việt Minh began to prepare for land reform in the area under its control. The heroic nature of the military campaign also made the soldier an ideal figure in all kinds of creative efforts. A large number of soldiers were peasants, of course, but many were also university students and urban youths. After the Việt Minh called for a general uprising in December 1946, Hanoi citizens were called on to leave the city while the Việt Minh set out to make it as difficult as possible for the French to return. Some four hundred young men and women of Hanoi decided to stay to defend their beloved city and actually managed to stave off the French for a few months before retreating and joining the Việt Minh troops.[22] The poems of Quang Dũng about this heroic and romantic image of Hanoi youths and Việt Minh soldiers, for example, personified the anti-French resistance and all that was transcendental and righteous about that historic period for generations of Vietnamese. The dominant concern of the writer Nguyễn Huy Tưởng, one of the original members of the Cultural Association for National Salvation, was with petit bourgeois Hanoians at the very point of having to make the decision to either join the Việt Minh or accept the return of the French to the city.[23] Early efforts to establish the image of the anti-French resistance, like the 1949 *Collection of Revolution and Resistance Literature,* was dominated by the figure of the soldier.[24]

One of the main subtexts of the sessions at the Conference of Debate in Việt Bắc was not, however, the proper construction of either the soldier or the peasant type in literature and the arts but the issue of form clashing with content. The writer Nguyễn Tuân, whose yearning for experience was the personification of the unattached intellectual in the prewar years, was preeminent in a literary form called *tùy bút,* literally meaning "following the pen." A *tùy bút* is an essay, but, as its name indicates, it is a highly personal and idiosyncratic one, allowing the voice of the author to dominate throughout. Even though he first achieved literary fame in 1940 with a collection of short stories, Nguyễn Tuân increasingly focused on the *tùy bút* genre in the years leading up to the August Revolution.[25]

At the time of the conference, he had just published a collection of essays called *Đường vui* (Happy roads), which recorded his travels during the resistance period. The collection was accepted as the work of a "new" Nguyễn Tuân, who now traveled with a goal and a belief, not merely to experience the world around him with detachment. For his peers and others at the conference, however, Nguyễn Tuân's level of involvement in the new life was inadequate. The writer Nguyên Hồng, a good friend, complained that *Happy Roads* "has a beautiful happiness but nothing raging. We love, hate, get angry, but we don't understand why we fight, how we fight, and what gains we achieve when we fight. *Happy Roads* lacks thinking about the people, of the bulk of the people who are shedding blood and tears."[26]

This lack of revolutionary fervor on behalf of the people was only the consequence of the personality of Nguyễn Tuân. Nguyên Hồng reproached him thus: "You love yourself too much, blow yourself up too much. You go looking for the appropriate beauty for yourself. If Nguyễn does not see something beautiful, would that thing still continue to be beautiful? . . . The objective truth is no longer objective."

The act of creation is being turned into an act of reflection, and the voice of Nguyễn Tuân is being condemned for precisely the emphasis that had made him the preeminent writer of the genre.

The clarity with which Nguyễn Tuân saw the direction of the discussion forced him to perform the self-preserving act of letting go of the form that hitherto had contained his person.

> Nguyên Hồng complains that in *Happy Roads,* there are some lovely emotions but they cannot speak of near and far causes. Correct. But, to stand on the side of the professional in the discussion, this failure is not because the author has no sensibility but because the technique of the *tùy bút* genre decides that kind of emotion. Therefore, I accept that not only do I fail in terms of consciousness but also of technique. *Tùy bút* makes people subjective. If we want to correct that subjectivity, the only way is to stop writing *tùy bút* and begin to write novels.[27]

Nguyễn Tuân's argument was unacceptable to the conference participants, however, because the problem was Nguyễn Tuân himself. He needed to let go of his old self and become a member of the masses, wherein his writing, whether in the form of an essay or a novel, would begin to achieve a level of authentic compassion for the people and the struggle. The session's published record noted that Nguyễn Tuân, at several points throughout the discussion, reiterated the point that "This is now the time to write novels; don't write *tùy bút* anymore" and "As for me, with *tùy bút* it is easy for me to run wild. Better to write novels."[28] In the end, Nguyễn Tuân continued to write *tùy bút*. He is the acknowledged master of the form, even though throughout his career he was criticized for the same reasons that he was being taken to task in 1949. Amazingly, the imprint of his voice in his writing never disappeared, though one wonders what heights of literary achievement he might have reached if he had not been so restricted.

Another session focusing on an individual intellectual was the session on the poetry of Nguyễn Đình Thi. Multitalented in music and art, as well as in poetry and prose, Thi was one of the earliest intellectuals to join the Việt Minh. He has consistently held high offices within the various intellectual organizations. At the time of the conference, he was experimenting with a nonrhyming form of poetry, and the session itself ended up focusing on the issue of whether or not poetry should rhyme.

This was one of the longer sessions of the conference. As in the case of Nguyễn Tuân's writing, the discussion came to focus on the aspect of form because the concern was with content and on a more subtle level with what was considered to be a reflection of the self of Nguyễn Đình Thi, the inner core that could not easily be cloaked in public service announcements. The issue of rhyme caught the interest of everyone partly because it coalesced a number of concerns for the Party and the intellectuals. The eminent scholar Ngô Tất Tố spoke about against Thi's poetry because, in his words, "nonrhyming poetry should not be called poetry," an opinion that sprang directly from his classical education.[29] Here the debate was also between two different generations. While Ngô Tất Tố's position did not concern ideology, it dovetailed with those who objected to Thi's poetry for ideological reasons. For one thing, nonrhyming poetry strayed from the bulk of Vietnamese poetry, which had always been rhyme dominant, particularly in popular poems and sayings. Thus, Thi's poetic style was quickly deemed to be too difficult for the masses to understand and remember.

There were other reasons to censure Thi's poetry, and these focused on the poet himself. The poet Thế Lữ complained that Thi's poetry was "vain and quiet, does not note clearly what moves it, and is confident that people will come to it in order to understand and be moved by it." Xuân Trường stated that he did not like Thi's poetry not because of its form but because "Thi's emotions are old emotions, even though he is a new person. The person of Thi does not fit the resistance." The writer Nguyễn Huy Tưởng was more detailed.

I see in [Thi] something very contradictory. At meetings, he is very proud, but at home he is very alone. His reasoning is clear and [in the interest of] the masses, but his poetry is complex and dark. Thi has a lot of capability, but the fundamental thing that makes his readers feel that the poetry is outdated is that he is far from the masses. He struggles much with himself, and his poetry is a reflection of part of his soul rather than the voice of the masses.[30]

It was this struggle of the inner self that was hard for Nguyễn Đình Thi's intellectual peers to bear. These comments on Thi's poetry are all the more amazing when we realize that those who disliked his poetry the most were those who already had significant literary stature and had come to fame during the height of the development of the novel and new poetry in the 1930s. The "newness" of Thi's poetry was essentially a further development of the New Poetry movement of the

1930s, but now that development could no longer be allowed to continue. It was as if the intellectuals were trying to set up a boundary between their old and new selves in order to stay on the correct path. There is something rather paranoid and self-centered about this fear. The poet Thế Lữ proclaimed that "there is a danger that Thi has scattered his style of poetry in the poetic village," as if it were a contagious disease.[31] At the heart of this fear was, ironically enough, newness, the desire to transcend an established boundary. That desire for newness, according to another participant at the conference, exemplified individualism or *cá nhân chủ nghĩa*.[32] The intellectual in the impending socialist new age, it turned out, would not be allowed to find his or her expression outside of the body of traditional forms.

Thi's response was an eloquent protest against the limits being placed upon intellectual inquiry. On the matter of content, he accepted the criticism that his poetry was not happy, but he argued that there was much that was painful in the resistance, or, in his words, "legitimate pains, . . . pains that are not of the pessimistic kind." There were hints, though, that there were other pains, besides legitimate ones, with which he was grappling in his poetry. Those pains would be precisely of the pessimistic kind that Thi could not reconcile with the public struggle: "The [painful] content [of my poetry], objectively speaking, is not appropriate for the current struggle; the pains of the resistance are not similar to the pains in my poetry." As for his experimentation with free form verse,

> Because the content [of the poetry] is already morose, when it is outwardly expressed it also has an austere and strict appearance. While I want to seek a free form, the content restricts me. I want to have something rough and simple, [but] it turns out ornate.[33]

Thi went on to present a defense of what he referred to as *thơ tự do*, or free poetry, a defense of the form itself. Here he came close to arguing for the separation of intellectual work from political exigencies, for a creative space in which different intellectual ideas and forms could be developed and gradually accepted (or not) over time because of their worth rather than the demand that creative works be tailored to the people's interests and ability to comprehend. Thi noted that the New Poetry movement of 1932 was also not accepted at first, and the issue of other "new poetries," meaning the future development of poetic forms, would continue to arise no matter what. He would accept that his sentiments were not strong enough to make his poetry successful, but he would not accept the argument that free form verse itself was problematic.

For all the different points Thi wanted to present in the discussion, the session was closed by the poet and Party cultural authority Tố Hữu, who defined the whole issue thus.

There are times when I love Thi's poetry, and there are many times when I hate it. When I am sad and fretful, tired or wistful, I like reading his poetry. Poetry is a melody of the soul, and similar spirits find their mates. But when I need to work, I very much hate Thi's poetry because I hate the return of the self to me. Then I would warn myself. Often I see that a poem is good, but I am not sure that it is good. Then what can we use as criteria for good poetry?

I cannot use the "I" as a criteria. The artist must ask himself: How do the masses view this poem? Are they moved by it? Is the pain of the masses being represented here?

If the work has not spoken or speaks in the opposite direction about the life of the masses, then we must consider it a bad work. I believe Thi's poems are not good because they have yet to speak for the innermost feelings of the masses.

. . . Another important thing is that Thi must reassess [how] his thoughts and feelings [will be accepted by] the masses. There are times when the spirit of the masses is tired or weak, and they can hear that weariness [in Thi's poetry].[34]

Tố Hữu was a dominant Party authority on culture and intellectual activities at this point in time, and his power grew after 1954. More clearly than ever, it was the self that Tố Hữu was reacting against, including his own. The very strength of poetry, its ability to reach out to kindred spirits, had come to be seen as its primary weakness. The private aspect had to become completely public, serving public needs and existing under public scrutiny. In this way, the poet could not maintain control over his or her own creation since at every step he or she must be guided by the public functions of the work. Yet while poets' control over their work had diminished greatly, they were held responsible for much more. Everything converged upon the correctness of their thoughts as the one thing that would measure the direction and the success of their lives and work.

The discussions on art, music, and theater displayed similar concerns over content and form, the difference between the intellectual's specific focus and the grander vision of the resistance, and the relationship between what was present in a creative work and the extent of its creator's ideological correctness. The intellectuals criticized themselves and were criticized for being too "intelligent" (*trí tuệ*) in their works and lacking the necessary "feelings" (*xúc cảm*) that would move their audience. Their works were therefore criticized variously for being still, cold, dead, outside the struggle, far from the people, too peaceful, too beautiful, not real enough, and so real as to be merely photographic accounts of events. These conflicting voices led to uneven results. In the area of music, the return to studying, preserving, and experimenting with folk songs brought about some notable achievements. In art, the traditional craft of lacquer did not receive good press at first, having been considered too time consuming to be appropriate for the new age and too dreamy (traditional lacquer is rendered primarily in shades of brown and gold) to reflect a revolutionary time. In the end, experimentation with lacquer, especially in paintings, was allowed to continue, mostly because lacquer was seen as a particularly Vietnamese medium as opposed to oil, but only as long as the time spent did not impinge upon the production of propaganda paintings.

Theater was more complicated. Given its ability to reach a wide audience, the matter of theater was even debated in a separate conference, the Conference of Debate on Theater in 1950. Modern theater, in the style of Western theater, gained support during the resistance because of the ease with which everyday conversations and current events could be portrayed. The form of "poetic play" (*kịch thơ*), which made its appearance only a few years before the August Revolution, combined aspects of traditional and modern theater with its distinguishing characteristic being an immersion in verse. The poetic disposition of Vietnamese literature gave *kịch thơ* a certain seamless sophistication, countering the often contrived dialogue and situations of modern theater. Not surprisingly, the predominant themes of *kịch thơ* were historical, exploiting the more heroic and dramatic dimension of episodes whose outlines were well known to the Vietnamese populace. It was a striking example of the indigenous development of a new form of art. It was, however, deemed to be slow and therefore not appropriate for the resistance by some top Party leaders and intellectuals, and *kịch thơ* disappeared from the Vietnamese stage. After 1954, one of the earliest efforts to write a Vietnamese literary history in the north was the Lê Quý Đôn Group's 1957 three-volume project, which enjoyed a high level of freedom of inquiry and expression before state control was tightened in 1958. The Lê Quý Đôn Group has this to say about the form of *kịch thơ*.

> *Kịch thơ* had a position similar to modern theater; after 1945, at times it even overshadowed modern theater. At the beginning of the resistance, many people still liked *kịch thơ*, but due to the lack of encouragement it died early and unexpectedly. [The critic] Hải Triều registered the death of *kịch thơ* while still in Interzone 4, [even though] the *kịch thơ* movement was actually on the rise.[35]

Other, more traditional forms of theater like *tuồng* and *chèo* were affected differently. *Tuồng*, a form that had always focused on luminary historical personages, was fervently denounced by some as impossible to maintain given its feudal character (an opinion held by Trương Tửu, Đoàn Phú Tứ, and Phan Khôi), while it was championed by others (such as Nguyễn Sơn and Đặng Thái Mai) as having real and practical uses.[36] It was not until after the Party issued a decree specifically restoring traditional art in late 1951 that the existence of *tuồng* was fully secured.[37] *Chèo*, another form of traditional theater, concentrated on popular characters and the village. Because of this perspective, *chèo* was maintained and even managed to grow throughout the resistance period. Like *tuồng*, old plays were greatly modified, and new ones were written to promote state-authorized campaigns such as rent reduction, land reform, and increased production.

Cải lương, a form of indigenous theater that came of age around the turn of the century in southern Vietnam, was more encompassing in its reach of topics. *Cải lương* has its stock of patriotic and moralistic historical plays, but at its height of popularity sentimental romantic plays were all the rage, catering to the taste of a growing urban population in the south.[38] Of the generally negative opinion of traditional forms of theater in 1949 and 1950, *cải lương* received more than criticism; it was banned. According to the southern writer Đoàn Giỏi, who joined the Việt Minh, in the early years of the resistance, when *cải lương* was banned in parts in the south under Việt Minh control, people would get in their boats and paddle deep into the fields to enjoy *cải lương* or they would quickly switch to playing other forms of music if a cadre happened to catch them singing *cải lương* in their houses.[39] Popular affection for the form never disappeared, and in 1952 *cải lương* and other traditional forms of theater regained official stature.

What are we to make of this harsh judgment of traditional theater? There is a sense of revolutionary fervor, later judged to be "ultra-leftist," a desire to destroy all old things in fear of their pernicious influence on the future. To be sure, ideological purity was an important concern, but revolutionary zeal was accompanied by deep ambivalence about the country's cultural heritage. Along the lines that I have argued, it seems that the distaste for and rather grudging acceptance of traditional theater forms point to disdain for aspects of the traditional culture, a mood that was prevalent at the time in spite of the Việt Minh's constant reiteration of concepts of the people and the nation.

Later communist commentators liked to highlight the Party leaders' support for *dân tộc* and placed the blame for the leftist mood of this period upon a number of intellectuals deemed to be reactionary or too Westernized.[40] I have emphasized otherwise in previous chapters, for prominent Party leaders like Trường Chinh and Tố Hữu and intellectuals like Đặng Thái Mai, Hoài Thanh, and Nguyễn Đình Thi all held very negative views of the Vietnamese classical past. Many in the intellectual community shared the same attitude. Thus, it was through a tentative trial and error kind of negotiation involving a complex set of motivating factors, from nationalist sentiment to revolutionary fervor to popular affection, that some cultural forms were retained and encouraged while others disappeared.

Rectification (Chỉnh Huấn) in the Educational System

At the beginning of the resistance, a Ministry of Education oversaw all matters relating to education. By the beginning of 1948, it had been organized along the lines of the interzones. The educational system during this period placed heavy emphasis on having a large number of schools widely dispersed geographically so that more students could attend and more teachers could be utilized given wartime conditions.[41] There was probably not much else that the Việt Minh could have done. Nevertheless, the content of education was always a contentious issue since it needed to operate with very specific goals. According to a 1948 report,

Right now the high school and elementary school curriculum [contains] fewer theoretical hours and more practical hours, emphasizing the subjects that relate to the resistance and generating a spirit of nationalism among the young people.[42]

By 1953, it was reported that in Interzone 4 there were 2,301 elementary schools (both public and private) with 120,011 students, 179 middle schools with 51,377 students, and 11 high schools with 2,507 students.[43] These numbers did not take into account the network of literacy classes for peasants, workers, and soldiers. By 1952, there was also a College of Literature (Đại Học Văn Khoa) in Thanh Hóa and Nghệ An. A number of courses in mathematics were being taught in Nghệ An and Việt Bắc, and a College Preparatory School (Trường Dự Bị Đại Học) had been established in Thanh Hóa.[44] Designed to provide the education that would prepare a number of young men and women to enter the university once the resistance was over, the College Preparatory School also represented recognition by the Việt Minh leadership that training for teachers and professors would be necessary in order to have the required staff for the new educational system. Indeed, many of those who graduated from the first years of the College Preparatory School went on to become prominent university professors, scholars, and creative intellectuals. The college had only two faculties at the time, one for the natural sciences and the other for the social sciences, with a total of about 200 students. There was also the Medical College run by the brilliant Dr. Tôn Thất Tùng.[45] In addition, some smaller schools were operating and classes on art, music, and writing were held at different times in the interzones.

Finally, a substantial educational structure for Vietnamese students had been established in 1951 in southern China. As of 1952, it was reported that in Nanning (Nam Ninh) there were 2,000 students enrolled in four schools: 27 students in the higher pedagogical school, 102 in the basic science school, 100 in Chinese language, and 1,400 in the middle pedagogical school. In addition, there was also a school for children of high-ranking cadres in Guilin (Quế Lâm) with 700 students.[46] Collectively referred to as Khu Học Xá Trung Ương (The Central Educational Facility), the schools in Nanning and Guilin were under the administration of Võ Thuần Nho, a brother of Gen. Võ Nguyên Giáp.

From the beginning, the proliferation of *quốc ngữ*, the romanized alphabet, was linked to Vietnamese nationalism. The Việt Minh linked education specifically with whatever campaign was being waged at the moment, be it to eradicate outdated practices or to boost production.[47]

Internal documents indicate that there was much impatience with the teachers, especially in the early years of the resistance, for clinging to the petit bourgeois notion of a "neutral education" or "pure culture." Education as an arena for free exchange of information and ideas was always a problematic notion under colonialism, but the space in which it had to operate was now enormously constricted. While acknowledging the enormous physical difficulties with which intellectuals and teachers had to cope, these reports disapproved of the lack of comprehension and/or application of Marxism in both teaching and intellectual activities. A 1949 report on the state of intellectual activities in Interzones 3 and 4, the areas with the largest concentration of both scientific and creative intellectuals, complained that in the social science arena "activities only *concentrate on general knowledge of the cadres rather than the application of Marxism in the research* of history and the current political, economic, and military situation of Vietnam."[48] As for the creative intellectuals, the lack of training courses and criticism sessions meant that "*theoretical issues on content, form, the people, the masses, and science are only understood in a vague and superficial way.*"[49] In education, it was generally more difficult for teachers at the higher levels of education to comprehend the spirit of the new education. Even when they agreed with the "scientific, democratic and popular" nature of the new education, it remained extremely difficult for them to express in practical terms the way to achieve such a spirit. In an exasperated tone, the report noted that "There are still naive assessments, for example, like the person who asked how to help peasants understand atomic theories."[50]

If ideological laxness among artists and writers was becoming untenable in the eyes of the Party by 1949, which led to the Conference of Debate in Việt Bắc, the move to tighten the ideological debate was a broad one aimed at other sectors of the society as well. The ideological setting had to be firm if the Party was to introduce land reform, which was seen as crucial in gaining mass support for the resistance.[51] Given the need for a united front, rent reduction and modification of the land system (the use of abandoned land, confiscation of church land, etc.) were viewed as necessary transitional methods. Ideological unity was necessary, however, and by 1951 it was deemed that the ideological situation thus far had been entirely too defensive. The Party must take the offensive, explicitly and concretely, in thought reform policy as it moved to prepare for land reform and eventual victory.[52]

The concepts of criticism and self-criticism (*phê bình và tự phê bình*) were touched upon briefly at the Conference of Debate in Việt Bắc, and in 1950 they were introduced into the educational system in order to dispel lingering notions of neutral education and the like.[53] There were to be other steps taken to move the teachers to a higher level of ideological comprehension and conformity: There were month-long courses in 1951 designed to inculcate in the teachers "the method of the people's democratic education," with full-scale rectification (*chỉnh huấn* in Vietnamese, *cheng feng* in Chinese) in 1952, which would emphasize "the consciousness of serving the people" and "determine the working-class position."[54]

The ideological battle was also being waged among the students. In a 1953 report issued by the Ministry of Education it was noted that since September 1951 there had been a rectification movement among the middle schools, high schools, and vocational schools. The students had "criticized their mistakes concerning the goals of education, conceptions about examinations, relationships with teachers and friends, and with social work and work for the resistance, and they resolved that going to school is serving the people."[55] Written by Nguyễn Văn Huyên, the minister of education, the report mentioned briefly that the rectification campaign in preparation for the later Phát Động Quần Chúng (Mobilize the Masses) campaign, itself part of the larger preparation for land reform, was causing upheaval within the school system. The report also raised the concern that "those cadres from the poor peasant classes who were assigned by the people to positions in the government and to mass organization tasks have very low level of culture. There are those who cannot read or write fluently and even some who are illiterate."[56] It was a problem that would plague the socialist state of Vietnam for years, but it is instructive to note that the dossier containing this report contains two versions. The one that was eventually sent on to the premier's office did not include the reference to badly educated peasant cadres being assigned leadership roles nor did it make any mention of the conflict in the schools caused by the rectification campaign. It would seem that at least in this instance the Party leadership was not receiving accurate or complete information.

The disturbance within the school system due to the rectification campaign was disruptive enough to merit some mention in reports that followed. The tame practice of "determining working-class position" (*xác định lập trường giai cấp*) of 1952 gave way to the much more revolutionary and consequential process of "political struggle" (*đấu tranh chính trị*) in 1953. Political struggle involved a fierce operation in which class position, already determined, was now used to criticize a person's life and work in order to achieve a specific goal, rent reduction, for example. Classism was no longer a mental exercise nor an issue of well-meaning belief. Political struggle demanded that classism be put into practice, and the classification inherent in the process came to the fore.

In 1953, the slogan ascribed to education was "lean on the people, strengthen organization, highlight quality" (*dựa vào nhân dân, củng cố tổ chức, đề cao chất lượng*).[57] The combination of land reform and the organizational rectification campaign from 1953 to 1956 was disastrous in Vietnam, especially since the Party membership had exploded between 1946 and 1954, from 20,000 to 700,000.[58] This extraordinarily rapid growth of the Party during the war years led its leaders to feel the need to purify the rank and file when the opportunity arose. The Chinese model was certainly powerful, but the widespread application of the organizational rectification campaign in Vietnam within a highly compressed time frame made Alexander Woodside's argument even more persuasive. The fragmentation of colonialism, Woodside contends, has made the Vietnamese extremely sensitive to the issue of organization, and the history of modern Vietnam can be seen as a quest for *đoàn thể*, or community.[59] The acute awareness of the need for organization coupled with the perception that the organization itself was being polluted by less than desirable elements produced a feverish urgency behind the prosaic term *political struggle.*

In Vietnam, the move to combine class with organizational rectification was also the case within the educational system. In Interzone 4, after a series of political struggles, a number of private Catholic schools were closed. It was reported that some one hundred teachers "with connections to reactionary activities" were arrested or lost their jobs. A number of those who belonged to the landowning class or had relations with landowners pressured their families to renounce their class status or publicly denounced family members for being landowners.[60] A more specific account puts the number at seventy-seven teachers and two students arrested in Thanh Hóa Province, sixty-eight teachers and forty-four students in Nghệ An, and four teachers and two students in Hà Tĩnh.[61] The students were clearly swept up in the campaign torrent. Many students from the poor peasant class became openly contemptuous of their classmates, and the student bodies of many schools organized their own struggle sessions, which the Ministry of Education later assessed privately as having been "fraught with mistakes that caused much harm."[62]

In Nghệ An, for instance, students beat another student for being a traitor when he was really nothing more than a petty thief. In Thanh

Hóa, the movement reached its height in February and March 1953, with all the schools organizing struggle sessions. One student ended up disclosing having had some contact with reactionary elements, and, "painfully hit, the student rashly confessed the names of one hundred people." In another instance, a student "was hit painfully and confessed to being a traitor and after being freed hanged himself." In another school, students organized a struggle session and beat the principal. Yet another school "used torture methods . . . and beat a student to death." The fever was widespread, not sparing even the Việt Bắc interzone, the seat of the Việt Minh government. One school there had organized a struggle session against a student who was the child of a landowner, torturing him three times. The student confessed to being a traitor and named fifty people, "causing confusion among the teachers, students, and people of the area."[63]

References to these events convey a very tense atmosphere and a sense of lack of control over the campaign by the authorities. In a number of localities in the early phase of the campaign, being marked as a traitor (*Việt gian*) was the same as being sentenced to death.[64] Being tortured or beaten to death was probably rare within the educational system, but students from poor peasant backgrounds took advantage of the situation and imposed their newfound, officially sanctioned power upon their classmates. In many instances, students who were the children of landowners and rich peasants were forced to sit separately without any communication with the rest of the class, a situation that was also causing apprehension among the children of the petite bourgeoisie and middle peasants.[65] Predictably, the dropout rate among students increased to 20 percent in the province of Thanh Hóa and 25 to 30 percent in the provinces of Hà Tĩnh and Nghệ An, affecting mostly the children of the landowning and rich peasant classes.[66]

The radical nature of the leftist emphasis on the poor peasant class in the educational system in North Vietnam in 1953 is clear. An earlier example exists. In 1952, the school for Vietnamese children of high-ranking officials and cadres in Guilin, southern China, was strongly criticized for being, of all things, rightist. Essentially military in organization, the school was directly under the Party's control, rather than that of the Ministry of Education, in its early years of existence. Seeing the school as having a special mission to develop future Party members and themselves as the forerunners of the proletarian class, the students took it upon themselves to reorganize the curriculum. Dismissive of the Party's united front agenda at the time, the students branded "Lê Lợi as a landowner who took advantage of the hardship of the peasants and the call for independence [from the Chinese]" and referred to Quang Trung and the Tây Sơn brothers as "a bunch of peasants learning to be kings."[67] Lê Lợi (who came from the upper class) and Quang Trung of the Tây Sơn brothers (who came from a less elitist background) are historical personages firmly ensconced in the Party's official history as national leaders who, with enormous popular support, successfully turned back the tide of Chinese invaders in the fifteenth and eighteenth centuries, respectively.

Political Education

The use of organization to carry out thought reform was authoritatively presented in a document entitled "Political Education," dated 4 September 1951 and written by someone who was clearly a high-ranking Party member.[68] A document of strict orthodoxy, its author aimed to have centralized the political education process that all sectors of society must undergo. The proposed program is shown in table 2.

TABLE 2. **The 1951 Proposed Political Education Curriculum**

	Content of the Curriculum	Composition of Students
Grade 1	Basic politics and education on citizenry	Elementary schools, people who just passed literacy exams, state employees of the lowest rank
Grade 2	Policies of the state and mass organizations	Middle schools, complementary education courses (i.e., post-literacy courses), state employees of the middle rank
Grade 3	Continue to study grade 2's program, with the addition of practice and a broad outline of Marxism-Leninism	High schools, university preparatory schools, higher complementary education courses, state employees of the highest rank
Grade 4	Marxism-Leninism	Universities and colleges, high-ranking state and mass organization employees
All grades	Revolutionary history of Vietnam, history of the Indochinese Communist Party, revolutionary histories of larger countries like the Soviet Union and China	For all, though revolutionary histories of countries like the Soviet Union and China should depend on educational level and how such a subject is presented

Source: Compiled from "Giáo dục chính trị" (Political education), Office of the Premier, dossier 2484.

The committee authorized to write and publish materials for political education would not be under the Ministry of Education but a central organ of the state. To oversee the application of the state's program of political education, a network of offices incorporated into the administrative structure at the provincial city level would focus on education and propaganda and receive directives from a central organ of the state.

Political education was to be complemented by the constant engagement of people going to the countryside to help with the harvest or participating in social and political campaigns. At the professional level, the emphasis on the practical nature of political education, according to the document's author, would be geared to specific problems relating to the different professions. For example, in the health care profession the focus would be on how to deal with patients. This would lead to greater consciousness about the masses, destroying the idea of prestige inherent in officeholders and changing the bureaucratic (*quan liêu*) work method. The kind of general political education provided thus far was simply not adequate to deal with the specific ills of the different professions.

The importance of political education was highlighted in the document's proposal to reorganize education into three branches: general, vocational, and political education. Increasingly, the Ministry of Education was left in the position of a participant in the decision-making process rather than that of a key player. Only in general education would the ministry have full authority. In vocational education, the ministry must work with other ministries, which had direct authority over vocational schools. In political education, the ministry would take part in shaping the curriculum, but ultimate authority would come from the state, or the Party more specifically. The new educational system was becoming distinctly unneutral.

There is in all of this a fervent belief that education could do much to change people's behavior. This was also a particular characteristic of Chinese communism, with its emphasis on thought reform, criticism and self-criticism, and rectification campaigns. Thought leads to deed; the correct thought leads to the correct deed. The idealistic, Confucian high regard for education as shaping men was very much in evidence. What was different was the focus on a very specific outcome, which led to the emphasis on organization as a way to bind people to the larger, desired view. Mass organizations were clearly seen as a way in which the primacy of the state's view could override those of the individual and the family. Schools functioned in this regard for children and youths, cooperatives for the countryside, and unions for others among the population who held state jobs. Key positions in state-run unions in turn were staffed by Party members, further securing its control over daily life. Given its control over resources (housing, employment, food coupons, etc.), the workplace, and unions, the Party exerted enormous power over people's lives. As this early document on political education contended, in the matter of Vietnamese women, who for a long time had functioned as petty traders in cities and villages,

> we must see the organizational form [of unions] not as for the workers alone but *for all of their families.* If [we cannot] organize [the women] directly into the unions of their husbands or brothers or fathers then [we must] use unions to gain influence over them to help them to have an organized life and therefore educate them.[69]

I want to emphasize less the specific form of an organization, like the unions, and more the insistence on organization as the way to encompass the population. Education was crucial in ideological transformation, but it was perceived as a long-term process, and therefore organization as the embodiment of correct ideology would have to be in place in order to structure both thought and behavior in the immediate as well as the long terms.

For all the emphasis on the united front and the role of intellectuals in the revolution, the contempt with which the Party leaders viewed the Vietnamese past also extended to intellectuals, although this was never stated publicly. The document on political education, however, voiced this contempt for intellectuals clearly and advocated tight organization of their activities as the primary means of transforming them. Well-known intellectuals must now be dealt with in an offensive manner, with the Party moving from the conciliatory stand previously used to persuade them to join the Việt Minh to an authoritative, mass-oriented position. All personal initiatives or actions must now give way to the opinion of the people embodied in the mass organizations.

With regard to the creative intellectuals, the author of the document declared, "It is a matter of embarrassment and pity that from the beginning of the resistance until now, in the literature and art of our country, there has not been a single creative work of value." As to why that should be the case, the document cited three reasons. The first had to do with the nature of the creative intellectuals, most of whom were young when they joined the resistance and therefore, lacking in life experience, education ("most are petite bourgeoisie who can write a few pieces of prose and a few poems with pleasing rhymes, and a few have published articles in the newspapers and therefore call themselves writers, not looking to study more"), and politics ("[the majority of our writers] are not like the majority of the writers in other countries, who have lived the lives of workers and peasants before writing. The opposite exists in our country"). The second reason was that "our country greatly lacks talent, so writers are launched on the path of life too easily, not encountering the difficulties endured by young writers in other countries (whose worth is many times that of our writers)." Finally, the third and final reason listed was education, meaning the lack of a proper educational effort leading these young, untalented, but brash writers to the right road. The policy toward these writers thus far, complained the author of the document, had been far too accommodating.

Rather then seeing the writers' trips to the countryside and the various military fronts as sincere participation in the resistance, the author judged them to be only a cover for the writers' recognition of their own modest capabilities. The method of going to other localities was not wrong, since that method had been used effectively in countries like China and the Soviet Union, but no credible result had resulted from these trips because they continued to stand upon their petit bourgeois background with regard to life. Once more, the document's author made his disdain for his own country's writers patently clear. Vietnamese writers

> use that method because they see that in other countries (like China and the Soviet Union), writers often go to other localities or military fronts. But the mistake is that they do not see the difference between them and their foreign peers. Those people can use that method, and the method is very useful for them, because on all three fronts, *politics, society, culture,* they have already lived a rich life. So when they confront a new situation they can still capture the main link, find the main characteristics. The writers of our country are new students on all three fronts, at the most just at the beginning of their practice, so how can they have a sufficient background?[70]

A frank voice within the Party is always rare, especially given wartime conditions and the Party's longtime emphasis on nationalism and a united front. It is easy to see that disdain for Vietnamese writers went hand in hand with great admiration for other nations' writers, who were better than their Vietnamese counterparts in every way. The disgust with Vietnamese writers went so deep that the author of the document could hardly see how the writers could be transformed. His one prescription for the situation was to exhort writers to go to the people but on these trips to make sure that they did specific tasks relating to whatever skills they had as opposed to simply recording events and gathering data for their next, worthless project. Whoever knew about agriculture, for example, should be made to do agricultural work in the villages and so on. Expecting opposition, the author added:

> Perhaps there are those who will ask: after a long time doing that, we will not have a group of people exemplifying our country's literature and art. But, I ask these people in return, if we leave things the way they are can the writers exemplify anything? What do they create that would exemplify anything? And leaving things like that is dangerous, because life moves on and they are retreating.[71]

Indeed, the author could not have cared less about any group of creative intellectuals who had established their reputations prior to the resistance because he aimed to install a new group of creative intellectuals born out of the struggle and drawn from among the people. The emphasis, therefore, should be on finding new talents among the people and providing them with the necessary support. Only they could truly exemplify art and literature in the new period.

Rectification and the Intellectuals

As the Việt Minh government became more stable, the number of translations and publications of works from the Soviet Union and China grew accordingly.[72] In addition, articles on intellectual issues, poems, and short stories were translated and circulated informally within the Party apparatus, government organizations, and the intellectual community. Given China's geographical proximity and its historical influence on Vietnam, many intellectuals recall that Chinese views on art and literature were circulating in North Vietnam with tremendous influence from 1950 onward after the success of the

Chinese revolution had opened the Sino-Vietnamese border. The works of the Chinese literary critic Chou Yang (Chu Dương in Vietnamese) were prominent in Vietnamese intellectual publications. Chou Yang, who became a member of the Central Committee of the Chinese Communist Party in 1956, was widely quoted as having the final say (after Mao) on all cultural matters by 1957.[73] Chou Yang's *Văn nghệ nhân dân mới* (The people's new literature and art) was translated and published in 1950, and his *Phấn đấu để sáng tạo những tác phẩm văn học nghệ thuật càng nhiều càng hay hơn* (Strive to create more and better works of literature and art) appeared in 1951.[74] In 1952, his recent speech to the Institute of Literacy Research in Beijing, which elaborated Mao Tse-Tung's directives on art and literature, was translated and given a prominent position in two issues of the journal *Văn Nghệ*, the organ of the Vietnamese creative community.[75]

These facts indicated that ideas and processes of the Chinese revolution itself were being introduced and studied in Vietnam as a model to follow, although high-level cultural officials in Vietnam have tended to downplay the Chinese influence. Hà Xuân Trường, for example, has stated that Mao's directives on literature and art did not have much influence in Vietnam at the time.

> For me, as for a number of other comrades also working around the central organizations [in the early years of the anti-French resistance] who were assigned to follow literature and art, we did read [Mao's "The New Democratic Culture" and "Talks at the Yenan Conference on Literature and Art"], but they were not the center of research for us. On the pages of the *Sự Thật* newspaper all those years, I remember that there was only one article by Lam Phong (Nguyễn Sơn) introducing Yenan literature and art, and then only its healthy and revolutionary character.[76]

Lam Phong, however, is none other than the influential Gen. Nguyễn Sơn of Interzone 4, famous for his participation in the Chinese Communist Party's Long March. He had lived in Yenan and was well known for being knowledgeable about Chinese literature and art. An iconoclastic revolutionary who did not always operate within the strict confines of rules and regulations, Nguyễn Sơn was well respected for inspiring command of Interzone 4, a hotbed of Vietnamese intellectual activity during the resistance.[77]

Nowhere was Chinese influence more evident than in the use of the rectification technique. I have mentioned that the technique was introduced into the educational system as early as 1950, coinciding with a hardening attitude toward intellectual and cultural issues in official reports and statements. Among intellectuals, the first formal rectification course was organized in the winter of 1951. The two-month course was taught to high-ranking cadres by instructors who had been trained in China and in turn would organize rectification courses for others. Trần Dần and Tử Phác were in charge of the course for intellectuals within the army. Đặng Đình Hưng and Lê Đạt, who worked in the central agency for propaganda, organized the courses for the intellectual community in general.[78] These names would recur in 1958, when these loyal children of the revolution would be branded antirevolutionary petit bourgeois for their roles in a brief moment of intellectual dissent, discussed in the next chapter. It is enough here to point out that they were among the first to be formally trained in rectification techniques in China. Their revolutionary credentials must have been impeccable at the time to be so chosen.

Tô Hoài's recollection of his first rectification session provides a sense of the organized solemnity of the scene.

> Waking up in the middle of the night, in the middle of the jungle hundreds of torches were lit, slogan bands of black cloth with white words glittering: *Disclose weaknesses . . . Measure loyalty. . . .* Gut-wrenching cold weather. Ink-dark jungle night. Filthy human beings, full of sins. Not enough. Not enough sincerity. Do it over. Do it over again. Each time doing it over, uneasiness and worry mounted. The wait to be cleared by the group remained long. Confessing to being degenerate [e.g., sleeping with someone to whom one is not married] was easiest, even if it were not true. Pounded the chest to say yes.[79]

No longer an earnest discussion of one's commitment to the people and revolution among friends or sympathetic comrades, as at the Conference of Debate in Việt Bắc in 1949, this description of rectification in 1951 was all austere organization with a menacing sense of enveloping authority. The analogy used by Tô Hoài was that of providing the cure for the patient, and there were patients who did not survive the treatment. At the newspaper *Cứu Quốc* (Save the nation), Tô Hoài recalled a young man who went into the jungle and hanged himself and another who swallowed a razor blade. There was, however, no escape, even in death: "Although dead, [he] was expelled [from the Party] because of the crime of escaping struggle."[80] These internal struggle sessions, never publicized to the larger community, culminated in a series of self-criticism statements by leading intellectuals that were finally published in 1953.[81]

Harsh, even by later official standards, these self-criticism statements testified to an ideological maelstrom, overpowering everyone with its intensely psychological core. One after another, the leading intellectuals of the day fervently denounced their creative works before and after the revolution for violating in one way or another the now painfully obvious prescriptions of the new situation. For the writer Tô Hoài, his pre-August Revolution short stories, which focused on his village's handicraft workers, who were disfigured and trapped by poverty and tradition, were in fact only "betraying the truth" since as a writer he did not see the strength of the people he wrote about, only their hopeless existence.[82] His work after the revolution, which focused on the ethnic highland people, was no better because even though he wrote of their enormous participation and sacrifice what the readers saw were only grinding poverty, diseases, and a mix of cadres that included "a few comrades cadres so subjective as to underestimate the enemies, botching the work, and another comrade cadre who pretended to be sick when faced with difficulties."[83]

The poet-playwright Thế Lữ, a prominent New Poetry writer who was also a leading member of the Self-Reliant Literary Group, denounced in absolute terms his connection to the group and Nguyễn Tường Tam, the real name of the writer Nhất Linh, who was its leader.[84] Thế Lữ now saw all of his major works during this period as "increasing the dose of poison in the minds of youth from 1932 to 1945. That influence has not ended. As for myself, passionate for fame at one time, I contracted the strange diseases of literature, leading to self-corruption and spreading it around me. I have been imprisoned for so long in the errors of self-conceit, self-satisfaction, and gratification."[85] The poet Xuân Diệu, another star of the New Poetry period, condemned his works as petit bourgeois, individualistic and therefore selfish, and antiprogress because of his emphasis on beauty, the temporal quality of life, and immediate sensation. Not only did they have no value, he said, but they were sinful because his poetry had poisoned the minds of susceptible urban youths, especially those of students.

Post–August Revolution works likewise did not escape harsh self-criticism. The critic Hoài Thanh decimated his 1951 *Talking about Resistance Poetry,* which had been one of the very first works of the revolution that recognized and highlighted poems written by peasants and soldiers. It turned out that he had only let readers see "a Vietnam in which everything is peaceful, beautiful, and cannot be more beautiful: everyone believes in Chairman Hồ, in the Party, in the government; everyone loves and supports one another; everyone only knows the business of fighting the French."[86] The reality was much starker. The country in fact was full of "deep contradictions between the land-owning class, increasingly recalcitrant and reactionary, and the working and peasant classes, which need to wrestle back their rightful economic and political powers in order to move forward to achieve the tasks of the resistance."[87] The revolution had firmly established its language, and the united front was but a mirage to be dispelled once and for all.

The condemnation of creative works focused on their wasteful lack of social purpose, and when they did have some social effects these were branded as poisonous to the population, antirevolutionary, and hopelessly bourgeois. Intellectuals admitted repeatedly to having been "emancipated from reality" (*thoát ly thực tế*). The notion of emancipation connotes the revolutionary capacity to let go of binding ties, especially familial ones, in order to move as one with the revolution. During land reform, those who could prove that they had *thoát ly* from their unfortunate class background to join the resistance could reestablish for themselves a new proletarian background, to the point of never acknowledging their landowning or bourgeois parents. They were allowed to wipe their embarrassing slates clean. A position in the new society was possible for people like them, but it came at a high price—complete renunciation of the past and the self that had been born and nurtured in that past.

In order to effect this rupture with the past, the past had to be demonized. This was a key method used during land reform, when the landowning class was accused of causing every conceivable ill in rural society. The analogy of a patient needing a cure was substantiated by the intellectuals' assessment of their past works as being not only of no worth to the society at large but "poisonous" to the population and therefore having a direct impact on the success or failure of the nation itself. The intellectual was therefore deeply sick within, so much so that only now did he or she begin to see the extent of the poison pen he or she had wielded to produce harmful works before and after the revolution.

The concept of "sin" (*tội lỗi*), mentioned in Tô Hoài's recollection of the first rectification session in 1951, reverberated throughout intellectuals' statements in 1953. The writer Nguyễn Tuân condemned his first and probably best known literary work, *Vang bóng một thời*, for containing "preliminary evidence of my sins toward the people, the revolution." His *Thiếu quê hương* represented "another sin among past creative works," and even the 1946 collection *Chùa đàn*, which he wrote with a sympathetic eye toward the revolution, was now a "non-political creation" that was "a big sin against the August Revolution and the rights of the people."[88] The poet Xuân Diệu judged his works to be "not only of no worth but also sinful to society."[89]

If their works were poisonous, nothing more than great sins against society, the people, and the revolution, then intellectuals had to be sinners themselves. Everything about their backgrounds, education, training, and even the creative impulses so crucial to the nature of their work were now viewed in extremely negative terms. The writer Nguyễn Tuân confessed that "I constantly need new sensations. Since objective reality does not provide enough novel sensations, I make them up, attempt to generate them for myself, even though I know that they are only illusions."[90] The writer Tô Hoài saw himself as a person whose "cowardice decides my indifferent and superficial view of the characters [in my works]."[91] The obsessive references to sin and to Việt Minh intellectuals as both conscious and unconscious sinners presented a new intellectual discourse with religious overtones. The so-called unconscious sin committed by the intellectual sinners is similar to Catholicism's Original Sin: having been born and matured in the old society, there was no escape from sin, and salvation could only be achieved through the recognition of the Party and the revolution. The ever-present possibility of committing future sins, however, would require constant vigilance.

The religious allusion made concrete the primacy of the state and the miraculous appearance of the twin figures of Party and revolution. Images of salvation and rebirth abounded. Tô Hoài wrote: "The August Revolution has saved me."[92] The writer Nguyễn Tuân claimed that "Because the Party guides me to stand by the one and only truth, I finally saw clearly my [bad] nature in my works."[93] The painter Tô Ngọc Vân stated that "Today, due to the light of the Party, which has been brought to me by the revolutionary community, shining into my soul, I see clearly that, although the revolution and the resistance have liberated me physically from the controlling reach of the enemy, my thoughts still are imprisoned by it."[94] The architects Nguyễn Cao Luyện and Hoàng Như Tiệp asserted that their work with the Self-Reliant Literary Group to generate well-built, inexpensive housing for low-income Vietnamese prior to the revolution was only playing into the hands of the colonial authorities and Vietnam-ese feudal and capitalist forces, and "we would have continued to go farther along that mistaken road, but the August Revolution and the resistance saved us."[95]

—•—

Images of light, the perception of truth, and of being saved and guided by a higher authority allowed intellectuals to be reborn as blank slates, children who would now be shaped into useful adults under the guidance of the Party. The love of the people became spe-cific, focusing on the differentiations of class and accompanied by a sharply defined hate for definite targets. The Party and its compan-ion, the revolution, became fully reified. In the intellectuals' self-critical statements, the intensely personal nature of their contact with Party members, which had led many of them to the revolution, had disappeared. Instead, the Party appeared to be a superhuman entity, godlike, and the relationship between the intellectuals and the Party became one of extreme inequality between leaders and followers.

Between 1948 and 1953, a transformation had taken place. A series of organizations and reorganizations had been carried out in the cul-tural and intellectual spheres, with the goal of radically reshaping the ideological content of the revolution in order to establish firm control over activities in these areas and prepare for the move toward land reform, the hallmark of a socialist state in the eyes of the Vietnamese communist leaders.

PART II

The Construction of a
Socialist State, 1954–65

— 4 —

Intellectual Dissent:
The Nhân Văn Giai Phẩm Period

The victory at Điện Biên Phủ in 1954 ended the anti-French struggle and provided the Việt Minh with enormous prestige and authority as it set about constructing a new state. Intended to be a temporary measure until the national election would be held two years later, the division of Vietnam into north and south at the Geneva Conference was nevertheless a great disappointment to the Việt Minh. Its leaders soon recognized that once established the American-backed government in the south would have few reasons to comply with the terms of the Geneva Accords. Having little room to maneuver since both the Soviet Union and China were also pushing Vietnam to accept those terms rather than antagonize the United States and its European allies, the Việt Minh turned to the task of establishing the framework of a socialist state in the north.

Land reform, which had been carried out in the areas under Việt Minh control since 1953, was now extended throughout the north. Pushed on in great haste, land reform was deemed to have been completed by mid-1956. Accompanied by a relentless organizational rectification campaign designed to purify the Party apparatus down to the villages, the twin processes of land reform and organizational rectification wreaked havoc not only on old structures in the village but on the Party apparatus, which might have provided some stability amid the chaos. In August 1956, Hồ Chí Minh himself acknowledged serious problems with land reform, and a subsequent Party announcement in October ushered in a period of correction of errors. Even then, official admission of land reform errors could not prevent, or perhaps finally gave vent to, a violent peasant rebellion in Nghệ An, Hồ Chí Minh's own home province, in November 1956. Throughout 1957, many who had been wrongly arrested during land reform were released and teams of correction cadres were sent to the villages to try to ease conditions in the countryside.

The year 1956 was one of upheaval for the nascent socialist state in North Vietnam. Not only was the countryside in disarray, but no sooner was land reform ended than the campaign to reeducate the capitalists (*cải tạo tư sản*) plunged the cities into fear.[1] The whole country was in turmoil, and the atmosphere was stoked by a series of developments that comprised the only instance of widespread intellectual dissent ever to occur in North Vietnam. Commonly referred to as the Nhân Văn Giai Phẩm (NVGP) period, the interlude received its name from two short-lived publications in which intellectuals voiced their concerns and criticisms of the Party and the government. Government suppression led to decades of professional and economic deprivation for the participants of NVGP, including long jail terms for a few who were considered to be the key leaders. Little was known about NVGP in the south, although some of its writings were well publicized, and the subsequent obliteration of the period from the public discourse also left generations of North Vietnamese ignorant of its development and issues it raised.[2] Under such circumstances, the period became shrouded in a mist of myth-making accounts and commentaries. This chapter seeks to delineate the domestic and international contexts in which the intellectual dissent arose, the issues that were raised by the intellectuals, and the state's responses to such concerns. Coming so soon after the establishment of the socialist state in North Vietnam and coinciding with a period of dramatic events in the communist world, the NVGP period came to exemplify the inherent conflict between the government's vision and the intellectuals' expectations of the new state and society.

Thắc Mắc versus Lập Trường

In his valuable account of the NVGP period, to which he was a firsthand witness, Georges Boudarel focused his first chapter on the concept of *thắc mắc*. According to the 1990 Vietnamese-English dictionary published by the Social Science Publishing House, *thắc mắc* is defined as (1) "to be still unclear about a point"; (2) "to worry, to be uneasy"; and (3) "to be at cross-purposes."[3] Boudarel traces the use of the word to a 1950 report by Đào Vũ, the first Vietnamese writer to witness land reform in China, on the concerns voiced by a peasant.[4] For Boudarel, from that point on, *thắc mắc* came to exemplify the whole world of subterfuge-speak that came into existence with the imposition of Marxism-Leninism and Maoism upon Vietnam's hard won national independence. One has certain *thắc mắc* or one is *thắc mắc* about the government, about one's boss in the workplace, about an announcement of the Party, or about a certain assignment of work or allocation of rations. Used as a noun or as a verb, the term indicates misgivings or discomfort without specifying the source of the concern. In short, according to Boudarel, *thắc mắc* characterizes nothing less than "la vie de Vietnam communiste depuis des decennies."[5] The existence of this indirect expression of opinion indicated clearly the oppressive nature of state power, but, as Boudarel has eloquently expressed, the term also spoke of the ability of the public to voice its discontent, no matter how limited.

> A condition d'entendre à demi-mot, de lire entre les lignes, de percevoir les sous-entendus et de déchiffrer les métaphores, une contestation certes timide, mais néanmoins réelle, a toujours existé au sien du régime communiste vietnamien.[6]

If *thắc mắc* encapsulates the Aesopian world of dissent, its opposite is embodied in the term and concept of *lập trường*, defined as "position, class position, class outlook, standpoint."[7] Coming into widespread use in the early 1950s, this socialist political term was soon employed in virtually every social and intellectual context. *Thắc mắc* by its nature was vague, and so was *lập trường*, even though it was closely associated with the class viewpoint. In time *lập trường* came to refer to any official line requiring support. Thus, one was constantly reminded to *giữ vững lập trường*, or "steadfastly maintain the viewpoint." The most common charge against someone seen as straying from the officially sanctioned course of behavior was that he or she had lost *lập trường*. If *thắc mắc* defined life in socialist Vietnam from the bottom up, with its pervasive questioning of established rules, then *lập trường* defined life in socialist Vietnam from the top down, with its enveloping sense of authority and its ubiquitous demand for compliance.

Land Reform and the New Society

The period of preparation for land reform, *phát động quần chúng*, or "mass mobilization," was carried out between 1953 and 1955. The first four waves of land reform covered about half the country between

December 1953 and December 1955, while one giant wave encompassed the rest of the country in 1956.[8] The establishment of a socialist state in North Vietnam with the Geneva agreements in June 1954 did not hamper land reform. Indeed, land reform could now be pushed to its conclusion all over the north, with the areas previously not under Việt Minh control now undergoing a compressed process of mass mobilization and then land reform proper. The pace of land reform in Vietnam was breathless, less than three years from start to completion compared to more than twenty years in the Chinese case.[9] The fifth wave, the most important of all, referred to as the "Điện Biên Phủ campaign in the delta," emphasized the urgency of the undertaking. The association with Điện Biên Phủ also supplied the last wave of land reform with a note of righteousness gained from the recent military victory, which had led to national independence and garnered enormous prestige and authority for the communists.[10]

In reality, however, the peace following Điện Biên Phủ had barely been celebrated when the Geneva Conference divided the country into two nations in 1954. A large number of North Vietnamese, aware of communism and/or fearful for their freedom to worship as Catholics, chose to go south. The chaos of a postwar society was intensified from late 1955 to early 1956, the height of the last massive wave of land reform, when, according to Edwin Moise, "leftish excesses and leftish paranoia, especially in the form of purges within the revolutionary movement, had reached astonishing levels."[11] The ferocity of the organizational rectification campaign perhaps can be understood in this light as the result of a conjunction of both a desire to dramatically increase the pace of the socialist revolution now that the Việt Minh had finally taken power and a deep sense of betrayal because the fruits of the victory were not forthcoming. Its enemies had succeeded in unexpected ways. They were faceless but omnipresent. Land reform and the accompanying organizational rectification campaign presented an opportunity to consolidate the Party's control down to the village level and to purify the Party apparatus, which had grown so rapidly during the anti-French resistance. Each village in northern Vietnam during this phase of land reform became a war zone. Private space was violently invaded and severely restricted. *Thắc mắc* did not have its moment here; *lập trường* was entirely in ascendance.

It was in this atmosphere of extreme vigilance, fear, and uncertainty that the first signs of intellectual dissent began to emerge. Intellectuals had also taken part in land reform, participating in many instances as members of reform teams. The writer Tô Hoài recalls the painter Nguyễn Tư Nghiêm's experience.

> Nguyễn Tư Nghiêm participated in a rent reduction program in Thái Nguyên. Work at the village level was tightly organized every moment of the day, the whole team was like a unit going to war. Two days to catch the roots, one day to string the beads. Rent reduction team member painter Nguyễn Tư Nghiêm tried all week but could not catch the root or string the bead of any poor peasant. Nguyễn Tư Nghiêm was so frightened that he went mad and left without remembering the way back to the village. The whole day he wandered about in the rice field, catching locusts and grasshoppers to eat. Painter Tạ Thúc Bình was sent by the work unit down to the team to bring Nguyễn Tư Nghiêm home. I have never asked if Nguyễn Tư Nghiêm really went crazy or was so scared of having to sit in the pen to self-criticize that he created that "Vân the crazy woman" scene.[12]

Bắt rễ, xâu chuỗi, or "catch the roots, string the beads," a crucial method borrowed from the Chinese, referred to the initial step in the land reform process in which members of the team made connections with key poor peasants (the roots), who would be the first to speak out against the landlords, inspiring other poor peasants to follow suit. This recollection from the vantage point of thirty years later allowed Tô Hoài a measure of levity and detachment, but one can sense the helplessness of the individual against the all-encompassing march of state policy. There is, however, also a rueful understanding of a time that the reader can only find incomprehensible and painful. Tô Hoài himself participated in three waves of land reform, partly because he was a writer-journalist whose presence in the village the Vietnamese government felt would ease the international community's concern for human rights. Tô Hoài, however, was also supposed to write reports on the miseries of the peasants and the crimes of the landlords for the Vietnamese press. This he did after attending sessions in which peasants were encouraged to relay their woes (*tố khổ*), but he also remembers a particular team leader, "bent on prevailing at all costs, fierce in every aspect," who after only a few days in the village organized a meeting to execute a landlord in order to uplift the peasants' spirits. This same team leader insisted on marrying a poor peasant to enhance his political credentials. Tô

Hoài remembers: "I was suspicious [of him]. But I could not open my mouth. He could imprison me in a buffalo pen anytime!"[13] The absolute power that a land reform team, particularly the team leader, possessed led to violence and opportunism. Intellectuals witnessed all this first hand, in addition to enduring the effects of land reform in their own villages.[14]

First Signs of Dissent: Trần Dần and the Army Intellectuals

In this environment of extreme uncertainty and fear, coming so soon after the hard won peace and nine years of enormous sacrifice, a brief flourish of dissent burst forth in 1956. The moment had its roots in 1955, and the spark was a poet and writer named Trần Dần, one of the first to have been trained in Chinese rectification techniques, who had led rectification sessions for creative intellectuals in 1951.

Trần Dần himself was not an established literary personality prior to 1945. The only literary note we have of him is when he and two friends founded a literary journal, melodramatically called *Dạ Đài* (The netherworld). *Dạ Đài* published its first and only issue on 16 November 1946, just before the Việt Minh's call for a general uprising against the French in December. *Dạ Đài* was not a well-known or lasting endeavor, but it does provide us with a glimpse into the person of Trần Dần in the days prior to the revolution. In a seven-page pronouncement, Trần Dần and his two poet friends grandly announced their "Bản Tuyên Ngôn Tượng Trưng" (Symbolic declaration). Setting themselves up as alienated intellectuals who happened to have been born at the wrong time, these young men proclaimed their weariness with living: "We have lived, lived all the earthly forms, had suffered all human sorrows and joys."[15] Trần Dần was twenty years old at the time.[16]

These young men proclaimed themselves "symbolic poets" and sought to create something new. The static, narrow world of the older generation must be replaced with something more authentic, a return to the primitive world:

By means of images, we will retell the old stories people have told us under the lamplight. We will seek to understand the spirit of folk songs and sayings. We will exemplify the excitement of the children hearing a fabulous legend and how a peasant is moved when he hears a simple children's song.

Far from the pessimistic image of national culture that was rampant among the intellectuals and Party theorists in the early days of the revolution, Trần Dần and his friends reveled instead in the "primitiveness" of nativist culture, seeing in it the sophistication and complexity of a culture that thus far had been shrouded by the classical veneer of gentility and cultivation. In the passage quoted above, however, it would be "we," meaning the authors, who would rediscover and present this worthy, ancient, nativist culture to the world. The power of creation, or at the very least re-creation, and interpretation rested entirely with the poets themselves.

The desire to find identity and worth in a vision of culture embedded in the native past made it easy to see why someone like Trần Dần would turn to the Việt Minh's nationalist vision. There was, however, a certain quality of boastfulness, intellectual confidence, and independent creativity evident even in this youthful literary declaration, which would bring Trần Dần into conflict with authority soon enough. According to his friend Hoàng Cầm, as early as 1947 Trần Dần was incurring official displeasure with his avant garde intellectual experimentation.

I knew of [Trần Dần] for a long time—among the soldiers in Sơn La, since the beginning of 1947, there was one famous Trần Dần who painted and wrote poetry with many interesting aspects. The art and literary friends around liked them very much, but it was rumoured that the soldiers did not understand them and a number of political cadres in the unit were irritated with him."[17]

Whatever it was that irritated a number of political cadres at the time about Trần Dần was not grave, however, since he joined the army and became a Party member in 1948. One of the first to be trained in Chinese rectification techniques, he led his own rectification courses in 1951 among creative intellectuals and performing troupes. He was a natural speaker on the subject of "the people's art and literature." Hoàng Cầm, in fact, would later ruefully acknowledge that Trần Dần himself was a fire and brimstone political cadre at this time, so Maoist that he was referred to by his peers as *thầy Tầu*, or the Chinese master.[18]

The victory at Điện Biên Phủ was more than a military one, and Trần Dần spent some months writing a book about the heroic individuals from all walks of life who had participated in it. Until Điện Biên Phủ, Trần Dần had only written a few poems and some newspaper articles. After his fall from grace, however, a hostile 1958 article complained: "The struggle demanded small and light [creative] products, sharp and to the point, to throw into the front. But Dần said: 'I am not used to making that kind of fare' and let his peers write them. Dần was filled with the eat-big idea."[19] The "eat-big" (ăn to) idea, a charge that became rampant during the last phase of the anti-French struggle and in the early years of the socialist state of Vietnam, accused any intellectual unable to respond to the demand for propaganda works of condescending to the masses. It was a charge that assailed writers who longed to do justice to the incredible drama of human will and sacrifice embodied in the anti-French resistance. They grew increasingly frustrated, however, by the constant state demand for propaganda pieces, which had to conform to established guidelines on how characters and events should be portrayed. In this context, Hoàng Cầm recalled Trần Dần's efforts to produce a worthy work on Điện Biên Phủ as breaking away from the formulaic writing that was already becoming a concern among the intellectuals.

After the Điện Biên Phủ victory, Trần Dần stayed up night and day to write the third draft of the book on the people who had generated that grand and historic victory. . . . He knew he was practicing so that his pen would be very sharp: "[it] has to be sharp to describe people and life" [he said]. He hated the easy way of writing, temporary, describing the soldiers and yet one can only see guns firing, fire raging, only noises but not people. He called that kind of writing smoke-and-fire literature. Looking at the written page, a reader searches forever and still will not find *a person*, not life events, only machines hanging around, repeating a set of empty nouns and images, the loud noise made by an empty barrel.[20]

This account was an effort to portray Trần Dần in a heroic light in response to the onslaught of criticism being launched against him at the time. Nevertheless, in both hostile and friendly accounts of Trần Dần's literary achievements we can catch a glimpse of a young, ambitious, and impatient writer who wanted to be faithful to his vision of life and literature, desiring to be more than a writer on commission and to achieve something unique. The loss of individuality was something that Trần Dần found difficult to accept. This complaint would be raised later by other intellectuals as well.

The book on Điện Biên Phủ, *Người người lớp lớp* (Men upon men, waves upon waves), was an inspiring work recalling the large number of ordinary but heroic Vietnamese who took part in the battle. Upon finishing it, Trần Dần was assigned the task of writing the narrative for a film on Điện Biên Phủ. He was sent to China for two months. In Hoàng Cầm's account of Trần Dần during this period, it was in China that he came into open conflict with the overzealous political cadre assigned to accompany him. The confrontation exemplified "the conflict between the creative intellectual and the political cadre [that] had begun to develop rather powerfully in the person of Trần Dần."[21]

Hoàng Cầm only described the Vietnamese context and Trần Dần's problem as mainly a personal issue. We do know, however, that Trần Dần was in China at the height of the Hu Feng crisis. In July 1954, Hu Feng, a literary critic and longtime member of the Chinese Communist Party, sent a letter to the Central Committee airing his grievances. The main points of his letter included his reaction against the domination of a few literary authority figures whose enforcement of the literary doctrine of socialist realism allowed for little creativity with its emphasis on peasants, workers, and soldiers and only the bright side of life. Socialist realism, Hu Feng contended, should not be an ideology set in stone but a flexible system of ideas capable of reflecting the constantly changing needs of society.[22] From late 1954 to the spring of 1955, the conflict between Hu Feng's and more orthodox views simmered. Overwhelming conservative pressure forced Hu Feng to write a self-criticism statement in January 1955, and by May an orchestrated campaign against him was in full swing. His personal letters to friends were confiscated, published, and presented as the main evidence of his counterrevolutionary ideas. Hu Feng was arrested in July 1955, and the campaign against him broadened into a campaign to reeducate the masses and reinforce the official line.

Official accounts would later emphasize Hu Feng's influence on Trần Dần, but Trần Dần's friends also wryly acknowledged the connection in a cartoon in the second issue of the *Nhân Văn* newspaper.[23] Nevertheless, I want to emphasize the fact that the concerns subsequently raised in the period of intellectual questioning in Vietnam had long been in existence. As I have discussed, the seeds of the conflict between the intellectuals and the Party's cultural officials had been sown as early as 1948. It would be misleading, therefore, to overemphasize the influence of Chinese dissent on the Vietnamese situation. As I will argue, Trần Dần became a focal point around which a number of intellectual concerns coalesced, and the state's violent reaction to him marked the moment when simmering intellectual questions burst into the open.

Trần Dần returned to Hanoi in late 1954 and rejoined his military unit. Beginning in 1949, many intellectuals had joined the army as a symbol of their solidarity with the people and their participation in the struggle. The army actively supported their work and nurtured a new generation of intellectual soldiers within its ranks, establishing an Army Office of Art and Literature and an influential literary journal, *Văn Nghệ Quân Đội* (Army art and literature). The Army Office of Art and Literature watched over the professional and personal lives of its intellectual soldiers. The office was independent of the ostensibly more professional organization of the Association of Art and Literature and reported directly to the higher command of the army and the ideological apparatus. The office's control over its intellectuals was rigid. They were to stay within the army's quarters, with movement in and out of bases strictly regulated by means of passes, Sunday being the one day of the week when most were allowed to leave.[24] Personal relationships, especially marriages, had to be approved by the political apparatus within the army. Topics of literary works were also tightly delineated, with the emphasis primarily on the soldier as a model hero.

Thus, it would be from among these army intellectuals that the first signs of questioning emerged. In February 1955, twenty of them gathered to speak to Gen. Nguyễn Chí Thanh, the head of the army's General Political Department (Tổng Cục Chính Trị), legendary for his heroic leadership of the difficult Bình Trị Thiên front during the anti-French resistance and respected for his down to earth nature. Given his background as a political cadre, his prior working relationship with Nguyễn Chí Thanh, his recent trip to China, and his zest for dramatic presentation, Trần Dần was a natural choice to be the group's spokesman.

The gist of the intellectuals' grievances was encapsulated in three main demands for creative freedom, for the army's art and literature branch to be associated directly with the professional Association of Literature and Art rather than under the control of the army's General Political Department and the Party's Propaganda and Political Education Department (Cục Tuyên Huấn), and for an end to the imposition of army laws and regulations upon art and literature.[25] Gen. Nguyễn Chí Thanh's fierce response stunned the group. According to the poet Hoàng Cầm, who was present, the general proclaimed: "The spirit of this statement of policy proposal is the unruly ideology of capitalism. It shows that capitalist ideology has begun to attack all of you comrades!"[26]

However naive in retrospect, these army intellectuals felt at the time that they had earned the right to speak about the deterioration of the intellectual environment given their heartfelt participation in the anti-French resistance. They simply believed that if they could convey the nature of their discontent to higher authority the situation would be remedied accordingly. Their respect for and close working relationship with Gen. Nguyễn Chí Thanh during the anti-French resistance had blinded them to the fact that he had been a primary force behind the establishment of the structure of political officers within the army in 1952.[27] Moreover, as the head of the army's General Political Department, he could hardly take a liberal stand when the existence of the new socialist state was under threat. The meeting with the general generated substantial doubt among these intellectuals. There was no recourse to a higher authority in the army, and the seeds of discontent were well and truly sown.

The New Literary Standards

Trần Dần's abhorrence of the new literature's tendency toward bland characters and unreal situations was evident in his vehemence as a critic of other people's works. Tố Hữu, who had been in charge of cultural and intellectual activities at the central level since 1947 and had become a full member of the Central Committee in 1955, was also a well-known revolutionary poet. At the end of 1954, his book of poetry entitled *Việt Bắc* was published with a printing of twenty thousand copies, a number unheard of in that period.[28] It was meant to be accessible to all, a tool for the propaganda effort as well as an example to intellectuals of the content and form of the new literature. The Party's cultural officials did not expect a lukewarm public reception or intellectual criticism of it.

Articles, many critical, began to appear in newspapers and journals discussing the worth of *Việt Bắc*. Wanting to set an example of the kind of intellectual exchange that the intellectual community could expect in the future, a session was convened by the Association of Art and Literature in early March to discuss *Việt Bắc*. Among those who voiced their disappointment with the collection, Trần Dần was one of the most vehement. He referred dismissively in Franco-Vietnamese to Tố Hữu's poetry as "tí ti la haine, tí ti l'amour" (a little hate, a little love).[29] Trần Dần judged Tố Hữu's poetry, in the recollection of one of his friends, as "small and bland in the face of the grandness of life and committing the grave mistake of the cult of personality, mythologizing leaders."[30] Another session was called, also in March, to discuss a wildly popular first novel by a young writer, Phùng Quán. Called *Escape from Côn Đảo*, it was reprinted four times in 1955 alone.[31] Based on a true story, the novel recounted the tragically heroic attempt of a number of Việt Minh soldiers to escape the infamous colonial prison on Côn Đảo island where generations of anticolonialist Vietnamese had been sent. Trần Dần was also vocal in his disagreement with aspects of the book, particularly with the sacrifice of lives in a botched and rather naive escape plan. He railed against the foolishness of such a venture.

> One cannot bring forth death and move us! I do not shed one single tear for people who die like that. That is the death of foolish people, who died because they lived according to adventurous emotions. That Party member is not a Party member. That soldier is not a soldier. . . . Those are warped images, with mouths proclaiming allegiance to the Party, to the people's army, but they cannot be the images of Party members and soldiers. They cannot be examples for us.[32]

Other critical voices were raised against *Escape from Côn Đảo*, but the intense fury of Trần Dần's public comments was striking and must be weighed against the escalating tensions in his personal life. At the time Trần Dần had fallen in love with a young Hanoi woman. Apparently it was the first major love of his life, and, as in everything else, he threw himself into the affair with abandonment. Soon after they met, he was already spending his days and nights at her home, violating army regulations by leaving the barracks. There could not be differentiated treatment even for one of the army's star writers, however. By this time, the third and last installment of Trần Dần's novel *Men upon Men, Waves upon Waves* had been published to great popular and critical success. It was one of the few full-length works being published in peacetime and one of the first to recount the heroic undertaking of Điện Biên Phủ.

The army also held the right to approve marital unions, and in this regard Trần Dần's chosen love was unacceptable. She was a Catholic, an orphan whose main source of income came from renting out the few houses she owned. She had also grown up in Hanoi, and Hanoi was suspicious ground. It was a colonial city where capitalist ideas were endemic. Moreover, Hanoi had remained under French control throughout the period of the anti-French resistance. Trần Dần's lover therefore was an amalgam of everything that was suspicious, dangerous, and potentially corrupting to the pure revolutionary army, whose stomping ground until recently had been the jungles, mountains, and villages.

Censured in both his personal and professional lives, Trần Dần asked to leave the Party and the army in May 1955. He was not the only one to do so. Hoàng Cầm, well known for his heartbreaking poem "On the Other Side of the Đuống River," which detailed his village's devastation during the anti-French resistance, had become the director of the National Theater Troupe in 1955. He, too, fell in love with a Hanoi woman, who also was deemed to be from a capitalist background and therefore untrustworthy. Ordered by a political cadre to end the relationship, Hoàng Cầm requested discharge from the army in June 1955. After five months of unsuccessful persuasion by top Party members, he became the first army intellectual to return to civilian life.

Hoàng Cầm was never a Party member, however, while Trần Dần was. He had even held the post of a political cadre at one time. His hot-tempered pronouncements as a critic, his flaunting of army rules, and now his petitions to leave the Party and the army led to what amounted to house arrest. For three months he was confined to a room at the army base to think about his erroneous ways and write self-criticism statements. He was not alone. Another army intellectual, Tử Phác, a friend of both Trần Dần and Hoàng Cầm, was undergoing similar discipline. It was during this period of incarceration that Trần Dần wrote his most famous poem, "Nhất định thắng" (We must win), which would bring even more disaster to him and force state-intellectual relations to a new stage.

At the same time, controversy erupted over the 1954–55 literary prizes. The only other prizes of similar stature had been awarded in 1951–52 to prominent figures in the literary firmament in recognition of their longtime labor. The scholar Phan Khôi's entire body of translation work, for example, had been given the translation prize. Upon returning to Hanoi in 1954, the Association of Art and Literature reestablished the process of awarding literary prizes, but this time to acknowledge and encourage the literary talents that had emerged during the anti-French resistance.

Far from being the first effort to establish a worthy tradition of national literary prizes befitting a newly independent state as many intellectuals had hoped, the selection of the 1954–55 prize winners was sloppily conducted and greatly compromised. The inclusion of many works in politically relevant categories forced the committee to labor throughout 1955. When the winners were finally announced in March 1956, immediate voices of dissent arose in the intellectual community.

Although Tố Hữu won first prize in the poetry category, the fiercest protest was voiced against the second and third prize winners, the collection *Ngôi sao* (Stars) by the established poet Xuân Diệu and the collection *Thơ chiến sĩ* (A soldier's poems) by the soldier Hồ Khải Đại. The intellectuals reacted strongly against Xuân Diệu's poetry collection because it was mediocre compared to his earlier works. As the range of intellectual topics had been increasingly curtailed, the works themselves became one-dimensional propaganda pieces for government campaigns and policies, populated by people whose actions and behavior were always beyond the reach of reality and human nature. Given his stature as one of the 1930s New Poetry movement's famed masters, Xuân Diệu's capitulation to this development in his new poetry collection was appalling to see. The fact that the collection was defended heavily by those who were at the helm of the intellectual apparatus, namely, the heads of the Association of Art and Literature and its journal, *Văn Nghệ*, further alarmed many intellectuals. Not only did those who governed the cultural and intellectual arena hold fundamentally wrong views about art and literature, but such views were becoming increasingly institutionalized.

If Xuân Diệu's poetry collection represented the visible decline of modern Vietnamese literature, Hồ Khải Đại's represented what the state had declared to be the examplar of things to come. Attacking the superficiality of Hồ Khải Đại's collection in a devastating critique, Hữu Loan noted that the poet had managed to cover just about all the major topics of the day, including love for Uncle Hồ and the Party, land reform, the relationship between the north and the south, a mother's love for her country, and a wife who placed responsibility above personal love. What was missing was the key ingredient that separated a literary work from a news report, namely, the art of literature. As Hữu Loan asserted,

> [While] performing the same task as the newspaper, the radio, or political data, which is promoting government policies, the specialty of a literary work is . . . to use art to go deep into feelings [so that] the reader is not bored by tedious events and the tight, headache-inducing structure of theory. The reader is

captivated without realizing it. We do not ask for that high level of artistic ability in the collection *A Soldier's Poems*, but in truth it lacks almost any artistic worth.[33]

Hữu Loan went on to expound on the collection's "unreal" portraits of people, events, and emotions. Confronted with life's larger moments, as when a mother said good-bye to her son as he was leaving for the front, Hồ Khải Đại's soldier-poet "has no heightened emotion or response; the author has gone beyond the norm, becoming a superman far removed from us." All vestiges of individuality disappeared, and all the characters populating Hồ Khải Đại's poetic landscape thought of every aspect of their lives in public terms. A young woman, for example, agreed with her beloved that their happiness could not come to pass when the country was not yet unified. They had their respective work to do: he to take care of "the country's business" (*việc nước*) and she "the village's business" (*việc làng*), meaning working in the field and on the looms in order to contribute taxes to the nation.

This monotonous constancy to the approved vision of life, work, and relationships enraged Hữu Loan, especially when such a mediocre work was being officially extolled as literature. Hữu Loan's insistence that "art and literature belong to the arena that clashes most with explanations and commentaries" is reminiscent of Tô Ngọc Vân's differentiation between art and propaganda in 1948–49, which was discussed in chapter 2. A poet, when practicing his craft properly, needs not chant mantras to generate an image. Noting that ten out of the fourteen poems in Hồ Khải Đại's collection mentioned the Party and Uncle Hồ, Hữu Loan commented tartly: "To explain [his emotions toward the Party and Uncle Hồ] in one poem marks the poet's impotence, but here he repeats it over and over again in many poems. It is sufficient, therefore, to read only one." By awarding Hồ Khải Đại's *A Soldier's Poems* the third prize, Hữu Loan argued that the prize committee not only had given him a false view of his talent but sent the wrong message to the reading public about the level of literary achievement to which they should aspire. Other intellectuals criticized the choices in other categories of the 1954–55 literary prizes and noted the conspicuous absence of Trần Dần's novel *Men upon Men, Wave upon Wave* from consideration.

By the end of 1955, therefore, the intellectual community was swirling with discontent. Still adjusting to being back in Hanoi, many intellectuals grew unhappy with the imposition of official views on their professional and personal lives. A common concern was that those who had the power to shape the structure of intellectual activity were dismissive of intellectual voices other than those that supported their agenda. Outspoken Trần Dần became the focus of official censure and therefore the focus of intellectual concerns as well. The disturbing outcome of the literary prizes of 1954–55 further illustrated to many intellectuals their lack of influence over an event that should have been a proud showcase of achievements for them and the new nation.

Giai Phẩm Mùa Xuân, the Masterpiece of Spring

According to Hoàng Cầm, the modest literary collection with the grand title *Giai Phẩm Mùa Xuân* (Masterpiece of spring) came into existence because a group of friends wanted to create something to celebrate the Vietnamese new year, Tết. Such a venture was very much a product of the pre-1945 intellectual era, when intellectuals left behind their provincial existence and gravitated toward cities to pursue careers as writers, journalists, editors, and publishers. The sense of experimentation was heady. Intellectuals with similar interests and beliefs banded together to bring out a book of poetry or a new journal while making their livings as journalists or petty bureaucrats in the colonial administration. The Vietnamese intellectual milieu of the 1940s was littered with these joint efforts of uneven quality, often existing for only a few issues because of colonial censorship, political turmoil, lack of readership, and the difficulty of finding financial support. Nevertheless, the literary and philosophical debates inherent in these intellectual ventures were lively and often acrimonious and on the whole exemplified a spirited milieu in which a national intellectual community came into existence.

This tradition inspired the Giai Phẩm group to produce their first literary effort in peacetime. These intellectuals wanted to inject fresh ideas into an intellectual environment increasingly dominated by formulaic writings. There was, of course, something boastful about this; they saw themselves as capable of issuing a challenge to their intellectual peers to rise above mediocrity. *Masterpiece of Spring*, however, was not meant to be a long-term venture but simply an interesting collection of short prose pieces, poetry, music, and art to celebrate the arrival of spring. It greeted the public in early February 1956.

It is difficult to read this slim, forty-eight-page collection and think that it was ever problematic with the authorities. The writers were earnest in asserting their belief in the Party and the revolution. They were, on the whole, young. Most of them were in their thirties, but several had had their professional debuts in the heady days of the 1940s and came of age during the anti-French resistance. The youthful mood of the collection was underlined by confidence gained through experience. Hoàng Cầm wrote a poem lauding the results of land reform, Nguyễn Sáng recalled a group of soldiers on the move in Việt Bắc, and the young Phùng Quán participated with a poem comparing a poet to a worker. The flamboyant poet Lê Đạt proclaimed the new industrialized society as envisioned in Party pronouncements in a poem entitled "Growing Bigger Each Day."

> The economy cannot walk carrying a backpack
> To achieve the two-year plan.
> The new life requires train trips
> Express trains,
> Rapid construction of
> The nation ten years tattered
> Bomb, bullets plowed on the body
> Tears reflecting smiles
> Shaking off blood walking toward construction
>
> . . . .
>
> What the colonialists did in twelve years
> We have achieved in four months
> Each day of a revolutionary contest
> Is equal to some tens of common days
> We collar time
> Lash it forward into a gallop.
> Pull tomorrow closer
> Shove life on the back
> Turn on the engine to move toward the communist horizon
> The whistle calls out in shining light
> Calling all aboard.[34]

These are images of an industrial age or at the very least of a kind of longing for modernity embodied in speed, a desire for newness and doing away with the past. In another poem, Lê Đạt issued a youthfully exaggerated cry against stagnation in order to be

New! New!
    Always new!
Fly high
    Fly far
Above the signs of the old
Above the deteriorating sidewalks
Surpassing today
Surpassing tomorrow, the day after,
                Always surpassing . . .[35]

This desire for a new world was not outside the Party but explicitly under its leadership. But this Party would be a perfect one, without the blemish of certain members whom the intellectuals saw as "untrue." Lê Đạt himself announced that "I would carry my pen to follow the Party / Push forward to the position at the front."[36] The young poet Phùng Quán, no less flamboyant, urged his poetic comrades to fulfill the role that the state had asked of them.

. . . .
We together with the worker comrades
Must make poems as uncouth as a broom
To clear away completely the trash
On the roads and in the souls
The responsibility is heavy but glorious
Which the Democratic Government has placed upon the
    poets.[37]

The contribution that came to define *Masterpiece of Spring*, however, turned out be a poem written by Trần Dần during his three-month penance duty at the army base. Apparently there was also an unofficial condition imposed upon Trần Dần during this time, prohibiting him from writing.[38] Trần Dần, therefore, had entrusted some of his poems to various friends, and Hoàng Cầm and Lê Đạt had in their possession the poems he had written during his self-criticism period. At the end of 1955 and the beginning of 1956, as another step in the army's effort to rehabilitate him, Trần Dần was sent to a village to work with a land reform team. Wanting to tweak the noses of a few hard liners who had imposed upon him the ridiculous prohibition on writing and also to include his friend in the new literary venture, Hoàng Cầm decided to include his poem "We Must Win" without Trần Dần's knowledge or approval. The collection also included another short story on a peasant character named Old Man Rồng, ostensibly told by Trần Dần and recorded by his friend Lê Đạt.

"We Must Win" is a long poem, in fact the longest contribution in the collection. It is an elegiac poem, expressing the poet's pain and ambivalence over the chaos of the new society, still raw from the vestiges of the war, in the midst of the confusing exodus of people to the south and the fear of unemployment among those who remained, like the poet's lover. The refrain is painful, echoing the poet's doubts and sense of isolation.

> I walk on
>   seeing no street
>   seeing no house
> Only the rain falling
>   upon the red flag.

The poem moves through the poet's doubt of himself and what his contribution means or whether it means anything at all in the chaos of postwar society. The moment of doubt passes, however, and the end of the poem moves toward a renewal of faith and of hope. From the image of the poet and his lover isolated and walking in the rain, the poem turns toward an image of them moving into a crowd, which surges on to demand peace and national reunification. The red flag now shines brightly in the sun, waving ghosts away, and for the poet the sad refrain has given way to

> The flag flutters
>   reddens the streets
>   reddens the houses
> The color of that flag is the medicine for my ailment.
> . . . .
> I walk on
>   seeing the streets and the houses
> Not the falling rain
> Only the sun rising
>   upon the red flag.

The poem is indeed the most notable contribution to *Masterpiece of Spring*. Its insistent, haunting rhythm pulls the reader into the poet's heart, a human one full of pain and worries but also of hope. The fact that the poem was never meant for publication made the interior view of the soul honest and raw, speaking to the experience of many that was not portrayed in the bulk of the works being published at the time, so intent were they on extolling the Party's achievements and the new society's numbing sunniness. "We Must Win," in the end, was also about hope, albeit of a different kind, a cautious hope tempered by the knowledge of difficulties past, present, and future.

Those who considered themselves to be the guardians of the new culture quickly reacted, arresting Trần Dần while he was still in the village with the land reform team. Meanwhile, copies of *Masterpiece of Spring* were confiscated. Articles began to appear criticizing it. The critic Hoài Thanh, now a member of the Executive Committee of the Association of Art and Literature, organized a criticism session for "We Must Win" without the author present. According to Hoài Thanh himself, the goal of the attack on Trần Dần was to send a message to the other writers who had written for *Masterpiece of Spring*.[39] Apparently the fierce campaign against Hu Feng in China had heightened the sense of vigilance in Vietnam. Hoài Thanh stated of his thinking at the time that "China has Hu Feng, perhaps we also have a Hu Feng." He denounced Trần Dần as a reactionary at the session and in a harshly critical opinion piece in a March issue of the literary journal *Văn Nghệ*, the organ of the Association of Art and Literature. Literary infractions were being viewed increasingly through a political lens.

The news of Trần Dần's arrest and his attempted suicide while incarcerated shocked the intellectual community. Top Party leaders, apparently unaware of the decision to arrest him, were disturbed at the drastic turn of events. Hoài Thanh disclosed that "my criticism [of Trần Dần] appeared in the paper in March, then in April the Party criticized us."[40] The state's more relaxed stance was also influenced by what was happening in the communist world. The de-Stalinization effect of the Twentieth Congress of the Communist Party of the Soviet Union in February 1956 and the emergence of the Hundred Flowers Movement in China in May 1956 allowed intellectuals in Vietnam the space to vigorously voice their concerns. A month-long study meeting convened by the Association of Art and Literature in August 1956, designed to study the Twentieth Congress and the new intellectual shift in China, provided the perfect moment for some three hundred Vietnamese intellectuals to call for a more relevant intellectual policy. Nguyễn Hữu Đang, who had gained fame as the organizer of the historic gathering at Ba Đình Square where Hồ Chí Minh proclaimed Vietnamese independence on 2 September 1945, spearheaded the intellectual group, which demanded a review of the Party's position on the relationship between politics and art. By extension, it was also a demand to reexamine the way in which the intellectual structure had been controlled by leaders appointed by the authorities rather than voted into office by the intellectuals themselves and how such a development had hampered intellectual criticism and creativity. There were admissions of guilt from the two highest ranking cultural cadres, Tố Hữu and Nguyễn Đình Thi.[41] Soon after, Hoài Thanh published an abject apology for denouncing Trần Dần as a reactionary, stating that he "had no reason to conclude so. To have no proof and yet reach such a conclusion was extremely dismissive of the political life of an individual."[42] Nguyễn Đình Thi also admitted to mistakes in the guidance of art and literature, validating numerous criticisms of the Association of Art and Literature and the inhibiting intellectual atmosphere.[43] Voices critical of the 1954–55 literary prizes were also finding a place on the pages of *Văn Nghệ*, the organ of the Association of Art and Literature.[44]

Intellectual Discontent and Private Publishing

A number of factors came together to push the intellectual community toward a more radical position regarding the authorities. By mid-1956, the overwhelming concern that dominated the intellectual discourse was the issue of *lãnh đạo văn nghệ* (leadership of art and literature). The increasingly authoritarian tone of those in charge of the intellectual apparatus had led to an extremely tense and restrictive intellectual atmosphere. The unacceptable selection of mediocre works as winners of the first national literary prizes in peacetime and the harsh reprisals against Trần Dần dispelled the celebratory and conciliatory mood. For the moment, however, private publishing activities were still allowed. New magazines and newspapers were not censored before printing; the publishers only needed to submit copies for the public record. Paper could still be bought on the open market, though the price was prohibitive. Certain ventures could convince the state to provide paper at a subsidized price.

The possibility of private publishing and the one-sided intellectual atmosphere provided the impetus for a return to the private publishing that had flourished in the years before 1945. New publishing houses, journals, magazines, and newspapers were appearing now in open competition with the state's publishing ventures. Most, if not all, intellectuals had already been assigned jobs in the state apparatus, the bulk of them working in various state publishing houses, for the

Ministry of Education, for the newly established Ministry of Culture, or for the Association of Art and Literature. Party and non-Party members alike, however, saw no conflict in pursuing private literary activities in their off hours.

Trần Thiếu Bảo, who had owned a publishing house before 1945, opened the Minh Đức Publishing House. The Xây Dựng Publishing House, owned by Đào Văn Ngọc, was another substantial player. According to a 1958 report by the Ministry of Culture, an incomplete survey conducted at the end of 1954 showed some eighty-four publishing houses, located mostly in Hanoi. In the changing political tide, many had stopped doing business, but by 1955 it was reported that there were altogether seventeen publishing houses in Hanoi, with four scattered in Bắc Giang, Vinh, Hải Phòng, and Thanh Hóa.[45] These new publishing houses were aggressive in competing with state-run operations. Minh Đức, for example, forcefully petitioned authors and their families for the rights to reissue well-known works written before 1945. It was also Minh Đức that published the literary collection *Masterpiece of Spring*. The writer Tô Hoài, who was in charge of the Association of Art and Literature's Văn Nghệ Publishing House, notes that during this time "Even at the work unit the feeling that only private publishing was progressive was contagious; the publishing house of the association was restrictive and seemingly outdated."[46]

If the authorities were troubled by the development, the structure of the state was still in the process of being formed and was ill equipped to deal with the rapid growth in private publishing. The Ministry of Culture, for example, was not founded until February 1955. The state attempted to influence these publishing ventures nevertheless, playing one against another when possible and using the resources it controlled such as paper and money.[47] Other independent intellectual undertakings did flourish, however, spurred by the more conciliatory official stance and the spirited intellectual atmosphere. *Masterpiece of Spring* was reprinted and had its successors. Also published by Minh Đức Publishing House, the momentum attracted other intellectuals to the enterprise, which produced four additional issues.[48] Around three thousand copies of each issue were printed, not an insubstantial number for a literary journal of this kind. Minh Đức also published a series called *Đất Mới* (New land) beginning in November 1956 for the university community, primarily targeting students. The number of university students at this point was small, and their guaranteed positions in the planned expansion of the educational system made them an important segment of the population.

The list of the writers in the *Giai Phẩm* series in particular was a virtual roll call of the most prominent names in intellectual circles. *Masterpiece of Spring*'s contributors were generally of a younger generation; a few had earned their reputations before, but most had come of age during the anti-French resistance. They included the poets Hoàng Cầm and Lê Đạt, the painters Sỹ Ngọc and Nguyễn Sáng, the poet-novelist Trần Dần, the composers Tử Phác and Tô Vũ, the young poet-novelist Phùng Quán, and the multitalented Văn Cao. Subsequent issues of the *Giai Phẩm* series would also include the venerable scholars Phan Khôi and Đào Duy Anh, the independent Marxist Trương Tửu, the lawyer Nguyễn Mạnh Tường, who held two doctorates from France at the age of 22, and the internationally know philosopher Trần Đức Thảo. One of the original founders of the influential French journal *Les tempes modernes*, who had engaged once in a fierce philosophical debate with his peer Jean-Paul Sartre, Trần Đức Thảo had returned to Vietnam to joint the revolution in the early 1950s. The participation of many writers, poets, painters, and composers made it seem as though the whole of the intellectual community was converging upon the pages of *Giai Phẩm* to voice their opinions and foster an environment in which new and interesting work could be achieved.

At the same time that *Giai Phẩm* was becoming a series, a number of intellectuals, many of whom were already contributing to *Giai Phẩm*, started a weekly newspaper called *Nhân Văn*. Intended to be a forum for the discussion of more topical issues, *Nhân Văn* was explicitly political. The name of the newspaper means "humanism." *Nhân văn* is a classical term, connoting the process of becoming a civilized human being through cultivation, especially through the learning provided by literature. Here once more is the expressed link between humanity and literature, a Confucian principle that has always given literature a substantial social role in China and Vietnam. The term *nhân văn* gradually took on the more modern and Western meaning of *humanism*, echoing the concept "socialism with a human face," which was the rage in Eastern Europe at this time. Whether nor not the Nhân Văn group actually derived that particular meaning from Eastern European developments at the time is not certain, but it does connote that they did believe that there was space to soften the harshness of the system that had just taken shape in Vietnam, allowing the human spirit room for expression while the public goals of society were being pursued. In fact, *Nhân Văn* closely followed events in China and Eastern Europe, supporting China's Hundred Flowers campaign and the liberalizing tendencies in Poland and Hungary.[49]

The *Nhân Văn* writers clearly felt that they were participating in a larger international movement, and domestically they were supported by other intellectuals in their effort to create a forum for discussions and debates pushing for change. Although published by Minh Đức and sold as a commercial newspaper, *Nhân Văn* was essentially speaking to the intellectual community and therefore it did not initially have a large press run. *Nhân Văn*'s readers and even those who were writing for it contributed funds to support its publication, from donations as small as 5,000 đồng to the largest amount, 300,000 đồng, given by a retired soldier.[50] There is no question that *Nhân Văn*'s impact went beyond the intellectual community. From a modest print run of two thousand copies of the first issue, the number grew to six thousand with the second, seven thousand with the third, and twelve thousand with the fourth. The Newspaper Office and the Central State Store, state agencies that coordinated the allocation of paper for publishing purposes at state prices, provided *Nhân Văn* with only enough for two thousand copies to print a fourth issue. That *Nhân Văn* managed to achieve an increasingly large print run, partly with money contributed from its readers and contributors, shows the considerable support many had for the venture.

In the short time that they were in existence, *Nhân Văn* and *Giai Phẩm* became the dominant forums in which a substantial number of intellectuals came together to present their views, which often differed from those of the state-sanctioned frame of reference. More generally, they spoke of the concern with the contraction of private space and the establishment of a "Party-governed regime" (*chế độ Đảng trị*). More specifically, they argued for more freedom within the intellectual sphere and demanded changes in the current leadership of art and literature. Toward the end of 1956, the discussions on the pages of *Nhân Văn* increasingly touched upon the issue of organization, advocating independent organization as a way to counter the abuses of power and make concrete the changes in intellectual policy intellectuals had been asking for.

The Contraction of Private Space and the "Party-Governed Regime"

It was the heavy weight of the state upon society that the intellectuals found unbearable. Barely two years after the establishment of the new socialist state, virtually every aspect of daily life was under its control.

Individual behavior was tightly regulated. Although land reform was devastating, intellectuals had little to say about it in their writings. After all, the state had admitted to land reform excesses. What the intellectuals increasingly reacted against in their works was the culture of land reform, which, once established, had become institutionalized in spite of the rectification of errors. The culture of land reform referred to governance by decrees and policies without an established legal system that could guarantee the people a just and impartial avenue for redress, the excessive concentration of power and authority in the hands of those who claimed to represent the Party, the single-minded interpretation of society through a class agenda, and the corresponding demand that all of society had to participate in carrying out this agenda to the fullest extent.

The concentration of power in the Party led directly to the rise of a group of people who claimed an intermediary position between the Party and the masses as interpreters of the Party's policies. Either already inhabiting or quickly making a move into the lower levels of the Party structure, these Party men wielded enormous power in their spheres of influence. Other members who joined when the Party was truly a meeting ground for idealists and nationalists did not fare well in the competition. Given the heightened emphasis on ferreting out hidden enemies and since many of these old time Party members came from backgrounds other than that of the working class or the peasantry, they were easy victims. The opportunists succeeded additionally because those in positions of power readily succumbed to their flattery. On this topic the contributors to *Nhân Văn* and *Giai Phẩm* were vehement; the hypocrisy of the life that went on around them extended to every nook and cranny of society and greatly affected their professional and personal lives. Hữu Loan derided the situation in a poem called "Again Those Who Sing Praises," arguing that the dangerous parasites who had flourished during the colonial period continued to exist in the new society, moving into positions of power and doing irreparable harm to the nascent structure of the state and the well-being of the people. It was difficult to differentiate them from the crowd because they cloaked themselves in "organization / with the people's point of view / with *lập trường* / official policy."[51]

It was this pervasive sense of the new society already being corrupted from within that dominated literary writing. The power that such corruptive agents could command was troubling. Those who learned to speak the language of the dominant discourse of "organization," "the people's point of view," the "class standpoint," and "official policy" became reliable and indispensable to the Party. Intellectuals grew increasingly alarmed as those who professed this dangerous and transparent brand of opportunistic political loyalty moved into positions of power as shapers of the new society in which they could literally command the lives of others. In a poem Phùng Quán cried out against the corruption and wastefulness of those in positions of leadership.[52] In a short story, Hữu Loan detailed the petty politics at a school in which a certain teacher, not well educated and uncouth, managed to become the secretary of the Party unit through lies, exploitation of the paranoia concerning the existence of "the enemy," and manipulation of the class standpoint.[53] In his new position, he held enormous power over people's lives because he controlled the allocation of jobs, housing, and food. The story paralleled the university students' own experiences, which filled the pages of the student journal, Đất Mới. Having to live on the grounds of the university, the students were subjected to the control and whims of the Party leaders. They spoke of relationships forced to end, friendships broken, scholarships taken away, and other blatant misdeeds committed by those who held important posts in the Party cells at the university. The students referred to this as the "Party-governed regime" (chế độ Đảng trị), where being a Party member took precedence over all other criteria, be it intelligence, hard work, or even compatibility and love in personal relationships.[54]

The short-sighted and narrow definition of *socialist development* imposed by the state did more than spawn this new class of men. The ideals of freedom for the people and the establishment of a new and just society, that had been fought for with the blood of so many Vietnamese, were fast becoming surreal prospects, mired in self-righteous and paranoid slogans, policies, and directives. The result was a nervous society, constantly looking over its shoulder for signs of "the enemy" and discounting the smallest joys in the act of living. The intense psychological maelstrom endured by the intellectuals in the last phase of the anti-French resistance, which had been constantly reiterated since then, was now imposed upon the society as a whole, demanding that each individual, no matter the level of education, background, class, sex or age, become an entirely political animal in ways dictated by the state. Hoàng Cầm, in a poem entitled "The Child of Six," told the story of a child slowly dying of hunger because no one in the village would feed her. Someone who had done so ended up being questioned for three days because it turned out that the child was a landowner's daughter.[55] In the case of Trần Dần's poem "We Must Win," one of the strongest criticisms was that he had portrayed average citizens as struggling to adjust to life without a clear political definition of the enemy. Indeed, by now, as Nguyễn Đình Thi indignantly charged,

> a child also knows how to differentiate an imperialist soldier or a spy of Ngô Đình Diệm from one of our soldiers or cadres. Our people have risen up, have resisted victoriously, have overcome the greatest difficulties precisely because our people understand very clearly who we are, who the enemies are. We are the just, the enemies are unjust; we move forward, the enemies decline. The ten years since the revolution have educated each person as much as hundreds of years of the old did.[56]

To present people, especially those who belonged to the working or peasant classes, as somehow removed from the political consider-ations that must dominate their lives was to risk being charged with "naturalism," a charge that was also levelled upon Trần Dần. In an account of a village drunk with a talent for composing biting verses about anyone who irritated him and whose death came at the hands of some hotheaded village youths, Trần Dần pondered how much class could explain the life of this old man.[57] Rather, he was an age-old element of village life, who suffered not so much at the hands of others but at his own and who could and did terrorize others while he was alive. The intricacy of life in the village and the many layers of hierarchy and structure within such a community quickly became evident to intellectuals who participated in land reform—themselves having grown up in the much more complex world of exploitation and reciprocity of the village than class alone could define. To later elevate the dead old drunk to the status of a class hero during land reform was an absurd and unnecessary act to Trần Dần. To his detrac-tors, however, his account of the village drunk exemplified only "the exploiting class's condescending and reactionary point of view."[58]

In the *Giai Phẩm* series, there were more nuanced portraits of the conflicts inherent within the souls of those who were trying to live up to the new society's standards. In a short play entitled *We Try to Raise the Children*, the playwright Chu Ngọc presented conversations be-tween a husband and a wife on a multitude of subjects. In some of them they took opposing views, while in others they conspiratorially spoke against the weight of public opinion and policy, making their marriage into the only private space in which they could express their views and concerns. The language they used was the official one, full of "class point of view," "love of the masses, of the working class," and "the progress toward socialism," and they generally believed in the vision of a better life under socialism. We never lose sight, however, of the concerns that they faced daily, from the endless meetings at work and in the neighborhood to constant criticism of their smallest acts. The wife wondered out loud about the innumerable intrusions into their lives, whereas her husband was more prone to accept the dominant views around them, partly because he was much more in tune with the political consequences. The last words of the play came from the husband, less fearful at the end of their conversation, trying to lull one of their children back to sleep: "Be good my child. And when you grow up don't be so narrow-minded!"[59]

Intellectual Freedom and the "Unwritten Agreement"

The contraction of private space and the rise of the Party men affected the intellectuals directly. The process had begun a few years before Điện Biên Phủ, but the clearly institutionalized nature of the development as it was embodied in the official reaction to the Trần Dần case alarmed the intellectuals and crystallized further the frustration they were feeling over their own experiences. More generally, political cadres wielded more power than they had any right to over what intellectuals should do and how they should do it. More specifically, intellectuals increasingly viewed Tố Hữu and the selected number of intellectuals who comprised the Executive Committee of the Association of Art and Literature as leaders in the cultural arena who were quick to dismiss any critical voice as reactionary. The independent Marxist Trương Tửu, in his essay on the deficiency of the leadership of art and literature, pointed to Tố Hữu as the culprit responsible for the current dreadful state of affairs.[60]

The matter went beyond a few bad apples in the Party, however. There had always been a fundamental distrust of intellectuals, and this tendency was more evident now than ever. The scholar Đào Duy Anh noted the intellectuals' participation in the country's history and the anti-French resistance and their compliance with Việt Minh policy to the point of sublimating the self in the various ideological rectification campaigns. He asked how there could be any question of trust with regard to the intellectuals, and cried plaintively that "Trust is the key to solving all the other details in the issue of intellectuals."[61] Lawyer and professor Nguyễn Mạnh Tường stated baldly that "TRUST is still better than DOUBT."[62] He demanded respect.

I only want to recall that in the history of the revolutions of the Soviet Union and China, when nation building moves into the decisive phase, the revolutionary regime cannot ignore the issue of intellectuals. The current struggle of the Vietnamese intelligentsia enters into the revolutionary framework, in concert with the movement of the struggle of intellectuals all over the world. To dismiss it is a mistake. To solve it in a cursory and superficial way, with the attitude of an adult giving a child a piece of candy so that he will not cry, is a grave blunder. To confront him, to oppose him . . . I will not continue because I believe that no revolutionary regime would act so.[63]

By emphasizing trust and respect, Nguyễn Mạnh Tường was insisting on returning state-intellectual relations to a more equal footing, one in which reciprocity was inherent. Thus far in public pronouncements, often written by the intellectuals themselves, the discussion of state-intellectual relations had been portrayed in orthodox terms: the intellectuals were grateful to the Party and the revolution for guiding them out of the darkness not only of feudal and colonial society but of their own minds.

The alliance between the state and intellectuals during the anti-French resistance was partly tactical, and the intellectuals' sense of betrayal was palpable as they struggled to regain a measure of balance lost. In his own dry, blunt style, the scholar Phan Khôi derided the development of the gap between the intellectual leadership and the intellectual community. The opinions of the intellectual community were constantly bypassed, and major decisions concerning the intellectual structure and its activities were in the hands of a few. In Phan Khôi's view, the issue was not that intellectuals must be guided, since they had already accepted the necessity of the Party's guidance. They only demanded freedom in their own sphere of art and literature. Following from this point, Phan Khôi expounded on the notion of an unwritten contract between state and intellectuals that had endured throughout the anti-French resistance.

It is a given that art and literature must serve politics, and thus politics must lead art and literature. But we must ask: if politics wants to reach its goal can it simply use slogans, banners, circulars, and decrees without art and literature? To answer this truthfully, [I think that] politics must tap art and literature on the shoulder and say: I am attached to you because I want to use your art. Once that is out in the open, art and literature agree. But this aspect of [the creativity needed by politics] is a separate component of art and literature. Politics cannot be in charge of that, too, and art and literature must demand freedom in that arena. As such, I think there is no reason for politics not to agree. "Both sides win": such a principle is applicable nowadays to any cooperative situation.[64]

The two years since peace, however, according to Phan Khôi, had seen the leadership violating that unwritten agreement (*giao ước bất thành văn*) with its ever greater invasion of the intellectuals' creative sphere. The space claimed by Phan Khôi was small; only in the intellectual arena did he demand freedom of creation and expression. All else remained under the Party's control, and intellectuals accepted Party guidance readily. Yet at the same time the notion of an unwritten agreement insisted upon a much more equal relationship between the Party and the intellectuals than was the case in the dominant view. By emphasizing the utilitarian nature of the agreement, in which not only did the intellectuals need the Party but the Party needed the intellectuals to carry out its agenda, Phan Khôi asserted the intellectuals' right to participate and not simply follow.

An Independent Structure of Organization

By invoking this unwritten agreement, which he contended the Party's leadership had violated, Phan Khôi emphasized a frame of reference in which the intellectuals had always been much more aware of what they had to give up in return for what they perceived as important, that which could only be gained under the Việt Minh banner of national unity and independence. The independent Marxist Trương Tửu went one step further than Phan Khôi, astutely placing the date of the deadening of the intellectual scene at 1949, the year of the Conference of Debates in Việt Bắc. Instead of allowing the force of the revolution to flower in each individual intellectual, resulting in works that would be commensurate with the age, Trương Tửu argued that since 1949 the opposite had occurred because the structure of intellectual organization had tightened its control over the intellectual community, with a few leaders ruling through narrow, bureaucratic measures and political dogma. To a large extent, they had succeeded in reining in intellectual freedom, but according to Trương Tửu an intellectual outburst was waiting to happen because Vietnamese intellectuals had never fully acquiesced to the power of the leadership. Trương Tửu reminded his readers that in one small form or another, a number of Vietnamese intellectuals had always fought to maintain their sphere of creativity and knowledge. Tô Ngọc Vân's debate with Trường Chinh in 1948 over the definitions of *art* and *propaganda* was one of the earliest examples. Even at the Conference of Debates in 1949, Trương Tửu emphasized,

> in the discussion sessions, intellectuals were completely free to express and defend their own opinions. Mr. Tố Hữu did participate in many of the sessions. But there was not one intellectual who thought that if Mr. Tố Hữu presented a particular point of view no one else could argue against it. I believe that if someone had flattered a leader who suppressed the free and democratic discussion during the conference then for certain he would have been attacked and spurned by his intellectual peers.[65]

If intellectuals had begun to push for a return to what they perceived to be their rightful position in the intellectual realm, the discussion also turned increasingly toward a structure of organization that would substantiate that position. Trương Tửu had pinpointed the moment when a gap opened up between the intellectuals and the Party as "the point when a number of [people in] the Party held the authority to command art and literature through organization."[66] Historian and professor Đào Duy Anh also emphasized that state control over the substance of research and the means of production and distribution effectively rendered any official proclamation of intellectual freedom meaningless.[67]

In that regard, Trương Tửu also pushed for a reexamination of the existing structure of intellectual organization by emphasizing that in this century progressive intellectuals had acted courageously on a variety of issues, although *"They were never forced by any organization to implement any guideline or policy of any workers' party."*[68] Trương Tửu argued that by not being shackled to any organization or policy these intellectuals retained the independence of mind to fight for issues important to the masses that the workers' party might not see. Furthermore, while literature for propaganda purposes must be controlled by the Party apparatus, Trương Tửu contended that Lenin only demanded that other progressive intellectuals accept the Party's general platform, not the direct leadership of the Party organization.[69] The implication of this argument for Vietnamese intellectuals was obvious, and Trương Tửu's position represented an attempt by an independent Marxist to hold on to the ideals of socialism against their unfortunate corruption in reality. Other intellectuals emphasized the need for a different structure of organization than what was in existence but in more specific terms, namely, a system of law in order to preserve and promote individual freedom and an independent method of redress. As the philosopher Trần Đức Thảo asserted, "The form of freedom is *individual freedom*. . . . The individual is in service to the community, but the community must be built by individuals, and [the existence of] the form of freedom within the realm of the people's law is a condition that enables each individual to truly build the community."[70]

The rampant lawlessness in society greatly troubled the corps of lawyers, and it was the Paris-trained lawyer Nguyễn Mạnh Tường who raised the issue. In a ringing speech delivered to the National Assembly on 30 October 1956, Nguyễn Mạnh Tường called for the establishment of an independent commission to investigate the excesses of land reform, the establishment of a system to verify the cadres' work, the promotion of mass organizations as true channels of people's opinions, and finally, the establishment of the freedoms of speech, publication, and the press as another way to esure that the voices of the masses would be heard. Throughout the speech, Nguyễn Mạnh Tường emphasized that the overriding importance of politics and politicians had led to devastating errors in land reform and paralysis in all areas from economics to culture. It was fine and good that top Party leaders like Trường Chinh and Hồ Việt Thắng admitted to land reform mistakes and took the blame for them, but, Nguyễn Mạnh Tường argued, such moves were only political and did not provide the substantive structure needed to prevent future mistakes from occurring.

> For my own part, as a lawyer, I confess that I am not yet able to determine that part of the responsibility that is Mr. [Hồ Việt] Thắng's. His responsibility may be very great; it may likewise be very small. According to a principle of justice, we cannot base ourselves on someone's confession of having assumed a particular responsibility. . . . We have to learn from past experience.[71]

Nguyễn Mạnh Tường insisted upon the separation of the legal from the political in order to check the abuses of power: "While they are arrogant and want to accumulate functions, our politicians are biased by their prejudice against legality, thinking that justice is only a spoke to be put into the wheel. They do not understand that, on the contrary, legality serves to prevent the car from being overturned; it prevents accidents."[72] To emphasize other independent channels of expression and checks and balances was to underscore the importance of and need for expertise, whether it was in law, economics, medicine, or literature. Technicians, as Nguyễn Mạnh Tường called them, wanted simply to play a role in national construction, and narrowly conceived political criteria coupled with intense distrust for their capacity for independent thought had driven many away from the revolution in the early years and reduced them to impotence in the new society. *Lập trường* (class standpoint) as the dominant, explicitly political criteria for judgment had rendered technical competence irrelevant, but its extreme application in daily life could be literally deadly. Such was the case with land reform, which continued to pose a grave problem even after the Party had admitted to errors. For Nguyễn Mạnh Tường, the profoundly idealistic nature of the revolution was a strength during the struggle for a national independence, but a functioning government could not rely on exhortations and vague but all-encompassing guidelines like *lập trường*. He opined: "Politics obsesses us so much that the word *lập trường* disturbs us day and night. If I may use an idealist analogy, I would describe *lập trường* as a wandering soul that incessantly haunts the one who murdered the body it formerly inhabited."[73]

The call for a codified system of law, therefore, clearly had implications for the entire society. In the fourth issue of *Nhân Văn*, Nguyễn Hữu Đang took up the issue.[74] *Lập trường* and self-criticism were no substitute for a court of law in which people would be held accountable for their actions and where others could seek redress. If Khrushchev's move toward de-Stalinization and Mao's Hundred Flowers Movement in the first half of 1956 coincided with a movement of official relaxation in Vietnam and gave the intellectuals the space to express their dissenting views, events in Hungary and Poland in the second half of the year further underlined the urgency of the situation. Nguyễn Mạnh Tường noted in his speech: "Now, after the Twentieth Congress of the Soviet Communist Party, after successive revolts in Berlin, Poznan, Czechoslovakia, and Hungary, we understand the problem a little better; we know how to solve it. . . ."[75] The solution lay in adequate structural change quickly achieved. An unsigned lead article in the fifth issue of *Nhân Văn*, pointedly entitled "Lessons of Poland and Hungary," emphasized that the state must move quickly to correct its mistakes, raise the standard of living, and increase democratic freedom.

The article attributed the mistakes to (1) Stalinism; (2) too rapid a move toward socialism, with heavy industry suppressing the development of agriculture and light industry and leading to dissatisfaction among the populace; and (3) the idea that the move toward communism must be accompanied by a heightened class struggle had led to overzealousness, decimating the rank and file of the Party and causing terrible transgressions of the law.[76]

The same issue of *Nhân Văn* took up the cause for freedom of speech, publishing, organization, congregation, and movement within and outside of the country. Freedom of congregation would guarantee the right to organize demonstrations. The fifth issue of *Nhân Văn* was its last. On 15 December 1956, Hanoi's Administrative Committee banned *Nhân Văn* and decreed that all five issues be taken out of circulation. The decision stated: "[In the] five issues of the newspaper *Nhân Văn* . . . there are many articles that distort the truth, slander, generate division, scatter doubts and ambivalence about the people's democratic regime, and in reality have caused much damage, affecting order and the security of the city."[77]

Reimposition of Intellectual Control

As *Nhân Văn* and the Minh Đức Publishing House were being closed down, the cities were undergoing a capitalist rectification (*cải tạo tư sản*) campaign. Urban dwellers were rigid with fear, while their relatives, escaping the chaos of the countryside, flowed into the cities. Hanoi was a city in turmoil, full of confusion and rumors. Meanwhile, all relevant organizations and work units initiated criticism and self-criticism sessions, targeting those who had written for, supported, or worked for *Nhân Văn* and *Giai Phẩm*. An anti-NVGP campaign dominated the press.

It must be said that there were always opposing voices to NVGP other than the official displeasure being displayed on the pages of such publications as *Nhân Dân* (People's daily). The independent journal *Trăm Hoa* (Hundred flowers), under the editorship of the poet Nguyễn Bính, for example, was not supportive of *Nhân Văn*. At one point, the authorities were actively providing Nguyễn Bính with money and a cheap supply of paper in an effort to persuade him to air even harsher views of *Nhân Văn*. The effort did not succeed because Nguyễn Bính wanted to maintain his independence.[78] Other intellectuals had become uncomfortable with the increasingly strident tone of

Nhân Văn, while personal and intellectual differences added to the split.

The press campaign against NVGP escalated after the two publications were banned in mid-December 1956. The *People's Daily* printed scores of letters from the public and the intellectual community condemning NVGP, claiming that it had received hundreds of such letters.[79] The *People's Daily* focused on Trương Tửu with a series of hardline articles criticizing his argument that intellectuals should not be under the direct leadership of a Party organization.[80] While references to the deleterious effects of NVGP continued to be mentioned in the press, the *People's Daily* itself quickly ended the anti-NVGP campaign in January 1957 after only two months. Although the state shut down *Nhân Văn* and *Giai Phẩm,* clearly it was also confident that it would not take much to rein in other troublesome voices. There was no other significant punishment of the NVGP intellectuals beyond self-criticism sessions and some demotion in the workplace. They continued to hold state jobs and, in some instances, leadership positions within the state publishing houses and even on the Executive Committee of the Association of Art and Literature itself. Such a situation testified to the small and highly informal nature of the intellectual community, where everyone knew everyone else. Additionally, the professional and personal lives of many intellectuals and high-level Party members had been interwoven into a dense network of relationships during the anti-French resistance. The cultural authorities had not deemed it necessary to make black and white distinctions within the intellectual community between true believers and corruptive remnants of the bourgeois mentality.

The Journal *Văn* and Continued Intellectual Discontent

The Second National Congress of Art and Literature was held from 20 to 28 February 1957 in Hanoi. Intended to summarize and assess past achievements and delineate future directions for the arts and literature, the resolution of the Congress did not mention NVGP but noted that there was a need to "struggle without concession against incorrect tendencies, like denying all achievements, demanding reexamination of fundamental principles of our art and literature, the tendency of art and literature to be removed from politics, from the masses and the leadership of the Party, [and] the tendency to return to the old ideas and feelings of the depraved capitalist art."[81] The resolution also noted that the intellectuals' theoretical level was still too low, resulting in simplistic works of art and literature, while criticism was still too weak to guide the public and counter incorrect ideas. In addition, the resolution stated that "the policy toward those who create and perform still lacks specifics, resulting in cases in which intellectuals were not treated appropriately." The leadership of the Executive Committee of the Association of Art and Literature was also gently criticized. Overall, however, the resolution emphasized the achievements that had been made in the last twelve years by correctly following the line of the Party and that "the immediate responsibility of art and literature is to serve in the task of consolidating the north, guide the north toward socialism, and step up the struggle to unify the country." The recent outburst of intellectual dissent had left no trace. The state would move toward socialism and national unification, and the intellectuals were cast firmly in the role of serving that agenda.

In order to organize the intellectuals, it was decided at the Second National Congress on Art and Literature that the different professions would now have their own associations and that intellectuals in the provinces would be gathered into associations of their own. Between 1957 and 1958, a series of congresses founded the Writers' Association, the Artists' Association, the Cinema Artists' Association, the Journalists' Association, the Architects' Association, and the Musicians' Association. The Writers' Association was the first to come into existence, and it quickly organized its own publishing house and journal. All the NVGP intellectuals were involved in these activities. Trần Dần and Hoàng Cầm, for example, both worked in the publishing house of the Writers' Association.[82]

The organ for the new Writers' Association was a weekly literary journal simply called *Văn* (Literature), whose first issue greeted the public on 10 May 1957. Criticism quickly surfaced after *Văn* published a two-part essay by Nguyễn Tuân on, of all things, *phở*, the ubiquitous Vietnamese noodle soup. Being a connoisseur of food, Nguyễn Tuân waxed lyrical about the different kinds of *phở*, which he had dearly missed while he was in Helsinki. A dish beloved by the rich and the poor, *phở* was truly a national treasure, and those who sold it had their own peculiar characteristics. Nguyễn Tuân mentioned that in Hanoi there was a *phở* seller whom people called "Mr. Phở of Rectification" because during land reform he had been wrongly categorized in his village. He had asked a friend to look after his *phở* stand and returned to his village. After rectification, when he came back to

Hanoi, the neighborhood leadership decided not to tax him for a while and gave him a good spot to sell his *phở*. [83]

It was the sort of throwaway but poignant human detail that had been Nguyễn Tuân's signature, but he was quickly criticized by other intellectuals for it. Above all, he was chided for thinking about food at a time when the people were struggling against so many other difficulties. While not all intellectuals agreed with the way in which NVGP pursued intellectual issues, the concerns that had animated NVGP continued to haunt and frustrate the intellectual community. A commentary on a recent book on land reform asserted that "the causes of [land reform] mistakes are all general, as in all the reports; the moods of the characters are superficial; details and situations are all here, as we have heard, but with little depth." [84] Simplistic characters and unreal circumstances were once more derided in literary works, even those that attempted to examine the mistakes of land reform. Meanwhile, those who had written for NVGP began to appear on the pages of *Văn*.

By July, *Văn* was harshly criticized in an article in *Học Tập* (Studies), the organ of the Party. Thế Toàn complained that "the ideological level in the first ten issues of *Văn* is generally low, love and hate [are] not clearly [presented], black and white [aspects] intermingle. . . . And we only see in *Văn* small, petty, and private emotions." Furthermore, "the journal is largely removed from reality, from life, distant from the primary responsibilities of the revolution." [85] These were harsh charges, and editor Nguyên Hồng, who nurtured *Văn* as his own literary child, quickly sprang to the journal's defense. The first shot against *Văn* had been fired, however, and the writer Nguyễn Văn Bổng offered another scathing review of *Văn*'s achievements in the pages of *Văn* itself. He argued that *Văn* had been distant from reality and the people and that "in *Văn* we hardly see people in *work*, in *public life*, in *work relations*, but much more in *love, private life, friendship, and familial relations*." [86] There was little on "people of the age" (*con người thời đại*), the men and women of the new society. He came to an inescapable conclusion: "The capitalist literary viewpoint is beginning to rise up." Another article critical of *Văn* appeared in the August issue of *Học Tập*, with the authors, Hồng Chương and Trịnh Xuân An, speaking as the authoritative voice of the masses. [87]

Now it would be up to the group of writers who had sided with the state against NVGP to defend *Văn* against the same kind of charges. The writer Tô Hoài argued that, rather than the constant discussion of theory, the emphasis should be on providing the structure necessary to promote creativity. [88] As for the stress on "people of the age," he made the point that coming from a feudal and colonial society, the evolution of these men and women must be portrayed in all its complexity rather than as fully formed characters appearing out of the blue.[89] Other articles, stories, and poems in *Văn* continued to draw criticism. A young writer's short story focused on wastefulness in a factory, whose imported machinery quickly rusted due to improper storage.[90] Apparently the criticism of the story was that it had been written by an engineer who wanted to speak badly of Vietnam's effort at modernization and slander international friendship.[91] It seemed that there were very few pieces in *Văn* that would please the growing decibels of critical voices.

The activities of the Writers' Association Publishing House also incurred condemnation. Headed by the writer Tô Hoài and the poet Hoàng Cầm, the publishing house set out to reprint a number of worthy pre-1945 literary works. A couple of novels by the late critical realist writer Vũ Trọng Phụng, whose works were condemned by Tố Hữu at the 1949 Conference of Debates in Việt Bắc, had already been reprinted. Now the publishing house also reprinted a work by Thạch Lam, a member of the Self-Reliant Literary Group, and Nguyễn Tuân's collection *Vang bóng một thời* (Echoes and shadows of an era), long considered to be a work extolling the mores and values of the feudalist upper class. The critical voices grew more indignant. Why reprint so many prerevolutionary works by those not considered to be model writers? Between the decline of the literary weekly *Văn* and the corruption at the publishing house, hard-liners within the intellectual community and representatives of the Party noted that the spirit of NVGP had not disappeared. After all, the intellectuals who had participated in NVGP were still there, working in the publishing house and writing for *Văn*. They had, in effect, managed to commandeer the structure of intellectual organization.

The state moved to rectify the situation. By the end of January 1958, *Văn* was shut down, replaced by a new weekly called *Văn Học* (Literary studies).[92] The Writers' Association Publishing House was consolidated into the Cultural Publishing House, and the whole intellectual community underwent study and criticism sessions. In addition, they were divided into teams and sent to other localities, some in the mines at Cẩm Phả, some in factories, and others in villages. Those considered to be prominent participants in NVGP would finally be judged.

Rather than seeing widespread discontent as an indication of the need to address the intellectual community's concerns, the Party saw that it had underestimated the danger of the ideas that had found

their moment in NVGP. The campaign against them was now renewed with particular fervor. First, the journal *Văn* was subjected to a
round of criticism on the pages of the *People's Daily* and elsewhere.
Intellectuals who had not spoken out against NVGP now entered the
fray. The scholar Đặng Thái Mai penned a two-part article in the
People's Daily, concluding that the problems of the past year were still
fundamentally an issue of *lập trường tư tưởng,* or ideological standpoint.[93] By the beginning of March, those who were responsible for
Văn began the process of public self-criticism. Editor Nguyên Hồng
admitted to not focusing on the national struggle and allowing *Văn* to
be used by the enemies in the south.[94] This self-criticism, however,
was in turn criticized in the *People's Daily* because Nguyên Hồng emphasized only the shortcomings of his work as opposed to admitting
to the graver error of not adhering to the Party's art and literary
directives.[95] The Party clearly wanted to subdue the intellectuals this
time, and nothing less than an unequivocal public statement of full
support for state organization and ideology would do. The writer Tô
Hoài and the poet Tế Hanh followed with articles reassessing the
opinions they had voiced in *Văn.*[96]

The campaign then turned to the participants of NVGP. The lawyer
and professor Nguyễn Mạnh Tường made an apology for his article
on the mistakes committed in land reform for *mất lập trường* (losing
standpoint) by not emphasizing the achievements of the Party, leading to the use of the article in the south as an indictment of the
north.[97] Statements of self-criticism by historian and university professor Đào Duy Anh and the philosopher Trần Đức Thảo were each
published in three parts in the *People's Daily.*[98] From mid-April to mid-
May 1958, a series of articles written by intellectuals appeared in the
People's Daily, criticizing those who had participated in NVGP.[99]
Lengthy articles of this kind, detailed and extremely harsh on their
respective subjects, were also published in *Văn Nghệ Quân Đội,* the
literary journal of the army.[100] The new literary journal with the more
academically sounding name of *Văn Học* (Literary studies), established to maintain the official line on art and literature, published its
first issue in May 1958 under the editorship of Nguyễn Đình Thi and
immediately launched a vociferous attack on the NVGP movement,
publishing the self-criticism statements of Trần Dần, Lê Đạt, Hoàng
Cầm, Trần Lê Văn, Sỹ Ngọc, and Tử Phác.

By now, the technique of self-criticism was entrenched as an effective method with which to rein in troublesome intellectuals and dis-
credit them by means of their own voices. Having had to write a

number of such critiques since the early 1950s, there was an extent to which intellectuals knew themselves to be participating in an exercise. What was different and devastating this time was the destruction of the intellectual community's cohesive unity and the camaraderie fostered by the anti-French resistance. Old friendships, mentoring relationships, personal ties through marriage, and no small measure of intellectual integrity were sacrificed not by unseen enemies but by a number of intellectuals who chose to accept the official stance. Politics subdued everything else, nullifying overnight all the various bases upon which professional and personal relationships within the intellectual community had been constructed over the years.

As for the Party, it now moved to establish its control over the intellectuals once and for all. Punishment and rewards were dispensed, marking the boundaries of future intellectual activities. Intellectuals associated with NVGP were removed from any important post they held on the executive committees of the creative intellectual associations and editorial boards of publishing houses. The Writers' Association suffered the most, with three members expelled (Thụy An, Trương Tửu, and Phan Khôi) and others dismissed for three years at most and banned from publication during that period (Trần Dần, Lê Đạt, Hoàng Cầm, and Phùng Quán). In reality, their membership in the Writers' Association and their right to publish their works would not be reinstated for another thirty years, in 1988. Similar prohibitions occurred in other organizations. A few were jailed, among them Nguyễn Hữu Đang, the writer Thụy An, and the publisher of Minh Đức Publishing House, Trần Thiếu Bảo. Many others were affected by NVGP, even when they were not cited officially. The writer Nguyên Hồng and the poet Hữu Loan, for example, chose to move their families to remote country locations. Scarred by the experience, they preferred facing economic privation and difficult working conditions to remaining within the central intellectual structure in Hanoi. The firm Party response also led to a tightening of the nascent literary effort to come to terms with the excesses of land reform, and those who had shown their loyalty by supporting the Party line and denouncing errant intellectuals and their works emerged in the aftermath to take up key posts within the intellectual structure.

— • —

From February 1955 to January 1958, from the time when the army intellectuals first broached the idea of a broader scope for intellectual creativity to the shutdown of the literary journal *Văn*, Vietnamese intellectuals were pulled into a confrontation from which there could emerge only one winner, the Party. The context of their dissent was complex. Having no room to maneuver at the 1954 Geneva Conference, the Party leadership reluctantly agreed to the division of the country into north and south. The victory thought to be finally at hand after nine years of struggle turned out to be incomplete. The enemy had been given a chance to regroup and was enticing a large number of northern Vietnamese to move south. Fresh from the war, society was plunged into chaos once more with the land reform and rectification campaigns. The zeal to move rapidly toward socialism and the intense effort to maintain vigilance against the enemy generated an environment in which politics ruled supreme, and those who knew how to function within the language and structure of this political discourse would ascend.

Society was being mobilized to an extent that it had never known previously. The rambling nature of intellectual discontent, however, coalesced in the case of Trần Dần, which exemplified the intellectuals' professional and personal concerns. The harshness of the official response to Trần Dần's activities sharpened the sense of grievance of many who were struggling to reconcile the heroic legacy of the revolution with the burdensome state structure. In that regard, the Hu Feng situation as it developed in China probably provided an impetus for the army intellectuals to express their concerns, which had been under discussion in one guise or another since the beginning of the revolution.

Events unfolding elsewhere in the communist world also indicated to the Vietnamese intellectuals that they were not alone. Intellectual discussion now focused on the need for systemic transformation, which forced the state to move against NVGP at the end of 1956. The relative mildness of the state's reaction, however, not only pointed to its confidence in its power but showed that it did not perceive NVGP to be genuinely threatening. Dissent, which increasingly demanded that the state examine the structure it had recently constructed, continued to be waged within the confines of the ideology that had brought the intellectuals to accept the revolution and the Party's leadership in the first place. For many intellectuals, that ideology did not correspond with the structure of the state that was now in place. They were in effect seeing themselves as trying to save the legacy of the revolution from being corrupted. By publicly expressing their opinions, they were also pushing for a better position for themselves in their relationship with the state.

The state, in turn, underestimated the intellectual community's fundamental concerns and what it would take to address them adequately. Soothing words and promises to provide more democratic guidance hardly responded to the problem. This became clear when even after *Nhân Văn* and *Giai Phẩm* were banned the same concerns continued to surface. That intellectuals began to reprint literary and scholarly works written before the revolution showed that they did not see the sharp political differentiation demanded by the state. By the same token, the state now recognized that an intense ideological campaign coupled with tight organizational control of the intellectual sphere were necessary to sharply define the framework guiding intellectual activities.

By the middle of 1958, the gray areas in state-intellectual relations had been removed. The NVGP period was no longer seen as an unfortunate error in judgment on the part of the participating intellectuals but the result of a much more sinister development. According to the 4 June 1958 definitive report of the newly established umbrella intellectual organization, the Association of Art and Literature, which summed up the "three years of struggle against the Nhân Văn-Giai Phẩm clique," presented by Tố Hữu himself,

> Through struggle, everyone has recognized that the Nhân Văn-Giai Phẩm clique is subversive, dangerously operating in the cultural and art and literary arena, intending to oppose the nation, the people, socialism, our regime, and our Party. Leading the clique are professional "intellectual agitators," long time Trotskyists, [and] sophisticated antirevolutionary characters . . . in collusion with some reactionary elements in the capitalist class. They rely on a number of intellectuals from the resistance, who since their return to the cities have been transformed by the depraved urban style of living and reactionary thought. From depravity in life, thought, and intellectual work, they have fallen into the antirevolutionary political path.[101]

The strident tone of the report marked the appearance of a new vocabulary. The period of intellectual dissent now had been designated as the struggle against "the Nhân Văn-Giai Phẩm clique." It had been given a proper name, and those who had been the most active participants were now termed reactionaries, traitors, and Trotskyists. Although it wanted to convey a black and white message to the intellectual community, the state was also careful in differentiating between politically dangerous components and those who were easily influenced. Intense study and criticism sessions and extended labor trips ensued, but in comparison with China, for example, there was no massive purge in the intellectual community, nor the loss of life.[102] The "intellectuals as lost lambs" image effectively dismissed their larger public roles as capable, independent voices and made the Party an even purer moral center whose firm political line was the only path to follow. The intellectuals' efforts to recover a more balanced relationship with the Party had been futile.

Intellectuals as servants of the state and culture as a weapon in the ideological struggle became the fundamental pillars governing all intellectual and cultural activities from 1958 on. The state reorganized the structure of intellectual organizations while constructing a network of cultural organizations extending to the remotest of villages, designed to continue the process of the transformation of society begun during land reform, in terms of content as well as form. Cultural work in the villages is the subject of the next chapter.

— 5 —

The Structure of a
Cultural Revolution:
The Ministry of Culture

The critical voices that briefly coalesced around the publications *Nhân Văn* and *Giai Phẩm* in 1956 highlighted the gap between many intellectuals and the new socialist state. Even though both publications were banned at the end of 1956, the Party maintained a moderate approach in intellectual matters throughout 1957, allowing for a measure of intellectual creativity and pushing for acquiescence through persuasion and dialogue. This flexible stance dramatically changed after 1958. Serious repercussions finally came to those who had participated in *Nhân Văn* and *Giai Phẩm,* and all other critical voices from within the intellectual community were stilled.

Several reasons have been offered to explain the sharp change in the official response to intellectual concerns. The antirevisionist movement resulting from the November 1957 Moscow conference in the aftermath of the upheavals in Eastern Europe provided the impetus in Vietnam to establish firm party control over the cultural arena, and the push in Vietnam to proceed to the period of socialist transformation made the issue of a cultural revolution an urgent one.[1] Socialist transformation, embodied in the 1958–1960 Three Year Plan for Economic Development and Transformation and Cultural Development, demanded the mobilization of the entire nation. Intellectuals were necessary in the ideological campaign, while education, both general and political, was crucial in the national effort to transform the country. Cultural work became enormously important in order to instill in the people "the importance of raising the people's awareness of their role as masters of the state; promoting a high regard for labor; educating the people in collectivism, organizational discipline, patriotism, and proletarian internationalism; and enhancing their caution against class enemies."[2]

The new society, whose composition and structure were subjects of great concern for so many intellectuals between 1955 and 1958, continued to be consolidated. The process had begun with land reform, the socialist state's single most revolutionary act, which aimed to transform the base of economic relations in the countryside, where the majority of the population resided, and represented a fundamental step in the attempt to radically alter the rural social structure. Party leaders underlined the importance of cultural work as they labored to overcome the mistakes committed during land reform and energize the population to participate in the intense efforts of economic and social transformation in the march toward socialism. The Nhân Văn–Giai Phẩm period had highlighted how deeply ingrained bourgeois ideas were among the intellectuals, even after then anti-French struggle, but Party leaders also argued for a long-term, sweeping cultural revolution to purge the deep-seated influence of feudalism upon the rural population. The victory against colonialism and feudalism had been achieved in physical terms, but the more difficult process of fully eradicating their pernicious influence in ideological and everyday terms still lay ahead.

To this end, the Ministry of Culture was established to coordinate and shape cultural activities. The importance of culture to the state can easily be seen in the ministry's varied interests and vast array of projects. As in other socialist states, through the control of the fundamental mechanisms of intellectual life, such as publishing and distribution and an administrative structure extending down to the village level, the Ministry of Culture came to have formidable power over the social and intellectual life of the country. The political nature that underlines most of the ministry's undertakings emphasized the level of official power it enjoys but is also the source of its strongest criticism.

The impression of extraordinary power certainly is not without substance, but confusion and conflict characterized the Ministry of Culture in the early years as it set out to formulate its agenda and goals. Immediately after the founding of the ministry in September 1955, there were many internal discussions and debates about cultural work and what it meant under socialism and in a primarily agrarian society. More specifically, there were conflicting inclinations within the ministry that pitted the professional emphasis against the more political focus of cultural work, beginning with the issue of choosing the most appropriate cadres for its staff.

Working with archival data from the files of the Ministry of Culture, I will examine its role and scope of activities in its early years as it struggled to establish an organizational structure and define its existence during a difficult period that encompassed not only land reform and the organizational rectification campaign but the state's efforts to correct land reform mistakes and the effects of Nhân Văn– Giai Phẩm. The more benign notions of ideological and cultural struggle that initially permeated the Ministry of Culture and allowed different views to be voiced gave way as the state consolidated its control over cultural activities. By the end of 1958, a major national campaign of criticism and self-criticism was under way, with the ministry playing a key role. The vigor with which the socialist vision was now being pursued effected a distinct shift in the tone and purpose of the ministry's undertakings.

The Definition of Culture

Tố Hữu, who had been in charge of propaganda, cultural, and literary work in the Party since 1947, was made full member of the Central Committee in 1955. At the National Congress on Culture in May 1956, he elaborated on the importance of cultural work in the revolution.

> The construction of a new society demands of the masses an increasing level of knowledge in order to protect and bolster the country [to make it] even more beautiful. That is a natural act; we all know that. We have often heard it said that "there is no revolution without revolutionary theory," and now I hear that you comrades are very surprised to hear it said that "the revolution will not be victorious without the mobilization of culture." Comrades! What is revolutionary theory? What is Marxism? [It is] science gained from the reality of the struggle. That is culture. The meaning of culture is very broad, covering all that belongs to the intellectual life of human beings. Medicine, education, society, literature and the arts, science, etc. . . . are all culture. We have not conceived [of culture] in such a broad manner, and that is why we are surprised. Our surprise is not without cause; [it is because] we view culture narrowly, understanding it in a way that could be said to be retrograde.[3]

This is the voice of a leader, confident of his views and impatient to impart them to the rank and file. Born into a poor mandarin family in central Vietnam, Tố Hữu joined the revolution at the age of sixteen and has long been considered the premier revolutionary poet. Given his top position in the Party and his control of the cultural arena, Tố Hữu's definition of culture deserves further elaboration.

Tố Hữu's broad definition of culture never mentioned intellectuals. He exalted instead in the populist definition to the point of denying culture any particular characteristic. Reflecting the mood of a postwar society, he opined:

> There are funny stories, as when we have a good meal we don't say that it was good but that this meal has "high culture," or when we wear a beautiful shirt we say that that way of dressing is "very cultured." The good meal and the well-tailored, beautifully colored shirt are precisely the bright ideas of the human intellect. That [they exist] is due to the existence of culture.[4]

These instances of everyday definitions of culture reflected the popular tongue in cheek response to the long years of material and spiritual deprivation during the anti-French resistance, but such general usage of the term sprang from the increasingly encompassing definition developed as part of the Party's effort to force a dramatic break with the past and institutionalize socialism. Party theorists and intellectuals such as Trường Chinh and Hoài Thanh had pondered the issue of national culture with disdain for high culture but ambivalence about popular culture. Men like Tố Hữu, however, whose life had been wholly committed to the revolutionary vision of state and society and who witnessed the extraordinary achievements of the socialist state, firmly held the view that culture must be defined as, and only as, popular culture. On this, he was emphatic.

> Culture is the product of the working class. . . . Culture is the spiritual sustenance of the masses. Those are the two sides of one issue. Our view is totally opposite the view of the ruling class. The exploiting ruling class did not accept culture as the product of the working class but as the product of genius, of God, of the creativity of a group of individual intellectuals, etc. . . . [The ruling class] did not see culture as being in the service of the people and the masses but as entertainment for those who "eat and do nothing" (*ăn không ngồi rồi*).[5]

This passage encapsulates many crucial points that would eventually define *culture* and *cultural work* from 1958 onward. For one thing, the individualism inherent in intellectual creativity was at odds with the cooperative era, seen by the Party as having no worth because it was disconnected from the masses and was primarily oriented toward providing entertainment for the ruling class. In such a view, intellectuals literally disappeared since they played no role in the populist definition. Second, the concept of culture now had a distinctly utilitarian air; it now served the masses, specifically to enable them to achieve the economic, social, and political goals defined by the Party. Finally, the class struggle aspect of culture was clearly enunciated. The Party might have admitted to land reform mistakes, but the class criteria pushed to the extreme during land reform would continue to be a central element in Party policy.

The rejection of the elite component of culture led to a definition of popular culture that would quickly come into conflict with the village world. To be sure, the elevation of popular culture brought about a heightened awareness of traditional art forms, although some of these had been denounced as feudal in the 1949 Conference of Debates. While Tố Hữu deemed culture to be the "spiritual sustenance of the masses," the push for increased economic output and the insistence on establishing a new socialist culture did away with much of what had informed the rhythm of village life. The popular culture of the new state excluded village festivals and fairs, ancestor worship, feasting at death anniversaries, and the rituals of funeral and wedding ceremonies.[6] These rituals and practices were seen as perpetuating superstitions, sustaining the unequal social hierarchy in the village, and being detrimental to agricultural output. Buddhist and Catholic activities were greatly curtailed. Increasingly, the popular culture referred to in official documents such as those of the Ministry of Culture was one that was still to be constructed. The "popular" aspect of this new culture insisted more on the participation of the masses in the interest of the common goals established by the state than on retaining the traditions, art forms, rituals, and practices of old. Where the old art forms were being preserved, they were used to broadcast the state's messages, from love of country to higher agricultural production to new hygienic practices.

The new view of culture as state-constructed popular culture prescribed no space for intellectuals' involvement. At the same time, however, in order to surge ahead with socialist economic transformation, the urgency to raise "the level of culture" (trình độ văn hóa) was deemed primary. In time, the level of culture came to mean simply the level of education. The masses, therefore, were rendered both active and passive. They were the producers of the only culture that could now be constituted as national, but they also must be taught to strive toward a higher level of culture befitting socialism in which their economic contribution was key. In this new stage, it was the Party that would guide the masses toward socialism, with intellectuals playing the intermediary role of transmitting the Party's agenda to them.

The Ministry of Culture's Roles and Responsibilities

The primary economic concern in cultural work can be seen most clearly in the four self-designated goals put forth by the Ministry of Culture at its founding in September 1955.

1. To develop optimistic and healthy cultural activities so as to generate the inspiration for productivity and the political struggle
2. To raise the cultural level of the masses
3. To raise the people's political level (patriotism, love of labor, love of class, the collective spirit, the internationalist spirit, and the will to strive to fulfill immediate responsibilities)
4. To construct the national culture, make good use of past heritage, combine with [the fight] against enslaving culture, eradicate vestiges of the enemy's culture, and study the progressive cultures of other countries[7]

This developmental agenda was to be backed up by an organizational structure that extended from the center down to the *xã*, or commune, level. Nationally, there were five main offices: the Bureau of Publication (Cục Xuất Bản), Bureau of Cinema (Cục Điện Ảnh), Department of Arts (Vụ Nghệ Thuật), Department of Mass Culture (Vụ Văn Hóa Đại Chúng), and Department of Cultural Liaison (Vụ Liên Lạc Văn Hóa). The wide-ranging cultural tasks under the Ministry of Culture's control can be gauged by examining the responsibilities of these offices. The Bureau of Publication was in charge of all the publishing houses, the printing presses, and the distribution network. The Bureau of Cinema oversaw the national film industry and the cinema theater network. The Department of Arts dealt with national troupes of all performing genres and of the schools teaching the performing arts. The Department of Mass Culture managed libraries, exhibits, cultural houses, museums, and the preservation of historical sites. Finally, the Department of Cultural Liaison organized international cultural exchanges. At the local level, the Ministry of Culture's network was to be an integral part of the local administrative structure, with offices in cities, provinces, districts, and communes.

Within a year of its founding, the Ministry of Culture proudly announced its achievements. It had distributed 8,321,482 books on all subjects and 27,431,588 copies of newspapers. Libraries had been established in twenty-nine cities compared to only three in all of Indochina in 1939 under colonial rule. Films had been made and shown, national troupes performed for millions of people, cultural cadres were being trained, many international performers had come to Vietnam, and scores of Vietnamese artists had gone abroad in cultural exchanges. As for mass culture, by September 1956, 1,784 cultural clubs in factories and cultural houses in the countryside, with 6,213 reading groups and 1,280 performing arts troupes, were said to be in operation.[8]

Such detailed statistics provided normative evidence of the achievements of the Ministry of Culture and the new society. Legions of cadres compiled these statistics, which saturated newspapers, the radio, and all government publications. The new state needed data to establish its standing and formulate its future plans, but the statistical preoccupation was also indicative of the government's view of culture as something concrete and utilitarian. Given that the Ministry of Culture's main task was to organize cultural activities with specific outcomes, increasingly *culture* was being defined as tasks seen in terms of and achieved by numbers.

The list of cultural tasks further conveyed a definite sense of purpose, and it was one way which the Ministry of Culture could translate concretely what needed to be done at the local level. In addition, the achievements exemplified in these statistics provided an impression of success gained very soon after the founding of the ministry that could be readily communicated to the Party, the state, and to the public. Yet the ministry's internal documents and reports evoke a different image. Far from being the unified organization that it was on paper, the ministry had great difficulty balancing the conflicting demands of the state while trying to engender within its own rank and file a firm sense of purpose and conviction. The problem was fundamental; it began with the organizational and ideological legacy inherited by the ministry from the beginning.

The Ministry of Culture's Organizational and
Ideological Legacy

The Việt Minh government initially created a Ministry of Information (Bộ Thông Tin), but during the anti-French resistance it became the Ministry of Propaganda (Bộ Tuyên Truyền). The change in name reflected a change in emphasis. As I have noted, *propaganda* as a term then did not have the overwhelmingly pejorative connotation that is associated with it today. Propaganda was viewed as the effort to broadcast the revolutionary message to the wider public through persuasion rather than brainwashing. Nevertheless, it was distinctly onesided, and the title of Ministry of Propaganda represented more appropriately the ministry's work. As the propaganda effort grew in scope and intensity, cultural work came to be considered part of propaganda work since, as the slogan for education during the anti-French resistance period proclaimed, it was "all for the front."

The Ministry of Culture inherited this difficult legacy. When the socialist state was established in the north in 1954, the Ministry of Propaganda was considered unnecessary since victory had been achieved. As a powerful ideological tool, however, propaganda continued to have a place in the new state. Propaganda work was now the purview of a small group of cadres, well trained and dedicated to the socialist state, who functioned within the Party structure. *Tuyên truyền* (propaganda) became part of the larger work of *tuyên huấn* (propaganda and ideological training). As propaganda work was moved into the Party's structure, the Ministry of Culture came to inherit the network of the now defunct Ministry of Propaganda.

On paper, therefore, the Ministry of Culture seemed to have appeared overnight, complete with an organizational structure that extended down to the villages. Reality was another matter. As one report from the province of Thanh Hóa noted:

> The newly established provincial cultural office only inherited from the provincial propaganda office a few cadres who were the least capable, and ever since the cultural unit was separated from propaganda and ideological work (*tuyên huấn*) the cultural machinery from the district down to the commune has been essentially nonexistent.[9]

The small number of cultural cadres meant that propaganda cadres continued to be in charge of the new cultural work in a number of places, adding to the general bewilderment about the nature of cultural work. The confusion in organizational structure was also galling to the Ministry of Culture's leadership, and it sought repeatedly to establish organizational independence from the propaganda machinery, which was now firmly integrated into the party apparatus. This was not merely a matter of establishing organizational integrity but an effort to prevent what was viewed as cultural work's professional concerns from being overwhelmed by pure propaganda work. During a conference on culture convened in September 1956, a year after the founding of the ministry, cultural cadres of Interzone 4 emphatically demanded that the ministry needed

> to put an end to the confusing situation between propaganda and ideological training and culture in terms of cadres, administrative regulation, and work style. [We must] officially proclaim the establishment of the provincial cultural office. The provinces need to have either a head or deputy head of the [provincial cultural office] officially and primarily in charge of culture. [We] should not prolong the situation in which those who are members of the Propaganda and Ideological Training Committee (Ban Tuyên Huấn) are also directly in charge of the provincial cultural office, causing problems for the leadership of the professional branch.[10]

The emphasis on professionalism pointed to aspects of cultural work that the ministry took on that demanded training far beyond what was required in propaganda work. For the cultural cadres in the provinces alone, for example, cultural work was supposed to include the formation of new troupes of performing artists with new songs and dances; the organization of film showings and exhibits; the construction of cultural clubs for factories and cultural houses for villages; the collection and preservation of historical data, relics, and structures; the collection and preservation of traditional songs and dances of different regions; the publication and distribution of books and newspapers; and, finally, the promotion of matters relating to the people's cultural and social life such as village festivals and sanitary education. The main beneficiaries of all these activities would be the peasants and workers, but the efforts were also meant to be national achievements. The recovery of Vietnam's historical and artistic past, for example, would provide the firm psychological base upon which to build the independent state. We have seen the tremendous ambivalence with which many intellectuals and early communist revolutionaries viewed the national culture, seeing it as heavily burdened with Chinese and French influences. Some of the Ministry of Culture's most important work would be in sketching out the shape and content of Vietnamese culture untainted by colonialism, finding, as it were, the authentic Vietnamese essence that would be a source of national pride.

From the beginning, however, cultural work was little understood by the larger administrative leadership. The general tendency was to equate cultural work with literacy programs or popular entertainment, which could be adequately covered by other mass organizations such as youth groups or women's associations. Moreover, swamped with directives and quotas of all kinds which had to be achieved and reported, leading cadres in the provinces tended to see cultural work as unimportant: "[Cadres are busy with] economic and social work such as reinforcing dikes, building roads, preparing against drought, constructing clinics . . . and are not paying attention to cultural work."[11]

The fundamental problem was that the number of trained cultural cadres was woefully inadequate to the tasks at hand. This partly explains why propaganda cadres continued to carry out cultural work in the first year of the ministry's existence. Moreover, the ministry had come into existence during the land reform and organizational rectification campaigns. At the height of land reform, cadres were assigned land reform work or were themselves being attacked. Older cadres often failed to satisfy the strict class requirements of the new society, while others were eager to take over important positions in the villages and provinces. On the whole, cultural work was impossible to carry out in 1956. According to the ministry itself,

the grave mistakes of land reform and organizational rectification have greatly harmed the machinery as well as cultural work (cultural cadres and artists were suspect, were punished wrongly; the nonprofessional performing troupes and the performing arts groups were disbanded; cultural and revolutionary data and evidence were destroyed, etc.)[12]

In the highly politicized atmosphere of the period, propaganda work and its new position in the Party apparatus were deemed more important than the new, broadly defined, and demanding cultural work. For one thing, propaganda work was seen as having a future whereas cultural work was seen as a dead end, to be assigned to those who could not get ahead or were not seen as politically loyal to the Party. Those who could do so, therefore, insisted on being transferred to propaganda units. High-ranking cadres themselves also sought to move those under their control out of cultural work. According to one 1956 report issued by the Ministry of Culture:

> Until now many leading cadres of the Party and the state appara-
> tus still do not correctly conceptualize the necessity of cultural
> work so that they have yet to care sufficiently, have yet to pro-
> vide appropriate cadres, have yet to help in constructing the
> machinery or the tasks, but instead often transfer cultural cadres
> to other tasks in a disorderly fashion (especially during the pe-
> riod of land reform and organizational rectification), creating
> great difficulties for cultural activities throughout 1956 (espe-
> cially in the first six months).[13]

Those left behind to do cultural work were therefore unfamiliar with the tasks at hand and uninspired. They were seen to be the least likely to rise to any notable position. In the province of Thanh Hóa, for example, those given the cultural tasks in the ministry's provincial office were the "least progressive [since cultural work was seen as] not glorious and lacking much relation to personal life, like land re-form work, [making] the task of cultural work in service of politics even more disorderly."[14] The view of cultural work as unimportant coupled with the emphasis on class during the purification of the Party led to the transfer of cadres from middle and poor peasant backgrounds to propaganda units, while those who were considered to have suspicious class backgrounds were sent to do cultural work.

This issue of class worked in contradictory ways. At the upper levels of the Ministry of Culture, up to the provincial levels at least, there were reports indicating that some cadres assigned to cultural tasks had complicated class backgrounds or had been disciplined dur-ing the party rectification campaign. They were generally well edu-cated, however, and it was their presence in the machinery of the ministry that stabilized its administrative structure during this early, difficult period. As noted in a lengthy and detailed report from Thanh Hóa Province,

> those who were disciplined are cadres with the ability to act and
> who have been active for a long time in [positions of] leader-

ship. . . . In the initial period, leadership was weak and confusing, but the cadres' ability to assimilate and their awareness were broad, so that even though they basically felt wronged they still tried to help the steering committee to develop its leadership aptitude [by] working, studying, and generating new ideas.[15]

A modicum of stability was critical in the aftermath of land reform since the Ministry of Culture, whose power was nonexistent in many areas because of the local land reform committees' complete control, was given the task of healing the wounds as well as institutionalizing the new social structure. The tense atmosphere in the countryside would have to be immediately defused: "In this period, all that which would arouse once more the fierce class struggle should be disregarded temporarily. . . . We need to introduce things to be read, performed, and talked about that can inspire healthy emotions from the past heritage; we should not restrict topics."[16] The mundane business of cultural work suddenly became important in order to calm down the countryside and create the stability necessary for production.

At the same time that the government was trying to correct land reform mistakes it was also consolidating the new social structure based on class criteria established during land reform. Excesses might have occurred, but the course of a class-defined social struggle in the new state had already been set and would continue. Land reform officially ended at the close of 1956, but soon after the cities were engulfed in a reform campaign that focused on the petite bourgeoisie and the capitalists. The countryside was in turmoil, but the cities also were thrown into a state of confusion and fear.[17] For the Ministry of Culture, if the more educated cadres had found refuge in cultural work at the upper reaches, the official policy at the local level was to increase the number of cadres who were *cốt cán*, or backbone elements, meaning those who had the appropriate class backgrounds and were considered to be politically pure.

The *cốt cán* were also the least likely to have been educated, and in many instances could not read or write well. Thanh Hóa Province complained that "the majority of the committee members in charge of cultural work ruined projects because of their low cultural level since most are women; there is even a lady district committee member in charge of culture who does not read and write well, as in Thạch Thành District."[18] In Quảng Bình Province, when the administrative committees were finally established at the *xã* level after land reform, the delegation of cultural and social tasks [often fall to] women, or those who have the least ability in the committees, so that even though there are people in charge, nothing gets done. This is not to mention the general situation of the *cốt cán*, which is that they are young (usually nineteen or twenty years old), do not understand life, lack prestige, and more or less had improper attitudes during land reform, such as making untruthful denunciations, so that the people became reproachful and do not trust them much.[19]

Even for those longtime cultural cadres who managed to ride out the stormy period of land reform and the organizational rectification campaign, it was difficult for them to understand what culture work really meant. After all, they were the ones who had shown the films and taught the songs that had generated such a high level of hatred and disorder in the countryside, and now they were given the task of "generating a happy and inspiring atmosphere in order to lessen tensions in the countryside and rely on that to motivate the people to achieve new tasks."[20] It was not surprising that the cultural cadres found that the people were distrustful of them and their work.

The Ministry of Culture's Activities

Under the circumstances, it was amazing that any cultural work was done at all. The task of preservation was hardest hit by land reform and the Party purification campaign. Since the local land reform committees held absolute power, the ministry's activities had to be coordinated with them. The thrust of land reform, however, resulted in immense destruction to cultural sites and made it impossible for the ministry to gather historical data relating to the various uprisings and the anti-French resistance. Temples and pagodas were already in need of restoration because of the war, and after 1954 they were used as storehouses, schools, or meeting places. Their interiors and exteriors were further neglected or destroyed. Land reform decreed that the bulk of the land belonging to the temples be divided among the peasants. What was left for the monks was often mediocre land far from the temples so that many simply gave up and left. In some places, land was taken away and temple gardens, courtyards, and even bell towers were given to the people. Even the tiles on their roofs and the trees in their precincts were sold. The move to rectify land reform mistakes could heighten the destruction. In one instance, "at the Trầm temple [in] Hà Đông, land around the temple was divided among peasants, and when the rectification of land reform mistakes began peasants were afraid of having to give back [the land], so they cut down twelve ancient trees."[21]

The fervor to build roads and dikes also devastated many well-known cultural and historical sites. Books were destroyed, regardless of their content, not only by land reform committees, which confiscated or burned them, but also by many of their owners who were fearful of being implicated as collaborators or reactionaries. In the process, much damage was done to the revolution's own history and image.

During land reform and organizational rectification, a number of the Party's big movements, like the Soviet Nghệ An and the history of the Party's struggle in Sơn Tây and Hà Đông, were incorrectly concluded to be the history of the reactionary Nationalist Party. A large number of the older Party members who fought for the revolution after 1930 were wrongly classified . . . as reactionaries. As such, the revolutionary and resistance data kept by these comrades were all seen by the land reform committees as belonging to the enemy, to the reactionary Nationalist Party in disguise, so they confiscated, destroyed, and burned them, tearing up the Soviet Nghệ An flag and burning revolutionary documents in Nam Định. Many Party members were afraid of being implicated, so they burned and destroyed the documents themselves or hid them and would not bring them out.[22]

The ministry's cadres were helpless. The lack of properly trained cadres and the general apathy toward cultural work in the early years did nothing to help the effort to research and preserve historic documents, art forms, and buildings. Such work was not carried out precisely because, as one document rightly assessed, it was "a task that is meticulous, urgent as well as long term."[23] Given the divergent interests of the land reform committees and cultural cadres, the resulting cultural work was abysmal. As one Ministry report revealed:

In wave 5 of land reform, [the ministry] coordinated with the Central Land Reform Committee, the local party groups, and the land reform committees to formulate the direction and the plan to collect [historical data]. The result did garner some evidence, but all it got were the spears, canes, and guns of landowners and other evidence that spoke of the misery of the peasants. Otherwise, no data, documents, written materials, or evidence that would speak of the struggle of the people against imperialism and feudalism [were collected]. And even the evidence that has been collected must be reevaluated after the rectification of land reform errors.[24]

The conflict between the ministry's professional impulse and the state's political demands echoed in other ministry activities. Books, for example, were carefully selected for general use. Out of 12,233 titles left behind by the French, only 1,500 were deemed fit to be used, though the number was bolstered subsequently with books donated by the Soviet Union and China.[25] The ministry was in control of all the publishing houses, printing presses, and distribution networks. Nevertheless, private publishing houses continued to exist until 1958, and the books that did get published under the ministry's direction were large in quantity but their contents were judged to be unsuitable for the people's needs and level of understanding, making the books inaccessible and costly.[26] Publishing houses were also criticized for only reporting the number of books intended to be published in their 1957 plan without disclosing the nature of their content, making it impossible to screen out potentially harmful works.[27] The reprint of a number of pre-1945 books and re-release of some pre-1945 films were denounced vociferously as politically dangerous.

The performing arts were also having difficulties. Instead of the traditional songs and dances that were an integral part of village festivals and ceremonies, the Ministry of Culture organized what came to be known as the mass performing arts movement (*phong trào văn nghệ quần chúng*). Talented and politically reliable members of a village were organized into small performance troupes, mostly to present songs and plays written about such things as literacy and agricultural production. Where possible, new content was provided for traditional art forms. The mass performing arts movement was envisioned as a means of bringing state policies to the people through new organizations composed of the people themselves. In practice, on the one hand, the Ministry of Culture was criticized for not properly guiding the mass performing arts movement so that performances were being presented everywhere, affecting the production schedule and wasting resources. On the other hand, the failure of the cultural house project, discussed below, led to a new emphasis on relying on the people's resources financially and artistically rather than on a top-down approach. In this regard, the ministry disbanded the provincial troupes in order to concentrate more resources on performance groups (*tổ văn nghệ*) at the village level.[28]

As with the situation regarding cadres, conflicting needs and goals often led to different strategies being implemented, which tended to cancel out the intended effects. If the requirements of a newly established ministry called for experienced and educated cadres at the upper levels, the policy at the lower levels was to increase the number of barely literate but politically pure cadres. Such a development allowed the Ministry of Culture to stabilize itself under extremely difficult conditions, but its directives were disregarded by the time they reached the villages. Similarly, the ministry's emphasis on the mass performing arts movement was deemed to be detrimental to the production schedule, but the state's stress on popular participation at the expense of experienced troupes undercut the ministry's efforts to professionalize the performing arts. The dilemma was therefore also being framed within the context of national versus regional development. One consequence of this was the distorted growth of the performing arts in socialist Vietnam in later years. In particular, a bias emerged against more talented artists, who gravitated toward Hanoi because of its intense intellectual atmosphere but suffered the risk of not being supported financially and in other ways, being, as they were, outside of the regional structure.[29]

A corollary of this dilemma was what has been referred to in various documents as the issue of popularization and elevation (*vấn đề phổ cập và đề cao*). The work of the Ministry of Culture was to encompass both, focusing on the needs of the people but at the same time working to raise their standards to a higher level. Hoàng Minh Giám (1904–95), a well-respected intellectual active in the nationalist cause in the 1930s and 1940s, became the first minister of culture. He held the post until July 1976. In a report summarizing and assessing the ministry's activities from 1955 to 1957, he stated:

> For more than three years now, our policy that *popularization is primary* has been correct, but we have one weakness in that we have not fully realized the importance of elevation, and at times elevation and popularization are still separate from each other. . . . Right now, we have literary, philosophical, and historical works by scholars and writers of the past, and a number

of ancient architectural and art works, but we have not re-
searched them enough to introduce them and assess their
value. . . . In our country's current situation, *popularization* is
still primary, but at the same time we must pay attention to
elevation, meaning that we must earnestly prepare the base (material and spiritual) on which to build a lasting new culture,
nation, and socialist society.[30]

Although the state's focus on providing for the people was important and necessary, Hoàng Minh Giám clearly believed that the country's cultural and literary heritage was being neglected. The professional side of cultural work was also clashing with the demands of
culture for the people at the expense of everything else. At so many
junctures, what the ministry perceived as important for cultural development in the long run was at odds with the new state's emphasis on
immediate problem solving and mass participation. While the ministry was hardly operating within a democratic or capitalist framework,
these early years did indicate that there was much conflict in terms of
how cultural work was being defined.

The Cultural House Project

For all the complaints about the leadership and cadres not fully understanding what cultural work was all about, the ministry itself was
also engulfed in its own vision of what cultural work was supposed
to be. This vision soon showed itself to be far removed from the
reality of the countryside. The ministry's project to construct a network of cultural houses and clubs in the early years is a potent
example of this misperception.

The creation of *nhà văn hóa*, or cultural houses, in the countryside,
with the counterpart being *câu lạc bộ*, or clubs, for the factories, was
a central project from its inception. There was to be a national network of these institutions catering to the needs of the peasantry and
the working class. In the Vietnamese context, a *xóm* is a neighborhood within a *thôn* (village), and a group of villages is called a *xã*, or
a commune. A *xã* is the unit upon which the state wanted to base
the cooperative process. Thus, as cultural clubs were being formed
in the factories, cultural houses were also being established at the *xã*
level.

What was a cultural house? At the Conference on Village Culture in late 1956, the Ministry of Culture defined it as follows.

> A cultural house can be big or small, of thatch or tiles. It can be a *đình* [village communal house] or a *điếm* [village watch house] or a room in a house borrowed from the people, depending on the needs of the specific locality. It is a place where the peasants of a village come to meet and talk, read books and newspapers, perform, play games, or exhibit agricultural products. In general, a cultural house is the public place where peasants come to discuss cultural activities. . . . But it is [also] the place meant to guide the cultural activities outside [the village], to guide the *xã*'s cultural movement.[31]

This definition is instructive for several reasons. First, the cultural house was to fulfill the ministry's responsibilities, namely, to structure cultural activities that would both educate and inspire people to emulate the ideals of nation, socialism, and production while constructing the new culture. It was clear that the activities of the cultural house were meant to support the state's agenda at the local level. More importantly, it was an attempt to break with old village ways and establish a new institution. The cultural house could take over a communal house, once the seat of village administration, the place where important village ceremonies took place.

The village communal house was not the only public structure being co-opted and transformed in the state's attempt to construct new social and political relations in the countryside. According to Shaun Malarney, there were differences in the kind of transformation these public buildings underwent, depending on their functions.

> Those structures which were either associated with the former elites, such as the *đình* [communal house] and *văn chỉ* [Confucian temple], or those whose ritual activities were considered superstitious, such as the *đền* [temple] and *điện* [temple], underwent the most violent transformation to mundane space. These structures were vandalized or defaced while their ritual objects were destroyed. Conversely, those spaces whose religious activities focused on kin, ancestors or Buddhism were transformed but in a non-violent fashion. Some ancestral halls were turned into residences but their altars were never destroyed. Family ancestral

altars were also not destroyed although there was strong social pressure to simplify ostentatious altars.[32]

Communal houses, temples, pagodas, and shrines were therefore desacralized and converted, most often into areas for drying paddy, warehouses, or even living spaces for poor village families. Recognizing that the elimination of these sacred and public structures' symbolic and social functions alone could not guarantee a transformation of the people's behavior, the state exerted much effort to ban or modify old practices and make sure that other kinds of activities took place. The establishment of cultural houses in every *xã*, for example, was meant to introduce a host of new activities into village life that would eventually transform it, contributing to the larger campaign of a cultural revolution in the countryside.

Although the establishment of cultural houses in every *xã* was an ambitious undertaking, the Ministry of Culture had intended them to be fairly modest. They were to be constructed using existing buildings or from the people's voluntary contributions. Nevertheless, the initial decree to build cultural houses sent to the provincial cadres included few specific instructions regarding how the structures were to be built and what activities they would offer. The ministry's definition of a cultural house, noted above, was offered at a conference on village culture a full year after their construction was under way.

The conference included provincial reports detailing the project's progress at the local level. Among the highly critical remarks, Vice Minister Đỗ Đức Dục's no nonsense report noted that the ministry had only been established in September 1955 and while its organization was still in its primary stages and land reform was making things difficult, the ministry was already presenting the concept of cultural houses to be included in the national plan, specifying a goal of 2,500 structures. Dục's conclusion was that the move made "local districts rush headlong into meeting the goal, wasting much labor in addition to causing difficulty with other tasks."[33]

Local cadres, intent on accomplishing their part in fulfilling the national plan, became obsessed with the structure rather than with what that structure meant. In certain areas, the people were asked to contribute heavily to the effort.

The people in Kiến An . . . have contributed 3,340 piastres and thousands of bricks with thirty-two roofing tin sheets; the people in the *xã* of Tân Tiến have gathered 14,525 piastres and one hundred workers for the cultural house; the people of the *xã* of Đặng Cường have organized fishing and work exchanges and used the money raised from performances to create an account for the cultural house's construction; the *xóm of* Đặng Cường raised 4,000 piastres to buy books for the cultural house; the *xóm* of Nhật Thường gathered 132 books, etc.[34]

Once the cultural houses were built, however, they offered few activities that attracted the peasants. First, their location at the *xã* level meant that the cultural houses were a fair distance from many villages. After the initial novelty wore off, peasants did not return to see the photographs, paintings, and "two-kilo potatoes" on display.[35] At the same time, the state's literacy campaign was being focused on the *xóm*, or neighborhoods. Essentially staffed by three to five young teachers and youngsters of the *xóm*, with thirty to one hundred books at their disposal, the reading group became important in the *xóm*'s activities and was effective in influencing work attitudes.[36]

The practical and personal nature of these reading groups supplanted some of the intended tasks of the cultural house. The Ministry of Culture was forced to refocus the cultural house concept on the smaller, more familial units of *thôn* and *xóm*, but, as Vice Minister Đỗ Đức Dục noted, local cadres continued to perceive cultural houses as their own achievements rather than as structures created for the people.[37] General opinions about the project were mixed. Some cadres pointed to poor content and lack of trained cadres. Others argued that the scheme was fairly well developed, needing only further consolidation of its organization and leadership.[38]

Most of the specific reports, however, were unenthusiastic. The cultural office in Quảng Bình Province, for example, complained of the lack of cooperation among the Ministry of Culture, other ministries, and other components of the state apparatus, which made it extremely difficult for the province to fulfill its tasks. On the matter of cultural houses, Quảng Bình officials were forthright: "We see that the construction of [cultural houses] is not appropriate to our current situation in the countryside and that we need only generate a wide and deep cultural movement *without the necessity of a 'house.'*"[39]

The cultural house project was a failure in the highlands. In Việt Bắc, 270 houses were stipulated; only 21 were built, and of these only 2 were active. The situation was bad enough that cadres protested, asking that the highland areas' special conditions be taken into consideration in the planning process rather than imposing a simple replication of what was being done in the lowlands. A report by the Ministry of Culture's Department of Mass Culture assessing the cultural houses project's achievement at the end of 1956 was bleak.

> In general the national plan was essentially achieved but largely only in terms of form. Activities are very haphazard and content is poor. There are even localities that built cultural houses worth more than a million piastres, only to close them down, such as the cultural house of Vũ Lạc in Thái Bình Province and a cultural house in Sơn Tây in which buffaloes and cows were allowed to sleep. Some places become headquarters for administrative committees or for literacy work or public meeting places, as in Lạng Sơn. In Vĩnh Linh the cultural house was built, and then there was no one in charge so that books were scattered. . . . Where there are activities, they are mainly focused on books and newspapers, with the audience being mostly students and very few people from the working class.[40]

The 1958 Assessment of Cultural Activities

The turning point came in 1958. I discussed the Nhân Văn–Giai Phẩm dissenting period and the hard-line state response of 1958 in the last chapter. The year also marked the consolidation of state power over all social activities, and Nhân Văn–Giai Phẩm provided the state with a powerful rationale. According to the Party, enemies had taken advantage of the intellectuals' naïveté and it had to assume a leadership position. A nationwide criticism and self-criticism campaign, which engulfed all sectors of society, began in late 1957 and lasted throughout 1958. The campaign was designed to educate people about their dangerously misguided thoughts and behavior during the last ideological storm. The Ministry of Culture was no exception, and given its responsibilities it assumed a large share of the task of reimposing the Party's notions of stability and truth. In the process, its activities and its vision of cultural work also underwent a major transformation.

In 1958 the ministry presented an assessment of its work during its first three years. Three pages of the twenty-seven-page report listed the publication of many books, the establishment of libraries in cities and provincial towns, the organization of cultural clubs in factories and cultural houses in the countryside, the production of documentaries and contemporary films that were shown to large audiences, the organization and stabilization of a number of national performing troupes, and the establishment of performing groups at the local level. Nothing gave more credence to these achievements than the words of Uncle Hồ, quoted in the report: "The Ministry of Culture has made a notable contribution: the people's cultural life has been raised one level [and] harmful cultural vestiges of the old regime are slowly being eliminated. A new culture is being constructed."[41]

The rest of the document was reserved for criticism (*kiểm điểm*). The point emphasized repeatedly was that the ministry had not recognized that culture was a weapon in the class struggle and that its own awareness of revolutionary culture and the transitional period to socialism in the north was "vague" (*mơ hồ*). That the ministry was new to the task was acknowledged, but there was no emphasis on professionalism nor any mention of the conflict with propaganda work that had been the preoccupation of earlier reports. The ministry's deficiencies were internal, related specifically to its "lack of responsibility on the ideological front, particularly in the storm of the very complex literary and arts movement of the past period."[42]

The report contended that the ministry failed to see that culture was first and foremost a weapon in the ideological struggle. Rather than emphasizing the struggle against capitalist thoughts and the need for socialist education, the ministry had designated as its first responsibility developing "optimistic and healthy cultural activities in order to generate the inspiration for productivity and the political struggle." The consequence of this misguided emphasis was that "in the past three years our cultural work has been heavy on entertainment and light on ideological education . . . light on opposing old ideas, especially capitalist ones, and lacking in awareness in the face of those ideas' reemergence." Whatever achievements the ministry might have gained, therefore, were inadequate and less than exemplary. Progress was judged to be slow, seen as moving at "an ordinary pace not appropriate to the forceful changes of a revolutionary era, with the fierce class struggle of the transitional period."[43]

Even though the slogans "culture in the service of politics" and "culture in the service of the people," specifically *công nông binh* (workers, peasants, and soldiers), were in place from the beginning, the report went one step further, stressing that the two slogans must be intertwined. Therefore, in the report's formulation, to speak of culture in the service of politics was to speak simultaneously of culture in the service of workers, peasants, and soldiers and vice versa. Why was such a point necessary? The report defined the issue of serving politics as follows.

> Serving politics first of all means serving the regime, participating in the construction of the regime, and protecting it. Especially in the revolutionary transitional period leading to socialism, where currently a fierce and difficult struggle is being played out . . . between capitalism and socialism, between the old and the new, then the issue of protecting the regime is being put forth in an urgent manner.[44]

Not paying enough attention to either the construction of a new socialist state in terms of ideological education or maintaining vigilance against the constant attacks by feudalist and imperialist ideologies, the Ministry of Culture had missed this critical situation entirely. This ideological laxness had allowed the emergence of prerevolutionary plays, films, and literary works and the revival of village festivals, which interfered with production and marked the return of vices like gambling, excessive eating and drinking, and superstitious beliefs. The ministry was criticized for being too simple in its approach to the preservation of the country's cultural heritage, highlighting only the good aspects without attacking outdated, feudal features. Moreover, the ministry was seen as too permissive in its policy regarding the private businesses that dealt in cultural products like the publishing houses, printing presses, bookstores, and movie theaters. In short, the ministry's failure to contribute to the defense of the regime went hand in hand with its vague understanding of who should be its intended target and therefore what purpose should be informing its work. The ministry's primary task, the report reiterated, was to bring culture to the people, with the emphasis on education rather than entertainment.

The report went even further than this in two crucial ways. The first was its demand that the ministry must work to bring the masses to the point at which they would become producers of culture. This was seen as "connecting with the issue of generating a new intellectual class born from the rank and file of the working class (which goes hand in hand with the issue of reeducating old intellectuals in order to serve workers and peasants)." Second, the working class must be given the central role in everyday life as "the primary characters in the content of culture and artistic and literary creations (and perhaps even in scientific discoveries)."[45]

What it meant the working class's role in scientific discoveries to be is far from obvious, but otherwise the thrust of the report's assessments was clear. The state's survival was a clear-cut struggle between capitalism and socialism, and there were no options but to reiterate the role of the working class and bring it to the forefront of society, notions much talked about but not yet achieved. The report demanded: "Why are new topics and new content still lacking in cultural products and on the stage? Why is it that the images of workers, peasants, and soldiers, of the new people, of the heroes of our era, are still so vague in literature and art?"[46] The structural development in which the proletariat would ultimately become society's cultural producer thus entailed a greatly circumscribed boundary on creativity. The intellectual was relegated to the role of facilitator from one level of development to another within a specified framework, one in which creativity was an external imposition.

Other major issues were similarly defined and decided. On the matter of popularization (*phổ cập*) versus elevation (*đề cao*), the culture minister previously had emphasized the need to preserve the national heritage from neglect and destruction. The 1958 report, on the other hand, was adamant that popularization had to take precedence over elevation. Since the renewed emphasis was on the working class and its ultimate role as cultural producer and arbiter, elevation had to be based upon popularization rather than being treated as a simultaneous consideration. The primary focus had to be on popularization. Hence the tasks of researching and safeguarding the national cultural heritage had to be done within the context of an ideological struggle and in the service of the working class.

The root cause of the cultural cadres' inability to respond appropriately in the recent intellectual storm was perceived to be their lack of political clarity. Too much capitalist thinking continued to permeate the thoughts of many ministry cadres who functioned as teachers in the ministry's schools of the performing arts, not to mention the large number of performers in troupes that remained under private ownership. Political education was indeed important, but the report also pointed out that more professional training should take place so that cultural cadres could be more confident about their work. After all, it was partly this lack of self-assurance about their tasks that made cadres hesitate, being on the defensive when they should be taking the offensive in the face of "the attacks of the saboteur element, [that] which is composed mostly of intellectuals with a certain level of culture."[47]

In sum, what was perceived as the Ministry of Culture's basic weakness was twofold. On the one hand, its stand on class (*lập trường giai cấp*) was not firm, and on the other it was out of touch with reality. Class struggle was at the very heart of this view; there was no other option except constant vigilance against the enemy. The Nhân Văn–Giai Phẩm affair had, more than anything else, confirmed the truth of this view and served as a warning that the threat to the state was ever present: "The painful experience of a number of our cadres (including Party members) in the past period exemplifies that simple truth [of the class struggle]. That is a lesson we will have to remember for the rest of our lives."[48]

Socialist ideology now provided both the cause and effect of cultural activities. The construction of cultural houses was once again put forth as an example of how far removed the ministry was from the people's situation. Yet, although its general failure had been mentioned often in regional reports and the ministry's own assessments, the project continued. The fact that other socialist states pursued such an undertaking did help to sustain it in Vietnam in spite of its lackluster performance.

> It can be said that the construction of cultural houses in the countryside and clubs in factories and work units is an issue basic to the goodness of our system. All our brother countries have done it, and in the beginning they also could not avert the difficulties [afflicting] our country today.[49]

In this regard, according to the report, the failure of the project rested squarely upon the Ministry of Culture, which needed to base its activities on the people's capabilities and stick close to the people in order to understand their needs. This explained why some cultural houses were more successful than others. Success was also due to the Party leadership; where Party leadership was coherent and strong, the cultural house was well organized and well attended. Thus, it became imperative that cultural cadres not only accept Party leadership but must "actively seek the leadership" of the Party at all levels.[50]

The Ministry of Culture's 1958 Going-down-to-the-People Campaign

In response to the ideological crisis in the aftermath of the Nhân Văn–Giai Phẩm period and to its own lack of a firm sense of cultural work, the Ministry of Culture organized an ambitious going-down-to-the-people campaign in 1958. The concept of going down to the people was not new; it had been utilized in China and by the Việt Minh. During the anti-French resistance, wartime conditions forced Việt Minh cadres to be on the move constantly and merge with the population. Restlessness, however, had long characterized the intellectual community. In the decades before the August Revolution, many intellectuals constantly moved about the country to search for ways to make a living, to participate in the emerging national intellectual scene, and to escape colonial repression.[51]

When intellectuals began to join the Việt Minh in large numbers during the resistance, they were often sent to work in villages or joined a troop of soldiers in order to publicize their military exploits. Since the French controlled Hanoi and other major cities, the intellectuals scattered and moved with Việt Minh troops.[52] For the intellectuals, working alongside of the people was an indication of their commitment to the revolution and the ideal that all Vietnamese would take part in the new society. As for the state, the process of going down to the people was necessary to keep the intellectuals aware of the people's needs and to shape their intellectual production accordingly.

The Ministry of Culture embarked on a major going-down-to-the-people campaign in August and September 1958, with cultural cadres going to thirty-five different locations, from factories to state farms to villages in the delta and highland areas. Given the pessimistic appraisal of cultural work in 1958, the goal of the new campaign was twofold. On the one hand, manual labor would help cultural cadres to reassess their own ideological stands regarding the people and the state. On the other, it was clearly necessary for cultural cadres to have a better understanding of local conditions and what had been achieved to that point in order to plan cultural work more effectively in the future.

The preliminary summary report of the campaign painted a mixed picture of the countryside. The easing of state control in the aftermath of the rectification of land reform errors had led to the return of old social vices such as child marriages, polygamy, alcoholism, opium addiction, and the reemergence of prerevolutionary books and plays. Still trying to recover from land reform but already being organized into work teams and in some locales into cooperatives, the peasants were greatly ambivalent, fearing the total communalization of the fruit of their labors and its effects on social relations. The view of cooperativization and socialism as primitive communism seems to have been widespread. People were worried that under socialism they would be criticized all the time, forced to go to many meetings, and forced to live in communal housing where marriage had no meaning. The extreme level of accountability would mean that, according to an idea floating around a village in Ninh Bình, "no matter where you go you must bring your own rice. Father visiting his children would still have to bring along rice. As such, there would not be any emotional bond."[53] Peasants clearly saw that economic and social relations would be changed dramatically, and many feared that the small joys of life would disappear as well. Moreover, chaos in China had forced thousands of Chinese to flee to Vietnam, and in border areas such as Cao Bằng it was known that "once we reach socialism, like in China, meat, rice, and alcohol will all be rationed. No freedom to go out and drink."[54]

People's bitterness and anger at state policies can be glimpsed throughout the report. In some instances, deliberate destruction of machinery or antigovernment leaflets were discovered. In other instances, people's responses indicated a high level of skepticism in the aftermath of land reform and with the effort to subdue the fierce independence of the village world. As one man in the village of Xuân Huy, Phú Thọ Province, reportedly said, "Everything is said to be under the leadership of the Party. No one is in charge of the crab or the fish, but they are all alive." The black humor of underground dissent also surfaced in the cities. As the report indignantly recounted, "in the neighborhood of the East Gate (Hanoi) when we mobilized the people to get their photos taken for identity cards, they voiced the opinion that it was 'to resolve the stock of moldy film,' and when we mobilized people to get their identity cards they said that it was 'to jail people.'"[55] "They" were the enemies resurfacing, and these sentiments and incidents of outrage, anger, and distrust were disheartening to the cultural cadres in their first efforts to understand the masses.

The final summary report of the first wave of the going-down-to-the-people campaign, written by the Vice Minister Cù Huy Cận, took a very different view of the weakness of cultural work, however. Cù Huy Cận's report painted a much more optimistic picture of the country in general.

> In summary, through the reflection of the thirty-five groups, we see clearly that our people in the north are in an optimistic mood, moving toward the construction of socialism. It is clear that the general situation grows brighter day by day, although

there are still many difficulties to overcome. The people see clearer everyday the good nature of our regime, supporting and energetically building socialism. The faith of the people in the Party, the government, and Chairman Hồ in the recent period has only increased with the good progress of the rectification of land errors, with the successful leadership of production. This situation signals a powerful transition in the north as we move toward the construction of socialism.[56]

The low-key, no-nonsense style of the preliminary report had disappeared, replaced with a breathless statement about socialism, the movement toward socialism, faith in the Party, and the brightness and clarity of views. The ideological emphasis in Cù Huy Cận's report contrasted sharply with the Minister of Culture Hoàng Minh Giám's report, detailed earlier. Even the "they" who represented the enemies became sharper and more monolithic in Cù Huy Cận's report: "they" worked with a unified plan to undermine the state by focusing on the people's doubts and the state's mistakes, "having no small effect on the people's thinking, especially in the Catholic areas, areas that were under French colonial control, in the border areas, and in the intermediate classes in the cities."[57]

The primary struggle in the north was presented as one between capitalism and socialism, which explained the opposition to nationalization of the private sector in the cities and the rich peasants' resistance to cooperativization in the countryside. In Cù Huy Cận's view, these kinds of opposition were worrisome but less important than the fact that for cooperativization to truly succeed two problems must be overcome: the conflict within the peasants between private and communal needs and their conservatism regarding technological change. The situation facing the country therefore concerned both a class struggle and a dramatic change in economic relations. Cultural work, in this view, could focus on only two issues: "what cultural work had done to defend socialism, defend the people's thoughts against the attacks of the enemies" and the fact that "cultural work at this time has very little connection to the task of educating [the people] about socialism and pushing for more production."[58]

Cù Huy Cận, one of the youngest stars of the New Poetry movement of the early 1940s, now speaking as the vice minister of the Ministry of Culture, had nothing to say about cultural work outside of what was primarily propaganda. He insisted that "production is the main front today in the north" and as such, unless cultural work dealt specifically with matters of production, it was not working toward the primary goal of the socialist revolution. For the performing troupes, for example, the issue came down to the question of "what kind of act [would] mobilize production, encourage technological reform, motivate [people to buy the state-produced] plough number 51, or inspire workers in the weaving factories to use more machines."[59] On a higher level, cultural work was closely connected to regime maintenance, and it was up to cultural cadres to institute measures that would counter the enemies' pernicious influence. For example, they should destroy reactionary reading materials while guiding the people more firmly and concretely in the content of songs, plays, and other activities in the cultural houses. The new content, however, must take into consideration the people's level of interest so as to ensure continued cultural activities long after the cadres were gone.

Whereas the preliminary summary report had stressed the objective difficulty of organization and leadership faced by the cultural cadres, Cù Huy Cận's final report emphasized the internal weakness of the cultural cadres themselves, from top to bottom. They did not understand the responsibility of cultural work in the socialist revolution, neglected the class struggle, and therefore neglected production. Second, the style of work of the Ministry of Culture had become bureaucratic and distant from the people. Therefore, the report concluded, in order to "resolve the issue of work methods" and "continue thought reform,"

> in the period ahead our cultural branch must assemble our forces to participate in manual work, join the masses, live within a number of key localities, motivate the people to work on their own cultural future under the firm leadership of the Party, and from those localities open up the movement in a stable way, moving to coordinate with the relevant branches in bringing the cultural revolution to the people.[60]

A second, even more ambitious going-down-to-the-people campaign began in late 1958 with four specific goals: (1) to reeducate the cadres in terms of class ideology and to encourage the habit of working side by side with the people; (2) to learn about and understand the people's cultural level, capabilities, and needs; (3) to check the ministry's work at all levels of the administrative apparatus and its working relationship with other mass organizations; and (4) to start the planning process for cultural work in 1959.[61]

The actual reports from the campaign, however, indicated that what the cultural cadres carried out was essentially a survey of the country's political, economic, social, and cultural conditions, testifying to the state's insecurity in the aftermath of land reform and the Nhân Văn–Giai Phẩm period. Cadres were supposed to investigate the ideological development of all sectors of society, from workers to students, locating the ideological factors specific to that group, which would indicate the extent of their loyalty to the state and the Party and in turn would aid or hinder production and the progress toward socialism. In addition, cadres were to assess the enemy's activities and what had been done to counter them. They would also investigate the economic situation after land reform, the ways in which government policies and Party directives had been executed, and, finally, the local area's social situation.[62]

The ideological education campaign was a national endeavor. After having gone through criticism and self-criticism sessions designed to address the ills of the Nhân Văn–Giai Phẩm period, intellectuals were sent to a number of places, from cooperatives to factories to highland villages, in August 1958.[63] In late 1958 members of national performing troupes spent some four months and students more than a month in the countryside participating in the people's work as well as performing, organizing exhibits, and teaching literacy courses. The campaign was carried out in two waves, with preparatory background work being done in the first so that cultural cadres could attempt to introduce activities tailored to local needs in the second. All in all, 155 cultural cadres, 300 performing artists, and more than 60 intellectuals in all disciplines were sent in the first wave. More than 200 cultural cadres, 350 students from the performing arts school under the direct control of the Ministry of Culture, and 65 intellectuals were dispatched in the second wave.[64]

The results of the fact-finding first wave were presented in a report by the culture vice minister, Cù Huy Cận.[65] It indicated that the state's policy continued to move in the direction of rapid cooperativization through the intermediate step of organizing peasants into work brigades (*tổ đội công*). It should be noted that work brigades were formed early in some areas but were greatly affected by land reform. Cận's report showed that by November 1958 the percentage of people in work brigades ranged from 60 to 90 percent in different communes. The report hoped that by the end of 1958 there would be more than four hundred cooperatives in operation, almost twice the number envisioned by the state.

The report also indicated a high level of resistance to the cooperativization effort. In the cities, efforts to resist state control could easily be attributed to the capitalist class, but in the countryside the class division of rich, middle, and poor peasants did little to explain the general reluctance to join cooperatives. Instances were noted in which rich and middle peasants had joined together to form work brigades rather than laboring with poorer peasants, but the report also noted other instances in which "a family joined and left the cooperative three or four times, [and there is] a cooperative of fourteen families in which twelve families of poor peasants left the cooperative once."[66]

Throughout the north, the conflict between the private and the communal continued. As the report recognized, this was partly a matter of overcoming the peasants' and workers' conservative nature when it came to technological change. The report complained that while peasants did work hard they did not understand the socialist work ethic since they "did not see that labor is glorious, did not fully recognize the worth of their labor so that the habit of active labor has not been entirely liberated."[67]

In terms of cultural work, the report underscored the need to structure cultural activities in a way that would meet the people's needs and capabilities so that such activities could be maintained without the cadres. It noted the ministry's weak organizational structure at local levels but with a noticeable change in tone. In previous reports and documents, the ministry had been more likely to indicate its helplessness due to neglect on the part of local Party leaders. Cù Huy Cận's report, however, took a different tack, arguing that cultural cadres, many of whom were also Party members, should take the main responsibility for the slow progress in cultural work thus far. He contended that "in comparing [the current situation] to the first experience of going to the localities, we see that the primary cause is still our ideology and behavior, from the ministry down to the provincial office and the cadres in charge of building the cultural movement in the villages and factories." The ministry was therefore reasserting control over its domain along harder socialist lines.[68]

The gist of the matter was ideology. The ministry had admitted that its weakness had been the lack of emphasis on culture as a weapon in the class struggle. It was not sufficient that cadres promote cultural activities and intellectuals produce their works with the people's needs and desires in mind. The people themselves must undergo an "ideological liberation" (*giải phóng tư tưởng*) to contribute to the overall vigilance against the enemy's constant subversive attacks, which could take many forms. In order to truly put the house in order, a much more thorough cleaning would be needed.

> Concerning the people in the coastal and ethnic minority areas, [we] must move them to liberate themselves from the idea of dependence on nature; [we] must, through the drive for techno-logical change, reinforce the people's belief in their own strength, in their own creative work. With regard to all the working people, [we] must motivate them to liberate themselves ideologically in terms of technology, destroy conservative ideas in order to bravely assimilate new techniques, and boldly introduce techni-cal innovations and improvements. With people in all areas, [we] must prompt them to liberate themselves from the ties of out-moded cultural vestiges, from the enslaving and degenerate feu-dal culture, from the influence of capitalist ideology.[69]

Only an ideological revolution could accomplish all this. Destroy-ing old beliefs while inculcating new ideas, cultural work had to gener-ate an unending, active enthusiasm in which love of country and socialism were tightly woven. The Ministry of Culture's immediate task was to begin the larger going-down-to-the-people campaign in order to acquire accurate data on a number of key localities. In these areas, the ministry's cadres would help the people to accomplish their own ideological liberation, at which point the ministry would open the process up to a cultural revolution with the cooperation of other government branches. On a practical level, this cultural revolution was to be conducted in tandem with the state's emphasis on increased production.

Wave two of the campaign included three steps. The first lasted roughly from November to December 1958, the second until Febru-ary 1959, and the third until June 1959. Each phase was specifically designed to mesh cultural work with the needs of the agricultural calendar. Cultural cadres first would take stock of economic, politi-cal, cultural, and social conditions in their specific localities, although reports prepared in the first wave would have provided them with some prior knowledge. Once the main physical, organizational, and ideological characteristics of an area had been assessed, the cadres could examine existing cultural activities and determine what needed to be done or revised to meet production needs. Teams of cultural cadres fanned out to many localities and covered all the different types of economic production units, from cooperatives to state farms, factories, and mines.

The reports that came back were very detailed. Geographical and population descriptions were provided, along with an assessment of the political situation before and after 1954 and the existing status of Party organization. A view of the post-land-reform countryside emerged. The extent of the wrongs committed in the name of land reform could be gauged using some simple recorded data. The rectification of land reform mistakes sought to reclassify those whose class backgrounds had been wrongly determined during land reform. In some instances, the number of landowners decreased by more than half.[70] Not surprisingly, in places where the extent of land reform upheaval was high, the Party structure suffered more. The reports also indicated that a large proportion of Party members had been inducted during land reform.

Party members recruited during land reform were mostly poor peasants. The fact that cultural work at the local level was executed by barely literate cadres meant that directives concerning cultural activities and other social projects often did not reach the people. As one report commented, "in general most of the intentions (*chủ trương*) and policies fell away by the time they reached the public because many of the cadres in the *xã* went to meetings but did not take notes and then came back to the *xóm* having little time to publicize so that the meaning and purpose of the issue were little known."[71]

These reports further indicated that the effort to persuade peasants to join work brigades (*tổ đội công*) prior to moving them into cooperatives had met much resistance. A report from Kiên An Province noted that the work brigade movement was started in 1955 through much hard work by cadres. By the end of 1955, for example, the *xã* of Hưng Tiến had forty-four work brigades comprised of 394 families. In 1956, during land reform, the number had increased to fifty-nine work brigades with 447 families.[72] Land reform proved to be devastating, however, and the report noted that "after land reform, the work brigade movement was only a shell." Rectification of land reform mistakes managed to maintain twenty-two brigades.[73] Under the circumstances, the move to form cooperatives would hardly be received with enthusiasm by the people. The cultural cadres noted that the main concern among the people was the fear of loss of profits, and one report was careful to stress that "the worry over loss [of profits] is an issue that [we] must persevere in resolving. It appears in many aspects and at any time; it is caused by very detailed calculations [by the people]."[74]

On the social and cultural side, the reports were very specific in detailing Buddhist and Catholic activities. There were also descriptions of the extent of belief in superstitions, vices such as drinking and gambling, outdated practices of marrying too early and demanding high brideprices, and assessments of the educational and health care situations as well as the state of existing cultural activities. In general, the reports noted that the organizational structure at the local level was too weak for them to carry out all the decreed cultural and social policies. Party members' understanding of policy goals was often too vague to make much headway in resolving numerous popular concerns about cooperatives. Furthermore, there continued to be lack of support for cultural work among provincial Party leaders. As for the reported enemies' activities, they were generally expressions of dissatisfaction rather than true subversive acts.[75] On the whole, the countryside seems to have been well under the control of the state.

In general, there were two recurring characteristics in these reports. One focused on the mediocre quality of cadres at the local level.

> In general cadres and Party members come from poor peasant backgrounds [while] our propaganda and education about socialism are weak [and not in accordance with] reality. Political and cultural levels are very low. . . . Due to their weak understanding of socialism, many comrades are not enthusiastically building work brigades and cooperatives. The unifying spirit within and outside the Party is weak, making it difficult for socialist reform to occur in the countryside.[76]

The second characteristic had to do with the devastating effects of land reform on the countryside, the consequences of which continued to be felt in many areas. Party structure was greatly weakened, making it difficult after land reform to carry out Party and state directives. In Kiến An Province, for example,

> the mistakes of land reform were prolonged. During that period many cadres were wrongly classified: three Party members were wrongly classified as rich peasants, six Party members were said to be members of the Nationalist Party . . . [and] thirteen Party members were expelled. Party organization and all the mass organizations are currently still weak, [and] activities have not returned to normal. . . . There are situations in which Party cad-

res who are middle peasants attack other cadres who are poor peasants. . . . Deeply conflicting aspects exist.[77]

In terms of actual cultural work, the cultural house project continued to be pursued, even as general failure was reported.[78] Cultural cadres spent much of their time reorganizing performing groups, sometimes expelling those deemed to be politically impure. They taught youngsters songs and organized cultural events aimed at increasing agricultural production. In addition, they established Committees to Wage a New Life (Ban Vận Động Nếp Sống Mới), designed to persuade peasants to relinquish old practices and outdated traditions. Such a committee would include local cadres, members of mass organizations, and a number of elder members of the biggest clans in the area. The main goal seemed to have been to prevent the practice of feasting at weddings and funerals and the reemergence of superstitious beliefs.[79]

In the end, the heavy agenda assigned to cadres in the 1958 going-down-to-the-people campaign and the long period of time required for it proved to be too much. Many reports indicated a conflict between the propaganda task (promotion of production and cooperativization) and the professional task (the nuts and bolts of organizing cultural houses, cultural activities, etc.) as time wore on. Cultural cadres were supposed to watch themselves and each other be transformed ideologically by the experience while at the same time carrying out a substantial agenda that demanded much more than their expertise in cultural work. In various reports, cadres voiced their fear of being disconnected professionally from their work back in the national offices and their concern with being away from their families for months in the provinces.

One report submitted to the Ministry's Department of Publication after four months of work in the province of Thái Bình was particularly frank: "Experience tells us that from now on we should not combine the two demands of doing labor in order to consolidate and reeducate thoughts and attempting cultural work in order to gain experience."[80] The report argued that for cultural work to be successful, cadres must be knowledgeable, politically reliable, and experienced from the start. There was no need for them to engage in labor in order to consolidate their ideological commitments. In short, the two tasks were important but should not be regarded as equal or be carried out simultaneously. It was, in effect, a rebuttal to the whole campaign's ambitious intentions.

In general, the appearance of cadres and intellectuals in the villages provided a genuine boost, instilling a sense that the state and the Party cared about the people. The experience also helped cadres and intellectuals become more aware of the peasants' situation. The harmonious view of socialism that cadres and intellectuals alike had to present to the people, however, often clashed with the harsh rural conditions they encountered. The insistence that going-down-to-the-people campaigns would reinforce the intellectuals' belief in socialism never quite achieved the goal. On the one hand, a few months of hard labor became a distant memory once a cadre or intellectual returned to his or her desk in the city. Over time, these trips came to be viewed as an obligatory component of the job, without the ideological implications with which they were imbued. On the other hand, the constant reminder of the discrepancy between reality and the idealized vision of socialism turned many intellectuals increasingly cynical toward the state in the long run. In this regard, the going-down-to-the-people concept may have had the opposite effect to what was intended.

Other Activities in 1958

The tighter state control over cultural activities in 1958 was evident. I discussed in chapter 4 how the state reined in and reorganized the intellectual community in the aftermath of the Nhân Văn–Giai Phẩm period. In particular, under the Ministry of Culture's administration, private publishing was phased out altogether. The ministry, moreover, was interested in curtailing all private cultural activities. To this end, by 1958, it had amassed detailed reports on private businesses operating in the areas it considered relevant: publishing; printing; distribution; film showing; photography; the arts; schools teaching music, painting, and crafts; painting for advertisements, portraits, and art; sculpture; making pins; toy making; street singing; and various kinds of fortune-telling. Of these, the main focus was on publishing, printing, distribution, film showing, and photography.[81] The goal was to nationalize these industries by controlling their business potential and needs and the growth of the industries as a whole. Private publishing houses and printing presses flourished between 1955 and 1957 since the state continued to need them, but the state's inhibiting approach was encapsulated in the slogan applied to these private enterprises: "utilize, restrict, reform" (*sử dụng, hạn chế, cải tạo*).[82]

By 1959, all private publishing houses had been eliminated. The state would have moved against them sooner if not for the fact that the continued existence of private publishing in the north was also seen as serving a political need in the propaganda war with the south.[83] Nhân Văn–Giai Phẩm, however, hastened the death of the private publishing industry. The other, less sensitive industries would take a few years longer to be nationalized. All in all, by 1966 a firm structure had emerged within the Ministry's Department of Publication to deal with control over the content of published materials. Of the nine committees dealing variously with the technical, financial, and organizational concerns of the publishing branch, one committee (tổ kế hoạch đề tài) set guidelines for topics considered to be important and assessed the books before they were published while another (tổ kiểm tra sách) examined all published books to make sure that no problematic volume slipped through. All the national publishing houses were under the Ministry of Culture's control by this time and were guided by this structure of planning and censorship. Books printed locally were submitted to the local party committees for approval.

The same strategy of "utilize, restrict, reform" was used with regard to the private theater troupes. The number of troupes was kept low; in 1957, there were thirty-one and in 1958, twenty-five. The ministry then tightened its control over the content of the plays these troupes could perform. By 1960, it was reported that these troupes had to have at least twenty plays in their repertoire, with a third of them "having topics reflecting the current activities and struggle" and another third composed of "[theatrical] acts that have been modified and transformed."[84]

Private theater troupes eventually disappeared altogether, but the ministry went one step further by ensuring that the performing arts would be under its firm control. The ministry operated a number of "creative camps" (trại sáng tác), bringing together promising playwrights for a short period in which they would be given some training, guidance in the proper topics, and toward the end communal criticism of their works. The report of one such camp in late 1958 tells us that "all the proposals of the seven playwrights were fundamentally broken down and constructively criticized by everyone" and "all the plays went through the whole camp twice, and from the initial proposal to the completion of a play the author must go through seven or eight revisions and also through the cadre in charge of the camp seven or eight times." Through these discussions and revisions, the budding playwrights learned to put primary importance on the ideological purpose of a play and that the rights and wrongs of laughter and tears depended on the author's class viewpoint. The participants concluded that there were three types of laughter, which all had their own class character: (1) "natural and happy laughter during regular activity," (2) ideological laughter over outdated behavior, and (3) laughter directed against the enemies. In short, "the comrades assess that the cause of the deficiencies and mistakes thus far in the writing process is immature thought, [class] standpoint, and political level. In addition, the authors are removed from the reality of the people's activity and their cultural levels are low." If at the end of camp time the cowed young playwrights came to the conclusion that "the community is clear-minded and mass creativity is an effective guide that can shorten the time and still achieve better results than working on one's own," they had come a long way toward achieving self-censorship.

The ministry also operated its own performing art and training schools. By 1963, it had established a total of eleven schools. At the college level, there were schools of art, music, library methods, and publishing. At the secondary level, there were schools in art, theater, dance, music, crafts, cinema, and professional training for cultural work.

The tumultuous early years of the Ministry of Culture between 1955 and 1958 provide us with a glimpse of the conflicting drama inherent in the ministry's effort to establish its organizational structure and define its purpose. The ministry's vision of a socialist cultural revolution was relatively benign in the beginning. Hampered by the devastating effects of land reform on the administrative machinery of the state and by the cadres' low level of understanding of cultural work, the ministry nevertheless pushed forward with the rudimentary tasks of cultural work by focusing on literacy courses, health education, libraries, exhibits, films, and live performances in both the cities and the countryside. Where the ministry tried to do more, as in the case of the cultural house project, it failed because it was imposing a socialist framework on the countryside without much of a basis on which to build. On the other hand, the ministry's lack of emphasis on the class struggle and the ensuing changes in economic relations in the countryside would not be tolerated in the aftermath of the Nhân Văn–Giai Phẩm period and given the state's insistence on moving rapidly toward socialism.

The ideological nature of cultural work would undergo a profound reorientation in 1958. Moving firmly to consolidate state power now

that land reform had been achieved, private enterprises were nationalized while cooperativization was the next stage to be implemented in
the countryside. In all of this, the Ministry of Culture had to play a
decisive role, and increasingly the political nature of cultural work
became dominant. Cultural work now had two main purposes: to
defend the regime and motivate production. Tight ideological control
over all cultural activities was absolutely necessary, and the ministry
projected its authority over publishing, the writing of plays, and the
education of the performers of the new songs, dances, and plays.
Workers, peasants, and soldiers were the main characters of cultural
productions, and from consumers of culture they must eventually be
raised to the level of its producers. Class background was to be the
determining factor in choosing key cadres, selecting students, and
deciding which kind of laughter a character in a play should have.
Popular culture, as defined by the state, became increasingly removed
from the popular culture of the countryside, and the gains in social,
political, and gender equality came at the cost of undermining the
complex fabric of village life.

The intense politicization of cultural work would have been less
problematic if it were not for the fact that cultural work continued to
include tasks that demanded a high level of professional training. The
conflict between professionalism and politics, which also plagued the
universities and research institutes, would trouble the ministry for
many years to come. On the issue of personnel, for example, a 1961
document from the ministry noted that "due to insufficient con-
ceputalization and realization, the task of organizing [the appropriate]
cadres for personnel work and other tasks is still simplistic; [the indi-
vidual] must have a firm ideological grounding, but otherwise it does
not matter whether he has any professional knowledge."[85] The reality
of cultural work, however, gave rise constantly to the observation that
a certain level of education and professional training was necessary in
a cultural cadre. In a lengthy fact-gathering mission in the provinces
of Vĩnh Phúc and Phú Thọ, the team from the Ministry of Culture
noted that

> the majority of the [cultural] cadres have been active for a long
> time, have a certain political level and experience in mobiliz-
> ing the masses, but their cultural and professional levels are
> weak. Cultural cadres of district Yên Lạc (Vĩnh Phúc) have not
> finished level 1 [comparable to the fourth grade.] Leading cadres
> of the provincial cultural office of Vĩnh Phúc tried very hard, and

up to now many have finished level 2 (complementary education) [comparable to the seventh grade]. Many cadres have not
been trained in basic theory and about the profession in a systematic manner, whether in the regular schools of the province or of
the ministry.[86]

The advent of the war against the United States in 1965 further expanded the cultural apparatus, and by 1970 there were again complaints that political standards were not being met.[87]

The dilemma was also reflected in another conflict, often voiced as
that between content and form. The overwhelming emphasis on politically correct content overshadowed artistic creativity, and this in turn
produced cultural works that drew no audiences. Thus, the ministry
constantly found that "literary and artistic activities still function at
the level of disseminating information or superficially stimulating
rather than going deeper into the art, emotionally persuasive."[88] The
kind of cultural performances and products produced by the localities, for example, were judged to be correct ideologically but were not
embraced by the people because their artistic quality was weak, which
in turn limited their popular appeal and educational value. Wall newspapers, a popular form of mass participation in cultural production in
the eyes of the state, were produced in large quantities, but no one
read them because "the content is poor and the form is not attractive."[89] In such a situation, the envisioned cultural club as a focal
point for ideologically uplifting cultural activities in the factory had
become just a place where meetings were held or where news was
disseminated.[90]

The ministry had tried to attack the problem at its roots by taking
over the education of those who would become the performers of new
songs, dances, and plays. They would be politically reliable and unencumbered by the bourgeois notions of intellectual freedom and individual creativity that had proved to be very resilient in the Nhân Văn–
Giai Phẩm period. They would also be chosen from the working class
and would be committed to the vision of a socialist state in which they
would play an exalted role. The effort to generate a new intellectual
class went beyond the Ministry of Culture to the heart of the nation's
educational system, the subject of the next chapter.

— 6 —

Education and the New
Intellectual Stratum

Although many intellectuals endured great hardships in joining the resistance and played an important role in various capacities as journalists and propaganda artists, they were often viewed by the Party leadership as undisciplined and difficult to control given their colonial education and their participation in the prerevolutionary environment. As early as 1951 there was a voice within the Party extremely disdainful of Vietnamese intellectuals' supposed achievements in comparison with their Soviet and Chinese counterparts and skeptical as to whether they could ever truly rid themselves of their petit bourgeois mentality to become the intellectuals of the socialist state.[1] Such a voice, therefore, was also forceful in arguing that the Party must now take the lead in the relationship with intellectuals rather than maintaining the more conciliatory stance once necessary to garner their support. Until the old intellectuals were fully reformed, a great effort must be made to locate talents from among the masses who would be nurtured to become members of the new intellectual stratum, ideologically clear about their role in society and unencumbered by such ideas as individual rights and creative freedom.

The desire to generate a new intellectual stratum was therefore very much connected to a general distrust of older intellectuals who had been educated in the Franco-Vietnamese system. As was discussed in chapter 2, colonial education in Vietnam was a confusing mix of traditional and colonial schools at the lower levels and highly elitist at the higher levels. Vietnamese who had full access to a secondary education were considered to be the cream of the society. Their number was minuscule. Given that many of the first generation of communist revolutionaries were former teachers, including Hồ Chí Minh, Võ Nguyên Giáp, Trường Chinh, and Phạm Văn Đồng, much attention was paid to the issue of education. Decades of clandestine work and the experience of maintaining Party discipline and organization in colonial prisons prior to 1945 had underlined further the importance of methods of transmitting the revolutionary message, of which education was a natural conductor. With the seizure of power in 1945, an educational system that was Vietnamese, popular, and capable of producing a new socialist intelligentsia was finally possible.

More specifically, *education* also came to be defined as "cultural level" (*trình độ văn hóa*). Even in today's Vietnam, a reference to someone's cultural level is most likely a reference to the level of education attained by the individual and nothing more. As with cultural work, detailed in the last chapter, education is being reduced to concrete statistical achievements. Yet at the same time the insistence in defining so many aspects of daily life as cultural achievements also indicated an exalted view of culture, one that could be constructed in the new socialist state. Critical in the establishment and consolidation of the new culture, education would further generate an intelligentsia from the people that would be commensurate with the new era.

Working primarily with archival data from the files of the Ministry of Education, I will examine the development of the educational system in North Vietnam between 1945 and 1965, its underlying goals and structure, its achievements, and its failures. As in the cultural arena, the political emphasis in the educational sector deepened in 1953 with the beginning of land reform. The achievement of peace in 1954 and a socialist state in North Vietnam allowed the educational system to grow in a much more explicitly socialist direction, and the dangerous effects of the dissenting Nhân Văn–Giai Phẩm period on students and teachers in 1957 only reaffirmed the correctness of the socialist agenda and the need for political education. Most notable in this regard was the dominance of class criteria in the selection process for higher education and the development of a program, called Worker-Peasant Complementary Education (Bổ Túc Văn Hóa Công Nông), aimed at the rapid emergence of a new worker-peasant intellectual stratum. Ideologically motivated and utilitarian, the ambitious new system quickly came into conflict with the more moderate desire to construct a worthy national educational system, popular but not at the expense of intellectual promise, which needed nurturing above all. The inherent dilemma faced by the educational system in these early years, exemplified in the distinction between quality and quantity, between a general education and a highly specialized one, and between political criteria and more academic standards, would continue to plague its development in the decades to come.

Education during the Resistance Period

The backbone of the educational effort in these early years was the Việt Minh's literacy campaign. The seriousness of the effort was mirrored in the slogan of the time: "Fighting against famine, fighting against illiteracy, fighting against foreign aggression." Displaying admirable spirit, such a slogan also showed the basic nature of the problems confronting the Việt Minh in 1946. Not only was an anticolonial, national independence struggle being waged, but food had to be secured for a population that had seen somewhere between one and two million dead in the horrific famine of 1945.[2] Hunger was physical, but hunger was also spiritual: 90 to 95 percent of the population was believed to be illiterate.

The mass education movement conducted in various forms by Vietnamese literati since the turn of the century had always carried an ideological component, namely, to counteract the Westernization embodied in colonial education and to reassert a sense of Vietnameseness. Such efforts reached only a small number of Vietnamese, but the new ground they broke served as the foundation for the Việt Minh's own endeavor. Given the wide network of cadres in the countryside, the Việt Minh's mass education movement helped to coalesce the community around the goals and demands of the resistance. The seizure and expansion of the mass education movement provided the Việt Minh with a structure in which to try to control and bolster food production and establish its political agenda at the most basic level of the population. In these early years, education could only be driven by political needs.

The beginning of the anticolonial resistance in December 1946 halted the Việt Minh's educational effort, but the Party quickly moved to reestablish literacy classes in 1947 in areas under its control. The slogans for education, such as "Each mass education class is a propaganda cell for the resistance" and "Each mass education teacher is a member of the resistance's propaganda committee," explicitly linked literacy with propaganda. The content of the literacy courses was geared toward the resistance, transmitting a newly constructed vocabulary of the revolution.

Many terms and topics of the resistance were brought into reading lessons at the elementary level. Mass education teachers taught words and also disseminated news and work goals of the localities such as support for "the soldiers' winter," "rice vats to feed the soldiers," and reported victories at Sông Lô and Là

Ngà. . . . Wherever the mass education movement was strong, the resistance's propaganda work was also pushed further.[3]

Given the wartime situation and the importance placed on the propaganda dimension of education, the emphasis during these early years was primarily on mass education. The number of literacy classes could grow quickly because minimum requirements were small. The vast effort needed many teachers in widely dispersed areas, and although the Ministry of Education provided trained teachers for important localities, mass education relied primarily on local initiatives to secure funds and teachers. Most of those involved in the mass education movement had only a limited elementary or secondary education, and in many instances they were barely literate themselves.[4]

The localized nature of education was the case with general education as well. The number of elementary and secondary schools grew, but they could not cope with the large number of students. Private schools came into existence, and schools run by the Catholic Church existed throughout the resistance period. In the second half of the resistance period, many localities set up their own schools. Referred to as "people-founded" (*dân lập*) schools, they were funded by the people themselves, from the construction of buildings to salaries for the teachers but with curriculums provided by the Ministry of Education. A number of private schools were eventually seminationalized in this way.

The educational system, therefore, was a localized and voluntary affair. The Ministry of Education provided a measure of overall direction, but given the difficult wartime situation it had to rely on local initiatives. Higher education was entirely staffed by intellectuals, who held classes where the students congregated. In areas of basic needs for the resistance, such as medicine and agriculture, classes were held aiming to provide as many technical cadres as possible so as to raise the level of self-sufficiency in food production and health care, especially for the soldiers at the front. In the creative arena, art and writing classes were conducted by well-known names in the intellectual firmament, but they were organized on a voluntary basis and without much guidance from the Ministry of Education. In 1949, the total number of cadres in the ministry was 118, with only 3 assigned specifically to the University Department (Nha Đại Học Vụ).[5]

As the resistance continued, a much more systematic approach to the development of the educational system was deemed necessary to better respond to the needs of the resistance and lay the foundation of the educational system in peacetime. The 1950 educational reforms sought to reshape both the content and the structure of the educational system. A nine-year school system replaced the colonial twelve-year system, with four years of level 1 (primary), three years of level 2 (lower secondary), and two years of level 3 (upper secondary). It was from the upper secondary level that the Việt Minh hoped to draw the required number of technical cadres. The urgent needs of the resistance coupled with the small number of existing colleges and university-level courses led to the development of a number of elementary and secondary vocational schools in pedagogy, medicine, agriculture, silviculture, communications, and public works.[6] Early specialization meant very short, specifically defined courses of study, and the vocational schools came under the guidance of the relevant ministries while the Ministry of Education "only has the responsibility to coordinate with the other ministries in order to provide leadership in terms of policy and direction and to unify organization."[7] While this development of a polytechnical emphasis and a ministry-controlled vocational system was not new, having been developed in the Soviet Union and adopted by other socialist countries such as China, it served a natural function for the Việt Minh during the resistance period.[8]

The academic track was maintained with the opening of the College Preparatory School (Dự Bị Đại Học) in Thanh Hóa in 1951, which had only two faculties, literature and science. The two-year program it offered was meant to provide an interim education for students who had finished the general secondary level, preparing them for the universities once those were established in peacetime. Only one college preparatory year was offered in the end, but the small number of students who did attend the College Preparatory School would become the first and most prominent generation of teachers and researchers when national universities and institutes were established after 1954.

The goal of education was also specified in the educational reforms of 1950: to train "'future working citizens' who would be loyal to the people's democratic regime and have all the quality and capability necessary to serve the resistance and the people."[9] The language reflected the political mode of the national front strategy that was in effect, but a more sharply defined political view was already expected of students and teachers alike. Political education was introduced into the system, along with the history of the Vietnamese revolution and the literature of the revolution and the resistance. Also beginning in 1950, all teachers and students took the first classes in criticism and self-criticism, which were aimed at dispelling the prevailing notion that education was neutral and presenting clearly the ideological motivations expected of teachers in the new educational system.

Under extremely difficult conditions, an educational system did emerge. The number of students grew quickly, and, although the number of teachers also grew, it was small and could not accommodate much growth.[10] The foundation for the network of pedagogical schools also was laid in 1950. Pedagogical schools were especially important because the lack of teachers had meant that instructors from the old school system had to be retained, and the conflict between need and political purity was inherent in the educational system from the beginning. With land reform beginning in 1953, the issue of ideology became even more important, and during this period "the educational branch considered rectification for teachers *its number one priority*, mobilizing all teachers and cadres to participate voluntarily in order to train themselves in the revolutionary standpoint and the class outlook."[11] Much attention also was paid to the training of teachers. Of the schools that were established in southern China in the second half of the resistance period, most were devoted to the training of future teachers. The students sent there were considered to be the most politically reliable; many were children of longtime cadres. Teaching materials were primarily Soviet or Chinese sources translated into Vietnamese.[12]

Although the educational system became increasingly politicized as the anti-French resistance was reaching its climax, prior to 1954 it did not mean the exclusion of students based on class background. The situation did become more stark by 1953, after the introduction of criticism and self-criticism sessions and the beginning of land reform, but the national front emphasis at the time meant that children of peasants, workers, and traders as well as petit bourgeois and landowning families that had supported the Việt Minh all intermingled in the school system. The elite nature of the College Preparatory School students was particularly notable. Cao Xuân Hạo (the son of the progressive mandarin Cao Xuân Huy), Phan Kế Hoành (the son of Viceroy Phan Kế Toại), and Phan Huy Lê (a member of the famous lineage of Phan Huy) were all students there. Overall, a more ideological line was emphasized with land reform toward the end of the resistance period, but class was not yet a determining factor in educational opportunities. In addition, while the educational system was extremely aware of the needs of the resistance, it continued to maintain a fairly academic course of study, especially at the higher levels.

The Ideological Foundation of the Post-1954 Educational System

With the Việt Minh victory in 1954, the new socialist state finally was able to pursue the development of a socialist educational system. Unified ideological control over the cultural and educational sectors was heightened by the fact that Trường Chinh, the main architect of the Việt Minh's cultural and intellectual policy, was also deeply involved in the structure of the new educational system. In 1947–48, creative intellectuals read his "Marxism and the Issue of Vietnamese Culture," and the document was assigned to all teachers and educational cadres as a fundamental theoretical exposition on the nature of the new educational system.[13] In his capacity as the general secretary of the Party, Trường Chinh also held forth on widely varied aspects of education, from kindergarten to mass education.[14]

Just as Lenin and Mao had played large roles in the development of the educational systems in the Soviet Union and China, Hồ Chí Minh was a prominent figure in the establishment of the new educational system in Vietnam. He was, in particular, an extraordinary human face of educational authority, with his letters and visits to the students and his initiation of inspiring competitive schemes such as the 1961 "two-good" (teach well and study well) campaign.[15] Hồ Chí Minh's talent at Vietnamizing the central tenets of a socialist education belied the extent to which the Vietnamese educational authorities looked to the Soviet Union and other socialist states in building a national educational system after 1954. Given that the educational authorities who mattered also happened to be top Party members, the political aspects of the educational system were prominent from the beginning.[16]

There was an early emphasis on maintaining tight Party control over the educational system. The vice minister of education, Nguyễn Khánh Toàn, was a longtime Party member, unlike the minister of education, the well-respected intellectual Nguyễn Văn Huyên, who held degrees in the humanities and law. In the first attempt at educational reform in the areas under Việt Minh control in 1950, Nguyễn Khánh Toàn was a key figure in shaping the ideological component. His essays and speeches, gathered in a book published by the Ministry of Education in 1950 entitled *Những vấn đề giáo dục* (Some issues on education), were widely disseminated within the teaching profession and were considered to be the "first theoretical works on [Vietnam's] new educational system."[17]

Moreover, it was Nguyễn Khánh Toàn who in a January 1954 report argued that the educational system had been put together primarily by means of a combination of individual ideas rather than from a clear and coherent developmental plan. He complained of insufficient Party attention to education. The Party's Ideological and Propaganda Department nominally oversaw educational issues but actually only provided some opinions on matters of daily activities, leaving the long-term direction up to the Ministry of Education.[18] In September 1954, Trường Chinh sent Nguyễn Khánh Toàn to China to study the Chinese educational system. The month-long trip was aimed at examining the Chinese experience in three areas: the direction of education, the structure of the educational organization, and the method of teaching. In particular, Nguyễn Khánh Toàn was to focus on general education and education for workers and peasants.[19]

Given the fact that the Chinese educational system was influenced most heavily by the Soviet Union in the years 1949–59, what Nguyễn Khánh Toàn learned was very much a reflection of the Soviet experience.[20] What was different, however, was the Chinese emphasis on peasant-worker education, which the Vietnamese found attractive. This aspect will be explored in greater detail later, but the trend toward further political socialization and a more utilitarian emphasis in education were highlighted at this point in time. If in his January 1954 report Nguyễn Khánh Toàn had argued that the stress should be on the formal general educational system, since complementary short-term courses could only be transitional, his report after his China trip placed the focus on complementary education for workers and peasants

> because [the program] is fundamental to the training of a new intellectual class, originating from the working classes: workers, peasants, and revolutionary cadres. [The program is] aimed at reinforcing [the education] of exceptional worker and peasant brothers in order to bring them into the higher level technical schools and universities.[21]

Furthermore, the attention paid to the experiences of the dominant socialist states could only put the Vietnamese educational experience in a bad light, even when the difference was only one of academic achievement. As Nguyễn Khánh Toàn exclaimed in one of his reports, the focus on technical education had led indeed to its growth, but *"the mathematics program of our ninth grade is even higher than the mathematics program of the tenth grade in the Soviet Union!"*[22] For Nguyễn Khánh Toàn, rather than being a notable achievement, such a development was bizarre because "our country is a backward agricultural country; stuffing [the students with] so much mathematics and having nowhere to use it is being abstract." In his view, Vietnamese students' higher mathematical skills were in fact only a continuation of the academic mode of the colonial educational system, which in turn exemplified how much "the schools still fundamentally have not been politicized."[23]

There is an echo here for the disdain for national achievement that had permeated the cultural and intellectual sphere documented earlier in this book. What dominated Nguyễn Khánh Toàn's view was the image of "our backward agricultural country" rather than the higher academic capability of Vietnamese students in comparison with their Soviet counterparts. In such a context, it was easy to accept the superiority of the Soviet model and ironically, in this particular instance, to call for limiting national academic achievement. Given such views, and with the arrival of Soviet educational advisers in 1955, the educational system in North Vietnam was reorganized and became increasingly politicized and polytechnically oriented.[24]

Vocational Education and Overspecialization

The 1956 educational reforms were therefore Soviet inspired. They unified the areas under Việt Minh control and areas under the colonial administration into a general educational system covering ten years: four years at the primary level (level 1), three years at the lower secondary level (level 2), and another three years at the upper secondary level (level 3). Given the fact that 90 percent of the country's population was illiterate, the number of students who made it through the secondary system was small. By another estimate, up to 1954 only one-tenth of level 1 students passed into level 2, and only one-twentieth of that number reached level 3.[25] The 1956 educational reforms actually reestablished exams between the different levels, making the move through the system even more academically rigorous. Nevertheless, at the same time the educational curriculum was standardized and simplified in order to produce a large number of technical cadres at the upper secondary level. The number of general secondary schools and especially vocational secondary schools greatly increased. The aim of the educational system was to train "workers who are owners of the country, cognizant of socialism, and have culture and technology, [in short,] those who are fully trained to construct a new society."[26]

Between 1954 and 1965, the concern was on structuring an educational system that would maintain a tight connection between life and work. The emphasis was on usefulness. The first graduates of the new system were viewed disdainfully in 1959 as not quite capable of carrying out the task of national construction. They were

> entering life very gingerly, it can even be said stupefied: not yet used to production nor work tasks, lacking independence in thinking and initiation, still heavily affected by the academic way, separating life from work. In short, [we can say that they are] "people with culture" but not yet "workers with culture."[27]

The insistent study-labor linkage led to a corresponding emphasis on vocational schools. Moreover, in a country where the majority of the population was illiterate, a university education was available to only a tiny number of students. Given the rapid expansion of the administrative apparatus in the new state, from the central down to the local level, especially with the move toward cooperatives in the countryside and the concerted effort to dramatically raise agricultural and industrial production, a large number of technical cadres was more necessary than ever. Thus, even though early specialization was problematic and the tension between too narrow an education and one that was not practical enough was a constant concern for the Ministry of Education, the situation, in which secondary vocational and college education remained under the management of specific ministries, was actually strengthened further.

Beginning with 3 colleges in 1954, by 1962 North Vietnam could boast of some 11 college-level institutions, most of which were under the guidance of various ministries.[28] Although the number of university-level institutions grew, the fastest growth was among the vocational secondary schools. In 1955, there were 8, but by 1960 there were 29 such schools.[29] The number would grow to 67 in 1961[30] and 112 by 1965.[31] Ministerial control was also most heavy in the vocational secondary school system since a specifically designed curriculum was required to produce competent young technical cadres in a relatively short time. Given the low level of industrial and agricultural development and the weak academic foundation of many students, the degree of specialization was overwhelming. The students' education also involved a large amount of time spent obtaining practical work experience in the factories, and the factories resented this as wasting their productive time. The 1961 Ministry of Education report ended with the conclusion that "specialization has come too early given our current practical needs" and asked mournfully at the end of the report what the responsibility of the Ministry of Education was in relation to that of the other ministries, what the correct relationship between quantity and quality should be, and how a student could obtain an education that was both deep and broad.[32] The report was responding in particular to a new demand on education that appeared in 1960; the new slogan regarding the training of cadres was "fast, numerous, good cadres, and by frugal means."

The Ministry of Education was at a loss in dealing with the other ministries. By 1963, the rapid growth in the number of vocational secondary schools and colleges controlled by other ministries had led to a chaotic situation in which "many schools overlap in terms of training responsibility, so that strengths are being dispersed (such as teachers, data, laboratories, etc.).[33] There was no shortage of examples: the Polytechnical College taught a number of courses on bridge and road construction that were also covered by the Ministry of Transportation; the Ministry of Education's Economic and Finance College taught courses on accounting, planning, and finance that other ministries also taught; and similar classes on auto mechanics and driving were being taught variously by the Ministry of Heavy Industry, the Ministry of Transportation, and the General Department of Silviculture.[34] Shifting demands and a chaotic vocational educational structure led to constant reorganization of universities, secondary schools, and their departments and faculties. In 1964, for example, the Silviculture Department of the College of Agriculture became a full College of Silviculture, while the architecture course of the Polytechnical College became a separate school under the control of the Ministry of Construction. The problem was particularly acute in the large number of vocational secondary schools, leading the Ministry of Education to complain that "the ministry does not grasp the number of vocational subjects [being taught in vocational secondary schools] because they are constantly changing, with many courses overlapping in terms of content, planning, and training programs. Their names are different and the schools have not fully reported [to the Ministry]."[35] The consequence was that "currently all the branches are discovering both excesses and needs [and] facing difficulties in assigning the employing [students.]"[36] In numerous conversations and interviews I conducted with professors and intellectuals in Hanoi between 1991 and 1993, a consensus emerged that, given the way education has been organized in Vietnam, to say that there were too many cadres was correct and that there were too few was also true. The educational system certainly has produced a substantial number of graduates with expertise suitable for positions within the state machinery and in the expected development of the economy, but their expertise did not always match the reality of the workplace. Indeed, the echo was resounding across three decades.

Teacher Training

Between 1954 and 1965, the dominant concern was political socialization. A new socialist educational system was being constructed with lessons drawn from the Soviet and Chinese experiences, while land reform and the intellectual discontent that coalesced around the publications *Nhân Văn* and *Giai Phẩm* in 1957 underlined the ideological emphasis. Given the rapid growth of the school system, teachers were overwhelmed with responsibilities. Faced with the constantly changing state agenda, they also had to deal with low wages, long hours, inadequate training to cope with new situations, and primitive working conditions. The lack of schools, desks, chairs, blackboards, books, paper, and fundamental teaching tools was ubiquitous.

Land reform was also devastating to the teaching profession. Teachers, whether in urban or rural areas and whether teaching at the universities or village schools, were all affected by the fierce anti-intellectual nature and the worker-peasant emphasis of land reform. According to a ministry report,

> There were many teachers who were wrongly punished, forced to stop working, and/or jailed. Land reform mistakes have, overall, greatly affected the ideology of teachers because [additionally] most teachers have relatives who were wrongly classified and therefore harbor many concerns since land reform.[37]

Not surprisingly, once rectification of land reform mistakes began, which coincided with dramatic events in Eastern Europe, many in the teaching profession were sympathetic to views being voiced in *Giai Phẩm* and *Nhân Văn*. Prominent intellectuals who were teaching in the university system such as Đào Duy Anh, Trần Đức Thảo, Trương Tửu, and Nguyễn Mạnh Tường actually wrote for both publications.

Influenced by the restless intellectual mood in particular, a number of university students also aired their grievances in their own publication, called *Đất Mới* (New land).

The rapid expansion of the educational system coupled with a small number of teachers meant that many intellectuals, bureaucrats, and even low-level civil servants of the former colonial administration were employed as teachers. While the Party insisted on the absolute ideological importance of the new educational system, ironically many who were considered to have problematic backgrounds were engaged in teaching. At the universities, a number of prominent intellectuals functioned with ease as authorities in both the academy and the creative intellectual community, a situation that has not existed to the same degree since. One document of the Ministry of Education noted in 1957 that

> the educational branch has many intellectuals. The Polytechnical College, the University of Hanoi, and the Teachers' Training College alone has 243 [intellectuals] from the level of assistant up, among them 5 Ph.D.s, 3 M.A.s, 8 engineers, 20 baccalaureates, 4 with degrees in higher pedagogy, 11 who completed their university education in China, and 140 who graduated from the Teachers' Training College. Intellectuals with a high level of knowledge, prestige, and societal influence numbers about 20.[38]

The involvement of many important intellectuals in Nhân Văn–Giai Phẩm and the generally politically unreliable nature of teachers at all levels sharpened the state emphasis on teacher training. Under the administration of the Ministry of Education, the teacher training school network developed rapidly. By 1960, there were some twelve secondary training schools throughout the country. The number of university professors increased rapidly as well, growing from around 30 in 1954 to 1,210 in 1960.[39] It was also noted that of the 1,210 teaching cadres at the university level in 1960, 120 were trained before 1945 in colonial schools, with 80 percent having participated in the resistance; 40 to 50 were educated in the Soviet Union and had returned since 1956; 90 to 100 were trained in China; a very small number were trained in other socialist countries; and the remainder had graduated from Vietnam's various colleges in 1956 and 1957 (250 from the Teachers' Training College and some 600 from other universities).[40]

While the number of university teachers had increased markedly, the data indicate that most of these early teachers were trained largely by the prominent group of colonial-educated intellectuals and professors between 1954 and 1957, when their influence, freedom to teach, and creativity were least encumbered by the state. The students themselves had entered the fledgling university system at a time when it did not yet have the motivation or the capability to pursue the class line vigorously. Therefore, their existence as the new university system's first generation of educators and the research institutes' first generation of scholars provided a measure of balance for decades to come in spite of the eventual dominance of the political criteria in both the content and structure of education and research.

Political criteria were even more important for students chosen for teacher training schools and colleges because they were the future "engineers of the soul" (*kỹ sư của tâm hồn*). By 1973, it was reported that nearly 100 percent of the teachers in the general educational system were children of cadres and soldiers and/or from worker and peasant backgrounds and that close to 25 percent of them were Party members.[41] To what extent the emphasis on political purity was achieved at the expense of the quality of teachers in general is unclear, but the report did note a low level of academic achievement and teaching capability as well as a modest sense of professional responsibility. Additionally, although the teaching profession was considered to be vital in the shaping of new generations, wages remained low in comparison with those of workers or members of other professions, so there were signs that the number of students who applied for teacher training was low. Trường Chinh's exasperated outburst at a 1966 meeting of the National Assembly Standing Committee on educational reforms is telling.

These last few years all the branches took all the good people and only gave the remaining people to education; that is not good. Teachers are engineers of the soul, and therefore we must take those who are morally strong and talented. It is a big revolution in education but if all those who are not capable of joining the factories are given places in teacher training schools, [then the situation] is very grave. [I hear that] in Hanoi out of 100 teachers, there are many who are not Party members or youth league members, of a low standard, too young, weak in pedagogical method, weak in moral character. . . . [I hear that] in Thanh Hóa Province out of 8,500 applications for universities and vocational secondary schools, only 2 requested teacher training. . . . The issue of material and spiritual compensation for teachers is still inadequate, and yet the work is difficult. This is against the tradition of our people, which respects teachers. . . . We must invest more and should not be frugal in this matter.[42]

One gets a sense that Trường Chinh no longer had the same control over the system that he once did, and this was less a matter of his political standing than the fact that the system was now in place with its inherent dilemmas. The constant talk of educational reforms over the years also pointed to a pervasive level of uneasiness among those involved in educational work at having to steer the system through the myriad of changing expectations and demands.

The Selection Criteria for General Secondary Schools and Universities

The clearest change in the educational system that conformed to a more explicitly socialist line after 1954 was the selection process. In May 1958, the Office of the Premier issued circular 257–TTg, which defined three main criteria for selection into the universities and vocational secondary schools: politics, culture, and health. Of these, "the political criteria should be placed first."[43] In this instance, the cultural criterion meant simply the educational level of the individual. Under this specific policy, beginning with the school year 1959–60, the selection process was to be divided among three pools of applicants, as shown in table 3.

The list of selection criteria provides a wealth of fascinating detail about official thinking on the subject at the time. The selection criteria were far from radical, exemplifying tensions over the expected ideological makeup of the school system along class lines. For one thing, the nature of the different pools of applicants and their varied treatment testified to the state's desire to compensate for the sacrifices made during the anti-French resistance. After all, the first group, preferential group 1, consisted of those who had spent a long time in the resistance. While their backgrounds were expected to be clear, the selection criteria did not demand that they be specifically from the peasant or working classes. They had proven their political loyalty and their ideological purity by spending at least six years of their youth carrying out revolutionary work on behalf of the Party and the people. Now the country was going to recognize their service by providing them with an education.

TABLE 3.   The 1959–60 Student Selection Criteria for Universities and Vocational Secondary Schools

Student Group	Criteria
Group 1 (40%)	*Exemplary Resistance Cadres* (six continuous years of work) (a) Clear background. (b) Show good grasp of ideology and standpoint in work. (c) Recommended by work unit and by superior. (d) Thirty-five years of age and younger, good health. (e) Has a tenth-grade certificate or the equivalent so as to be exempt from the university entrance exam (if only seventh grade, then allow the person into a vocational secondary school). If not, candidate must take an exam. If it is felt that the individual can follow the course of study, he or she will be given preference regardless of the score achieved on the exam. *Exemplary Worker-Peasant Youths* • Workers (four continuous years of work). (a) Background: the individual is a worker, not from the exploiting class (also b, c, d, and e as above). • Peasants: because cooperativization is just beginning only include heroes and soldiers of peasant background in this group. *Minority Cadres* Similar to exemplary resistance cadres, but they do not need to have minimum years of work.
Group 2 (35%)	• Cadres (four continuous years of work) who meet the other criteria similar to those in the exemplary resistance cadre category. • Students who are Party members. • Students who are children of workers, poor and middle peasants, revolutionary martyrs, or resistance cadres. • Students who are youth cadres. • Students who are from the south. • Students who are female and not from an exploiting class.
Group 3 (25%)	Select according to educational level, but do not accept more than 3 percent of the exploiting class.

Source: "Dự thảo tuyển sinh vào các trường Đại Học và Chuyên Nghiệp Trung cấp năm 1959" (Draft plan of student selection into the universities and vocational secondary schools in 1959), Ministry of Education, dossier 17.

To be sure, the list of selection criteria gave preferential treatment to worker and peasant youths, other cadres, Party members, and children of workers, peasants, revolutionary heroes, and cadres, but what is striking is the overall emphasis on a certain level of education at the outset. It was expected that all these new students would have at the very least a tenth-grade education, or in other words had completed secondary school. This would hardly seem to constitute preferential treatment, but there were many young Vietnamese who had completed their secondary education but did not have a chance to attend a university because of the war. Moreover, the elite nature of the university system during the colonial period would have made such an education an impossibility for most secondary school graduates. Therefore, there was a sizable pool of students ready for the universities and the specialized secondary schools in the general population, and this number was to be accommodated in group 3, which was allotted 25 percent of the admissions.

Groups 1 and 2, with 75 percent allotted to them, comprised the bulk of the new student body. The detailed selection criteria indicated their special status, a mix of resistance and cadre work, Party affiliation, and worker-peasant background. Such a list, however, continued to maintain the demand that these students must also have attained a minimum level of education prior to entering the university system and the more specialized secondary schools. To be sure, how such a minimum level of education was to be proven or judged satisfactory was another matter, but such a demand even of these favored pools of applicants underlined the official desire to maintain academic integrity in the higher educational system, even while insisting that the political criteria be placed first.

A brief examination of the number of students selected for the major universities between 1955 and 1959 will provide a better sense of the makeup of these schools according to the Ministry of Education. Table 4 presents the percentage of students in the categories considered to be important by the ministry in tracking its selection process.

Table 4 indicates that the categories of students who were given special emphasis by the state increased but that the increase was small and gradual. Not surprisingly, the largest amount of growth was in

TABLE 4.   Categories of University Students between 1956 and 1959 (in percentages)

Student Categories	1956	1957	1958	1959
Female	8.05	7.22	10.34	11.08
Children of workers and peasants	23.39	28.66	29.10	40.71
From the south	13.12	16.24	17.38	16.65
Cadres and soldiers	11.83	16.54	11.88	23.30
Party members	5.73	6.64	9.09	11.22
Ethnic groups	0.62	0.58	1.40	1.68

Source: "Tỷ lệ phần trăm (%) các thành phần có trong tổng số các sinh viên ở các trường đại học chính quy" (Percentage of students in existing categories attending universities full-time), Ministry of Education, dossier 1815.

the category of children of workers and peasants, reaching 40 percent of the student body by 1959. It should be noted, however, that in this particular table the category of children of workers and peasants is the only one that specifically mentions class. In fact, in a more detailed statistical table compiled on the universities between 1956 and 1959 there were two distinct types of category. One referred to family backgrounds, which could be workers, laboring people, petit bourgeois/ poor people, rich peasants, capitalists, and landowners. The other had to do with the students themselves such as their status as southerners, members of ethnic groups, Party or Youth League members, and cadres or soldiers. Female students were set apart from the rest, indicative of the state's effort to promote the number of females in the educational system.[44] Finally, from data taken from table 5, we actually get additional data for the years 1958 and 1959, which give us information on the number of students coming from classes other than worker and peasant.

Given the requirement of a minimum level of education for entrance into the universities, the pool of qualified students drawn strictly from the working and peasant classes was very small. Additionally, the ministry's list of selection criteria (presented in table 4) specifically indicated that the number of students coming from the peasant class should not be increased markedly because they were needed for the cooperativization process, which was just beginning in the countryside. As for those students who came from the working class, the number was small, as indicated in table 5, and so it was lumped in with the larger category of "laboring people" (*nhân dân lao động*) to produce the category "children of workers and peasants." The largest number of qualified students therefore came from two

TABLE 5.   Class Backgrounds of University Students in 1958 and 1959 (in percentages)

Categories of Students	1958	1959
Workers	2.45	3.65
Laboring people	26.66	37.06
Petit bourgeois/poor people	50.46	45.16
Rich peasants	2.57	1.76
Capitalists	2.76	2.47
Landowners	10.17	5.57
Unclear	4.94	4.33

Source: "Số sinh viên chia theo thành phần gia đình và phân loại học sinh (số giữa năm học)" (Number of university students divided by family and student categories [number at middle of school year]), Ministry of Education, dossier 1815.

main categories, those of laboring people and petit bourgeois/poor people (*tiểu tư sản/dân nghèo*). These categories were the least specific about class, reflecting the fluid world of the colonial cities, where many Vietnamese from diverse backgrounds congregated. It is worth noting that among the categories there was none assigned to the mandarin class. It was enough for those of the mandarin class to be captured in the capitalist or landowner category; otherwise, for many of Vietnam's most intellectual and best known literati lineages, they were part of those catchall categories of working people and petit bourgeois/poor people. The large number of writers and poets active in the prerevolutionary intellectual world would end up in these same categories.

Moreover, although these categories reflected the students' backgrounds, for the most part the selection process focused on the students themselves. Occupations as cadres or soldiers, membership in the Party or the Communist Youth League, minority group status, and having been regrouped from the south seems to have been decisive factors. Although originally from the landowning class, for example, a young man could be classified as a poor peasant if during the anti-French resistance he had renounced his family to join the revolution and had demonstrated his political loyalty and work value. Given the heavy emphasis on class categorization, there were widespread political and economic negotiations to make sure that friends and families gained the proper advantageous class status. The class criteria, therefore, was greatly tempered by many factors, among them revolutionary achievements, educational levels, and personal connections.

The recent colonial experience may have been another factor contributing to the dilution of class criteria. The early documents of the Ministry of Education were obsessed with detailing the comparison between the colonial educational system's meager offerings and the growing number of schools in the new socialist state, which served thousands of Vietnamese instead of a handful. The antifeudal impulse was certainly present, but it was never quite as strongly felt as the anticolonial one. The psychological nature of the educational enterprise must be understood in this light: when the Ministry of Education was founded in the days after the brief but glorious August Revolution of 1945, one of its earliest official documents demanded that Vietnamese language be used because "it is regrettable that the Ministry of Education still receives a number of documents or letters written in French."[45] By 1950, the ministry had succeeded in fully establishing Vietnamese over French as the medium for teaching. Given the experience of other colonized states, the breathtakingly rapid pace at which North Vietnam was able to do this testified to the unanimous determination among many Vietnamese to construct an educational system that they could call their own, especially at the higher levels, where the colonial influence was most dominant.

The growth of the educational system after 1954, therefore, was achieved with the recent colonial experience in mind. At the lower level elementary and secondary education would consolidate and supplement the gains made in the literacy campaign, leading eventually to universal education for all Vietnamese, while at the highest level a new intellectual and scientific elite would emerge, confident in its abilities and aware of its special responsibility in the new socialist state. The accelerated pace of growth, the enormous demands made of the educational system, and the increasingly restrictive emphasis on class criteria, however, made balanced development of the educational system very difficult, as the remainder of this chapter will show. If the selection process for the university and specialized secondary school levels did not show a dramatic class orientation in the early years, the ideology of the new state did pursue such a strategy in a different form.

Complementary Education (*Bổ Túc Văn Hóa*) and Its Changing Goals

One of the greatest achievements proclaimed by the Việt Minh during the years of the anti-French resistance, and one that attracted immense popular and intellectual support, was its illiteracy eradication campaign. Whether at the military front or in the village, rudimentary literacy courses were organized by the thousands, at times taught by youths who barely knew how to read themselves. There was a heroic dimension to the undertaking, and cadres and students were urged to find inventive ways to teach without infringing upon the production schedule. Many cadres began their careers by participating in the literacy campaign in their own villages. It was truly a marriage of political and social needs at the most basic level.

After its founding in September 1945, one of the Ministry of Education's first tasks was to consolidate the gains achieved by the literacy campaign. Between 1946 and 1950, the ministry viewed complementary education (*Bổ túc văn hóa*) as the natural follow-up after the achievement of universal literacy. It was envisioned that complementary education would entail two additional levels. First, there was the *bậc dự bị bình dân* (popular preparatory level), which would make sure that people would not forget what they had learned in the literacy classes, such as rudimentary reading and writing skills and the four calculation methods, while providing them with a basic level of education comparable to the third grade. The ambitious second level would eventually lead to the achievement of an education comparable to that of the sixth grade, or the level at which a regular student entered secondary school. This level was referred to as the *bậc bổ túc bình dân* (popular complementary level), and this was viewed as "the basic educational foundation of the people."[46]

It seems that this initial effort to consolidate the literacy campaign and push it further was not successful. The number of people attending school at the popular complementary level was low: the highest was 50 percent of the graduates of the literacy classes in some areas; in others, it was only 11 percent.[47] The effort was also greatly hampered by the lack of teachers, and there was no indication that the popular complementary level ever bore any real fruit. The popular complementary level was eventually abandoned, and the literacy campaign would involve only basic classes bolstered by simple follow-up classes.

Complementary education soon found a new mission. From the focus on the general population and the emphasis on the postliteracy campaign, the new targets of complementary education between 1951 and 1954 were "cadres and workers who have already had some level of general secondary education and who need to acquire a certain level of knowledge in order to carry out their work."[48] The continued growth and consolidation of a bureaucracy even during the anti-French resistance, the eventual establishment of a socialist state, and the growing emphasis on new cadres being from the peasant and working classes underscored the need to upgrade the level of education to provide the necessary training. The *Phổ Thông Lao Động Trung Ương* (Central General Work) school, established in 1951, brought together mid- and high-ranking cadres for an intensive period of education and training, and soon a network of general work schools was established in the different zones. As envisioned by the government, the education and training provided in these schools were meant to be ideologically clear but highly flexible and practical to ensure success but also local funding and support. The three criteria demanded of complementary education in 1952 were:

1. Unify theory and reality, learning goes hand in hand with work, studying for utilitarian purposes
2. Make use of time in order to be of service to the resistance, at the same time preparing for further education
3. Rely on the people, specifically and appropriately for each period, locality, and group[49]

Between 1951 and 1954, complementary education became increasingly organized in both content and structure. It included two levels. Level 1 contained two grades, comparable to elementary and middle school education, while level 2 covered three grades, comparable to a secondary level of education. Complementary education had two forms. Besides the network of general work schools, which would bring the cadres together in a full-time school setting, there was a series of complementary education courses organized at the work units for leading administrative cadres who could not get away from their posts in the factories and the countryside. The nature and goals of complementary education would change again after 1954, and this time with the radical aim of generating nothing less than a new intellectual class.

Complementary education was greatly expanded in 1954 as the state gained complete control over the economy and the bureaucracy. Between 1955 and 1959, the number of students enrolled in complementary education courses at work units and factories reportedly increased ten times.[50] The policy of placing politically pure cadres in positions of importance at the local level required the expansion of complementary education since the majority of these new cadres barely knew how to read and write. Complementary education, therefore, broadened its intended target to include lower level cadres and ordinary workers. In the process, its goals also became more encompassing and political. According to a report on the Conference on Complementary Education in October 1959, the purposes of complementary education were

1. To support the literacy campaign
2. To provide education about socialism and disseminate state and party policies
3. To train people for positions involving administrative or mass organization tasks and to become literacy and elementary school teachers, health cadres, etc.
4. To raise the level of education of workers and cadres in order to raise production levels and to provide the political

and professional education necessary to allow a number of workers and cadres to enter vocational schools

5. [Through worker-peasant complementary education schools, to send a number of students to the universities in order to] transform the existing students in those schools and generate a new intellectual class of workers and peasants.[51]

These goals far surpassed the strictly utilitarian criteria demanded of complementary education in 1952, exemplifying the program's ambitious growth. Next to the general school system, which took on a more class-based character although academic achievement continued to be emphasized, complementary education became a vast second educational system composed of programs designed to meet the specific needs of different groups. At the most basic level, complementary education still conducted postliteracy courses for the general population, but this basic goal was meshed with the state's need to raise the level of education of its cadres at all levels of the bureaucracy. Out of the ten grades in general education, the majority of rural cadres was at the second- or third-grade level. Moreover, according to the report, "the more restrictive focus on the backbone elements [shows that more of them] are at the second-grade level, and among the principal elements the number of those who just escaped illiteracy is not small."[52] The situation improved at the upper reaches of the bureaucracy, but the generally low level of education remained the dominant concern for the new state. At the same time that the state was emphasizing political criteria in the expansion of the bureaucracy, it was obsessively keeping track of these new recruits' educational status, finding it wanting. It was estimated that many leaders at the district and provincial levels did not have an education beyond the third grade, and even among the highest ranking cadres in central organizations the majority did not go beyond the seventh grade.[53]

The statistics regarding the educational levels of cadres, workers, and peasants concerned the state in two ways, political and economic. The low level of education often meant a low level of understanding of socialist goals and methods, resulting in an undisciplined approach to the political aspects of life in the new society. The low level of education also meant a slow pace of economic development in both agriculture and industry. Complementary education was seen as the solution to both of these problems, and specific targets were set. The goals expected to be achieved by 1960 are shown in table 6.

The desire to combine both political and technical education for varied constituencies of students led to the development of a number of specialized education programs. In the countryside, for example, the general education component included the basics of reading, writing, grammar, and mathematics and information on sanitation, agriculture, animal husbandry, and the like. The political education component included lessons on the desirability of technical change, the construction of cooperatives, the bad influence of outdated practices and beliefs, and the struggle for national unification and international friendship. For the factories, the general education component would be the same but with a focus on factory production, machinery, and fundamental scientific information on air, heat, electricity, and metals. The political education component would emphasize socialist labor, the idea of the mastery of the people, the idea of class, and so on.[54] Only a small number of cadres would be sent to the general labor schools for a full-time education; the bulk of the population attended the complementary education courses organized outside of working hours. The Ministry of Education designed the contents of these different curricula and assigned teachers to the more important local levels, and those who were sent for full-time education were provided with financial support from the central government or the provinces. The majority of the complementary education courses in factories, state farms, and the like were expected to be funded by the work units themselves.

TABLE 6. Categories of Complementary Education Students and Their Expected Educational Achievements in 1960

Category of Students	Expected Educational Achievement
Leading cadres of communes	Completion of fourth grade
Leading cadres of districts	Completion of sixth grade
Leading cadres of provinces (including army cadres)	Completion of seventh grade
Technical workers	Completion of fourth grade and in a number of branches completion of seventh grade
Leading cadres of factories and state farms, technical cadres	Completion of seventh grade
Army soldiers	Completion of fourth grade, and completion of higher grades in a number of branches

Source: "Hội nghị Bổ Túc Văn Hóa ngày 8–10–1959 (Bộ Giáo Dục tổ chức)" (Conference on complementary education held on 8 October 1959 [organized by the Ministry of Education]), Ministry of Education, dossier 1284.

Worker-Peasant Complementary Education (*Bổ Túc Vãn Hóa Công Nông*)

It was the last goal of complementary education after 1954 that was truly radical. The achievement of an independent state made possible the return of an issue that had been discussed as early as 1951, that of generating a new, pure intellectual class from the worker and peasant classes. The discussion of a new worker-peasant intellectual class led in 1956 to the establishment of the Worker-Peasant Complementary Education Program (WPCE) and its network of schools designed to "train students up to the middle and secondary levels of general education in order to take the exam for the vocational secondary schools and the universities."[55] The Chinese influence in this development was obvious. China had established the first Peking Experimental Worker-Peasant High School in 1950 with the aim of providing the students with three years of education and preparing them for the universities. One year later, there were thirty-seven such schools throughout China.[56] As mentioned earlier, Vice Minister of Education Nguyễn Khánh Toàn's trip to China in September 1954 seems to have greatly influenced his subsequent emphasis on worker-peasant complementary education.

In Vietnam, the Worker-Peasant Complementary Education Program was a component of the larger complementary education effort, but its own network of schools and organized curricula focused on a specific pool of students, cadres, peasants, and workers who were politically pure but educationally disadvantaged. The WPCE would provide these students with an intense and compressed education within a period of a few years that would be comparable to the ten-year general secondary education, preparing them for the university or additional specialized training. The aim of the WPCE schools was to produce the following.

> The socialist revolution in the north requires that there must be a worker-peasant intellectual group that is loyal to the revolution and has firm control of progressive technology and science [so as] to build the nation. The primary core of this cadre [of intellectuals] must be those who came from worker and peasant backgrounds, those who have revolutionary achievements, and those who are exemplary in production and the struggle.[57]

By 1959, under the general rubric of complementary education, there were really three different programs at work. There were the twenty-five General Labor schools where some 3,978 cadres from the district level up were sent full time for a period of training. There were nine WPCE schools providing a full-time secondary education to 4,699 students, preparing them for the universities and vocational secondary schools. And there were hundreds of complementary education classes in work units, factories, and villages that provided a more basic education in general knowledge, fundamental technical information, and administrative training to some 14,635 low-level cadres and workers.[58]

It was the WPCE program that was the most ambitious in its scope and growth. Beginning only in 1956, it included nine schools by 1959 and at its height grew to fourteen schools by 1961. The rapid growth also meant rapidly changing education programs and shifting timetables, as indicated in table 7.

In a regular ten-year secondary education, level 1 referred to grades one to four (elementary level), level 2 contained grades five to seven (lower secondary level), and level 3 included grades eight to ten (upper secondary level) during which students chose their specialization. At level 3, however, there was also a network of more specialized and technically oriented schools operated by the different ministries, and these were referred to as vocational secondary schools (*trung học chuyên nghiệp*). Depending on the planning needs at the time and on the students' aptitude and educational achievements, students could take the exam for entrance into the universities or be diverted to these vocational secondary schools.

The complementary education program was supposed to provide a

TABLE 7.   The Worker-Peasant Complementary
Education Program between 1956 and 1962

School Year	Length and Coverage of Program	
1956–58	9 months	level 3
1958–59	2 years	level 2
	2 years	level 3
1959–62	1 year	level 2
	2 years	level 3
	2 years	level 2
1962–	3 years	level 3

Source: "Báo cáo của Bộ Giáo Dục tổng kết kinh nghiệm các chủ trương của Bộ về trường Bổ Túc Công Nông và phương hướng mới đối với trường Bổ Túc Công Nông năm 1964" (Ministry of Education's report summarizing the experience of the ministry's policy on worker-peasant complementary education schools and the new direction concerning the worker-peasant complementary education schools), Ministry of Education, dossier 217.

comparable education to that of the ten-year secondary school, but with its dramatically shortened time frame it could only approximate the ten-year system. As table 7 indicates, in the early years of the program the students were ushered through nine months of intense studying that provided a comparable education to level 3, in other words, three full grades. Those who were selected for the first WPCE school had relatively good educational backgrounds, and therefore the compressed time frame of nine months was possible. Between 1956 and 1958, the central WPCE school took in 1,958 students and during these same years it sent 789 to the various universities.[59]

In order to dramatically increase the number of these worker-peasant students in the universities and professional secondary schools, the WPCE school network expanded rapidly. There were nine such schools around the country in 1959, with 4,600 students. By 1961, thirteen schools enrolled 7,564 students.[60] The qualified pool of students, however, shrank markedly. Nine months became an impossible time frame to prepare the new students given their lower starting level, and the program was quickly expanded to four years for the 1958–59 school year and then cut back to three between 1959 and 1962. If it took three WPCE school years to prepare the students for the universities, they now would need only a fourth-grade education to enter the WPCE schools. The intense program would usher the students through the remaining six grades in three years.

It was truly a Herculean task, and not surprisingly the WPCE students found it hard to compete successfully in the university entrance exams. Between 1959 and 1961, it was reported that some 3,642 WPCE students entered the university system, with the largest number of close to 2,000 students coming in the 1960–61 school year.[61] Another document of the Ministry of Education reported that "out of 2,600 [WPCE] students taken into the first year [in 1960–61], close to 40 percent have to be saved [i.e., given additional points in order to pass] and 20 to 30 percent [also have to be saved] this year, 1961–62."[62] The abysmal rate of success was not surprising, and the Ministry of Education's own assessment of the WPCE students in 1962 was hardly optimistic. Only 15 percent were considered to be good, with none in this category achieving exemplary status; 45 percent were considered to be average; and an astounding 40 percent were viewed as weak or barely average.[63] Another assessment made by principals and vice principals of the WPCE schools themselves noted in 1961 that "[the students'] level of general education is weak overall; if chosen for the universities, it is feared that it cannot be guaranteed that they will keep up [with the other students.]"[64]

The students simply had had too little and too unsystematic an education prior to their arrival at the WPCE schools to be expected to plow through a comprehensive and compressed educational program. The weakness of their educational foundation became obvious after 1958 as the pool of qualified students dramatically contracted. In addition, the emphasis on a quick and effective educational program also demanded specially trained, or at least good, teachers, of whom there were few in the educational system as a whole. The ambitious nature of the WPCE program also demanded certain teaching tools, especially in the natural sciences, and these were sorely lacking. By the end of 1962, the Ministry of Education was greatly troubled by the WPCE schools' lack of success. Among the various suggestions forwarded to and debated at the ministry, one actually suggested ending the recruitment for these schools and maintaining only those students already in the system. After all, the number of worker-peasant students in the regular secondary school system had grown over the years, and these had both political and academic credentials needed to satisfy the tasks assigned to the WPCE schools. The amount of money being spent on a WPCE student from the fourth to the seventh grade (if he or she were to enter a professional secondary school) and from the eighth to the tenth grade (if he or she were to enter a college) was very high, while the existing educational system could be used more effectively.[65]

The emphasis on students from the working class was also a failure because, as one ministry document belatedly noted, the large number of students from the peasantry and those who were cadres and soldiers in the WPCE school system simply reflected the fact that Vietnam was primarily a peasant society. The document went on to suggest that the number of students drawn from the working class should not matter because "the working class nature of the [particular student] is exemplified more in political virtue than class background."[66] Therefore, whether a student was from the peasant or the petit bourgeois class, and perhaps even from the hated capitalist class, if he or she had fought for the revolution and become a loyal cadre or heroic soldier he or she would have achieved working class status. It was a rare moment of repudiation of the harsh politics of class.

Once it had become institutionalized, however, the system was difficult to eliminate. The failure of the three-year WPCE Program between 1959 and 1962 did lead to changes, chief among them the increase of the school years from three to five because, as one ministry document stated, "the level of knowledge of the students is low while professional demands are increasing."[67] More WPCE students were being channeled into the vocational secondary schools rather than the universities from the early 1960s onward.[68] The push for cooperativization and greater industrial production in the early 1960s also prompted an educational system that would rapidly produce a large number of basic technical cadres. The slogan for complementary education during this period was "studying whatever necessary" (*cần gì học nấy*), and the heightened utilitarian tendency further steered more WPCE students toward the professional secondary schools rather than the universities. At the height of its development in 1961–62, the WPCE system boasted a total of fourteen schools throughout the country, but the ambitious expansion belied the essential weakness of the system and its inability to reach the set goal of producing worker-peasant students who were qualified for higher education.[69] The official enthusiasm for the WPCE program seems to have waned markedly from 1962 on, as the number of students from the peasant and working classes continued to increase within the regular secondary school system while the selection pool for WPCE schools became even more complex. In 1964, it was reported that the quality of WPCE students remained low, making the effort to move them into the university system increasingly difficult.[70]

Achievements and Failures of the Educational System

There is no doubt that the new state had managed to provide education to an unprecedented number of Vietnamese of all backgrounds. In particular, the complementary education program made an effort to reach out to Vietnamese living in the villages and highland areas, making available a basic level of education where none had existed previously. In addition, it was an attempt to provide a continuous level of training for the large number of administrative and technical cadres required to carry out the state's numerous tasks and goals while cementing their continued commitment to the state's agenda. At the political level, the complementary education program in its various guises was an effort to bring the people as a whole into a unified ideological system. The state alone could not fund the vast educational effort, but many aspects of the program were supported locally. It was a strategy that guaranteed the growth of the program without an enormous cost to the state.

The structure and ambitious goals of the complementary education program, however well meaning and flexibly envisioned, proved to be unrealistic. For one thing, the local emphasis left the funding, the selection of students, and the development of the classes up to the work units in the villages, factories, state farms, and state organizations. The state's heavy emphasis on production, however, clashed resoundingly with the motives of complementary education since local leaders, too busy trying to fulfill quotas and satisfy a host of other demands by the state, did not always see the long-term importance of these classes and sometimes actively worked against them. As early as 1960, the Ministry of Education reported that in the many central administrative organizations there was no one specifically responsible for complementary education. It was usually left to the union cadres to push people to attend classes, without much success, and therefore "in many places, the lower level did whatever possible without the upper level knowing anything about it."[71] The situation had not changed a decade later, with the Ministry of Education noting in 1971 that in factories and cooperatives the organization and management of complementary education classes were left up to the cadres in charge of production without any directives as to how to carry out the tasks, so that given the cadres' production responsibilities, complementary education had come to be seen as a sideline. In a number of work units, cadres and workers interested in complementary education classes were actually discouraged from enrolling.[72] Moreover, after the initial period of enthusiasm most people did not want to attend the complementary education classes because there was no established system of encouragement (such as a salary structure based on educational level), and so the classes became a burden of time and energy in a day that was already filled with production demands and political meetings.

The success of the complementary education program also depended on the availability of good teachers and teaching tools, both of which were sorely lacking even for the general educational system. Furthermore, one of the most consistent criticisms of complementary education was that the program "did not respond to the reality and needs of the new situation" and "the content of complementary education has not married technical information with economic administration."[73] Simply put, one of the biggest goals of complementary education was to quickly produce technical and administrative cadres, but this goal was, for the most part, beyond the capability of the system itself.

As for the most ambitious goal of complementary education, to produce a new intellectual class from the peasant and working classes, which was embodied in the WPCE effort most notably between 1956 and 1962, the program's failure to produce quality students who could compete against other students in the university system led to its gradual downgrading. By the beginning of the 1960s, more WPCE students were already being channeled into the vocational secondary school system rather than the universities as initially envisioned, and a decade later the Ministry of Education had stopped mentioning WPCE altogether. It would be in the regular secondary school system itself that the state sought to impose the political criteria more fervently from 1960 onward to ensure that it had a politically reliable pool of students for the universities.

The dilemma between the desire to have a large number of politically pure students and the need to maintain a high level of academic quality was ever present, which in turn made class-based statistics unreliable. Similar statistics reported in different documents of the Ministry of Education varied widely and often seem exaggerated. One document reported that the number of students who were children of workers and peasants had grown to 40 percent of the total student body of the university system in 1959.[74] By 1964, that figure was claimed to have risen to 99 percent, with those from the exploiting classes occupying a mere 1 percent.[75] Elsewhere, the ministry had reported that the number of students from the exploiting classes of rich peasants, capitalists, and landowners in 1958 was 15.5 percent and, while it did drop to 9.8 percent in 1959, it is difficult to believe that the number would have decreases to only 1 percent in 1964.[76] In short, as much as the composition of the student body changed dramatically after 1954 to provide students from peasant and working class backgrounds with more opportunities, especially at the higher levels, the state never excluded students from other classes. The strict class emphasis, therefore, was often diluted by other criteria also considered to be important in the selection process, gender being one and status as cadres or soldiers being another.

— • —

The development of the educational system in Vietnam between 1945 and 1965 aligned itself with the development of educational systems in other socialist states, following the system first developed and refined in the Soviet Union. The ideological requirement of the Vietnamese revolution had emphasized a radical approach to make sure that children of workers and peasants would occupy an exalted place in the new intellectual stratum, and class became one of the most dominant criteria in the selection process. In the end, however, the nationalist impulse, the long literati tradition, and the reality of a country in which the majority of the population was barely literate greatly tempered the ideologically motivated trend toward a radical transformation of the educational system.

The primary conflicts in the educational system—between professionalism and political reliability, between general and more technical training, and between quality and quantity—were never fully resolved. Additionally, the devastating war against the United States beginning in 1965 led to some further tightening in the political realm but at the same time sparked a renewal of the national front strategy that was so successful during the anti-French resistance. The state simply needed personnel to fill the many positions left vacant by those who went to war. According to Douglas Pike, officers in the People's Army of Vietnam often came from the working class because of the official distrust of those who came from a petit bourgeois background.[77] Those whose personal histories were tainted by familial connections, religious affiliations, and the like were funneled into other work, such as work at research institutes, publishing houses, and universities. Many intellectuals who came from suspect classes therefore came to hold positions of some importance within the intellectual structure that they probably would not have had access to if it were not for the war against the United States.

The Ministry of Education's report on the university selection process for the school year 1971–72 is also telling. On the one hand, the report noted that with regard to the children of those with political problems and from the exploiting classes the Politburo had emphasized that only the status of parents, spouses, and siblings could be taken into account when determining students' qualifications. Nevertheless, the local administrative offices and the schools used even the status of grandparents, aunts, and uncles in the selection process. Therefore, many good students who actually came from good political backgrounds were not chosen. On the other hand, the report also noted that the number of those belonging to preferential groups (e.g., children of revolutionary martyrs, ethnic minority children, and children of southern cadres) had dropped dramatically because "the universities tend to focus on academic criteria and entrance examination grades rather than conforming to policies." Finally:

> Almost all the preferential targets tend to be weak students. Having failed the entrance examinations, they are not viewed by the schools in more comprehensive ways in the selection process. Currently there is the opinion among the people that children of soldiers, cadres, and those who have done much for the resistance do not get into the universities [while] children of those who contribute nothing, children of capitalists and the exploiting classes, are selected by the universities, attending this or that school.[78]

The document itself does not seem to note the irony of the reported situation, but the image it presents is hardly one of unqualified political purity. One can easily imagine the furious behind the scenes politicking that must have gone on to subvert the strident emphasis on class categorization.

The general educational system had managed to provide a formal education to many Vietnamese in a relatively short time and under exceedingly difficult circumstances. While the state was successful in imposing a socialist line in the content of education, it never managed to fully resolve the inherent dilemma between the purer socialist direction and the more nationalist approach. The result was an educational system that was populist and vocational in large part but continued to show a commitment to academic achievement, particularly at the higher levels.

Conclusion

More than a quarter of a century has passed since the end of the Vietnam War and the reunification of the country. In so many ways, however, the direction taken by the Vietnamese revolution continues to haunt the country today. In the midst of rapid economic and social changes brought on since late 1986 when the Vietnamese Communist Party adopted a market-oriented development strategy and set out to integrate Vietnam into regional and international networks, issues about culture, tradition, modernity, intellectual freedom, and national identity have returned to the public arena to be discussed and debated with passion. That these were the same concerns that dominated intellectual discourse in the 1930s and 1940s points to the unsatisfactory resolution of the modernizing experience for many Vietnamese. The Vietnamese Communist Party's extraordinary success in steering the country though the struggle for independence and the carnage of warfare in the twentieth century has given it the power to impose a specific political vision, but the alternative views that were evident in the decades before the revolution and justified the existence of a separate state in the south for some twenty years are emerging to challenge anew the content of state and society for Vietnam in the new century.

It is difficult to clearly discern the shape and the continuing impact of this effort to construct a national identity in modern terms from the way in which nationalism has been defined for the country by the Vietnamese communists and many Western writers on Vietnam. To be sure, the overwhelming factor of warfare cannot be understated in the unfolding of modern Vietnamese history and politics. More specifically, the anticolonial nature of the First Indochina War and the anti-imperialist nature of the Second Indochina War forced the issue of survival to the forefront. In this context, the communist victory was possible because the socialist discourse was tightly interwoven with the nationalist discourse, but such a victory also allowed the Party to equate socialism with the nation. Over time, however, the construction of this socialist nation narrative came to project a linear development of the revolutionary consciousness in moral and semireligious terms: an awakening from deep slumber (*thức tỉnh*), deliberation over the correct path to take (*nhận đường*), a transformation moment in which the revolution and all its meanings are clearly understood (*giác ngộ cách mạng*), an abandonment of the old life (*thoát ly*), and then the act of following the revolution itself (*đi theo cách mạng*). This narrative was totalizing. Countless numbers of individual accounts of discovering the revolution depicted in memoirs, autobiographies, and the self-generated personal histories (*lý lịch*) that are part of people's official dossiers add up to a kind of state-organized national reckoning of socialism. Whatever conflict was inherent in the revolutionary process has been subliminated to the only possible outcome.

As I discussed in the introduction, however, warfare has also left a deep imprint on the scholarship on Vietnam. Motivated by the desire to counteract the simplistic view of Vietnamese society assumed by American policy with its cold war preoccupations, a number of early works set out to recover history for the country.[1] Much attention was also devoted to understanding the complex sociopolitical context of the emergence of the revolution and how the communists managed to come to power, with a view to better delineating the implications of the American strategy in Vietnam.[2] Over time, however, the looming presence of the Vietnam War led to the emergence of what David Marr has referred to as the "continuity thesis," the tendency to attribute Vietnamese success in repelling foreign domination largely to the traditional strengths of a country that possessed an ancient civilization and a strong sense of national identity.[3] In this view, the communists' ability to take control of the nationalist movement was due to their success in representing the needs of the bulk of the population within a political vision that deeply appreciated the influence of the past upon the present as well as the future. At its extreme, the logic of such an argument invests the Vietnamese revolution with extraordinary power in its seemingly unique ability to generate radical political and social transformation without having to make a fundamental break with the past.[4]

In comparison with the tremendous upheavals in the Chinese case, the Vietnamese revolution certainly seemed much more centered in and comfortably connected to the nation's history and cultural achievements. In the works of such communist intellectuals as Nguyễn Khắc Viện, which became well known in the West, ideology seemed much less of a concern than the ultimate goal of national independence.[5] The image of the communists as the rightful inheritors of the nationalist tradition and the most credible guardians of the country's history and culture came to coincide with later communist efforts to ensconce the achievements of the anticolonial struggle and the revolution within the state's socialist narrative.

At the risk of oversimplification, it seems to me that the result is a curious disjuncture in these various descriptions of Vietnamese history and revolutionary politics: it is as if the raucous prerevolutionary debate on the nation (which has become increasingly well documented) somehow just drained into the organized structure of the socialist state as the embodiment of nationalism after 1954. The dominant focus on the anticolonial and anti-imperialist dimensions of nationalism inherent in both the continuity thesis and the socialist nation narrative overlooks the internal dynamics of revolutionary politics that continued to play out in the early years of the socialist state. This is precisely why this book focuses on the period between 1945, when the communists took firm control of the anticolonial struggle, and 1965, when the escalation of the Vietnam War marked a new phase in the life of the Democratic Republic of Vietnam.

What I have concentrated on is the political culture that first gave rise to the revolution and later informed the construction of a socialist state in the north. Rather than focusing on the outcome of the socialist state, I have explored instead the process of becoming a socialist state to better capture the complexities of a period fraught with contradictory possibilities and tensions that have continued to act as points of reference for so many of the current discussions on politics, culture, and national identity. Rather than accepting the existence of nationalism as having been consolidated by struggles against external enemies, I wanted to make better sense of the internally directed, diverse, and painful questioning of self, culture, and national essence that dominated the prerevolutionary intellectual discourse and haunted the Party's early cultural pronouncements. Although national survival was clearly the primary consideration, the extraordinary power and enduring meaning of revolutionary politics for so many Vietnamese have to be understood not only in light of the struggle for national independence but as driven by an intense desire for radical change that would lead to the necessary modernization of state and society.

In the years immediately preceding the revolution, modernization was conceived of in basic and visceral terms: how to effect the transformation from a perceived cultural stagnancy, if not utter defeat, to a new life marked with vitality and possibilities. Many of the debates of the 1930s and early 1940s converged on the painfully self-conscious awareness of the lack of a true and worthy national legacy of cultural achievements, that what thus far had been accepted as Vietnamese was actually only a second-rate derivation of Chinese culture with an overlay of the more recent French influence. Voices defending traditional Vietnamese culture were castigated by a younger generation demanding fundamental change through Westernization. The enormous political confusion and physical impoverishment within the context of waning French colonialism, dying imperial power, and the taxing Japanese occupation deepened in 1944 and 1945 and rendered such discussions academic. The very survival of the country was visibly under threat, and the shift away from the more elitist and Western-oriented direction toward the peasantry, or at least the larger population, was clearly discernable in the intellectual discourse.

The powerful moment of unity between the communists and many within the intellectual community therefore was not in the preservation of the nation's past and cultural achievements but in their very destruction in order for a new Vietnam to emerge into the modern world. Far from the discourse of historical continuity and national confidence with which we have become familiar, what I want to draw out is the profound ambivalence about the worth of national culture that pervaded not only the intellectual community but important Party writings on cultural and intellectual issues. What the Việt Minh managed to achieve was to successfully embody contemporary intellectual concerns within a more coherent and action-oriented worldview, encapsulated in the key constructs of the cultural policy *dân tộc hóa, đại chúng hóa, khoa học hóa* (nationalization, popularization, and scientific orientation). From the outset, the introduction of a new language, which gradually brought to life land reform, cultural revolution, classism, and criticism and self-criticism within the context of nationalism, egalitarianism, and popular culture, was immensely powerful and effective. It did nothing less than establish the base for a radically new political culture in which the explicit egalitarian character of socialist ideology spoke to the emergent mass politics. This in turn allowed the Việt Minh to wage an anticolonial war with all the necessary and syncretic nationalist language and symbols precisely within the promise of the new culture to be generated.

The importance of the Party's organizational capability in this context cannot be overemphasized because it provided cohesiveness while the consensus on the content of national identity and culture was still being reached. Once it possessed political power, however, the definitions of *national culture* and *identity* were increasingly formulated along socialist lines. A number of intellectuals were well aware of the cost of this shift even at the beginning of the transition, and, although some did leave the Việt Minh–controlled areas and returned to French-governed cities, most continued to be persuaded by the Việt Minh's political platform, its united front strategy, and its cohesive organizational structure. The frame of reference for Party-intellectual relations remained one of comradeship, and intellectuals still had the ideological space needed to enter into discussions with Party authorities on a wide range of issues. Their tacit acceptance of the Party's leadership recognized the primary needs of the resistance and was predicated on a belief in the promise of a just and open society once national independence became a reality.

The second half of the book laid out the consequences of the logic of revolutionary politics established between 1943 and 1954 in the postwar period and the societal reactions against the new policies. Once power had been achieved in 1954, radical new institutions were seen as the key to effecting fundamental political, economic, social, and cultural transformation in postwar society. For intellectuals, it was disheartening to realize that peace had not brought a relaxation of the controls of the war years or allowed for the broadening of intellectual creativity. The sharply curtailed private sphere and the politicization of daily life were in fact characteristics of the new regime. The growing power of those who claimed to represent the Party was first viewed by intellectuals as an aberrant development that could be rectified and only later as a deep systemic flaw that must be addressed by more objective reliance on the rule of law. In response to the escalating voices of dissent, the net of institutions tightened and grew even more encompassing. In both the cultural arena and the education system, discussed at length in the last two chapters of the book, we see the efforts on the part of the state to bypass what it considered to be unreliable societal groups to create new, more loyal ones. The attempt to generate a new intelligentsia from the working class is a clear example.

Yet it is fascinating to discern the internal conflicts that plagued the state's various efforts at radical transformation. The discontent that gave rise to dissident voices embodied in the 1956 publications *Nhân*

Văn and *Giai Phẩm* also greatly affected the official intellectual organs, and even what we would consider to be staunch instruments of the state, like the Ministry of Culture and Ministry of Education, were deeply troubled internally by contradictory views about culture and society in those early years. What this underlines is the extent to which the larger societal debate on national identity and culture continued to affect many, including those who were given the task of implementing the Party's radical vision. At a more general level, precisely because the system is intensely bureaucratized we should be cautious in making too sharp a distinction between state and society, which may prevent us from recognizing the deeper underlying tendencies and their impact.[6]

Partha Chatterjee has argued that the emphasis on nationalism as an anticolonial political movement dominant in Western scholarship as well as in standard nationalist history misses completely the internal dynamics of nationalism in what he refers to as "its most powerful, creative, and historically significant project: to fashion a modern national culture that is nevertheless not Western."[7] We can see glimpses of this fragmented and painful effort at constructing a modern Vietnamese national culture in the years before the revolution, but it is a process that never had the political space to be fully deliberated and in fact is reemerging. The long-term internal negotiation over the form and content of nationalism is crucial to our understanding of the enduring meaning of the revolution. Such a process continues to resonate today, but I do not think we have shifted our vision adequately from the externally oriented dimension of nationalism in Vietnam to better address the current domestic dynamics of change. Contemporary Vietnam is beyond the scope of this book, but let me illustrate my point with one example.

Since late 1986, Vietnam's adoption of market-oriented reforms and a broader view of external relations have generated wide-ranging efforts to discover suitable political, economic, and social strategies for the country in the new regional and international contexts. Even premodern statecraft ideas are being revived as state power is reconceptualized.[8] This more open environment has also allowed a space for activities that are more internally directed, constituting, as it were, a process of recovery and reassessment of recent history. A new generation of writers has come to national and international prominence since the late 1980s with their sharp portraits of life in the socialist state and critical explorations of the meaning of extraordinary human sacrifice, particularly during the Vietnam War.[9] More important for my purpose here are the quietly determined efforts of individuals and institutions to return forgotten or previously banned intellectual works to public circulation.[10]

After long years of being viewed as decadent, petit bourgeois, and even antirevolutionary, the works of the Self-Reliant Literary Group and the New Poetry movement of the 1930s and 1940s, discussed in chapter 1, have now been reprinted numerous times. The reading public's appetite for these works has yet to wane, even if they still have not been fully embraced in the teaching curriculum. In addition to these two dominant literary movements of the prerevolutionary period, collections of all kinds are being published to capture other intellectual ventures or debates of decades past.[11] In recent years, works produced by intellectuals who lived under the southern regimes increasingly are being reprinted in the country, although they are generally limited to the less politically sensitive subjects of literary history or local customs and traditions.[12]

The fact that many of the works being reprinted are research projects and compilations of past intellectual debates on a particular subject indicates that the motivating factor is not commercial. The target audience for these publications is much smaller than the reading public interested in the literary works of the Self-Reliant Literary Group and the New Poetry movement. It seems to me, therefore, that underneath the seemingly diverse efforts to reprint earlier intellectual works there is an impulse toward true national integration on the one hand and the reassessment of history on the other. Certain research projects of the past are now being introduced as Vietnamese achievements worthy of preservation and dissemination.[13] The subtle emphasis on Vietnamese as opposed to northern or southern reminds us that the "we" remains elusive, although it also points to a conscious desire to address this problem. Often presented as simply preserving data that are threatened by the passage of time rather than stimulating any critical commentary or analysis of these earlier works, their reprinting is in fact putting into public circulation a wide range of views on intellectual creativity, state, and society that do not conform to the Party's socialist nation narrative. In this context, the focus has been particularly noticeable on the period immediately preceding the revolution precisely because this was when the most dynamic and contradictory questioning of national identity and culture took place.[14]

History casts a long shadow over the present. The shape of the current societal impulse to come to terms with the past and notions of national identity and culture has points of reference in the past and will be reflected in the ongoing discussion of what Vietnam ought to be in the new century. Such is the implication of this book. But at the very least, by returning in this book to the revolutionary politics of a historical period that constituted the key movement from a range of ideational possibilities to the structural institutionalization of a specific discourse of state and society, I hope to have given voice to the tangled web of intellectual concerns and expectations that motivated the heartfelt participation of a generation in the revolution. It came of age at a time when Vietnamese society was at its most Westernized but also its most agonized over what truly constituted national identity and culture. The beginning of such tormented questioning of national worth led to discussions of culture in essentialist terms, although this was the generation of intellectuals most at ease with world literature and philosophy.[15] Revolutionary politics and socialist ideology offered them a way to return to the more involved and exalted role of Vietnamese literati in the past while they were surging toward a radically new conception of nationhood and people in modern terms. They would be in the thick of change rather than watching forlornly from the sidelines as many in the former generations of literati had to do, preserving their integrity in the process but becoming impotent and irrelevant in the new world. It was a rare moment in which intellectuals felt the inspiring unity of their creative and social roles. They could fulfill their professional ambition while actively participating in the construction of a new political community for all Vietnamese.

As such, for many of those who participated in the revolution and who bravely held on to their integrity and professionalism against the encroachment of state authority in the early days of the socialist state, the legacy of the revolution was far more powerful and complex than the simplistic view of a struggle between capitalism and communism that underlined the American policy in Vietnam or the predetermined socialist nation narrative insisted upon by the Party. They have paid a heavy price for their faith and their insistence on the validity of the revolutionary experience, which utterly transformed the world they knew.

Appendix A: List of Archival Fonds and Dossiers

The following list provides information regarding the fonds and dossiers in the National Archives I (Hanoi) that I consulted for this study. Since a dossier often contains a number of items, only the names of the specific documents are cited in the body of the text. This appendix provides the full names of the dossiers. If the name of the dossier is the same as that of the document cited in the text, either the dossier contains only one document or the title of the document was used to name the dossier itself.

The fond of the Office of the Premier is divided into two sections. I was given access to section 2, which contains materials dated between 1945 and 1956. Information on culture, society, and education is included in this fond up to 1956. Thereafter, one must refer to the fonds of the appropriate ministries.

The fond of the Ministry of Education contains dossiers that are categorized as temporary or permanent. The temporary dossiers, according to the staff of the National Archives, were considered unimportant and would eventually be destroyed, although there was no indication as to when. The temporary dossiers often contain drafts of documents or reports, and that is probably the main reason why they are considered to be expendable. On the other hand, the existence of drafts of reports that were never finalized or the different draft versions of a particular document provides fascinating materials with which a researcher can get a glimpse of the debates and discussions that went on behind the scenes. I have utilized both temporary and permanent dossiers in this study.

The fond of the Ministry of Culture was newly established during my research period at the archives. I was the first foreign researcher given access to the fond of the Ministry of Culture, using a temporary catalog. The reader is advised that the numbers and names of dossiers cited in this study may change as they are integrated into the archives' current holdings.

Dossier Number	*Title of Dossier*

Fond of the National Assembly (Phông Quốc Hội)

Box 40/Dossier 564	Hồ sơ phiên lập thứ 31 của UBTVQH nước VNDCCH khóa II ngày 23-23/3/1966 về vấn đề CCGD và việc chuẩn bị kỳ họp thứ 3 của QH.

Fond of the Office of the Premier (Phông Phủ Thủ Tướng)

2408	Hồ sơ tổng kết 1000 ngày kháng chiến (23/9/1945 đến 19/6/1948)
2409	Báo cáo tình hình hoạt động của Hội Văn Hóa và Văn Nghệ VN 1949
2410	Báo cáo về công tác văn xã, y tế và tuyên truyền 1952
2412	Báo cáo thành tích về công tác giáo dục trong 8 năm kháng chiến của BGD
2419	Tập báo cáo của UBKCHC LK4 về tình hình công tác văn xã 53, 54, 55
2434	Báo cáo công tác 1953 của BDG
2435	Báo cáo của đồng chí Nguyễn Khánh Toàn về công tác giáo dục năm 1954
2438	Biên bản đại hội văn hóa toàn quốc 16–20/7/1948
2471	Hồ sơ về cải cách giáo dục 1950: Tập I
2477	Tập biên bản, nghị định, quyết định, đề án và báo cáo về tình hình công tác, học tập và sinh hoạt của học sinh, cán bộ Khu Học Xá Nam Ninh và trường trung học Quế Lâm 1952
2484	Công văn và chương trình giáo dục bổ túc của BGD năm 1951

Fond of the Ministry of Culture (Phông Bộ Văn Hóa)

2	Báo cáo của Bộ Văn Hóa về hoạt động của nước VNDCCH công tác của BVH 2 năm 1955–1956
3	Báo cáo công tác năm 1956 của BVH (bản thảo)
4	Hội nghị văn hóa toàn quốc từ 25/5–1/6/56 (không đủ)
5	Hội nghị văn hóa nông thôn của BVH năm 1956
7	Báo cáo của các Sở, Ty Văn Hóa và Hội nghị văn hóa ở các địa phương năm 1956
9	Chương trình, báo cáo công tác năm 1956 của các đơn vị trực thuộc BVH
14	Báo cáo công tác văn hóa năm 1956 của các Ty văn hóa Nghệ an, Hà tĩnh, Quảng bình, Vĩnh linh
19	Báo cáo của BVH, tổng hợp tình hình công tác văn hóa 3 năm 1955–1957
41	Báo cáo của BVH, các vụ chức năng, các ty văn hóa về tình hình tư doanh văn hóa năm 1958
122	Báo cáo của các đoàn cán bộ của BVH về tình hình hoạt động văn hóa văn nghệ ở một số tỉnh năm 1965
667	Báo cáo công tác tổ chức cán bộ 6 năm (1955–1961) và năm 1961 của BVH
843	Báo cáo công tác năm 1969 và kế hoạch từng quỹ năm 1970 của Vụ Tổ Chức BVH
901	Đề án, kế hoạch, báo cáo, thông báo của BVH, Đảng Đoàn BVH, Tiểu Ban Văn Nghệ về việc văn nghệ sĩ đi thực tế ở cơ sở năm 1955–1959
908	Hội nghị tổng kết văn nghệ sĩ đi công tác thực tế ở các cơ sở năm 1958 (11/1958)
909	Báo cáo của các ty văn hóa về cán bộ văn hóa đi thực tế ở cơ sở năm 1958

911	Kế hoạch, báo cáo của các đoàn cán bộ văn hóa đi thực tế ở các cơ sở là hợp tác xã nông nghiệp năm 1958 (11/1958)

Fond of the Ministry of Education (Phông Bộ Giáo Dục)

1 (temporary)	Sưu tập nghị định, thông tư, sắc lệnh năm 1945 của BGD
32 (temporary)	Tập tài liệu về nhân sự của Bộ QGGD và các cơ quan trực thuộc Bộ 1950–51
117 (temporary)	Công văn BGD về công tác cải cách giáo dục năm 1959–1960
525 (temporary)	Dự thảo báo cáo về thực hiện chính sách đối với giáo viên dân lập và trí thức năm 1957 của BDG
708 (temporary)	Thông tư của PTT về việc tuyển sinh vào các trường ĐH&THCN 1958
17	Công văn, chỉ thị của Ban Chấp Hành Trung Ương Đảng, Đảng Đoàn BGD về qui chế tuyển sinh đại học và trung học chuyên nghiệp, in lịch công giáo và xin khai giảng chủng viện 59–60
34	Tập tài liệu của Tiểu Ban Giáo Dục chính phủ, Đảng Đoàn BGD về đề án cải cách giáo dục và hoạt động của Tiểu Ban Cải Cách Giáo Dục 1965
43	Dự thảo báo cáo của Đảng Đoàn BGD về tình hình đội ngũ cán bộ và công tác xây dựng đội ngũ cán bộ của ngành giáo dục 1973
174	Báo cáo về tình hình đào tạo, bồi dưỡng cán bộ khoa học của BGD năm 1961
197	Tờ trình báo cáo của BGD về trường Bổ Túc Công Nông 1962
217	Báo cáo của BGD tổng kết kinh nghiệm các chủ trương của Bộ về trường BTCN và phương hướng mới đối với trường BTCN năm 1964

1279	Báo cáo tổng kết phong trào BTVH và thanh toán nạn mù chữ năm 1959 và phương hướng nhiệm vụ năm 1960 của Vụ BTVH của BGD
1280	Báo cáo thống kê của Ban Tổ Chức Trung Ương về trình độ văn hóa của cán bộ trường cao cấp năm 1959
1284	Hội nghị BTVH 8–10/1/1959
1361	Tờ trình lên Ban Bí Thư Trung Ương Đảng, Hội Đồng Chính Phủ về công tác BTVH 54–71 và phương hướng nhiệm vụ 5 năm 71–75 của BGD
1811	Danh sách các trường trung học chuyên nghiệp mở trong thời gian kháng chiến
1815	Thống kê tình hình tuyển sinh vào các trường đại học, chuyên nghiệp năm 55–59 của BGD
1836	Văn bản của Vụ ĐH&CN về tình hình yêu cầu đảm bảo số lượng và chất lượng tuyển sinh vào các trường đại học 61–62
1851	Báo cáo tổng kết công tác các trường ĐH&CH 1964
1860	Bác cáo về giải quyết công tác tuyển sinh vào các trường ĐH&CN 65–66

Appendix B: Number and Types of Vocational Secondary Schools in 1960

Agency in Charge	Name of School (and Specialization)
Ministry of Education (Bộ Giáo Dục)	* Foreign languages * Teacher training (12 schools)
Ministry of Heavy Industry (Bộ Công Nghiệp Nặng)	* Technology I (machinery, electricity, metallurgy, culture) * Technology II (chemicals, geology) * Technology III (weaving, fibers) * Mining (electrical mechanics, exploration, etc.)
Ministry of Forests and Agriculture (Bộ Nông Lâm)	* Central forests and agriculture (cultivation, breeding, veterinary medicine, silviculture, fisheries, fishing, staff organization) * Forests and agriculture, Việt Bắc * Forests and agriculture, Tây Bắc * Forests and agriculture, Nam Đàn * Forests and agriculture, Nghĩa Đàn
Ministry of Transport (Bộ Giao Thông)	* Rail transport (bridges, roads, carriages, transportation) * Water transport (land roads, waterways) * Merchant marine (ships' decks, ships' machinery) * Post (general technology, general professional knowledge)
Ministry of Construction (Bộ Kiến Trúc)	* Architecture (design, construction)
Ministry of Waterworks (Bộ Thủy Lợi)	* Waterworks (hydrography, geography, irrigation, etc.)
Ministry of Culture (Bộ Văn Hóa)	* Fine Arts, Hanoi (decorative arts, painting, sculpture) * Music * Arts and crafts (lacquer, ceramic, stone, cloth decoration)

Agency in Charge	Name of School (and Specialization)
	* National Theater (traditional theater forms *tuồng, cải lương, chèo*) * Cinema (direction, performing)
Ministry of Health (Bộ Y Tế)	* Health, Hanoi (medicine, dentistry, pharmacy) * Health, Hải Phòng * Health, Viêt Bắc * Health, Tây Bắc
Sports Commission (Ban Thể Dục và Thể Thao)	* Exercise and sports
Office of the Premier (Thủ Tướng Phủ)	* Economics and finance

Source: "Danh sách các trường Trung Học Chuyên Nghiệp trong thời gian kháng chiến (19–12–46 đến 7–1954) (không kể các trường ở Nam Bộ và miền Nam Trung Bộ hiện nay không có số liệu) (List of vocational secondary schools opened during the resistance period [19 December 1946 to July 1954] [not including those in the south and southern central regions currently without statistics]), Ministry of Education, dossier 1811.

Appendix C: Educational Levels of the 630 Highest Ranking Cadres in Central Organizations as of June 1959

Level and Grade	Total Number of People	Percentage in Each Grade	Number of People in Level	Percentage in Level
Level 1			63	10.5
(elementary)				
Grade 2	3	5		
Grade 3	3	5		
Grade 4	57	9.5		
Level 2			321	50
(lower secondary)				
Grade 5	81	13		
Grade 6	98	16		
Grade 7	142	21		
Level 3			103	16.5
(upper secondary)				
Grade 8	46	7.5		
Grade 9	24	4		
Grade 10	33	5		
University	31	8	143	23
Completed university	92	15		

Source: "Báo cáo thống kê của Ban Tổ Chức Trung Ương về trình độ văn hóa của cán bộ trường cao cấp năm 1959" (Statistical report of the Central Organization Committee on the cultural level of cadres in high-level schools in 1959), Ministry of Education, dossier 1280.

Note: Includes ministers and vice ministers, heads and deputy heads of committees and committee members, heads and deputy heads of ministry offices, and heads and deputy heads of bureaus and institutes of all central organizations belonging to the mass organizations, the state, and the party.

Notes

Introduction

1. See, for example, David G. Marr, *Vietnamese Anticolonialism, 1885–1925* (Berkeley: University of California Press, 1971); David G. Marr, *Vietnamese Tradition on Trial, 1920–1945* (Berkeley: University of California Press, 1981); Alexander B. Woodside, *Community and Revolution in Modern Vietnam* (Boston: Houghton Mifflin, 1976); Huynh Kim Khanh, *Vietnamese Communism, 1925–1945* (Ithaca: Cornell University Press, 1982); and Hue-Tam Ho Tai, *Radicalism and the Origins of the Vietnamese Revolution* (Cambridge: Harvard University Press, 1992).

2. Colonial era scholarship aside, the development of Southeast Asian studies as a field of which Vietnam became a part truly took off in the United States in the 1950s, driven by the reality of decolonization and by the American role in the cold war. For a succinct history, see the introduction to Benedict Anderson, *The Spectres of Comparisons: Nationalism, Southeast Asia, and the World* (London: Verso, 1998), 1–26.

3. Marr, *Vietnamese Anticolonialism,* xix.

4. Woodside, *Community and Revolution in Modern Vietnam,* ix.

5. Respectively, see Woodside, *Community and Revolution in Modern Vietnam,* 2; Keith Weller Taylor, *The Birth of Vietnam* (Berkeley: University of California Press, 1983); Truong Buu Lam, *Patterns of Vietnamese Response to Foreign Intervention, 1858–1900* (New Haven: Council on Southeast Asian Studies, Yale University, 1967); and John K. Whitmore, *Vietnam, Ho Quy Ly, and the Ming (1371–1421)* (New Haven: Council on Southeast Asian Studies, Yale University, 1985).

6. David W. P. Elliott, "Revolutionary Re-integration: A Comparison of the Foundation of Post-liberation Political Systems in North Vietnam and China," Ph.D. diss., Cornell University, 1976, 8.

7. Marr, *Vietnamese Tradition on Trial,* x.

8. Ibid.

9. Nguyen Khac Vien, "Confucianism and Marxism," in *Tradition and Revolution in Vietnam* (Berkeley: Indochina Resource Center, 1974), 45. This article was published previously in Jean Chesneaux, Georges Boudarel, and

Daniel Hemery, eds., *Tradition et révolution au Vietnam* (Paris: Editions Anthropos, 1971).

10. Nguyen Khac Vien, "Confucianism and Marxism," 50.

11. David Marr has elaborated further on this issue.

Why the continuity thesis has been so pervasive is an interesting question in itself. Presumably some historians have found in it a comfortable reaffirmation of their own conservative philosophy of life. Others have tended to confuse the wish to condemn imperialism morally with the more objective question of determining exactly what factors helped or hindered the imperialist and anti–imperialist causes. Among Vietnamese Marxists there has been the additional desire for historiography always to serve politics—both when employed as an analytical tool and when used as propaganda. (*Vietnamese Tradition on Trial,* x).

12. Paul Mus, *Sociologie d'une guerre* (Paris: Editions du Seuil, 1952). For a revised version in English, see John T. McAllister and Paul Mus, *The Vietnamese and Their Revolution* (New York: Harper and Row, 1970).

13. Frances FitzGerald, *Fire in the Lake: The Vietnamese and the Americans in Vietnam* (Boston: Little, Brown, 1972).

14. Ngo Vinh Long, *Before the Revolution: The Vietnamese Peasants under the French* (New York: Columbia University Press, [1973] 1991), ix.

15. John K. Whitmore, "Communism and History in Vietnam," in *Vietnamese Communism in Comparative Perspective,* edited by William S. Turley (Boulder: Westview, 1980), 32.

16. I have in mind the writings of Alexander Woodside, David Marr, and Huynh Kim Khanh already cited as examples of some of the early works on Vietnam. In the past decade, among others, see Hue-Tam Ho Tai, *Radicalism and the Origins of the Vietnamese Revolution;* Shawn Frederick McHale, "Printing, Power, and the Transformation of Vietnamese Culture, 1920–1945," Ph.D. diss., Cornell University, 1995; David G. Marr, *Vietnam, 1945: The Quest for Power* (Berkeley: University of California Press, 1995); Christoph Giebel, "Ton Duc Thang and the Imagined Ancestries of Vietnamese Communism," Ph.D. diss., Cornell University, 1996; and Peter B. Zinoman, "The Colonial Bastille: A Social History of Imprisonment in Colonial Viet Nam, 1862–1940," Ph.D. diss., Cornell University, 1996.

17. A quick perusal of a recent bibliography on Vietnam compiled by David Marr, for example, shows very clearly that for the period 1945 to 1975, and especially 1954 to 1975, the bulk of the materials concerns the south, international diplomacy among the various capitals, and the increasingly polarizing debate on American policy in Vietnam. Politics and society in North Vietnam barely appear. See David G. Marr, *Vietnam* (Oxford: Clio, 1992).

Recent works, however, have begun to address this gap in the literature. In the United States alone, see, for example Hy V. Luong, *Revolution in the Village: Tradition and Transformation in North Vietnam, 1925–1988* (Honolulu: University of Hawaii Press, 1992); Shaun Kingsley Malarney, "Ritual and Revolution in Vietnam," Ph.D. diss., University of Michigan, 1993; Thaveeporn Vasavakul, "Schools and Politics in South and North Vietnam: A Comparative Study of State Apparatus, State Policy, and State Power (1945–1965)," Ph.D. diss., Cornell University, 1994; and Russell Hiang-Khng Heng. "Of the State, for the State, Yet against the State: The Struggle Paradigm in Vietnam's Media Politics," Ph.D. diss., Australian National University, 1999.

18. Partha Chatterjee, *Nationalist Thought and the Colonial Discourse: A Derivative Discourse?* (London: Zed, 1986), 50.

19. Lynn Hunt, *Politics, Culture, and Class in the French Revolution* (Berkeley: University of California Press, 1984), 14.

20. Woodside, *Community and Revolution in Modern Vietnam*, 5.

21. David W. P. Elliott, "Institutionalizing the Revolution: Vietnam's Search for a Model of Development," in *Vietnamese Communism in Comparative Perspective*, edited by William S. Turley (Boulder: Westview, 1980), 217.

22. Katherine Verdery, *National Ideology under Socialism: Identity and Cultural Politics in Ceausescu's Romania* (Berkeley: University of California Press, 1991), 91 (emphasis in original).

23. Vietnamese intellectuals are well aware of this excessive demand on literature. In conversations, intellectuals often trade ironic comments about the basic powerlessness of literature concerning social and political issues, but at the heart of their thinking there is still a tremendous faith and an almost sacred view of the role of literature in daily life. Note, for example, this extraordinary comment made by the writer Phạm Thị Hoài on the occasion of being awarded a German literary prize in November 1993:

> I come from a civilization which bears heavily the mark of literature. There, literature generally carries many more responsibilities regarding the entire social life than a mother with her new-born child, more missions than a liberation army, more ties than blood connections, and can create more miracles than magical power. There, literature is a moral born to consolidate other morals, and with the character of morals, it has to be more than art.

Hoài is hardly a writer who conforms to the tenets of socialist realism, and yet her characterization of literature as a moral that "has to be more than art" is very much the way the state has defined literature. For Hoài's statement in Vietnamese, see Kim Thi, "Phạm Thị Hoài với giải Liberaturpreis" (Phạm Thị Hoài and the Liberaturpreis Prize), *Hợp Lưu*, no. 14 (December 93–January 94: 193).

24. Among others, see Ralf Dahrendorf, "The Intellectual and Society: The Social Function of the 'Fool' in the Twentieth Century," in *On Intellectuals: Theoretical Studies/Case Studies*, edited by Philip Rieff (New York: Doubleday, 1970); Raj P. Mohan, ed., *The Mythmakers: Intellectuals and the Intelligentsia in Perspective* (Westport, Conn.: Greenwood, 1987); and Lewis S. Feuer, *Ideology and the Ideologists* (New York: Harper and Row, 1975).

25. For an influential explication of the view of intellectuals in socialist systems as constituting a new class fully embedded in the power structure, see George Konrad and Ivan Szelenyi, *The Intellectuals on the Road to Class Power* (New York: Harcourt Brace Jovanovich, 1979).

26. Dina Spechler, *Permitted Dissent in the USSR: Novy Mir and the Soviet Regime* (New York: Praeger, 1982).

27. Carol Lee Hamrin and Timothy Cheek, eds., *China's Establishment Intellectuals* (Armonk, N.Y.: M. E. Sharpe, 1986).

28. The fact that intellectuals were at the forefront of the demand for democratic change that swept across the Soviet Union and Eastern Europe in the late 1980s was largely unanticipated by many analysts, who had come to accept the dominant view of intellectuals in socialist systems as fully embedded in the power structure. See Lewis A. Coser, "The Social Role of Eastern European Intellectuals Reconsidered," in *Culture, Modernity, and Revolution: Essays in Honour of Zygmynt Bauman,* edited by Richard Kilminster and Ian Varcoe (New York: Routledge, 1996).

For remaining socialist states like China and Vietnam, a number of recent works have begun to examine dissent from a different perspective. On China, see X. L. Ding, *The Decline of Communism in China: Legitimacy Crisis, 1977–1989* (Cambridge: Cambridge University Press, 1994). On Vietnam, see Russell Hiang-Khng Heng, "Of the State, for the State, Yet against the State: The Struggle Paradigm in Vietnam's Media Politics."

29. It should be noted that since a dossier can contain a number of documents, only the names of the specific documents are cited in the body of the text. The reader is referred to appendix A for a list of all the fonds and dossiers consulted in this study.

Chapter 1

1. See, for example, *Văn nghệ vũ khí sắc bén* (Art and literature: A sharp weapon) (Hanoi: NXB Văn Học, 1962).

2. *Một chặng đường văn hóa: Tập hồi ức và tư liệu về Đề Cương Văn Hóa của Đảng và đời sống tư tưởng văn nghệ, 1943–1948* (A cultural stage: A collection of memoirs and documents on the Party's 'Theses on Culture' and the ideological and intellectual life, 1943–1948) (Hanoi: NXB Tác Phẩm Mới, 1985), 29, 51.

3. Ibid., 88.

4. Đỗ Ngọc Quang, "Việt Nam sẽ có 'Đề Cương Văn Hóa' Mới" (Vietnam will have a new "Theses on Culture"), *Lao Động Chủ Nhật,* 13 December 1992.

5. Noting Trường Chinh's wide-ranging interests in political, economic, and military affairs, Gen. Võ Nguyên Giáp recently paid this tribute to his revolutionary comrade: "Uncle Hồ is the soul of the anti-French struggle, but Trường Chinh was the one who put forth the concrete direction and strategy in his work *The Resistance Will Win.*" See Võ Nguyên Giáp, "Cách Mạng Tháng Tám, kháng chiến, đổi mới: Những cống hiến sáng tạo nổi bật của anh Trường Chinh" (The August Revolution, the resistance, renovation: Trường Chinh's notable creative contributions), in *Trường Chinh và Cách Mạng Việt Nam* (Trường Chinh and the Vietnamese Revolution), edited by Viện Nghiên Cứu Hồ Chí Minh và Các Lãnh Tụ của Đảng (Hanoi: NXB Chính Trị Quốc Gia, 1997), 31.

6. Besides his numerous works on culture, Trường Chinh published a number of poetry collections. For a succinct description of his involvement and influence in the ideological and cultural arenas, see the entry under his

name in Đỗ Đức Hiểu et al., eds., *Từ điển văn học* (Literary dictionary), vol. 2 (Hanoi: NXB Khoa Học Xã Hội, 1984).

7. Vũ Ngọc Phan, *Những năm tháng ấy* (Those years) (Hanoi: NXB Văn Học, 1987), 130–31.

8. For a comprehensive discussion of the Franco-Vietnamese educational system, see Gail Paradise Kelly, "Franco-Vietnamese Schools, 1918–1938," Ph.D. diss., University of Wisconsin-Madison, 1975.

9. For a short discussion of the issue of romanization of writing systems based on Chinese characters, see John DeFrancis, "Vietnamese Writing Reform in Asian Perspective," in *Borrowings and Adaptations in Vietnamese Culture,* edited by Truong Buu Lam (Honolulu: Southeast Asian Studies, Center for Asian and Pacific Studies, University of Hawaii-Manoa, 1987). A longer work is John DeFrancis, *Colonialism and Language Policy in Vietnam* (The Hague: Mouton, 1977).

10. This refers to the famous Đông Kinh Nghĩa Thục (Eastern Capital Free School), founded in 1907 by reform-minded classical scholars. The school was part of a radical educational movement that aimed to give members of the general population a more vigorous and practical education than the classical and colonial versions provided. It was privately funded and within nine months was teaching more than forty classes for hundreds of students at all levels. Students were provided with books, pens, and paper as well as room and board. Realizing the school's anticolonial nature, the authorities shut it down in early 1908 and jailed a number of prominent scholars involved with it. See Vũ Ngọc Khanh, *Tìm hiểu nền giáo dục Việt Nam trước 1945* (Understanding the Vietnamese education system prior to 1945) (Hanoi: NXB Giáo Dục, 1985), 192–99.

11. There is a tendency to gloss over the achievements in disseminating *quốc ngữ* in the south because of the dominance of the Self-Reliant Literary Group and the New Poetry movement in the 1930s, which were Hanoi based but had enormous national influence. In historical terms, given the early introduction of *quốc ngữ* in the south, it was the breeding ground for the first *quốc ngữ* newspaper, the first *quốc ngữ* novel, and so on. Nevertheless, the point of takeoff for *quốc ngữ* as a feasible medium for communication came at about the same time for both north and south, requiring as it were the development of an audience knowledgeable in *quốc ngữ*, which only came into existence in the 1920s. For a detailed and judicious discussion of *quốc ngữ* in the south, See Bằng Giang, *Văn học quốc ngữ ở Nam Kỳ, 1865–1930* (*Quốc ngữ* literature in the south, 1865–1930) (Ho Chi Minh City: NXB Trẻ, 1992).

12. Phạm Thế Ngũ, *Việt Nam văn học sử giản ước tân biên, Tập III, Văn học hiện đại, 1862–1945* (A new outline history of Vietnamese literature, vol. 3, Contemporary literature, 1865–1945) (Saigon: Anh Phương, 1965), 426.

13. The voice belonged to Đức Lạng, who made these comments in an article in the Saigon newspaper *Journal d'Extrême-Orient* on 6 November 1953, quoted in Bằng Giang, *Văn học quốc ngữ ở Nam Kỳ,* 356.

14. Nguyễn Vỹ, *Văn thi sĩ tiền chiến: Chứng dẫn của một thời đại* (Prewar writers and poets: Testimony to an era) (Saigon: Khai Trí, 1970), 27.

15. Quoted in Phạm Thế Ngũ, *Việt Nam văn học sử,* 427.

16. Victor Hugo's *Les Miserables,* Alexander Dumas's *Les Trois Mousque-*

taires, Balzac's *La Peau de Chagrin,* and Molière's plays are some of the works Nguyễn Văn Vĩnh translated into *quốc ngữ,* introducing many young Vietnamese intellectuals and students to French literature. Vĩnh's energetic journalistic and publishing ventures did not prevent him from being engulfed in the Great Depression of 1920–30. From around 1934 to 1935, he tried to recoup his devastating financial losses by embarking on a search for gold in Laos. The harshness of the trips did him in, and he died in Laos in 1936. It was a sad end to a productive life. See the section on Nguyễn Văn Vĩnh in Phạm Thế Ngũ, *Việt Nam văn học sử,* 101–22.

17. Nguyễn Văn Vĩnh made this statement in the preface to the first book published by his publishing house, Phan Kế Bính's *quốc ngữ* translation of the Chinese classic *Three Kingdoms* (ibid., 116).

18. Quoted in ibid., 176.

19. Ibid., 219.

20. Neil Jamieson, *Understanding Vietnam* (Berkeley: University of California Press, 1993), 97, 98.

21. Ibid., 99.

22. The other nine concepts also reflect a fervent desire to move away from what Hoàng Đạo felt to be the backward and stagnant past: people should believe in the possibility of progress; live life with some kind of ideology rather than simply following what had gone before; engage in social work to break away from the closed nature of village and family; complement education with a strong will; provide a more equal role for women in society; attempt to gain a scientific mind and break away from superstitions; know that a career is more important and useful than fame; maintain a healthy body; and recognize the need for an organized mentality. See Hoàng Đạo, "Mười điều tâm niệm" (The ten concepts), first printed in several issues of the journal *Ngày Nay* (Today) between late 1936 and early 1937. Excerpts have been reprinted in Trung Tâm Nghiên Cứu Quốc Học, *Luận về quốc học* (Debate on national culture) (Danang: NXB Đà Nẵng và Trung Tâm Nghiên Cứu Quốc Học, 1999), 139–55.

23. Ibid., 143.

24. The influence on contemporary intellectual life of the Self-Reliant Literary Group was enormous and wide ranging. A detailed study of the group's literary output and other activities in the context of the time is still lacking. There are a few works in Vietnamese, but none that does full justice to the Self-Reliant Literary Group's pioneering literary and social importance. For a Vietnamese attempt to synthesize the group's development and achievements, see Doãn Quốc Sỹ, *Tự Lực Văn Đoàn* (The Self-Reliant Literary Group) (Saigon: Hồng Hà, 1960). In English, see Jamieson, *Understanding Vietnam,* esp. chap. 3.

25. Phạm Thế Ngũ, *Việt Nam văn học sử,* 423.

26. Thanh Lãng, *Phê bình văn học thế hệ 1932* (Literary criticism of the generation of 1932), 2 vols. (Saigon: Phong Trào Văn Hóa, 1972–73).

27. Hoài Thanh and Hoài Chân, *Thi nhân Việt Nam, 1932–1941* (Vietnamese poet, 1932–1941) (Hanoi: NXB Văn Học, [1942] 1988), 42.

28. Ibid., 43.

29. Ibid., 46.

30. The use of *new* and *old* here in labeling poets of the time concerns their adherence to poetic modes, not to their age. The classically trained older scholar Phan Khôi, for example, is credited with having been the first to bring New Poetry to life, and rank and file supporters on both sides of the poetic divide included both younger and older writers. Nevertheless, the majority of the poets supporting the new poetic movement was of a younger generation and primarily educated in the Franco-Vietnamese colonial education system.

31. Hoài Thanh and Hoài Chân, *Thi nhân Việt Nam*, 52–54, quoted in Jamieson, *Understanding Vietnam*, 185. I have translated additionally the last paragraph of the quote, which did not appear in Jamieson's book.

32. Hoài Thanh and Hoài Chân, *Thi nhân Việt Nam*, 55.

33. Marr, *Vietnamese Tradition on Trial*, 279–80.

34. Ibid., 280.

35. Phạm Thế Ngũ, *Việt Nam văn học sử*, 615.

36. *Xuân thu nhã tập* (reprint, including articles on *Xuân Thu Nhã Tập* selected by Nguyễn Bảo) (Hanoi: NXB Văn Học, [1942] 1991).

37. Nguyễn Hoành Khung, "Nhóm Thanh Nghị" (The Thanh Nghị Group), in *Từ điển văn học* (Literary dictionary), edited by Đỗ Đức Hiểu et al., vol. 2 (Hanoi: NXB Khoa Học Xã Hội, 1984), 125.

38. Phạm Thế Ngũ, *Việt Nam văn học sử*, 621.

39. David G. Marr, *Vietnamese Anticolonialism, 1885–1925* (Berkeley: University of California Press, 1971), 6.

40. On Hòa Hảo, see Hue-Tam Ho Tai, *Millenarianism and Peasant Politics in Vietnam* (Cambridge: Harvard University Press, 1983). On Cao Đài, see Jayne Susan Werner, *Peasant Politics and Religious Sectarianism: Peasant and Priest in the Cao Dai in Viet Nam* (New Haven: Council on Southeast Asian Studies, Yale University, 1981).

41. Nam Mộc, in *Một chặng đường văn hóa*, 86.

42. Huynh Kim Khanh, *Vietnamese Communism, 1925–1945* (Ithaca: Cornell University Press, 1982), 264.

43. Trường Chinh, "Đề Cương về Văn Hóa Việt Nam," in *Một chặng đường văn hóa*, 15.

44. Ibid., 15, 18.

45. Marr, *Vietnamese Tradition on Trial*, 364.

46. Mao Tse-Tung, *On New Democracy* (Peking: Foreign Language Press, 1967), 12.

47. Ibid., 58.

48. Ibid., 60.

49. Marr, *Vietnamese Anticolonialism*, 6.

50. The attempt to recruit Nguyễn Tuân is recounted by Tô Hoài, one of the first members of the Cultural Association for National Salvation, in his memoir. Tô Hoài became one of Nguyễn Tuân's closest friends, and the bulk of his memoir presents a loving but honest portrait of Nguyễn Tuân, one of Vietnam's most talented modern literary voices as well as one of its most distinctive personalities. See Tô Hoài, *Cát bụi chân ai* (Dust upon whose feet) (Hanoi: NXB Hội Nhà Văn, 1992).

51. Nguyễn Tuân, *Tùy bút* (Essays) (Glendale, Calif.: Đại Nam, [1941, 1943] 1986?), 25, 26.

52. Ibid., 239.

53. Tô Hoài, *Cát bụi chân ai*, 23.

54. Nhật Chí Mai's article in the journal *Ngày Nay* (Today), quoted in Vũ Đức Phúc, *Bàn về những cuộc đấu tranh tư tưởng trong lịch sử văn học Việt Nam hiện đại (1930–1954)* (On discussing the ideological battles in modern Vietnamese literary history (1930–1954) (Hanoi: NXB Khoa Học Xã Hội, 1971), 119.

55. Vũ Trọng Phụng's response to Nhật Chí Mai in the pages of the journal *Tương Lai* (Future), 25 March 1937, quoted in Vũ Đức Phúc, *Bàn về những cuộc đấu tranh tư tưởng*, 119.

56. Phạm Thế Ngũ, *Việt Nam văn học sử*, 425.

57. Ibid., 467. Khái Hưng's last novel is known variously as *Thanh Đức*, the name of one of the novel's protagonists; *Băn khoăn* (Apprehension); or the more forthright *Tội lỗi* (Sins).

58. Ibid.

59. Nguyễn Đăng Mạnh, introduction to *Tuyển tập Nguyễn Tuân* (Selected works of Nguyễn Tuân), vol. 1 (Hanoi: NXB Văn Học, 1981), 87–88.

60. There are diverse views on the period 1939–45. The literary historian Phạm Thế Ngũ, writing in the south in 1965, believed that the vibrant intellectual activities of the time indicated a period of renaissance and also maturity. He pointed to the return to many national concerns that were cast aside during the Westernized 1930s, the rise in interest in philosophy and science, and finally the emergence of many intellectual groups like Thanh Nghị, Tri Tân, and Hàn Thuyên, among others, rather than the dominance of one group over a period of time, as was the case with the Self-Reliant Literary Group. On the other hand, Nguyễn Đăng Mạnh, a northern literary critic, saw the period prior to the August Revolution as essentially bleak and hopeless, leading many intellectuals to feel a tremendous psychological crisis. Indeed, the period were inundated with escapist and sensational novels. All these conflicting moods and trends did exist within an extraordinary confusing period, but in the end even Phạm Thế Ngũ had to concede that at that time the Marxist view appealed to many intellectuals, like those in the Hàn Thuyên group, because "Since the French first occupied our country, the lamentable drama of the struggle has been played out between two cultures in which all that was beautiful in the old culture has disappeared and whatever is good in the new culture has yet to be discovered" (Nguyễn Đăng Mạnh, introduction to *Tuyển tập Nguyễn Tuân*; Phạm Thế Ngũ, *Việt Nam văn học sử*, 628).

61. For more details about these authors and translations of chapters from their works, see Ngo Vinh Long, *Before the Revolution: The Vietnamese Peasants under the French* (New York: Columbia University Press, [1973] 1991). Additional translations of works of the critical realist school can be found in Greg Lockhart and Monique Lockhart, *The Light of the Capital: Three Modern Vietnamese Classics* (Kuala Lumpur and New York: Oxford University Press, 1996).

62. Trường Chinh, "Đề Cương về Văn Hóa Việt Nam," in *Một chặng đường văn hóa*, 18.

63. For a rare portrait of an early Vietnamese scientist and what motivated him, see the succinct memoir of Dr. Tôn Thất Tùng, an internationally known

doctor who pioneered the study and surgery of the liver. (*Đường vào khoa học của tôi* [My path to science] [Hanoi: NXB Thanh Niên, 1978]).

64. Kim Lân, in *Một chặng đường văn hóa*, 72, 70.

65. Trường Chinh, "Mấy nguyên tắc lớn của cuộc vận động văn hóa mới Việt Nam lúc này" (Some major principles of the current movement of new Vietnamese culture), written 23 September 1944, published in the newspaper *Tiên Phong* (Vanguard), 1 December 1945, and reprinted in Trường Chinh, *Về văn hóa và nghệ thuật* (On culture and the arts), vol. 1 (Hanoi: NXB, Văn Học, 1985), 30.

66. Ibid., 31.

67. Ibid., 31–32.

68. Nguyễn Tế Mỹ, *Hai Bà Trưng khởi nghĩa* (The Trưng sisters' uprising) (Hanoi: Hàn Thuyên, 1944?).

69. Nguyễn Bách Khoa, *Kinh thi Việt Nam* (Vietnamese classical odes) Houston: Xuân Thu, [1945] 1976); *Văn chương Truyện Kiều* (The literature of *The Tale of Kiều*) (Hanoi: Hàn Thuyên, 1945); *Nguyễn Công Trứ* (Hanoi: Thế Giới, [194?] 1951).

70. The classically trained scholar Nguyễn Văn Tố, a writer for the journal *Tri Tân*, was the first to react against Nguyễn Tế Mỹ's book. His grievances against the Hàn Thuyên group's use of historical facts and interpretations were numerous. He delved into classical writings and surviving steles to argue, for example, against the assertion that the society of the Trưng sisters' time was ever a matriarchal one and that king Quang Trung, who waged what amounted to a proletarian peasant revolution and then turned against it, was killed by a group of his own military men in order to deceive the people and gain fame and power. In retaliation for these criticisms, the Hàn Thuyên group irreverently shot back: "The youth of today do not expect from you (this kind of) useless endeavor; they ask what is more useful, more practical. . . . Of what use is your kind of criticism to the progress of Vietnamese thought and literature at this time?" (quoted in Phạm Thế Ngũ, *Việt Nam văn học sử*, 639).

71. Trường Chinh, "Một con quỷ đội lốt Mác Xít" (A devil under the Marxist guise), *Cờ Giải Phóng*, 28 January 1945, reprinted in Trường Chinh, *Về văn hóa và nghệ thuật*, 1:34.

72. Marr, *Vietnamese Tradition on Trial*, 363.

73. Trần Độ, "Từ bản Đề Cương Văn Hóa Việt Nam năm 1943 nghĩ về văn hóa Việt Nam hiện nay" (From the 1943 "Theses on Vietnamese Culture" to thinking about contemporary Vietnamese culture), in *Bốn mươi năm Đề Cương Văn Hóa Việt Nam* (Forty years of the "Theses on Vietnamese Culture") (Hanoi: NXB Sự Thật, 1985), 58.

74. For English translations of Xuân Diệu's and Trường Chinh's poems, see Huynh Sanh Thong, *An Anthology of Vietnamese Poems: From the Eleventh through the Twentieth Centuries* (New Haven: Yale University Press, 1996), 297–98, 302–5.

75. Trần Độ, "Hai cuộc 'vận động văn hóa'" (Two "cultural campaigns"), in *Một chặng đường văn hóa*, 93.

76. Sóng Hồng, *Thơ* (Poetry) (Hanoi: NXB Văn Học, 1983).

77. Ibid., 8–12.

78. Nguyễn Tuân, "Trò chuyện" (Conversation), in *Cách mạng, kháng chiến, và đời sống văn học (1945–1954)* (Revolution, resistance, and the literary life resistance [1945–1954]), edited by Viện Văn Học, vol. 3 (Hanoi: NXB Tác Phẩm Mới, 1985–93), 18, 19.

79. Trường Chinh, "Chủ nghĩa Mác và văn hóa Việt Nam" (Marxism and Vietnamese culture), in *Về văn hóa và nghệ thuật*, vol. 1 (Hanoi: NXB Văn Học, 1985), 60.

80. Ibid., 65.

81. In addition to Hồ Chí Minh, four members of the Central Committee were present: Trường Chinh, Hoàng Quốc Việt, Hoàng văn Thụ, and Phùng Chí Kiên. For reasons unknown, Phạm văn Đồng, Võ Nguyên Giáp, and Vũ Anh did not attend, even though they were closely involved with the plenum's preparation. See Huynh Kim Khanh, *Vietnamese Communism*, 257–59.

82. Woodside, *Community and Revolution in Modern Vietnam*, 221.

83. Ibid., 165.

84. Trần Độ, "Hai cuộc vận động văn hóa," in *Một chặng đường văn hóa*, 98.

85. Mao Tse-Tung, Talks at the Yenan Forum on Literature and Art," in *Selected Works of Mao Tse-Tung*, vol. 3 (Peking: Foreign Language Press, 1967), 80.

86. Ibid., 74.

87. Ibid., 70, 81–82.

88. Huynh Kim Khanh, *Vietnamese Communism*, 328.

89. Le Duan, *This Nation and Socialism Are One* (Chicago: Vanguard, 1976).

90. Trường Chinh, "Chủ nghĩa Mác và văn hóa Việt Nam," 70, 72.

91. Ibid., 92.

92. Ibid., 104.

93. Ibid., 113.

94. Ibid., 121.

95. Ibid., 115.

96. Ibid.

97. Ibid., 116.

98. Ibid.

99. Ibid., 73.

100. Trường Chinh, "Marxism and Vietnamese Culture," quoted in Marr, *Vietnamese Tradition on Trial*, 364.

101. Marr, *Vietnamese Tradition on Trial*, 364.

102. E. J. Hobsbawm, *Revolutionaries: Contemporary Essays* (New York: New American Library, 1973), 3 (emphasis in the original).

103. These are phrases used in "Marxism and Vietnamese Culture," but they are also common in countless other works.

Chapter 2

1. Gail P. Kelly, *Franco-Vietnamese Schools, 1918–1938: Regional Development and Implications for National Integration* (Madison: Center for Southeast Asian Studies, University of Wisconsin, 1982), 46.

2. Nguyễn Công Hoan, *Đời viết văn của tôi* (My writing life) (Hanoi: NXB Văn Học, 1971).

3. Gail Paradise Kelly, "Franco-Vietnamese Schools, 1918 *to* 1938," Ph.D. diss., University of Wisconsin-Madison, 1975.

4. Đặng Thái Mai, *Hồi ký* (Memoir) (Hanoi: NXB Tác Phẩm Mới, 1985), 254.

5. Ibid., 286.

6. Ibid., 326. Chu refers to Chu Hsi (1130–1200) and Trinh to the brothers Cheng Yi (1033–1107) and Cheng Hao (1032–85), who were the leading exponents of Sung neo-Confucianism. Kháng Lương refers to the thinkers Kang Youwei (1858–1927) and Liang Qichao (1873–1929).

7. Thanh Lãng, *Phê bình văn học thế hệ 1932* (Literary criticism of the generation of 1932), vol. 1 (Saigon: Phong Trào Văn Hóa, 1972–73), 44.

8. Mã Giang Lân, "Quá trình hiện đại hóa văn học Việt Nam, 1900–1945" (The modernizing process of Vietnamese literature, 1900–1945) in *Quá trình hiện đại hóa văn học Việt Nam*, edited by Mã Giang Lân (Hanoi: NXB Văn Hóa Thông Tin, 2000), 36.

9. Kelly, *Franco-Vietnamese Schools*, 32.

10. Ibid., 40.

11. Thanh Lãng, *Phê bình văn học thế hệ 1932*.

12. Kelly, *Franco-Vietnamese Schools*, 91.

13. Trinh Van Thao, *Vietnam du Confucianisme au Communisme* (Paris: L'Harmattan, 1990), 62, 92, 108.

14. Đặng Thái Mai, *Hồi ký*, 164.

15. The first subgroup of the Cultural Association for National Salvation, founded in 1943 in an attempt to capture urban support, included the writers Tô Hoài, Nguyễn Đình Thi, Nam Cao, Nguyên Hồng, and Nguyễn Huy Tưởng and the critic Như Phong.

16. Lê Quang Đạo, "Nhớ lại việc truyền đạt bản 'Đề Cương về Văn Hóa Việt Nam' ở Hà Nội" (Remembering the transmission of the "Theses on Vietnamese Culture" in Hanoi), in *Một chặng đường văn hóa: Tập hồi ức và tư liệu về Đề Cương Văn Hóa của Đảng và đời sống tư tưởng văn nghệ, 1943–1948* (A cultural stage: A collection of memoirs and documents on the Party's "Theses on Culture" and on the ideological and intellectual life, 1943–1948) (Hanoi: NXB Tác Phẩm Mới, 1985), 38.

17. Như Phong, "Hoạt động của Hội Văn Hóa Cứu Quốc" (The Activities of the Cultural Association for National Salvation), in *Một chặng đường văn hóa*, 67.

18. Ibid., 66.

19. The situation concerning Đặng Thái Mai's *Văn học khái luận* (An outline of literature) is a case in point. As the first systematic attempt to examine literary activities from an explicitly Marxist viewpoint, *Văn học khái luận* is claimed to be the major result of the influence of the "theses." The fact that the work was published by the vilified Hàn Thuyên group was later explained away as a tactic necessary to get Marxist thought into the public arena. Mai himself claimed that he had read a copy of the theses in late 1943 and wrote the book afterward (*Một chặng đường văn hóa*, 83–84), although the person who transmitted the "Theses" to Mai noted that he did so in the middle of

1944 (43). *Văn học khái luận* itself was published in 1944, so the issue of the influence of the "Theses" on the book seems moot, especially since Đặng Thái Mai, a well-respected scholar in his own right, had explored Marxist works on his own much earlier and was entirely capable of writing such a work without the supposed guiding influence of the theses.

20. I differ here from Neil Jamieson's positive assessment of the Việt Minh's work within the intellectual community prior to the August Revolution. Jamieson writes:

By the end of 1944 [the Việt Minh's] interlocking networks of front organizations and covert agents had successfully introduced large numbers of urban intellectuals and students into the Vietminh network, bringing them under the influence of the ICP. In the cities of Vietnam, the tide was turning toward the Vietminh. Curiously enough, little has been written about this, one of the more important and successful of all party programs. The Communist Party itself has been strangely reticent about the National Salvation Cultural Association. (*Understanding Vietnam* [Berkeley: University of California Press, 1993], 190–91.)

There is no doubt that there was a great deal of sympathy for the Việt Minh's goal of national independence, but there was also much ambivalence concerning the socialist aspects of its agenda among the intellectuals. The Việt Minh did make a number of converts among the intellectuals, but these men and women proved to be crucial only *after* the August Revolution. My reading of memoirs of those who later joined the Việt Minh reinforces this. The Cultural Association for National Salvation was not important at the time, and this is precisely why the Communist Party has been reticent about it.

21. Đặng Thái Mai, "Vấn đề lập trường trong văn nghệ" (The issue of standpoint in art and literature), *Tiên Phong*, 1 October 1946, cited in Phong Lê, Vũ Tuấn Anh, and Vũ Đức Phúc, *Văn Học Việt Nam kháng chiến chống Pháp (1945–1954)* (Vietnamese literature in the anti-French resistance [1945–1954]) (Hanoi: NXB Khoa Học Xã Hội, 1986).

22. It was a short-lived association since Nguyễn Tường Tam was fervently anticommunist and bitterly opposed the Việt Minh's constant maneuvering (Jamieson, *Understanding Vietnam*, 200–201).

23. A number of key articles that entered into the debate on *quốc học* from the 1930s and 1940s have been collected and published recently in one volume. See Trung Tâm Nghiên Cứu Quốc Học, *Luận về quốc học* (The debate on national culture) (Danang: NXB Đà Nẵng and Trung Tâm Nghiên Cứu Quốc Học, 1999).

24. Thanh Lãng, *Phê bình văn học thế hệ 1932*, 1:154–55.

25. The Marxist critic Hải Triều argued that Phan Khôi was essentially writing as an idealist and did not see that material achievements reflect not so much spiritual values as the economic system. In subsequent exchanges, Phan Khôi would only accept the terms of *duy vật* and *duy tâm* as philosophical categories and not as the scientific methodologies insisted upon by Hải Triều (ibid., 10–20).

26. Phạm Duy, "Những bước đầu (trong nửa thế kỷ tân nhạc)" (The first steps [in a half century of modern music]), *Hợp Lưu* (Garden Grove, Calif.), no. 17 (June–July 1994): 23–41.

27. Articles on popular culture in this vein appeared in the journals *Tri Tân* and *Thanh Nghị*, both of which flourished between 1942 and 1945. Nguyễn Bách Khoa of the Hàn Thuyên group was most explicit on this subject, defining Vietnamese classical culture as popular culture. See Nguyễn Bách Khoa, *Kinh thi Việt Nam* (Vietnamese classical odes) (Hanoi: Houston: Xuân Thu, [1945] 1976).

28. Thanh Lãng, *Phê bình văn học thế hệ 1932*, 1:185.

29. Ibid., 226.

30. Quoted in ibid., 390.

31. For an English translation, see Huynh Sanh Thong, trans., *The Tale of Kieu* (New Haven: Yale University Press, 1983).

32. This view of *The Tale of Kiều* was emphasized in the 1920s by Phạm Quỳnh, but there were others among the classical scholars who passionately fought against the elevation of it to this grand status, arguing that Kiều was nothing more than a prostitute. For Phạm Quỳnh's role and the bitter debate around Kiều, see Phạm Thế Ngũ, *Việt Nam văn học sử giản ước tân biên*, Tập 3, *Văn học hiện đại, 1862–1942* (A new outline history of Vietnamese literature, vol. 3, Contemporary literature, 1862–1945) (Saigon: Anh Phương, 1965), 150–60.

33. Hue-Tam Ho Tai, *Radicalism and the Origins of the Vietnamese Revolution* (Cambridge: Harvard University Press, 1992), 110.

34. Nguyễn Bách Khoa, *Văn chương Truyện Kiều* (The literature of *The Tale of Kiều*) (Hanoi: Hàn Thuyên, 1945).

35. Ibid., 122.

36. Ibid., 168, 171.

37. In Vietnamese, the phrase is "Âm điệu lục bát tiến đến chỗ tuyệt diệu là một âm điệu báo tin sự diệt vong vậy" (ibid., 186; emphasis in original).

38. Ibid., 199.

39. Đặng Thái Mai, *Văn học khái luận* (An outline of literature) (Hanoi: Hàn Thuyên, 1944).

40. Ibid., 131.

41. Ibid., 133.

42. Dave Laing, *The Marxist Theory of Art* (Sussex: Harvester, 1978), 25.

43. Mao Tse-Tung, "Talks at the Yenan Forum on Literature and Art," in *Selected Works of Mao Tse-Tung*, vol. 3 (Peking: Foreign Language Press, 1967), 82 (emphasis is mine).

44. Trường Chinh, "Chủ nghĩa Mác và văn hóa Việt Nam" (Marxism and Vietnamese culture), in *Về văn hóa và nghệ thuật* (On culture and the arts), vol. 1 (Hanoi: NXB Văn Học, 1985), 84.

45. Nguyễn Hữu Đang and Nguyễn Đình Thi, *Một nền văn hóa mới* (A new culture) (Hanoi: Hội Văn Hóa Cứu Quốc Việt Nam, 1945).

46. Ibid., 30.

47. Ibid., 31.

48. Ibid., 44.

49. See chapter 1; and Hoài Thanh and Hoài Chân, *Thi nhân Việt Nam, 1932–1941* (Vietnamese poets, 1932–1941) (Hanoi: NXB Văn Học, [1942] 1988).

50. Nguyễn Hữu Đang and Nguyễn Đình Thi, *Một nền văn hóa mới*, 41.

51. Hoài Thanh, *Có một nền văn hóa Việt Nam* (There is a Vietnamese culture) (Hanoi: Hội Văn Hóa Cứu Quốc, 1946), 7.

52. Ibid.

53. Ibid., 17.

54. Ibid., 18.

55. Nguyễn Bách Khoa, *Kinh thi Việt Nam*.

56. Alexander B. Woodside, *Community and Revolution in Modern Vietnam* (Boston: Houghton Mifflin, 1976), 170.

57. Hoài Thanh, *Có một nền văn hóa Việt Nam*, 29.

58. Đặng Thái Mai, "Cần phải tu dưỡng nghệ thuật về phần chính trị" (The need to strengthen the arts in terms of politics), *Tiên Phong*, 1 April 1946.

59. Đặng Thái Mai, "Vấn đề lập trường trong văn nghệ" (The issue of standpoint in art and literature), *Tiên Phong*, 15 May 1946, quoted in Vũ Đức Phúc, *Bàn về những cuộc đấu tranh tư tưởng trong lịch sử văn học Việt Nam hiện đại (1930–1954)* (On discussing the ideological battles in modern Vietnamese literary history [1930–1954]) (Hanoi: NXB Khoa Học Xã Hội, 1971), 147.

60. Phong Lê, Vũ Tuấn Anh, and Vũ Đức Phúc, *Văn học Việt Nam kháng chiến chống Pháp (1945–1954)* (Vietnamese literature during the anti-French struggle [1945–1954]) (Hanoi: NXB Khoa Học Xã Hội, 1986), 31.

61. Vũ Đức Phúc, *Bàn về những cuộc đấu tranh tư tưởng*, 148.

62. Trotskyism as a branch of radical politics came to Vietnam through a number of students who studied in France in the 1920s and 1930s. For various reasons, prominent Vietnamese Trotskyists were southerners, and for a period roughly between 1930 and 1937 Trotskyists and communists worked fruitfully together in the south against the colonial authorities. Great ideological differences, however, emerged over time. The Trotskyists' advocacy of working-class interests and a direct move toward the dictatorship of the proletariat coupled with their intense distrust of the bourgeoisie contrasted starkly with the communists' emphasis on a nationalist revolution to be achieved through a popular front in which the bourgeoisie would play a role and peasant interests be taken into account. Proving no match for the Việt Minh's clandestine operations and extensive rural contacts, the Trotskyists were devastated by colonial repression in late 1939. Surviving remnants were decimated by the southern communists in 1945.

There was no real Trotskyist tendency in the north to speak of. The northern Hàn Thuyên group was a congregation of independent Marxist thinkers with diverse opinions. They were scholars, not revolutionaries, products of the Franco-Vietnamese education system if not self-taught. Their independence of thought and their desire for intellectual experimentation often clashed with the communists' demand for acquiescence. Thus, over the years a number of intellectuals came to be branded as Trotskyists in the north more often because of their intransigence than because they were Trotskyists.

For a brief discussion of the southern Trotskyists, see David G. Marr, *Vietnamese Tradition on Trial, 1925–1945* (Berkeley: University of California Press, 1983), 387–400. For a fuller description, see Hue-Tam Ho Tai, *Radicalism and the Origins of the Vietnamese Revolution* (Cambridge: Harvard University Press, 1983).

63. Trương Tửu, *Tương lai văn nghệ Việt Nam* (The future of Vietnamese art and literature) (Hanoi: Hàn Thuyên, 1945), quoted in Phong Lê, Vũ Tuấn Anh, and Vũ Đức Phúc, *Văn học Việt Nam kháng chiến chống Pháp (1945–1954)*, 35.

64. These comments would later come back to haunt Trương Tửu when the government moved to suppress the Nhân Văn–Giai Phẩm movement, which arose during a brief period of intellectual dissent in socialist Vietnam in 1956, in which he was a participant.

65. Khái Hưng, *Câu chuyện văn chương* (The conversation on literature), *Chính Nghĩa*, 7 October 1946, quoted in Vũ Đức Phúc, *Bàn về những cuộc đấu tranh tư tưởng*, 153.

66. Ibid.

67. The importance of Nguyễn Đình Thi's "Nhận đường" was highlighted when it was selected to lead off the first of the three volumes of collected documents and personal reminiscences on intellectual activities between 1945 and 1954. See Viện Văn Học, *Cách mạng, kháng chiến và đời sống văn học (1945–1954)* (Revolution, resistance, and the literary life [1945–1954]), vol. 1 (Hanoi: NXB Tác Phẩm Mới, 1985–93).

68. Viện Văn Học, *Cách mạng, kháng chiến và đời sống văn học*, 1: 9.

69. Ibid., 11.

70. Ibid., 18 (Emphasis in original).

71. Mao Tse-Tung, "Talks at the Yenan Forum on Literature and Art," 72, 73.

72. Nguyễn Đình Thi, "Nhận đường," 12.

73. Quoted in Phan Cự Đệ, introduction to *Tuyển tập truyện ngắn Việt Nam (1945–1954)* [Selected Vietnamese short stories (1945–1954)], edited by Phan Cự Đệ and Hà Văn Đức (Hanoi: NXB Đại Học và Giáo Dục Chuyên Nghiệp, 1988), 4.

74. Đỗ Đức Hiểu et al., eds., *Từ điển văn học* (Literary dictionary), vol. 2 (Hanoi: NXB Khoa Học Xã Hội, 1984), 8.

75. Ibid.

76. Phan Cự Đệ, introduction to *Tuyển tập truyện ngắn Việt Nam (1945–1954)*, 4.

77. Nam Cao, "Đôi mắt" (Pair of eyes), in *Tuyển tập truyện ngắn Việt Nam (1945–1954)*, 257.

78. Ibid., 254.

79. Ibid.

80. Lê Lợi and Quang Trung are revered kings in Vietnamese history. With tremendous popular support, they successfully repelled tides of Chinese invaders in the fifteenth and eighteenth centuries, respectively.

81. Nam Cao, "Đôi mắt," 255.

82. Nam Cao is reputed to have based the character of Hoàng on his friend the writer Vũ Bằng, who was already a journalist of some prominence when he left for the south in 1954. Vũ Bằng (1914–84) became an intellectual figure in the south, writing for numerous publications, but it was recently disclosed that he went south in 1954 as a secret agent for the north." See Nguyễn Quang Thiều, "Nhà văn Vũ Bằng: Người tình báo mang bí số X10" (The writer Vũ Bằng: Secret agent X10), *Nhân Dân*, 21 April 2000.

83. Nam Cao, "Bốn cây số cách một căn cứ địch" (Four kilometers from the enemy's base), in *Tuyển tập truyện ngắn Việt nam (1945–1954)*.

84. Quoted in Jamieson, *Understanding Vietnam*, 101.

85. Tô Ngọc Vân, "Tranh tuyên truyền và hội họa" (Propaganda art and art), *Tự Do*, no. 1 (July 1947), quoted in Vũ Đức Phúc, *Bàn về những cuộc đấu tranh tư tưởng*, 183.

86. Đặng Thái Mai, "Vài ý nghĩ về nghệ thuật" (Some thoughts on the arts), *Cứu Quốc*, special spring issue (January 1948), quoted in Vũ Đức Phúc, *Bàn về những cuộc đấu tranh tư tưởng*, 185.

87. Ibid.

88. Tô Ngọc Vân, "Vẫn tranh tuyên truyền và hội họa" (Still on propaganda paintings and art), *Văn Nghệ*, no. 2 (April–May 1948): 14.

89. Ibid., 15.

90. Ibid., 16.

91. Đặng Thái Mai, "Kháng chiến và văn hóa" (The resistance and culture), *Văn Nghệ*, no. 3 (June–July 1948): 3–10.

92. Ibid., 10.

93. Ibid.

94. Trường Chinh, "Mấy vấn đề thắc mắc về văn nghệ" (Some issues of concern in literature and art), *Văn Nghệ*, no. 6 (October–November 1948): 1–8.

95. As listed in issue no. 6 (October–November 1948) of *Văn Nghệ*, the editorial staff included Nguyễn Tuân, Hoài Thanh, Nguyễn Huy Tưởng, Xuân Diệu, Nguyễn Đình Thi, Tố Hữu, Đoàn Phú Tứ, and Nguyễn Xuân Khoát, with the collaboration of Đặng Thái Mai, Trần Huy Liệu, Ngô Tất Tố, Phan Khôi, Tô Ngọc Vân, Văn Cao, Huy Cận, Nguyên Hồng, Trần Văn Cẩn, Tô Hoài, Trần Huyền Trân, Như Phong, Nguyễn Công Hoan, Anh Thơ, Thanh Tịnh, Ngô Quang Châu, Trần Đình Thọ, and Nguyễn Tử Nghiêm.

96. Trường Chinh, "Mấy vấn đề thắc mắc về văn nghệ," 1.

97. Ibid., 2.

98. Ibid., 6.

99. Hoài Thanh, "Một thái độ cần xét lại" (An attitude that needs to be revised), *Văn Nghệ*, no. 7 (December 1948): 2–5.

100. Nguyễn Đình Thi, "Tìm nghĩa hiện thực mới" (Seeking the meaning of the new realism), *Văn Nghệ*, no. 10 (March 1949): 2.

101. Ibid., 7 (emphasis in original).

102. Tô Ngọc Vân, "Học hay không học?" (Study or not?), *Văn Nghệ*, no. 10 (March 1949): 54–58.

103. Ibid., 55.

104. Ibid., 53.

Chapter 3

1. Quoted in Phong Lê, Vũ Tuấn Anh, and Vũ Đức Phúc, *Văn học Việt Nam kháng chiến chống Pháp (1945–1954)* (Vietnamese literature in the anti-French Resistance [1945–1954]) (Hà Nội: NXB Khoa Học Xã Hội, 1986), 51 (emphasis is mine).

2. Ibid., 57.

3. Ibid.

4. Tố Hữu, "Đẩy mạnh phong trào văn hóa" (Pushing the cultural movement forward), *Sinh Hoạt Nội Bộ* (Internal activities), no. 13 (January 1949), quoted in Phong Lê, Vũ Tuấn Anh, and Vũ Đức Phúc, *Văn học Việt Nam kháng chiến chống Pháp (1945–1954)*, 57.

5. Nguyễn Tuân in the weekly journal *Văn Nghệ* (Literature and art), 29 August 1987, quoted in Nguyễn Hưng Quốc, *Văn học Việt Nam dưới chế độ Cộng Sản* (Vietnamese literature under the communist regime) (Stanton, Calif.: Văn Nghệ, 1991), 22, 23.

6. Nguyễn Hưng Quốc, *Văn học Việt Nam dưới chế độ Cộng Sản*, 23.

7. Edwin E. Moise, *Land Reform in China and North Vietnam: Consolidating the Revolution at the Village Level* (Chapel Hill: University of North Carolina Press, 1983), 147, 185.

8. Interzone 2 was the only one not to have an office of the Association of Art and Literature, understandable given its high concentration of ethnic minority groups. The total number of members in all the interzonal art and literature associations was stated to be 400 in 1949, with the largest concentration in interzone 4 (129 members), followed by interzone 3 (67 members) and interzone 1 (34 members). Associations of Art and Literature in interzones 5 and 6 were not created until 1950. See Hoài Thanh, "Báo cáo tình hình hoạt động của Hội Văn Hóa và Văn Nghệ Việt Nam năm 1949" (Report on the situation of the activities of the Association of Culture and Art and Literature on Vietnam in 1949), Office of the Premier, dossier 2409.

9. Phạm Duy, *Hồi ký thời cách mạng kháng chiến* (Memoir of the resistance period) (Midway City, Calif.: PDC Musical Productions, 1989), 198.

10. Ibid., 200.

11. Ibid., 181–82.

12. "Hội nghị tranh luận văn nghệ tại Việt Bắc 25–26–27–28 tháng 9–1949" (The conference of debate on literature and art in Việt Bắc, 25–28 September 1949), *Văn Nghệ* nos. 17–18 (November–December 1949): 3.

13. Ibid., 5.

14. Văn Tâm, "'Vũ Như Tô' trong cuộc đời 'bát nháo'" ("Vũ Như Tô" in the "Chaotic" Life), paper presented at a conference commemorating the life and works of the writer Nguyễn Huy Tưởng, Institute of Literature, Hanoi, 12 May 1992), 13 (emphasis in original).

15. "Hội nghị tranh luận văn nghệ tại Việt Bắc," 8, 9.

16. Ibid., 12.

17. Hoài Thanh and Hoài Chân, *Thi nhân Việt Nam, 1932–1941* (Vietnamese poets, 1932–1941) (Hanoi: NXB Văn Học, [1942] 1988), 195.

18. Anh Thơ, *Từ bến sông Thương* (From the quay of the river Thuong) (Hanoi: NXB Văn Học, 1986).

19. Tô Ngọc Vân, "Vẫn tranh tuyên truyền và hội họa" (Still on propaganda paintings and art), *Văn Nghệ*, no. 2 (April–May 1948): 9–18.

20. Edward Shils also has noted this dilemma with regard to Indian intellectuals in the 1950s in postcolonial India. The sincere sense of alienation many English-educated intellectuals felt with regard to their own people led them to promote complete "Indianization," although Shils emphasized the extent to which the cultural traditions of India lived on in its intellectuals in

spite of the alienation they felt and that was insisted upon by many commentators. See Edward Shils, *The Intellectual between Tradition and Modernity: The Indian Situation* (The Hague: Mouton, 1961), 65–68.

21. The guilt-ridden aspect of intellectual life whenever the focus was on the countryside had also been a strong component of the prerevolutionary period in both Russia and China. For the Vietnamese case, this has been noted by Vietnamese thinkers of different political persuasions. See South Vietnamese lawyer Nghiêm Xuân Hồng, *Phong trào quốc gia Việt Nam* (The Vietnamese nationalist movement) (Saigon: Quan Điểm, 1958), and a more recent article by northern literary critic Vương Trí Nhàn, "Mặc cảm-tha hóa-phân thân trong tâm lý người cầm bút" (Complex-corruptiveness-self division in the psychology of writers), *Cửa Việt* 15 (June 1992): 65–71.

22. Phạm Duy, *Hồi ký thời cách mạng kháng chiến*, 191.

23. Writing primarily on historical themes prior to the August Revolution, Nguyễn Huy Tưởng turned to more contemporary ones afterward. One of his best-known plays, *Những người ở lại* (Those who stayed), detailed the final days of 1946 when members of a Hanoi family must decide to either stay in Hanoi under French occupation or leave to join the Việt Minh. The title of the play refers to the young Hanoians' heroic decision to stay in Hanoi in order to defend the city, even if they had to die in the process. The defense of Hanoi was a theme Nguyễn Huy Tưởng returned to again in a 1961 novel entitled *Sống mãi với thủ đô* (Live forever with the capital). He was never fully satisfied with these efforts, feeling that he had yet to capture the enormous sacrifice and the epic nature of the struggle that played out in Hanoi. He once said, "[I] only like to describe the petit bourgeois class, only like to go deeply into the petit bourgeois psychology (generally like the characters in my play *Those Who Stayed*)." The critic Hà Minh Đức, maintaining the Party's orthodox view of literature, was therefore critical of such work as *Those Who Stayed* because they "did not pay enough proper attention to the role of the working people in the struggle in Hanoi" and because in "depicting petit bourgeois characters Nguyễn Huy Tưởng exploited too much of their complex relationships, especially love and marital relationships." The decadent urban image presented by such individualistic touches was criticized for not fully focusing on the struggle of the soldiers and as such not inspirational enough for the audience. See Hà Minh Đức, introduction to *Tuyển tập Nguyễn Huy Tưởng* (Selected works of Nguyễn Huy Tưởng), edited by Hà Minh Đức, vol. 1 (Hanoi: NXB Văn Học, 1984–86), 29.

24. *Tập văn cách mạng và kháng chiến* (Collection of revolutionary and resistance literature) (N.p: Hội Văn Nghệ Việt Nam, 1949).

25. The collection of short stories, an accepted classic of modern Vietnamese literature, is *Vang bóng một thời* (Echoes and shadows of an era) (Hanoi: Tân Dân, 1940).

26. "Hội nghị tranh luận văn nghệ tại Việt Bắc," 24.

27. Ibid., 25.

28. Ibid., 25, 26.

29. Ibid., 48.

30. Ibid., 50.

31. Ibid., 51.

32. Ibid., 52.

33. Ibid., 54.

34. Ibid., 56.

35. Nhóm Lê Quý Đôn, *Lược thảo lịch sử văn học Việt Nam* (A summary of Vietnamese literary history), vol. 3 (Hanoi: Xây Dựng, 1957), 359.

36. Phong Lê, Vũ Tuấn Anh, and Vũ Đức Phúc, *Văn học Việt Nam kháng chiến chống Pháp (1945–1954)*, 237, 238.

37. Ibid., 240.

38. Ibid., 250.

39. Ibid., 252.

40. See, for example, Vũ Đức Phúc, *Bàn về những cuộc đấu tranh tư tưởng trong lịch sử văn học Việt Nam hiện đại (1930–1954)* (On discussing the ideological battles in modern Vietnamese literary history [1930–1954]) (Hanoi: NXB Khoa Học Xã Hội, 1986).

41. The most comprehensive effort to date to examine the educational system in Vietnam between 1945 and 1965 is Thaveeporn Vasavakul, "Schools and Politics in South and North Vietnam: A Comparative Study of State Apparatus, State Policy, and State Power, 1945–1965," Ph.D. diss., Cornell University, 1994.

42. "Báo cáo về tình hình giáo dục trong 1,000 ngày kháng chiến" (Report of the education situation during the 1,000 days of the resistance), Office of the Premier, dossier 2408.

43. "Báo cáo về văn hóa xã hội trong năm 1953" (Report on culture and society in 1953), Officer of the Premier, dossier 2419.

44. *Đại Học Tổng Hợp Hà Nội: Lược sử* (The University of Hanoi: A historical summary) (Hanoi: Đại Học Tổng Hợp, 1991), 15.

45. "Báo cáo về công tác văn hóa–xã hội 1952" (Report on cultural and social work in 1952), Office of the Premier, dossier 2410.

46. Ibid.

47. Ngô Văn Cát, *Việt Nam chống nạn thất học* (Vietnam against illiteracy) (Hanoi: NXB Giáo Dục, 1980).

48. "Báo cáo các địa phương gửi Thường Vụ Trung Ương" (Reports from the localities to the Central Standing Committee), Office of the Premier, dossier 2409 (emphasis in original).

49. Ibid. (emphasis in original).

50. Ibid.

51. Moise, *Land Reform in China and North Vietnam*, 156.

52. "Giáo dục chính trị" (Political education), Office of the Premier, dossier 2484.

53. "Báo cáo về công tác giáo dục từ 1945 đến 1953" (Report on education work from 1945 to 1953), Office of the Premier, dossier 2412.

54. Ibid.

55. Ibid.

56. Ibid.

57. "Báo cáo về văn hóa xã hội trong năm 1953," Office of the Premier, dossier 2419.

58. David W. P. Elliott, "Institutionalizing the Revolution: Vietnam's Search for a Model of Development," in *Vietnamese Communism in Comparative Perspective*, edited by William S. Turley (Boulder: Westview, 1980), 204.

59. Alexander Woodside, *Community and Revolution in Modern Vietnam* (Boston: Houghton Mifflin, 1976).

60. "Báo cáo về văn hóa xã hội trong năm 1953," Office of the Premier, dossier 2419.

61. Bộ Giáo Dục, "Báo cáo công tác giáo dục năm 1953," Office of the Premier, dossier 2434.

62. Ibid.

63. Ibid.

64. Xuân Hoàng, *Âm vang thời chưa xa* (Echoes of a recent era) (Hanoi: NXB Văn Học and Hội Văn Học Nghệ Thuật Quảng Bình, 1995), 416.

65. Ibid.

66. "Báo cáo về văn hóa xã hội trong năm 1953," Office of the Premier, dossier 2419.

67. "Tập biên bản, nghị định, quyết định, đề án và báo cáo về tình hình công tác, học tập và sinh hoạt của học sinh, cán bộ Khu Học Xá Nam Ninh và Trường Trung Học Quế Lâm 1952" (Collection of minutes, decisions, proposals, and reports on the work, education, and activity situation of students and cadres in the Nanning Education Area and in the Guilin Middle School in 1952), Office of the Premier, dossier 2477.

68. This document, entitled "Giáo dục chính trị" (Political education), can be found in the fond of the Office of the Premier, dossier 2484. Of the official documents of this period that I have come across in the National Archives, many were brief, handwritten, personal notes from one Party official to another. Typed documents were relatively rare, and paper quality was poor. In contrast, this document was typed on good paper, thirteen pages in length, and written in a clear and confident style. It was signed "LINH," obviously an alias, which I have not been able to identify. It is for certain not the work of the recent Party general secretary Nguyễn Văn Linh, since all the people I have consulted agree that he did not have a high Party position at that time and would not have been involved in matters relating to culture, education, and ideology.

69. "Giáo dục chính trị," Office of the Premier, dossier 2484 (emphasis in original).

70. Ibid. (emphasis in the original).

71. Ibid.

72. Between 1949 and 1954, some twenty-one such works were published by the Literature and Art Publishing House, the main publishing house of the anti-French resistance period: fourteen from the Soviet Union, six from China, and one from North Korea. The data were compiled from Nhà Xuất Bản Văn Học, *35 năm văn học, 1948–1983* (Thirty-five years of literature, 1948–1983) (Hanoi: NXB Văn Học, 1983).

73. Merle Goldman, *Literary Dissent in Communist China* (Cambridge: Harvard University Press, 1967), 199.

74. Nhà Xuất Bản Văn Học, *35 năm văn học, 1948–1983*, 206, 208.

75. Chu Dương, "Phải thấm nhuần đường lối văn nghệ Mao Trạch Đông"

(We must absorb Mao Zedong's direction on literature and art), *Văn Nghệ*, nos. 36–37 (October–November 1952): 3–12.

76. It should be further noted that Hà Xuân Trường's comment was published when there was much hostility and distrust between China and Vietnam after the 1979 Chinese military attack on Vietnam for its invasion of Cambodia to oust the Khmer Rouge. See Hà Xuân Trường, "Văn học và đời sống văn hóa-văn nghệ mấy năm đầu kháng chiến chống Pháp trên trang báo Đảng" (Literature and literary and artistic life in the early years of the anti-French resistance on the pages of the Party's newspapers), in Viện Văn Học, *Cách mạng, kháng chiến và đời sống văn học (1945–1954)* (Revolution, resistance, and the literary life [1945–1954]), vol. 2 (Hanoi: NXB Tác Phẩm Mới, 1987), 46, 47.

77. See Phạm Duy, *Hồi ký thời cách mạng kháng chiến.*

78. Additionally, according to Tô Hoài, a number of those who were trained in these first sessions were sent to other places to begin the rectification process and the preparation for land reform. One group did arrive in Interzone 5, and another managed to reach the eastern part of the south when the Geneva Accords were signed. See Tô Hoài, *Cát bụi chân ai* (Dust upon whose feet) (Hanoi: NXB Hội Nhà Văn, 1992), 100.

79. Ibid.

80. Ibid.

81. The exaggerated harshness of these self-flagellating statements can be ascertained in the reserved judgment made in a 1986 work by the Institute of Literature on this period.

> Here we would like to note that the self-criticism statements made by the writers published in the newspapers in 1953 and 1954 are historical data, containing correct aspects but also those that need to be rectified, mainly when the writers demeaned themselves and denounced many of their own worthy literary works. Later many other writers did not accept those self-criticism statements. (Viện Văn Học, *Văn học Việt Nam kháng chiến chống Pháp*, 67)

82. Tô Hoài, "Nhận xét về tư tưởng của tôi" (Assessment of my thoughts), *Văn Nghệ*, no. 45 (November 1953): 10.

83. Ibid., 13.

84. In 1936 Thế Lữ wrote his most famous poem "Nhớ rừng" (Remembering the forest), which describes the frustrated and agonized feelings of a trapped tiger. The poem was written for Nhất Linh, the leader of the Self-Reliant Literary Group ostensibly to praise his strong will and commitment to change despite the fact that he was trapped in a difficult and mundane time. See Lê Hữu Mục, *Thân thế và sự nghiệp Nhất Linh* (The life and work of Nhất Linh), vol. 2 (Huế: Nhận Thức, 1957), 136.

After the miserable failure of the attempt at political coalition building with the Việt Minh after the August Revolution, Nhất Linh eventually settled in South Vietnam and renounced political activity and party affiliation of any kind. He began writing again, enjoying great prestige among intellectuals and the public. In 1963, he committed suicide to protest the Diem regime. Nhất

Linh's last days are briefly recounted in Jamieson, *Understanding Vietnam*, 241–44.

85. Thế Lữ, "Những sợi dây trói buộc tôi trên đường phục vụ cách mạng" (The ties that bind me on the road in the service of the revolution), *Văn Nghệ*, no. 41 (July 1953): 20.

86. Hoài Thanh, "Tự phê bình về quyển *Nói chuyện thơ kháng chiến*" (Self-criticism on the volume *Talking about Resistance Poetry*), *Văn Nghệ*, no. 42 (August 1953): 23, 24.

87. Ibid., 24.

88. Nguyễn Tuân, "Nhìn rõ sai lầm" (Seeing the errors clearly), *Văn Nghệ*, no. 41 (July 1953): 4–8.

89. Xuân Diệu, "Dứt khoát" (Decisively), *Văn Nghệ*, no. 41 (July 1953): 25.

90. Nguyễn Tuân, "Nhìn rõ sai lầm," 4.

91. Tô Hoài, "Nhận xét về tư tưởng của tôi," 10.

92. Ibid., 8.

93. Nguyễn Tuân, "Nhìn rõ sai lầm," 9.

94. Tô Ngọc Vân, "Tâm sự một người bị đầu độc" (Confidences of one who has been poisoned), *Văn Nghệ*, no. 41 (July 1953): 36.

95. Nguyễn Cao Luyện and Hoàng Như Tiệp, "Thực chất của 'Nhà Ánh Sáng'" (The reality of the "House of Light"), *Văn Nghệ*, no. 41 (July 1953): 49.

Chapter 4

1. Tô Hoài, *Cát bụi chân ai* (Dust upon whose feet) (Hanoi: NXB Hội Nhà Văn, 1992), 49.

2. The major sources in print in Vietnamese on NVGP continue to be Hoàng Văn Chí's volumes on the subject. See his *Tâm trạng của giới văn nghệ ở miền Bắc* (The disposition of the intellectual circle in the north) (Saigon: N.p., 1956); *The New Class in North Vietnam* (Saigon: Công Dân, 1958); and *Trăm hoa đua nở trên đất Bắc* (One hundred flowers bloom in the north) (Saigon: Mặt Trận Bảo Vệ Tự Do Văn Hóa, 1959).

3. Đặng Chân Liêu and Lê Khả Kế, *Từ điển Việt-Anh* (Vietnamese-English dictionary) (Hanoi: NXB Khoa Học Xã Hội, 1990), 647.

4. Georges Boudarel, *Cent fleurs écloses dans la nuit du Vietnam: Communisme et dissidence, 1954–1956* (Paris: Editions Jacques Bertoin, 1991), 12.

5. Ibid., 19.

6. Ibid., 18.

7. Đặng Chân Liêu and Lê Khả Kế, *Từ điển Việt-Anh*, 401.

8. Edwin E. Moise, *Land Reform in China and North Vietnam: Consolidating the Revolution at the Village Level* (Chapel Hill: University of North Carolina Press, 1983), 178.

9. Ibid., 280.

10. In recent years there have been more literary works dealing more openly with the devastating effects of land reform. See for example, Ngô Ngọc Bội, *Ác mộng* (Nightmare) (Hanoi: NXB Lao Động, 1990).

11. Moise, *Land Reform in China and North Vietnam*, 178.

12. *"Vân dại,"* or "Vân the crazy woman," is a well-known character in the traditional *chèo* theater of north Vietnam (Tô Hoài, *Cát bụi chân ai,* 101).

13. Ibid., 104.

14. See, for example, the writer Võ Văn Trúc's reminiscence of the devastating effects of land reform on his own village in *Chuyện làng ngày ấy* (Village stories in those days) (Hanoi: NXB Lao Động, 1993).

15. Trần Dần, Trần Mai Châu, and Vũ Hoàng Địch, "Bản tuyên ngôn tượng trưng" (Symbolic declaration), *Dạ Đài* (The netherworld), 16 November 1946.

16. Hữu Mai, "Để rõ thêm chân tướng phản động của Trần Dần" (To better understand Trần Dần's reactionary profile), *Văn Nghệ Quân Đội* (May 1958): 58.

17. Hoàng Cầm, "Tiến tới xét lại một vụ án văn học: Con người Trần Dần, hồi ký của Hoàng Cầm" (Toward a reassessment of a literary case: The person of Trần Dần, a memoir of Hoàng Cầm), *Nhân Văn,* 20 September 1956. For a full translation of this article into French, see Georges Boudarel, *Cent fleurs écloses dans la nuit du Vietnam,* 26–46.

18. Personal conversation, Hà Nội, July 1992.

19. Hữu Mai, "Để rõ thêm chân tướng phản động của Trần Dần," 58.

20. Hoàng Cầm, "Tiến tới xét lại một vụ án văn học," 2 (emphasis in the original).

21. Ibid.

22. Merle Goldman, *Literary Dissent in Communist China* (Cambridge: Harvard University Press, 1967), 140.

23. Boudarel, *Cent fleurs écloses dans la nuit du Vietnam,* 51.

24. Trần Công, "Về vấn đề lãnh đạo của Phòng Văn Nghệ Quân Đội" (On the leadership of the Army Office of Art and Literature), *Văn Nghệ,* no. 136 (30 August–5 September 1956).

25. Vũ Tú Nam, "Sự thực về con người Trần Dần" (The truth about the person of Trần Dần), *Văn Nghệ Quân Đội* (April 1958), 50.

26. Hoàng Cầm, "Tiến tới xét lại một vụ án văn học," 2.

27. Douglas Pike, *PAVN: People's Army of Vietnam* (Novato, Calif.: Presidio, 1986), 158–59.

28. Boudarel, *Cent fleurs écloses dans la nuit du Vietnam,* 119.

29. Vũ Tú Nam, "Sư thực về con người Trần Dần," 52.

30. Hoàng Cầm, "Tiến tới xét lại một vụ án văn học," 2.

31. Phùng Quán, *Vượt Côn Đảo* (Escape from Côn Đảo) (Huế: NXB Thuận Hóa, [1955] 1987).

32. Quoted in Vũ Tú Nam, "Sự thực về con người Trần Dần," 53.

33. Hữu Loan, "Phê bình 'Thơ chiến sĩ' của Hồ Khải Đại (Giải Thưởng Văn Học 54–55 của Hội Văn Nghệ Việt Nam)" (Critique of "A Soldier's Poems" by Hồ Khải Đại [Winner of Literary Prize 54–55 of the Association of Art and Literature of Vietnam]), *Văn Nghệ,* no. 142 (11–17 October 1956).

34. Lê Đạt, "Mỗi ngày mỗi lớn" (Growing bigger each day), in *Giai Phẩm Mùa Xuân, 1956* (Masterpiece of spring, 1956) (Hanoi: Minh Đức, 1956), 35, 36.

35. Lê Đạt, "Mới" (New), in *Giai Phẩm Mùa Xuân, 1956,* 29.

36. Lê Đạt, "Làm thơ" (Writing poetry), in *Giai Phẩm Mùa Xuân, 1956,* 4.

37. Phùng Quán, "Thi sĩ và công nhân" (Poets and workers), in *Giai Phẩm Mùa Xuân, 1956,* 27.

38. Hoàng Cầm, "Tiến tới xét lại một vụ án văn học," 2.

39. Hoài Thanh, "Tôi đã sai lầm như thế nào trong việc phê bình bài 'Nhất định thắng' của anh Trần Dần" (How I was wrong in criticizing Trần Dần's poem "We Must Win"), *Văn Nghệ*, no. 139 (20–26 September 1956).

40. Hoài Thanh, "Tôi đã sai lầm như thế nào."

41. "Một đợt học tập và đấu tranh" (A wave of studying and struggling), *Nhân Văn*, no. 1 (20 September 1956).

42. Hoài Thanh, "Tôi đã sai lầm như thế nào."

43. Nguyễn Đình Thi, "Một vài sai lầm khuyết diểm trong sự lãnh đạo văn nghệ" (Some mistakes and errors in the leadership of art and literature), *Văn Nghệ*, no. 140 (27 September–3 October 1956).

44. For example, see Hữu Loan, "Phê bình 'Thơ chiến sĩ' của Hồ Khải Đại."

45. "Báo cáo về những nét lớn về tình hình tư nhân kinh doanh trong ngành xuất bản và hướng cải tạo họ" (Report on some general aspects of the situation of private enterprises in the publishing business and the way to rectify them), Ministry of Culture, dossier 41.

46. Tô Hoài, *Cát bụi chân ai*, 51.

47. See, for example, Tô Hoài's account of how he tried to carry out the order to win over the poet Nguyễn Bính, who was the editor of the independent journal *Trăm Hoa*, which was not sympathetic to the *Nhân Văn* effort. (ibid., 56).

48. *Giai Phẩm Mùa Thu, Tập I* (Masterpiece of autumn, 1956, vol. 1) was published on 29 August 1956; *Giai Phẩm Mùa Thu, Tập II* (Masterpiece of autumn, 1956, vol. 2) on 30 September 1956; *Giai Phẩm Mùa Thu, Tập III* (Masterpiece of autumn, 1956, vol. 3) on 30 October 1956; and the last, *Giai Phẩm Mùa Đông, Tập I* (Masterpiece of winter, vol. 1), on 28 November 1956.

49. See, for example, "Bài học Ba lan và Hungari" (The lessons of Poland and Hungary), *Nhân Văn*, 20 November 1956.

50. *Nhân Văn*, 15 October 1956.

51. Hữu Loan, "Cũng những thằng nịnh hót" (Again those who sing praises), in *Giai Phẩm Mùa Thu, Tập II* (Hanoi: Minh Đức, 1956), 62.

52. Phùng Quán, "Chống tham ô lãng phí" (Against corruption and waste), in *Giai Phẩm Mùa Thu, Tập II*, 39–42.

53. Hữu Loan, "Lộn sòng" (Fraudulence), in *Giai Phẩm Mùa Đông* (1956), 36–44.

54. Q. Ngọc and T. Hồng, "Phê bình lãnh đạo sinh viên" (Criticism of the leadership of the university students), *Đất Mới*, 10 November 1956, 11.

55. Hoàng Cầm, "Em bé lên sáu" (The child of six), in *Giai Phẩm Mùa Thu, Tập II*, 17.

56. Nguyễn Đình Thi, "Những sai lầm về tư tưởng trong tập sách *Giai phẩm*" (Ideological mistakes in the *Giai Phẩm* volume), *Văn Nghệ*, no. 118 (26 April–3 May 1956).

57. Trần Dần, "Lão Rồng" (Old man Rồng), in *Giai Phẩm Mùa Xuân, 1956*, 45–47.

58. Nguyễn Đình Thi, "Những sai lầm về tư tưởng."

59. Chu Ngọc, "Chúng ta gắng nuôi con" (We try to raise the children), in *Giai Phẩm Mùa Thu, Tập III* (Hà Nội: Minh Đức, 1956), 56.

60. Trương Tửu, "Bệnh sùng bái cá nhân trong giới lãnh đạo văn nghệ"

(The sickness of the cult of personality within the leadership of the arts and literature), in *Giai Phẩm Mùa Thu, Tập II,* 11.

61. Đào Duy Anh, "Muốn phát triển học thuật" (To foster scholarship), in *Giai Phẩm Mùa Thu, Tập III,* 40.

62. Nguyễn Mạnh Tường, "Vừa khóc vừa cười" (Crying and laughing simultaneously), in *Giai Phẩm Mùa Thu, Tập III,* 23 (emphasis in the original).

63. Nguyễn Mạnh Tường, "Vừa khóc vừa cười," 25.

64. Phan Khôi, "Phê bình lãnh đạo văn nghệ" (Criticizing the leadership of art and literature), in *Giai Phẩm Mùa Thu, Tập I* (Hanoi: Minh Đức, 1956), 8–9.

65. Trương Tửu, "Bệnh sùng bái cá nhân trong giới lãnh đạo văn nghệ," 6–7.

66. Ibid., 9.

67. In an interview published in *Nhân Văn,* 30 September 1956, 1, Đào Duy Anh stated:

> No one denies another the freedom to conduct research and create, but if you do not have the means to conduct research and create then in reality you do not have any rights. No one denies a person the freedom of expression, but if you do not have the means to print books and newspapers then in reality you do not have any rights. Moreover, if you have the special and fortunate condition that enables you to print books and newspapers but you do not have the means to distribute them, then you should not speak forcefully of freedom. Since in reality the bulk of the means of publishing, distribution, and all the means of research and creation have been consolidated in government units, the issue is not so much the struggle to demand what kind of freedom but the struggle to win the genuine support of the government so as to generate conditions favorable to achieving those freedoms, like truly helping private individuals to publish easily, supporting the distribution end, providing favorable conditions for creativity and research, nurturing the broad publication of literary works, and paying special attention to the publication of scientifically researched works.

68. Trương Tửu, "Văn nghệ và chính trị" (Literature and art and politics), in *Giai Phẩm Mùa Thu, Tập III,* 17 (emphasis in the original).

69. Trương Tửu, "Tự do tư tưởng của văn nghệ sĩ và sự lãnh đạo của Đảng Cộng Sản Bôn-Sê-Vích" (Freedom of thought of intellectuals and the leadership of the Bolshevik Communist Party), in *Giai Phẩm Mùa Dông, Tập I* (Hanoi: Minh Đức, 1956), 3–10.

70. Trần Đức Thảo, "Nỗ lực phát triển tự do dân chủ" (The effort to foster democratic freedom), *Nhân Văn,* no. 3 (15 October 1956) (emphasis in original).

71. Nguyễn Mạnh Tường, "Concerning Mistakes Committed in Land Reform," speech delivered to the National Assembly on 30 October 1956, translated in Hoàng Văn Chí, ed., *The New Class in North Vietnam* (Saigon: Cong Dan, 1958), 159.

72. Ibid., 148.

73. Ibid., 149.

74. Nguyễn Hữu Đang, "Cần phải chính quy hơn nữa" (Need for more regularization), *Nhân Văn*, no. 4 (5 November 1956).

75. Nguyễn Mạnh Tường, "Concerning Mistakes Committed in Land Reform," 155.

76. "Bài học Ba lan và Hungari," *Nhân Văn*, (20 November 1956).

77. Quoted in *Nhân Dân*, 19 December 1956.

78. Tô Hoài, *Cát bụi chân ai*, 56.

79. The list of names of journalists and writers who signed a letter against *Nhân Văn* includes: Tô Hoài, Thế Lữ, Nguyễn Tuân, Nguyễn Huy Tưởng, Võ Huy Tâm, Nguyễn Bính, Học Phi, Hoàng Trung Thông, Hoa Bằng, Mộng Sơn, Vân Đài, Bùi Hiển, Nguyên Hồng, Thanh Tịnh, Đào Vũ, Nguyễn Ngọc, Bửu Tiến, Đặng Thái Mai, Từ Bích Hoàng, Phạm Hổ, and Trần Huyền Trân. See *Nhân Dân*, 16 December 1956.

80. See the three-part article by Xuân Trường, "Cần xác định tự do của văn nghệ sĩ" (The need to assess the freedom of creative intellectuals), *Nhân Dân*, 6–8 January 1957; and the three-part article by Trần Thanh Mai, "Quan điểm và lập trường tư tưởng của một người tự xưng là Mác-Xít-Lê-Ni-Nít" (The views and ideological standpoint of a person who claimed to be Marxist-Leninist), *Nhân Dân*, 2–14 January 1957.

81. "Nghị quyết của Đại Hội Văn Nghệ Toàn Quốc lần thứ hai" (Resolution of the Second National Congress of Art and Literature), *Nhân Dân*, 5 March 1957.

82. Tô Hoài, *Cát bụi chân ai*, 76.

83. Nguyễn Tuân, "Phở," *Văn*, (10 and 17 May 1957).

84. Huy Châu's criticism of Hữu Mai's book *Những ngày bão táp* (The turbulent days), *Văn*, 24 May 1957.

85. Quoted in Nguyên Hồng, "Tuần báo Văn và một số bài cần được nhận định như thế nào?" (How should the weekly *Văn* and a number of articles be assessed?), *Văn*, 6 August 1957.

86. Nguyễn Văn Bổng, "Nhận lại phương hướng qua việc phê bình tuần báo VĂN" (Reassessing direction through the criticism of the weekly VĂN), *Văn*, 20 September 1957 (emphasis in original).

87. As mentioned in Nguyễn Tuân, "Phê bình nhất định là khó" (Criticism is definitely difficult), *Văn*, 11 October 1957.

88. Tô Hoài, "Tổ chức phát triển lực lượng sáng tác trước nhất" (Organize to promote the creative body first and foremost), *Văn*, 1957, quoted in Tô Hoài, *Cát bụi chân ai*, 114.

89. Tô Hoài, "Góp thêm vài ý kiến về con người thời đại" (To contribute a few thoughts on the people of the age), *Văn*, 4 October 1957.

90. Minh Hoàng, "Đống máy" (The pile of machines), *Văn*, 27 December 1957.

91. Tô Hoài, *Cát bụi chân ai*, 77.

92. In his 1992 memoir, the writer Tô Hoài noted in a footnote that even in the 1992 collection issued by the Writers' Association in commemoration of its thirty-five years of existence the weekly *Văn* was never mentioned as the first journal of the Writers' Association (*Cát bụi chân ai*, 77).

93. Đặng Thái Mai, "Căn bản vẫn là vấn đề lập trường tư tưởng" (Funda-

mentally still an issue of ideological standpoint), *Nhân Dân,* 6–7 February 1958.

94. See Nguyên Hồng's statement under the column entitled "Các đồng chí ở báo 'VĂN' bắt đầu tự phê bình" (The comrades at the paper "VĂN" begin self-criticism), *Nhân Dân,* 2 February 1958.

95. *Nhân Dân,* 9 March 1958.

96. Tô Hoài, "Nhìn lại một số sai lầm trong bài báo và công tác" (Reconsidering a number of mistakes in newspaper articles and work), *Nhân Dân,* 12 March 1958; Tế Hanh, "Quan niệm siêu giai cấp của tôi về nhật tính và con người mới" (My transcendent class view on humanity and the new person), *Nhân Dân,* 14 March 1958.

97. *Nhân Dân,* 10 April 1958.

98. For Đào Duy Anh's self-criticism statement, see *Nhân Dân,* 19–21 May 1958; for Trần Đức Thảo's, see *Nhân Dân,* 22–24 May 1958.

99. Mạnh Phú Tứ on Nguyễn Hữu Đang (15 April 1958); Bùi Huy Phồn on Trương Tửu (16 April); Hoàng Châu Ký on Phan Khôi (17 April); Thế Lữ on Phan Khôi (21 April); Phạm Văn Khoa on Nguyễn Hữu Đang (23 April); Huy Vân on Trần Dần (25 April); Chính Hữu on Lê Đạt (26 April); Phạm Huy Thông on Trần Đức Thảo (4–5 May); Như Phong on Nguyễn Hữu Đang (11–12 May).

100. In the April 1958 issue of *Văn Nghệ Quân Đội* alone, there were three articles of this kind: Vũ Tú Nam, "Sự thực về con người Trần Dần" (The truth about the person of Trần Dần); Vũ Cao, "Ý thức phá hoại và tư tưởng đồi trụy của Hoàng Cầm" (Hoàng Cầm's destructive tendency and depraved ideology); and Nguyên Ngọc, "Con đường đi của Phùng Quán, con đường sai lầm điển hình của một người viết văn trẻ" (Phùng Quán's path, the model of the incorrect path of a young writer).

101. Tố Hữu, "Tổng kết cuộc đấu tranh chống nhóm Nhân Văn-Giai Phẩm" (Summarizing the struggle against the Nhân Văn-Giai Phẩm clique), *Văn Học,* 15 June 1958.

102. For a description of his own labor trip to a village in the aftermath of NVGP, see the memoir of the writer Tô Hoài, *Chiều chiều* (Evening) (Hanoi: NXB Hội Nhà Văn, 1999), chap. 1.

Chapter 5

1. Hirohide Kurihara, "Changes in the Literary Policy of the Vietnamese Workers' Party, 1956–1958," in *Indochina in the 1940s and 1950s,* edited by Takashi Shiraishi and Motoo Furuta (Ithaca: Southeast Asia Program, Cornell University, 1992), 2:186–87.

2. Ibid., 190.

3. "Bài nói chuyện của đồng chí Tố Hữu tại Hội Nghị Văn Hóa ngày, 25–5-56" (Comrade Tố Hữu's speech at the Congress of Culture, 25 May 1956), Ministry of Culture, dossier 4.

4. Ibid.

5. Ibid.

6. Shaun Kingsley Malarney, "Ritual and Revolution in Viet Nam," Ph.D. diss., University of Michigan, 1993.

7. "Báo cáo tổng quát tình hình hoạt động văn hóa của nước Việt Nam Dân Chủ Cộng Hòa trong hai năm hòa bình (từ tháng 1 năm 1955 đến tháng 9 năm 1956)" (General report of the Democratic Republic of Vietnam's cultural activities in the two years of peace [from January 1955 to September 1956]), Ministry of Culture, dossier 2.

8. "Báo cáo tóm tắt tình hình công tác của Bộ Văn Hóa trong 2 năm hòa bình (từ 1–1955 den 9–1956)" (Abridged report of the Ministry of Culture's work situation in the two years of peace [from January 1955 to September 1956]), Ministry of Culture, dossier 2.

9. Ty Văn Hóa Thanh Hóa, "Báo cáo tổng kết công tác văn hóa năa 1956 (ở Thanh Hóa])" (Summary report on cultural work for 1956 [in Thanh Hóa]), Ministry of Culture, dossier 14.

10. "Phòng Văn Hóa, UBHC LK4, "Biên bản Hội Nghị Văn Hóa LK4 ngày 27 and 28/9/56" (Record of the proceedings of the Conference on Culture of Interzone 4, 27–28 September 1956), Ministry of Culture, dossier 7.

11. Ty Văn Hóa Thái Bình, "Nghị quyết Hội Nghị Văn Hóa Thái Bình từ ngày 21 đến 23/8/56" (Resolution of Thái Bình's Conference on Culture from 21 to 23 August 1956), Ministry of Culture, dossier 7.

12. "Báo cáo công tác văn hóa của Bộ Văn Hóa năm 1956" (Report on cultural work of the Ministry of Culture for 1956), Ministry of Culture, dossier 3.

13. Ibid.

14. Ty Văn Hóa Thanh Hóa, "Báo cáo tổng kết công tác văn hóa năm 1956 (ở Thanh Hóa)," Ministry of Culture, dossier 14.

15. Ibid.

16. Phòng Văn Hóa, UBHC LK4, "Biên bản Hội Nghị Văn Hóa Liên Khu 4 ngày 27 & 28–9–56," Ministry of Culture, dossier 7.

17. For an evocative portrait of the intellectual community and Hanoi during this stormy period, see the two memoirs of the writer Tô Hoài, *Cát bụi chân ai* (Dust upon whose feet) (Hanoi: NXB Hội Nhà Văn, 1992), and *Chiều chiều* (Evening) (Hanoi: NXB Hội Nhà Văn, 1999).

18. Ty Văn Hóa Thanh Hóa, "Báo cáo tổng kết công tác văn hóa năm 1956 (ở Thanh Hóa)," Ministry of Culture, dossier 14.

19. Ty Văn Hóa Quảng Bình, "Báo cáo tổng kết công tác văn hóa năm 1956 ở Quảng Bình" (Summary report of cultural work in Quảng Bình in 1956), Ministry of Culture, dossier 14.

20. Phòng Văn Hóa, Ủy Ban Hành Chính LK3, "Biên bản hội nghị cán bộ văn hóa toàn khu ngày 2, 5/9/1956" (Record of the conference of cultural cadres of the interzone from 2 to 5 September 1956), Ministry of Culture, dossier 7.

21. Ibid.
For a frank account of this kind of destruction, which also occurred in a number of villages before 1954 in areas controlled by the Việt Minh, see Võ Văn Trực's memoir of what happened in his own village (*Chuyện làng ngày ấy* [Village stories in those days] [Hanoi: NXB Lao Động, 1993]).

22. Ibid.

23. Ty Văn Hóa Thái Bình, "Nghị quyết Hội nghị văn hóa Thái bình từ ngày 21 đến 23/8/56," Ministry of Culture, dossier 7.

24. Vụ Văn Hóa Đại Chúng, Bộ Văn Hóa, "Báo cáo công tác một năm 1956" (Work report for 1956), Ministry of Culture, dossier 9.

25. In 1956, the Soviet Union provided 159,991 books while China supplied 36,857. See "Báo cáo công tác một năm 1956 (của Vụ Văn Hóa Đại Chúng)" (Work report for the year 1956 [of the Department of Mass Culture]), Ministry of Culture, dossier 9.

26. "Báo cáo tổng kết công tác văn hóa trong ba năm hòa bình" (Summary report of cultural work in three years of peace), Ministry of Culture, dossier 19.

27. "Báo cáo tổng kết công tác năm 1956 của Cục Xuất Bản" (Summary report of the Bureau of Publication's work in 1956), Ministry of Culture, dossier 9.

28. "Báo cáo tổng kết công tác văn hóa trong ba năm hòa bình," Ministry of Culture, dossier 19.

29. This point was reiterated at a November 1993 conference celebrating the twenty-fifth anniversary of the founding of the Association of Art and Literature in the province of Quảng Ninh by Ngô Thảo, a member of the National Executive Committee of the Association of Theater Artists. He noted that it was important to maintain regional support for writers and artists in a place like Quảng Ninh. Given the country's limited resources, however, he argued that it was also necessary to reallocate financial support in a way that would aid the greater talents currently languishing outside the regional structure. He contended that the time had come to put an end to the process of, in his words, "amateurization in art and literature."

30. "Báo cáo tổng kết công tác văn hóa trong ba năm hòa bình," Ministry of Culture, dossier 19 (emphasis in original).

31. "Hội nghị văn hóa nông thôn" (Conference on culture in the countryside), Ministry of Culture, dossier 5.

32. Malarney, "Ritual and Revolution in Viet Nam," 297.

33. "Vấn đề nhà văn hóa nông thôn" (The issue of the cultural house in the countryside), Ministry of Culture, dossier 5.

34. "Báo cáo công tác một năm 1956" (Work report for 1956), Ministry of Culture, dossier 9.

35. "Vấn đề nhà văn hóa nông thôn," Ministry of Culture, dossier 5.

36. For example, in the case of a *xóm* in the *xã* of Hoàng Lộc it was reported that a passage in the book *Stories about the Active Life of Chairman Hồ* made people think and then volunteer beyond their capacity to build dikes. See Ty Văn Hóa Thái Bình, "Báo cáo tổng kết công tác văn hóa năm 1956 (ở Thanh Hóa)," Ministry of Culture, dossier 14.

37. "Vấn đề nhà văn hóa nông thôn," Ministry of Culture, dossier 5.

38. Ty Văn Hóa Hà Nam, "Báo cáo tổng kết của hội nghị tổng kết công tác văn hóa Hà nam 1956 (họp ngày 12–14/2/1957)" (Summary report of conference summarizing cultural work in Ha Nam in 1956 [meeting of 12–14 February 1957]), Ministry of Culture, dossier 7.

39. Ty Văn Hóa Quảng Bình, "Báo cáo tổng kết công tác văn hóa năm 1956 ở Quảng Bình," Ministry of Culture, dossier 14 (emphasis is mine).

40. "Báo cáo công tác một năm 1956," Ministry of Culture, dossier 9.

41. "Kiểm điểm công tác văn hóa trong ba năm qua (1955–57) và hướng công tác văn hóa trong ba năm tới (1958–60)" (Criticism of cultural work in the past three years [1955–57] and the direction of cultural work for the next three years [1958–60]), Ministry of Culture, dossier 19.

42. Ibid.

43. Ibid.

44. Ibid.

45. Ibid.

46. Ibid.

47. Ibid.

48. Ibid.

49. "Vấn đề nhà văn hóa nông thôn," Ministry of Culture, dossier 5.

50. Ibid.

51. For a glimpse of the restless atmosphere of the journalistic community in Vietnam in the 1930s and 1940s, see Vũ Bằng's affectionate memoir of his years as a journalist in both North and South Vietnam, *40 năm "nói láo"* (Forty years of "lying") (Saigon: Phạm Quang Khải, 1969).

52. To this day, for example, the Vietnamese Writers' Association continues to maintain relations with Battalion 54, which it adopted in the days of the anti-French resistance. Battalion 54 was part of the Capital Regiment (*trung đoàn Thủ Đô*) during the resistance. It was so named because it was composed of young men from Hanoi.

53. "Báo cáo tổng hợp tình hình kinh tế, văn hóa, xã hội ở 35 cơ sở có Tổ cán bộ văn hóa xuống lao động trong 2 tháng 8 và 9–1958" (Report summarizing the economic, cultural, and social conditions in thirty-five locales where cultural cadre groups worked for two months in August and September 1958), Ministry of Culture, dossier 908.

54. Ibid.

55. Ibid.

56. "Báo cáo tổng kết chung đợt đầu tham gia lao động, làm công tác văn hóa ở cơ sở của cán bộ căn hóa (do đồng chí thủ trưởng Cù Huy Cận báo cáo)" (General summary report of the first wave of work participation and cultural work in the localities by cultural cadres [reported by Comrade Leader Cù Huy Cận]), Ministry of Culture, dossier 908.

57. Ibid.

58. Ibid.

59. Ibid.

60. Ibid.

61. "Đề án đi xuống cơ sở tham gia lao động và nghiên cứu công tác của cán bộ ngành văn hóa" (Proposal to go down to the bases to participate in labor and conduct research by cadres of the cultural branch), Ministry of Culture, dossier 901.

62. Ibid.

63. "Báo cáo tình hình văn nghệ sĩ đi thực tế" (Report on the situation of artists and writers going down to the people), Ministry of Culture, dossier 901.

64. These numbers were compiled from reports contained in the Ministry of Culture's dossier 908.

65. "Báo cáo tổng kết chung đợt đầu tham gia lao động, làm công tác văn hóa ở cơ sở của cán bộ văn hóa (do đồng chí Thủ trưởng Cù Huy Cận báo cáo)," Ministry of Culture, dossier 908.

66. Ibid.

67. Ibid.

68. Ibid.

69. Ibid.

70. In the village of Khắc Niêm in Bắc Ninh Province, for example, out of thirty-one landowners classified during land reform, only twelve were so considered after rectification. See Ty Văn Hóa Bắc Ninh, "Báo cáo tình hình xã Khắc Niêm huyện Võ Giang" (Report on the situation of Khắc Niêm Commune of Võ Giang District), Ministry of Culture, dossier 909.

71. "Báo cáo những nét chung về công việc đã làm trong đợt công tác từ 18–11–58 đến 15–3–59 tại huyện Đông Quan (Thái Bình)" (Report on some main aspects of work done during the work wave from 18 November 1958 to 15 March 1959 in Đông Quan District [Thái Bình]), Ministry of Culture, dossier 911.

72. "Báo cáo sơ kết công tác bước 1 từ 1 đến 10/8" (Summary work report of step 1 from 1 to 10 August), Ministry of Culture, dossier 911.

73. Ibid.

74. Ibid.

75. One report from Thái Bình Province noted "distortions of socialism . . . , erasure and alteration of slogans . . . , dissemination of untruthful leaflets, tearing up of the flag, and the cutting of street lights' electric cables" (Báo cáo những nét chung về công việc đã làm trong đợt công tác từ 18–11–58 đến 15–3–59 tại huyện Đông Quan [Thái Bình])," Ministry of Culture, dossier 911.

76. "Báo cáo tình hình công tác bước hai, bổ xung báo cáo số 2 (về Kiên An)" (Report of the work situation in step 2, adding to the second report [on Kiên An Province]), Ministry of Culture, dossier 911.

77. Ibid.

78. "Báo cáo công tác bước 1 (từ 26–11 đến 15–12–1958)" (Work report on step 1 [from 26 November to 15 December 1958]), Ministry of Culture, dossier 909.

79. "Báo cáo sơ kết bước ngắn I của đợt II (từ 1–12 đến 30–1–1959) của tổ công tác thí điểm xã Tâm Đồng (tại Vĩnh Phúc)" (Summary report of step 1 in wave 2 [from 1 December to 30 January 1959] on the working group of the model commune of Tâm Đồng [in Vĩnh Phúc province]), Ministry of Culture, dossier 909. See also Malarney, "Ritual and Revolution in Viet Nam," 283–89.

80. "Báo cáo sơ kết bước ngắn I của đợt II (từ 1–12 đến 30–1–1959) của tổ công tác thí điểm xã Tâm Đồng (tại Vĩnh Phúc)," Ministry of Culture, dossier 909.

81. "Mấy nét tình hình chung" (Some aspects of the general situation), Ministry of Culture, dossier 41.

82. "Báo cáo những nét lớn tình hình tư nhân kinh doanh về nghề in và hướng cải tạo họ" (Report of some main aspects of the situation among

private enterprises in the printing business and the way to rectify them), Ministry of Culture, dossier 41.

83. Ibid.

84. "Củng cố thắng lợi một năm qua, tiến hành cải tạo xã hội chủ nghĩa các đoàn ca kịch dân doanh, hướng các đoàn thực sự phục vụ xã hội chủ nghĩa phục vụ công nông binh" (Bolster the victory of the past year, move forward to carry out socialist rectification of the people's performing troupes, and direct them to truly serve socialism, workers, peasants, and soldiers), Ministry of Culture, dossier 41.

85. "Nhận xét và kiểm điểm mấy nét chính về công tác tổ chức cán bộ từ trước đến nay" (Assess and criticize some main aspects of the work of organizing cadres from the beginning up to the present), Ministry of Culture, dossier 667.

86. "Mấy nét về tình hình hoạt động văn hóa văn nghệ của hai tỉnh Vĩnh Phúc-Phú Thọ từ 5–8–1964 đến cuối tháng 11–1965" (Some aspects of the situation concerning cultural, artistic, and literary activities in the two provinces of Vĩnh Phúc and Phú Thọ from 5 August 1964 to the end of November 1965), Ministry of Culture, dossier 122.

87. "Báo cáo tổng kết công tác của Vụ Tổ Chức Cán Bộ năm 1969" (Summary report of the work of the Cadre Organization Department in 1969), Ministry of Culture, dossier 843.

88. "Nhận xét về tình hình hoạt động văn hóa văn nghệ ở 3 cơ sở công nghiệp Hà Nội, Hải Phòng, Quảng Ninh và một số vấn đề cần giải quyết: Một số ý kiến đề ra" (Assessments of the situation of cultural, artistic, and literary activities in three work units in Hanoi, Hải Phòng, and Quảng Ninh and a number of issues to be resolved: Some opinions voiced), Ministry of Culture, dossier 122.

89. Ibid.

90. Ibid.

Chapter 6

1. "Giáo dục chính trị" (Political education), Office of the Premier, dossier 2484. For a detailed discussion of this document, see chapter 3.

2. Edwin E. Moise, *Land Reform in North China and Vietnam: Consolidating the Revolution at the Village Level* (Chapel Hill: University of North Carolina Press, 1983), 154.

3. Võ Thuần Nho, ed., *35 năm phát triển sự nghiệp giáo dục phổ thông* (Thirty-five years of development in general education) (Hanoi: NXB Giáo Dục, 1980), 30.

4. "Tập tài liệu về nhân sự Bộ Quốc Gia Giáo Dục và các cơ quan trực thuộc Bộ, 1950–51" (Documents on personnel of the National Ministry of Education and the organizations under the ministry, 1950–1951), Ministry of Education, dossier 32 (temporary).

5. "Về cải cách giáo dục năm 1950, Tập I: Đề án, thuyết trình, công văn của Bộ Giáo Dục và đồng chí Trường Chinh" (On the 1950 educational reforms,

volume 1: Proposals, lectures, and documents of the Ministry of Education and comrade Trường Chinh), Office of the Premier, dossier 2471.

6. Nguyen Van Huyen, *Sixteen Years' Development of National Education in the Democratic Republic of Vietnam* (Hanoi: Foreign Languages Publishing House, 1961), 19.

7. "Tập biên bản họp bàn về vấn đề Đại Học của Bộ Giáo Dục năm 1954" (Proceedings of Ministry of Education's meetings on the issue of the universities in 1954), Office of the Premier, dossier 2448.

8. For a general introduction to education in the Soviet Union, see Herbert C. Rudman, *The School and State in the USSR* (New York: Macmillan, 1967); and Joseph I. Zajda, *Education in the USSR* (Oxford: Pergamon, 1980). For a general introduction to education in China, see Stewart E. Frazer, ed., *Education and Communism in China: An Anthology of Commentary and Documents* (Hong Kong: International Studies Group, 1969); R. F. Price, *Education in China* (New York: Praeger, 1970); and Ruiqing Du, *Chinese Higher Education: A Decade of Reform and Development (1978–1988)* (New York: St. Martin's, 1992).

9. Võ Thuần Nho, ed., *35 năm phát triển sự nghiệp giáo dục phổ thông*, 3–4.

10. Between 1945 and 1954, the number of students in level 1 grew from 284,314 to 633,718 and the number of teachers rose from 3,534 to 12,589; in level 2, the number of students increased from 4,849 to 63,209 and teachers from 89 to 1,305; and in Level 3 the number of students and teachers rose from 735 and 31, respectively, in 1950 to 3,423 and 96 in 1954. See Võ Thuần Nho, *35 năm phát triển sự nghiệp giáo dục phổ thông*, 58.

11. Ibid., 60 (emphasis in original).

12. Ibid., 62.

13. Ibid., 28.

14. Ibid., 54.

15. Hồ Chí Minh, *Bàn về công tác giáo dục* (On discussing educational work) (Hanoi: NXB Sự Thật, 1972).

16. See, for example, Lê Duẩn, Trường Chinh, Phạm Văn Đồng, and Tố Hữu, *Về đường lối giáo dục xã hội chủ nghĩa* (On the methodology of socialist education) (Hanoi: NXB Sự Thật, 1979).

17. Võ Thuần Nho, *35 năm phát triển sự nghiệp giáo dục phổ thông*, 43.

18. Nguyễn Khánh Toàn, "Báo cáo về tình hình giáo dục" (Report on the educational situation), Office of the Premier, dossier 2435.

19. Nguyễn Khánh Toàn, "Báo cáo trình Trung Ương Đảng về kết quả nghiên cứu một số vấn đề giáo dục ở Trung Quốc" (Report to the central committee on the results of the research on a number of educational issues in China), Office of the Premier, dossier 2435.

20. Price, *Education in Communist China*, 101.

21. Nguyễn Khánh Toàn, "Báo cáo trình Trung Ương Đảng về kết quả nghiên cứu một số vấn đề giáo dục ở Trung Quốc," Office of the Premier, dossier 2435.

22. Nguyễn Khánh Toàn, "Báo cáo về tình hình giáo dục," Office of the Premier, dossier 2435 (emphasis in original).

23. Ibid. (emphasis in original).

24. Bộ Đại Học và Trung Học Chuyên Nghiệp, *Đại học và trung học chuyên*

nghiệp, 1945–1985 (Universities and second vocational schools, 1945–1985) (Hanoi: Đại Học và Trung Học Chuyên Nghiệp, 1985), 12.

25. Nguyễn Khánh Toàn, "Báo cáo về tình hình giáo dục," Office of the Premier, dossier 2435.

26. Vụ Nghiên Cứu Giáo Dục, "Một số ý kiến về vấn đề tiến tới một cuộc cải cách giáo dục" (Some suggestions on the issue of moving toward educational reform), Ministry of Education, dossier 117 (temporary).

27. Ibid.

28. The eleven college-level institutions in 1962 and their guiding ministries were: the University of Hanoi (Ministry of Education), Polytechnical College (Ministry of Education), Teacher Training College Hanoi (Ministry of Education), Teacher Training College Vinh (Ministry of Education), Agriculture and Forestry Institute (Ministry of Agriculture and Forestry), Hydraulic and Electric Power Institute (Ministry of Hydraulics), College of Medicine (Ministry of Health), College of Pharmacy (Ministry of Health), College of Communications and Transportation (Ministry of Communications and Transportation), College of Economics and Finance (originally Office of the Premier, now Ministry of Education), and the Higher School of Arts (Ministry of Culture). See "Tài liệu giới thiệu các trường đại học và chuyên nghiệp nước VNDCCH năm 1962" (Data introducing universities and secondary vocational schools of the Democratic Republic of Vietnam in 1962), Ministry of Education, dossier 762.

29. "Danh sách các trường Trung Học Chuyên Nghiệp trong thời gian kháng chiến (19–12–46 đến 7–1954) (không kể các trường ở Nam Bộ và miền Nam Trung Bộ hiện nay không có số liệu)" (List of vocational secondary schools opened during the resistance period [19 December 1946 to July 1954] [not including those in the southern and southern central regions currently without statistics]), Ministry of Education, dossier 1811. See appendix B for further information concerning the structure of specialization and ministerial control of the vocational secondary school system and the number and types of vocational schools that existed in 1960.

30. Nguyen Van Huyen, *Sixteen Years' Development of National Education*, 27.

31. Nguyen Minh Duong, "The System of Middle Technical Schools and Vocational Schools," in *Education in Vietnam, 1945–1991*, edited by Pham Minh Hac (Hanoi: Ministry of Education and Training, 1991), 84.

32. "Báo cáo về tình hình đào tạo, bồi dưỡng cán bộ khoa học của BGD năm 1961" (Ministry of Education's report on the situation of training and supporting scientific cadres in 1961), Ministry of Education, dossier 174.

33. "Đề cương trao đổi ý kiến về một số vấn đề trong hệ thống đào tạo cán bộ" (Proposal to exchange ideas on a number of issues regarding the system for training cadres), Ministry of Education, dossier 702.

34. Ibid.

35. "Báo cáo tổng kết công tác các trường đại học và trung học chuyên nghiệp năm 1964 của Bộ Giáo Dục" (Ministry of Education's report summarizing the work of the universities and vocational secondary schools in 1964), Ministry of Education, dossier 1851.

36. "Đề cương trao đổi ý kiến về một số vấn đề trong hệ thống đào tạo cán bộ," Ministry of Education, dossier 702.

37. "Chính sách cụ thể đối với thầy giáo" (Specific policy toward teachers), Ministry of Education, dossier 525 (temporary).

38. Ibid.

39. "Báo cáo về tình hình bồi dưỡng cán bộ khoa học của Bộ Giáo Dục năm 1961," Ministry of Education, dossier 174.

40. Ibid.

41. "Dự thảo báo cáo của Đảng Đoàn Bộ Giáo Dục về tình hình đội ngũ cán bộ và công tác xây dựng đội ngũ cán bộ của ngành giáo dục năm 1973" (Draft report of the Party Committee of the Ministry of Education on the situation concerning cadres and the work to build up the rank and file of educational cadres in 1973), Ministry of Education, dossier 43.

42. "Lược ghi ý kiến phát biểu của đồng chí Trường Chinh trong phiên họp cuối cùng của UBTVQH bàn về vấn đề cải cách giáo dục (ngày 30/3/1966)," (Summary of comrade Trường Chinh's statement at the last meeting of the Executive Committee of the National Assembly on Education Reform (March 30, 1966) National Assembly, box 40, dossier 564.

43. "Thông tư về việc tuyển sinh vào các trường Đại Học và Trung Học Chuyên Nghiệp năm 1958" (Circular on student selection into the universities and vocational secondary schools in 1958), Ministry of Education, dossier 708 (temporary).

44. "Số sinh viên chia theo thành phần gia đình và phân loại học sinh (số giữa năm học)" (The number of university students divided according to family categories and student categories [number at the middle of the school year]), Ministry of Education, dossier 1815.

45. "Sưu tập nghị định, thông tư, sắc lệnh năm 1945 của Bộ Giáo Dục" (A collection of the Ministry of Education's decisions, circulars, and decrees of 1945), Ministry of Education, dossier 1 (temporary).

46. "Đề cương dự thảo tổng kết công tác Bổ Túc Văn Hóa trong 30 năm qua (sơ thảo lần thứ 1, tháng 11/1977)" (Proposed draft summary of complementary education of the past 30 years [first draft, November 1977]), Ministry of Education, dossier 1156 (temporary).

47. Ibid.

48. Ibid.

49. Ibid.

50. Ibid.

51. "Hội nghị Bổ Túc Văn Hóa ngày 8–10–1950 (Bộ Giáo Dục tổ chức)" (Conference on complementary education held on 8 October 1950 [organized by the Ministry of Education]), Ministry of Education, dossier 1284.

52. Ibid.

53. For the educational levels of the 630 highest ranking cadres in central organizations as of June 1959, see appendix C. These cadres included ministers and vice ministers, heads and deputy heads of committees, committee members, heads and deputy heads of ministry offices, and heads and deputy heads of bureaus and institutes of all central organizations belonging to mass organizations, the state, or the Party.

54. Ibid.

55. "Dự thảo quy chế trường BTVHCN" (Draft regulations of the worker-peasant complementary schools), Ministry of Education, dossier 1018.

56. Price, *Education in Communist China*, 64.

57. "Báo cáo của Bộ Giáo Dục tổng kết kinh nghiệm các chủ trương của Bộ về trường Bổ Túc Công Nông và phương hướng mới đối với trường Bổ Túc Công Nông năm 1964" (Ministry of Education's report summarizing the experience of the ministry's policy on worker-peasant complementary education schools and the new direction concerning the worker-peasant complementary education schools), Ministry of Education, dossier 217.

58. "Báo cáo tổng kết phong trào Bổ Túc Văn Hóa và Thanh Toán Nạn Mù Chữ năm 1959" (Summary report on the complementary education and completion of the eradication of illiteracy movements in 1959), Ministry of Education, dossier 1279.

59. "Báo cáo về tình hình đào tạo, bồi dưỡng cán bộ khoa học của Bộ Giáo Dục năm 1961," Ministry of Education, dossier 174.

60. Ibid.

61. "Báo cáo về tình hình đào tạo, bồi dưỡng cán bộ khoa học của Bộ Giáo Dục năm 1961," Ministry of Education, dossier 174.

62. Note that the number of WPCE students entering the university system in the 1960–61 school year provided in this document is 2,600, which is higher than the figure of 1,925 students for the same year provided in the report contained in dossier 174. Since dossier 197 contains documents specifically on WPCE schools, I am inclined to take the figure of 2,600 as more representative. The fact that so many students were given additional points to allow them to enter the university system may account for the higher number in the end. See "Tờ trình Bộ Giáo Dục về chất lượng các trường BTVHCN," Ministry of Education, dossier 197.

63. "Báo cáo chất lượng các trường BTVHCN và những đề nghị nhằm nâng cao chất lượng những trường này" (Report on the quality of the WPCE Schools and suggestions for raising the quality of these schools), Ministry of Education, dossier 197.

64. "Văn bản của Vụ ĐH and CN về tình hình yêu cầu đảm bảo số lượng và chất lượng tuyển sinh vào các trường Đại Học năm 61–62" (Documents of the University and Vocational Department on the need to guarantee quantity and quality in the selection of students for the universities in the school year 61–62), Ministry of Education, dossier 1836.

65. "Tờ trình Bộ Giáo Dục về nhiệm vụ và hướng phát triển các trường BTVNCN" (Document presented to the Ministry of Education on the responsibility and development direction of the worker-peasant complementary education schools), Ministry of Education, dossier 197.

66. "Báo cáo của Bộ Giáo Dục tổng kết kinh nghiệm các chủ trương của Bộ về trường BTCN và phương hướng mới đối với trường BTCN năm 1964" (Report by Ministry of Education summarizing experience of ministry's policies concerning worker-peasant complementary education schools and their new direction in the year 1964), Ministry of Education, dossier 217.

67. Ibid.

68. Ibid.

69. "Tờ trình Bộ Giáo Dục về chất lượng các trường BTVHCN," Ministry of Education, dossier 197.

70. "Báo cáo của Bộ Giáo Dục tổng kết kinh nghiệm các chủ trương của Bộ

về trường BTCN và phương hướng mới đối với trường BTCN năm 1964," Ministry of Education, dossier 217.

71. "Báo cáo tổng kết phong trào BTVH năm 1959 ở địa bàn cơ quan trung ương" (Summary report on the complementary education movement in 1959 at the central work units), Ministry of Education, dossier 1279.

72. "Tờ trình lên Ban Bí Thư Trung Ương Đảng, Hội Đồng Chính Phủ về công tác BTVH từ năm 1954 đến 1971 và phương hướng nhiệm vụ 5 năm 71–75 của Bộ Giáo Dục" (Document presented by the Ministry of Education to the Secretariat of the Central Committee and Government Council on complementary education work from 1954 to 1971 and the direction and responsibilities of the five years 1971 to 1975), Ministry of Education, dossier 1361.

73. Ibid.

74. "Tỷ lệ phần trăm (%) các thành phần có trong tổng số các sinh viên ở các trường đại học chính quy" (Percentage of existing categories in the total number of university students attending the regular universities), Ministry of Education, dossier 1815.

75. "Báo cáo về giải quyết công tác tuyển sinh vào các trường ĐH và THCN năm học 65–66 của Bộ Giáo Dục" (Ministry of Education's report on the resolution of the work of student selection for the universities and the vocational secondary schools for the school year 65–66), Ministry of Education, dossier 1860.

76. "Số sinh viên chia theo thành phần gia đình và phân loại học sinh (số giữa năm học)," Ministry of Education, dossier 1815.

77. Douglas Pike, *PAVN: People's Army of Vietnam* (Novato, Calif.: Presidio, 1986), 190.

78. "Dự thảo báo cáo công tác tuyển sinh năm học 1971–1972" (Draft report on the work of student selection for the school years 1971–1972), Ministry of Education, dossier 1323.

Conclusion

1. On early Vietnamese history, see, for example, Keith W. Taylor, *The Birth of Vietnam* (Berkeley: University of California Press, 1983); and John K. Whitmore, *Vietnam, Ho Quy Ly, and the Ming (1371–1421)* (New Haven: Council on Southeast Asia Studies, Yale University, 1985).

2. Although primarily American and French, scholars from other countries also participated. See the comprehensive bibliography provided in David Marr, *Vietnam, 1945: The Quest for Power* (Berkeley: University of Cailfornia Press, 1995).

3. David G. Marr, *Vietnam's Tradition on Trial, 1920–1945* (Berkeley: University of California Press, 1981), x.

4. See John K. Whitmore, "Communism and History in Vietnam," in *Vietnamese Communism in Comparative Perspective,* edited by William S. Turley (Boulder: Westview, 1980).

5. Nguyen Khac Vien, *Tradition and Revolution in Vietnam* (Berkeley: Indochina Resource Center, 1974).

6. This view has been furthered recently by Russell Heng, who examined

state-media relations in five specific cases in Vietnam over time and found that dissent could often be found within the state-controlled media. See Russell Hiang-Khng Heng, "Of the State, for the State, Yet against the State: The Struggle Paradigm in Vietnam's Media Politics," Ph.D. diss., Australian National University, 1999.

7. Partha Chatterjee, *The Nation and Its Fragments: Colonial and Postcolonial Histories* (Princeton: Princeton University Press, 1993), 6.

8. Alexander Woodside, "The Struggle to Rethink the Vietnamese State," in *Culture and Economy: The Shaping of Capitalism in Eastern Asia,* edited by Timothy Brook and Hy V. Luong (Ann Arbor: University of Michigan Press, 1997).

9. I have in mind writers like Nguyễn Huy Thiệp, Phạm Thị Hoài, Bảo Ninh, and Dương Thu Hương, whose works have been translated into English and French.

10. Perhaps the marker for the beginning of the process of recovering history is the eight-volume *Văn xuôi lãng mạn Việt Nam, 1930–1945,* published by the Social Science Publishing House in 1989, which reprinted many of the prerevolutionary works that the Party once viewed as petit bourgeois if not antirevolutionary. See Nguyễn Hoành Khung et al., eds., *Văn xuôi lãng mạn Việt Nam, 1930–1945,* (Vietnamese romantic prose [1930–1945]), 8 vols. (Hanoi: NXB Khoa Học Xã Hội, 1989–90).

11. For example, the 1942 symbolist declaration of the Xuân Thu Nhã Tập group was reprinted in 1991. See *Xuân thu nhã tập* (Hà Nội: NXB Văn Học, 1991). A number of articles by those who participated in the heated intellectual debate of the 1930s on whether Vietnam had ever had a distinctive national culture can be found in Trung Tâm Nghiên Cứu Quốc Học, *Luận về quốc học* (The debate on national culture) (Danang: NXB Đà Nẵng và Trung Tâm Nghiên Cứu Quốc Học, 1999).

12. The works of Sơn Nam, Nguyễn Hiến Lê, and Vương Hồng Sển have been reprinted since the late 1980s. More recently, the literary historian Phạm Thế Ngũ's masterful three-volume work on Vietnamese literature, written in 1961, has been reprinted. See Phạm Thế Ngũ, *Việt Nam văn học sử giản ước tân biên* (A new outline history of Vietnamese literature) ([Sa Dec]: NXB Đồng Tháp, 1997–98).

13. See Trần Hữu Tá's preface to the reprint edition of Phạm Thế Ngũ's literary history volumes, "Một công trình nghiên cứu đáng quí" (A respected research endeavor), in Phạm Thế Ngũ, *Việt Nam văn học sử giản ước tân biên,* 1:9–12.

14. In addition to the reprinted works already cited, the 1939 magazine *Tao Đàn,* an imprint of the Tân Dân publishing house, was collected and reprinted in two volumes in 1998. See Nguyễn Ngọc Thiện and Lữ Huy Nguyên, eds., *Tao Đàn, 1939* (Hanoi: NXB Văn Học, 1998). The Writers' Association's own publishing house is also bringing out titles that focus on prominent publishing houses during the first half of the twentieth century. See, for example, Mai Hương, ed., *Nhà Xuất Bản Mai Lĩnh* (The Mai Lĩnh Publishing House) (Hanoi: NXB Hội Nhà Văn, 1997).

15. The tendency toward an essentialist definition of *culture* began in the 1930s and was particularly prominent in the early years in the life of North

Vietnam. Note, for example, the debate in the 1930s over *quốc học* (national culture) in Vietnam (whether Vietnamese scholars ever managed to formulate an ideological system that was specifically Vietnamese in comparison with those of Korea and Japan) and the debate over the definition of *Hán học* in 1955, which dominated the early volumes of the journal *Nghiên Cứu Văn Sử Địa* (whether works written in Chinese could be accepted into the corpus of classical Vietnamese works). In both of these instances, the more syncretic view of Vietnamese cultural development and borrowing eventually dominated, but the fierce debate around these issues showed the profound need to define a more concrete sense of self. It is also interesting to note that currently in Vietnam intellectual discussions, in the works of Phan Ngọc, for example, are increasingly framed in a more syncretic mode, taking into consideration Vietnamese borrowing not only from French and Chinese but from local ethnic minorities. See, for example, his *Văn hóa Việt Nam và cách tiếp cận mới* (Vietnamese culture and the new approach) (Hanoi: NXB Văn Hóa and Thông Tin, 1994).

Bibliography

National Archives Center No. 1 (Trung Tâm Lưu Trữ Quốc Gia-1), Hanoi

Fonds consulted:

Fonds of the National Assembly
Fonds of the Office of the Premier
Fonds of the Ministry of Education
Fonds of the Ministry of Culture

The reader is referred to appendix A for a complete list of dossiers in these fonds that were consulted for this study.

Journals and Newspapers (issues or years consulted)

Đất Mới (New land) (no. 1, 5 February 1956)

This was the only issue published by the Minh Đức Publishing House. It aimed to provide a forum for university students as part of the fervor of the Nhân Văn–Giai Phẩm period.

Giai Phẩm series (1956)

Five volumes in this series were published by Minh Đức Publishing House before it were banned by the state:

Giai Phẩm Mùa Xuân, 1956 (Masterpiece of spring, 1956) (5 February 1956)
Giai Phẩm Mùa Thu, Tập I (Masterpiece of autumn, vol. 1) (29 August 1956)
Giai Phẩm Mùa Thu, Tập II (Masterpiece of autumn, vol. 2) (30 September 1956)
Giai Phẩm Mùa Thu, Tập III (Masterpiece of autumn, vol. 3) (30 October 1956)

Giai Phẩm Mùa Đông, Tập I (Masterpiece of winter, vol. 1) (28 November 1956)

Nhân Dân (People's daily) (1956–58)

Nhân Văn (Humanism) (1956)

Published by the Minh Đức Publishing House in 1956, this weekly newspaper reached issue 5 before it was banned by the state: no. 1 (20 September); no. 2 (30 September); no. 3 (15 October); no. 4 (5 November); and no. 5 (20 November).

Nghiên Cứu Văn Sử Địa (Research on literature, history, and geography) (1954–59)

Tiên Phong (Vanguard) (1946)

As the official organ of the Hội Văn Hóa Cứu Quốc (Cultural Association for National Salvation) *Tiên Phong* was the first public intellectual forum of the anti-French resistance. It was superseded by the journal *Văn Nghệ*.

Văn (Literature) (1957–58)

Established as the first magazine of the Writers' Association in May 1957, *Văn* lasted less than a year. After thirty-seven issues, the state shut down the publication in January 1958. *Văn* was replaced by *Văn Học*.

Văn Học (Literary studies) (1958–63)

As the journal replacing *Văn*, *Văn Học* had an explicitly political origin. Its name was chosen to emphasize the more academic aspects rather than the independent creative tendencies of literary work. The journal's first year was devoted primarily to attacking the Nhân Văn–Giai Phẩm group. *Văn Học* was consolidated into *Văn Nghệ* in early 1963, and the Writers' Association would not have its own journal again until 1978.

Văn Nghệ (Literature and art) (1948–63)

This celebrated intellectual publication had a long and complicated history. Begun in 1948 during the anti-French resistance, this monthly literary journal continued to publish until 1957, for a total of 162 issues. In June 1957, *Văn Nghệ* was renumbered and reached issue number 71 in April 1963. After a consolidation with the journal *Văn Học* in 1963, *Văn Nghệ* was renumbered again, and this numbering continues to this day. *Văn Nghệ* was under the control of the umbrella intellectual organization Hội Liên Hiệp Văn Hóa Nghệ Thuật (Union of Cultural and Art Associations) until January 1978 when it became the official organ of the Writers' Association, its current status.

Văn Nghệ Quân Đội (the army's literature and art) (1956–58)

Books and Articles

Anderson, Benedict. *Imagined Communities: Reflections on the Origin and Spread of Nationalism*, London: Verso, 1983.

————. *The Spectres of Comparisons: Nationalism, Southeast Asia, and the World*. London: Verso, 1998.

Anh Thơ. *Từ bến sông Thương* (From the quay of the river Thương). Hanoi: NXB Văn Học, 1986.

"Bài học Ba lan và Hungari" (Lessons from Poland and Hungary). *Nhân Văn*, 20 November 1956.

Bằng Giang. *Văn học quốc ngữ ở Nam Kỳ, 1865–1930 (Quốc ngữ* literature in the south, 1865–1930). Ho Chi Minh City: NXB Trẻ, 1992.

Bốn mươi năm Đề Cương Văn Hóa Việt Nam (Forty years of the "Theses on Vietnamese Culture"). Hanoi: NXB Sự Thật, 1985.

Berman, Marshall. *All That Is Solid Melts into Air: The Experience of Modernity*. New York: Simon and Schuster, 1982.

————. *The Politics of Authenticity: Radical Individualism and the Emergence of Modern Society*. New York: Atheneum, 1970.

Boudarel, Georges. *Cent fleurs écloses dans la nuit du Vietnam: Communisme et dissidence, 1954–1956*. Paris: Editions Jacques Bertoin, 1991.

Brinton, Crane. *The Anatomy of Revolution*. New York: Vintage, 1957.

Brown, Archie, ed. *Political Culture and Communist Studies*. Armonk, N.Y.: M. E. Sharpe, 1984.

Brown, Edward J. *Russian Literature since the Revolution*. London: Collier-Macmillan, 1969.

"Các đồng chí ở báo 'VĂN' bắt đầu tự phê bình" (The comrades at the paper "VĂN" begin self-criticism). *Nhân Dân*, 2 February 1958.

Chatterjee, Partha. *The Nation and Its Fragment: Colonial and Postcolonial Histories*. Princeton: Princeton University Press, 1993.

————. *Nationalist Thought and the Colonial Discourse: A Derivative Discourse?* London: Zed, 1986.

Chesneaux, Jean, Georges Boudarel, and Daniel Hemery, eds. *Tradition et révolution au Vietnam*. Paris: Editions Anthropos, 1971.

Chu Dương. "Phải thấm nhuần đường lối văn nghệ Mao Trạch Đông" (We must absorb Mao Zedong's direction on literature and art). *Văn Nghệ*, nos. 36–37 (October–November 1952).

Chu Ngọc. "Chúng ta gắng nuôi con" (We try to raise the children). In *Giai Phẩm Mùa Thu, Tập III*, 48–56. Hanoi: Minh Đức, 1956.

Churchward, L. G. *The Soviet Intelligentsia: An Essay on the Social Structure and Roles of Soviet Intellectuals during the 1960s*. London and Boston: Routledge and Kegan Paul, 1973.

Connor, Walker. *The National Question in Marxist-Leninist Theory and Strategy*. Princeton: Princeton University Press, 1984.

Coser, Lewis A. "The Social Role of Eastern European Intellectuals Reconsidered." In *Culture, Modernity, and Revolution: Essays in Honour of Zygmunt Bauman*, edited by Richard Kilminster and Ian Varcoe. New York: Routledge, 1996.

Dahrendorf, Ralf. "The Intellectual and Society: The Social Function of the

'Fool' in the Twentieth Century." In *On Intellectuals: Theoretical Studies/Case Studies,* edited by Philip Rieff. New York: Doubleday, 1970.

Đại Học Tổng Hợp Hà Nội: Lược sử (University of Hanoi: A summary history). Hanoi: Đại Học Tổng Hợp Hà Nội, 1991.

Đặng Chân Liêu and Lê Khả Kế. *Từ điển Việt-Anh* (Vietnamese-English dictionary). Hanoi: NXB Khoa Học Xã Hội, 1990.

Đặng Thái Mai. "Căn bản vẫn là vấn đề lập trường tư tưởng" (Fundamentally still an issue of ideological standpoint). *Nhân Dân,* 6–7 February 1958.

———. "Cần phải tu dưỡng nghệ thuật về phần chính trị" (The need to strengthen the arts in terms of politics). *Tiên Phong,* 1 April 1946, 18–19.

———. *Hồi ký* (Memoir). Hanoi: NXB Tác Phẩm Mới, 1985.

———. "Kháng chiến và văn hóa" (The resistance and culture). *Văn Nghệ,* no. 3 (June–July 1948): p 3–10.

———. *Văn học khái luận* (An outline of literature). Hanoi: Hàn Thuyên, 1944.

Đào Duy Anh. "Muốn phát triển học thuật" (To foster scholarship). In *Giai Phẩm Mùa Thu, Tập III,* 33–46. Hanoi: Minh Đức, 1956.

———. *Nhớ nghĩ chiều hôm: hồi ký* (Twilight remembrances: A memoir). Ho Chi Minh City: NXB Trẻ, 1989.

DeFrancis, John. *Colonialism and Language Policy in Vietnam.* The Hague: Mouton, 1977.

———. "Vietnamese Writing Reform in Asian Perspective." In *Borrowings and Adaptations in Vietnamese Culture,* edited by Truong Buu Lam. Southeast Asia Papers, no. 25. Honolulu: Southeast Asian Studies, Center for Asian and Pacific Studies, University of Hawaii-Manoa, 1987.

Ding, X. L. *The Decline of Communism in China: Legitimacy Crisis, 1977–1989.* Cambridge: Cambridge University Press, 1994.

Đỗ Đức Hiểu et al., eds. *Từ điển văn học* (Literary dictionary). 2 vols. Hanoi: NXB Khoa Học Xã Hội, 1983–84.

Đỗ Ngọc Quang, "Việt Nam sẽ có 'Đề Cương Văn Hóa' mới" (Vietnam will have new "Theses on Culture"). *Lao Động Chủ Nhật,* 13 December 1992.

Doãn Quốc Sỹ. *Tự Lực Văn Đoàn* (The Self-Reliant Literary Group). Saigon: Hồng Hà, 1960.

Du, Ruiqing. *Chinese Higher Education: A Decade of Reform and Development (1978–1988).* New York: St. Martin's, 1992.

Duiker, William J. *The Communist Road to Power in Vietnam.* Boulder: Westview, 1981.

———. *The Rise of Nationalism in Vietnam: 1900–1941.* Ithaca: Cornell University Press, 1976.

Elliott, David W. P. "Institutionalizing the Revolution: Vietnam's Search for a Model of Development." In *Vietnamese Communism in Comparative Perspective,* edited by William S. Turley. Boulder: Westview, 1980.

———. "Revolutionary Re-integration: A Comparison of the Foundation of Post-liberation Political Systems in North Vietnam and China." Ph.D. diss., Cornell University, 1976.

Feuer, Lewis S. *Ideology and the Ideologists.* New York: Harper and Row, 1975.

FitzGerald, Frances. *Fire in the Lake: The Vietnamese and the Americans in Vietnam.* Boston: Little, Brown, 1972.

Frazer, Stewart E., ed. *Education and Communism in China: An Anthology of Commentary and Documents.* Hong Kong: International Studies Group, 1969.

Gella, Aleksander, ed. *The Intelligentsia and the Intellectuals.* London: Sage, 1976.

Gellner, Ernest. *Nations and Nationalism.* Ithaca: Cornell University Press, 1983.

Giebel, Christoph. "Ton Duc Thang and the Imagined Ancestries of Vietnamese Communism." Ph.D. diss., Cornell University, 1996.

Goldman, Merle. *China's Intellectuals: Advise and Dissent.* Cambridge: Harvard University Press, 1981.

———. *Literary Dissent in Communist China.* Cambridge: Harvard University Press, 1967.

———. *Modern Chinese Literature in Communist China.* Cambridge: Harvard University Press, 1977.

Hà Minh Đức. Introduction to *Tuyển tập Nguyễn Huy Tưởng* (Selected works of Nguyễn Huy Tưởng). Vol. 1. Hanoi: NXB Van Hoc, 1984.

———, ed. *Tuyển tập Nguyễn Huy Tưởng* (Selected works of Nguyễn Huy Tưởng). 3 vols. Hanoi: NXB Văn Học, 1984.

Hà Xuân Trường. "Văn học và đời sống văn hóa-văn nghệ mấy năm đầu kháng chiến chống Pháp trên trang báo Đảng" (Literature and the literary and artistic life in the early years of the anti-French resistance on the pages of the Party's newspapers). In *Cách mạng, kháng chiến và đời sống văn học (1945–1954),* edited by Viện Văn Học. Vol. 2. Hanoi: NXB Tác Phẩm Mới, 1987.

Hamrin, Carol Lee, and Timothy Cheek, eds. *China's Establishment Intellectuals.* Armonk, N.Y.: M. E. Sharpe, 1986.

Heng, Russell Hiang-Khng. "Of the State, for the State, Yet against the State: The Struggle Paradigm in Vietnam's Media Politics." Ph.D. diss., Australian National University, 1999.

Hingley, Ronald. *Russian Writers and Soviet Society, 1917–1978.* London: Methuen, 1981.

Hồ Chí Minh. *Bàn về công tác giáo dục* (On discussing educational work). Hanoi: NXB Sự Thật, 1972.

Hoài Thanh. *Có một nền văn hóa Việt Nam* (There is a Vietnamese culture). Hanoi: Hội Văn Hóa Cứu Quốc, 1946.

———. "Một thái độ cần xét lại" (An attitude that needs to be revised). *Văn Nghệ,* no. 7 (December 1948), p 2–5.

———. "Tôi đã sai lầm như thế nào trong việc phê bình bài 'Nhất định thắng' của anh Trần Dần" (How I was wrong in criticizing Trần Dần's poem "We Must Win"). *Văn Nghệ,* no. 139 (20–26 September 1956).

———. "Tự phê bình về quyển 'Nói chuyện thơ kháng chiến'" (Self-criticism concerning the volume *Talking about Resistance Poetry*). *Văn Nghệ,* no. 42 (August 1953).

Hoài Thanh and Hoài Chân. *Thi nhân Việt Nam, 1932–1941* (Vietnamese poets, 1932–1941). Hanoi: NXB Văn Học, [1942] 1988.

Hoàng Cầm. "Em bé lên sáu" (The child of six). In *Giai Phẩm Mùa Thu, Tập II,* 15–19. Hanoi: Minh Đức, 1956.

———. "Tiến tới xét lại một vụ án văn học: Con người Trần Dần, hồi ký của Hoàng Cầm" (Toward a reassessment of a literary case: The person of Trần Dần, a memoir of Hoàng Cầm). *Nhân Văn*, no. 1 (20 September 1956).

Hoàng Ngọc Thành. *Những phản ảnh xã hội và chính trị trong tiểu thuyết miền Bắc* (Social and political reflections in North Vietnamese novels). Saigon: Phong Trào Văn Hóa, 1969.

Hoàng Văn Chí. *Tâm trạng của giới văn nghệ ở miền Bắc* (The disposition of the intellectual circle in the north). Saigon: N.p., 1956.

———. *Trăm hoa đua nở trên đất Bắc* (One hundred flowers bloom in the north). Saigon: Mặt Trận Bảo Vệ Tự Do Văn Hóa, 1959.

———, ed. *The New Class in North Vietnam*. Saigon: Cong Dan, 1958.

Hobsbawm, E. J. *Radicalism and the Origins of the Vietnamese Revolution*. Cambridge: Harvard University Press, 1992.

———. *Revolutionaries: Contemporary Essays*. New York: New American Library, 1973.

"Hội nghị tranh luận văn nghệ tại Việt Bắc 25–26–27–28 tháng 9–1949" (The Conference of Debate on literature and art in Viet Bac, 25–28 September 1949). *Văn Nghệ*, nos. 17–18 (November–December 1949).

Hội Nhà Văn Việt Nam. *Nhà văn Việt Nam hiện đại* (Contemporary Vietnamese writers). Hanoi: NXB Hội Nhà Văn, 1997.

Hunt, Lynn. *Politics, Culture, and Class in the French Revolution*. Berkeley: University of California Press, 1984.

Hữu Loan. "Cũng những thằng nịnh hót" (Again those who sing praises). In *Giai Phẩm Mùa Thu, Tập II*. Hanoi: Minh Đức, 1956, 59–62.

———. "Lộn sòng" (Fraudulence). In *Giai Phẩm Mùa Đông, 1956*. Hanoi: Minh Đức, 1956, 36–44.

———. "Phê bình 'Thơ chiến sĩ' của Hồ Khải Đại (Giải Thưởng Văn Học 54–55 của Hội Văn Nghệ Việt Nam)" (Critique of "A Soldier's Poems" by Hồ Khải Đại [Winner of Literary Prize 54–55 of the Association of Art and Literature of Vietnam]). *Văn Nghệ*, no. 142 (11–17 October 1956).

Hữu Mai. "Để rõ thêm chân tướng phản động của Trần Dần" (To better understand Trần Dần's reactionary profile). *Văn Nghệ Quân Đội* (May 1958).

Huynh Kim Khanh. *Vietnamese Communism, 1925–1945*. Ithaca: Cornell University Press, 1982.

Huynh Sanh Thong, trans. *The Tale of Kieu*. New Haven: Yale University Press, 1983.

———, trans. *An Anthology of Vietnamese Poems: From the Eleventh through the Twentieth Centuries*. New Haven: Yale University Press, 1996.

Jamieson, Neil. *Understanding Vietnam*. Berkeley: University of California Press, 1993.

Johnson, Chalmers A. *Peasant Nationalism and Communist Power: The Emergence of Revolutionary China, 1937–1945*. Stanford: Stanford University Press, 1962.

Jowitt, Kenneth. "An Organizational Approach to the Study of Political Culture in Marxist-Leninist Systems." *American Political Science Review* 68, no. 3 (September 1974).

Kelly, Gail P. "Franco-Vietnamese Schools, 1918 to 1938." Ph.D. diss., University of Wisconsin-Madison, 1975.

————. *Franco-Vietnamese Schools, 1918–1938: Regional Development and Implications for National Integration.* Madison: Center for Southeast Asian Studies, University of Wisconsin, 1982.

Kerkvliet, Benedict J. Tria. "Village-State Relations in Vietnam: The Effect of Everyday Politics on De-collectivization." *Journal of Asian Studies* 54, no. 2 (1988).

Kim Thi. "Phạm Thị Hoài với giải Liberaturpreis" (Phạm Thị Hoài and the Liberaturpreis prize). *Hợp Lưu,* no. 14 (December 1993–January 1994): 193.

Konrad, George, and Ivan Szelenyi. *The Intellectuals on the Road to Class Power.* Translated by Andrew Arato and Richard E. Allen. New York: Harcourt Brace Jovanovich, 1979.

Kurihara, Hirohide. "Changes in the Literary Policy of the Vietnamese Workers' Party, 1956–1958." In *Indochina in the 1940s and 1950s,* edited by Takashi Shiraishi and Motoo Furuta. Vol. 2. Ithaca: Southeast Asia Program, Cornell University, 1992.

Laing, David. *The Marxist Theory of Art.* Sussex: Harvester, 1978.

Lê Đạt. "Làm thơ" (Writing poetry). In *Giai Phẩm Mùa Xuân, 1956.* Hanoi: Minh Đức, 1956:3–4.

————. "Mới" (New). In *Giai Phẩm Mùa Xuân, 1956.* Hanoi: Minh Đức, 1956: 28–29.

————. "Mỗi ngày mỗi lớn" (Growing bigger each day). In *Giai Phẩm Mùa Xuân, 1956.* Hanoi: Minh Đức, 1956:35–36.

Le Duan. *This Nation and Socialism Are One.* Chicago: Vanguard, 1976.

Lê Duẩn, Trường Chinh, Phạm Văn Đồng, and Tố Hữu. *Về đường lối giáo dục xã hội chủ nghĩa* (On the method of socialist education). Hanoi: NXB Sự Thật, 1979.

Lê Hữu Mục. *Thân thế và sự nghiệp Nhất Linh* (The life and career of Nhất Linh). Hue: Nhận Thức, 1958.

Lê Quang Đạo. "Nhớ lại việc truyền đạt bản 'Đề Cương Về Văn Hóa Việt Nam' ở Hà Nội" (Remembering the transmission of the "Theses on Vietnamese Culture" in Hanoi). In *Một chặng đường văn hóa: Tập hồi ức và tư liệu về Đề Cương Văn Hóa của Đảng và đời sống tư tưởng văn nghệ, 1943–1948* (A cultural stage: A collection of memoirs and documents on the Party's "Theses on Culture" and on the ideological and intellectual life, 1943–1948). Hanoi: NXB Tác Phẩm Mới, 1985.

Lockhart, Greg, and Monique Lockhart. *The Light of the Capital: Three Modern Vietnamese Classics.* Kuala Lumpur and New York: Oxford University Press, 1996.

Luong, Hy V. *Revolution in the Village: Tradition and Transformation in North Vietnam, 1925–1988.* Honolulu: University of Hawaii Press, 1992.

Mã Giang Lân. "Quá trình hiện đại hóa văn học Việt Nam, 1900–1945" (The modernizing process of Vietnamese literature, 1900–1945). In *Quá trình hiện đại hóa văn học Việt Nam, 1900–1945,* edited by Mã Giang Lân. Hanoi: NXB Văn Hóa Thông Tin, 2000.

MacFarquhar, Roderick. *The Hundred Flowers Campaign and the Chinese Intellectuals.* New York: Praeger, 1960.

Mai Hương, ed. *Nhà Xuất Bản Mai Lĩnh* (Mai Lĩnh Publishing House). Hanoi: NXB Hội Nhà Văn, 1997.

Malarney, Shaun Kingsley. "Ritual and Revolution in Viet Nam." Ph.D. diss., University of Michigan, 1993.

Mao Tse-Tung. *On New Democracy*. Peking: Foreign Language Press, 1967.

———. "Talks at the Yenan Forum on Literature and Art." In *Selected Works of Mao Tse-Tung*. Vol. 3. Peking: Foreign Language Press, 1967.

Marr, David. *Vietnam*. Oxford: Clio, 1992.

———. *Vietnam, 1945: The Quest for Power*. Berkeley: University of California Press, 1995.

———. *Vietnamese Anticolonialism, 1885–1925*. Berkeley: University of California Press, 1971.

———. *Vietnam's Tradition on Trial, 1925–1945*. Berkeley: University of California Press, 1983.

McAllister, John T., and Paul Mus. *The Vietnamese and Their Revolution*. New York: Harper and Row, 1970.

McHale, Shawn Frederick. "Printing, Power, and the Transformation of Vietnamese Culture, 1920–1945." Ph.D. diss., Cornell University, 1995.

Medvedev, Roy. *On Soviet Dissent: Interviews with Piero Ostelino*. New York: Columbia University Press, 1980.

Minh Hoàng. "Đống máy" (The pile of machines). *Văn*, 27 December 1957.

Mohan, Raj P., ed. *The Mythmakers: Intellectuals and the Intelligentsia in Perspective*. Westport, Conn.: Greenwood, 1987.

Moise, Edwin E. *Land Reform in China and North Vietnam: Consolidating the Revolution at the Village Level*. Chapel Hill: University of North Carolina Press, 1983.

Một chặng đường văn hóa: Tập hồi ức và tư liệu về Đề Cương Văn Hóa của Đảng và đời sống tư tưởng văn nghệ, 1943–1948 (A cultural stage: A collection of memoirs and documents on the Party's "Theses on Culture" and on the ideological and intellectual life, 1943–1948). Hanoi: NXB Tác Phẩm Mới, 1985.

"Một đợt học tập và đấu tranh" (A wave of studying and struggling). *Nhân Văn*, 20 September 1956.

Mus, Paul. *Sociologie d'une guerre*. Paris: Editions du Seuil, 1952.

Nam Cao. "Bốn cây số cách căn cứ địch" (Four kilometers from the enemy's base). In *Tuyển tập truyện ngắn Việt Nam (1945–1954)*, edited by Phan Cự Đệ and Hà Văn Đức. Hanoi: NXB Đại Học và Giáo Dục Chuyên Nghiệp, 1988.

———. "Đôi mắt" (Pair of eyes). In *Tuyển tập truyện ngắn Việt Nam (1945–1954)* (Selected Vietnamese short stories [1945–1954]), edited by Phan Cự Đệ and Hà Văn Đức. Hanoi: NXB Đại Học và Giáo Dục Chuyên Nghiệp, 1988.

"Nghị quyết của Đại Hội Văn Nghệ Toàn Quốc lần thứ hai" (Resolution of the Second National Congress of Art and Literature). *Nhân Dân*, 5 March 1957.

Nghiêm Xuân Hồng. *Phong trào quốc gia Việt Nam* (The Vietnamese nationalist movement). Saigon: Quan Điểm, 1958.

Ngô Ngọc Bội. *Ác mộng* (Nightmare). Hanoi: NXB Lao Động, 1990.

Ngô Văn Cát. *Việt Nam chống nạn thất học* (Vietnam against illiteracy). Hanoi: NXB Giáo Dục, 1980.

Ngo Vinh Long. *Before the Revolution: The Vietnamese Peasant under the French*. New York: Columbia University Press, [1973] 1991.

Nguyễn Bách Khoa. *Kinh Thi Viet Nam* (Vietnamese classical odes). Houston: Xuân Thu, [1945] 1976.

———. *Nguyễn Công Trứ*. Hanoi: Thế Giới, [194?] 1951.

———. *Văn chương Truyện Kiều* (The literature of the *Tale of Kiều*). Hanoi: Hàn Thuyên, 1945.

Nguyễn Cao Luyện and Hoàng Như Tiệp. "Thực chất của 'Nhà Ánh Sáng'" (The reality of the "House of Light"). *Văn Nghệ*, no. 41 (July 1953).

Nguyễn Công Hoan. *Đời viết văn của tôi* (My writing life). Hanoi: NXB Văn Học, 1971.

Nguyễn Đăng Mạnh. Introduction to *Tuyển tập Nguyễn Tuân* (Selected works of Nguyễn Tuân). Vol. 1. Hanoi: NXB Văn Học, 1991.

Nguyễn Đinh Thi. "Một vài sai lầm khuyết điểm trong sự lãnh đạo văn nghệ" (Some mistakes and errors in the leadership of art and literature). *Văn Nghệ*, no. 140 (27 September–3 October 1956).

———. "Nhận đường" (Recognizing the way). In *Cách mạng, kháng chiến và đời sống văn học (1945–1954): Hồi ức-kỷ niệm*, (Revolution, resistance, and the literary life [1945–1954]: Reminiscences-memories), edited by Viện Văn Học. Vol. 1. Hanoi: NXB Tác Phẩm Mới, 1985.

———. "Những sai lầm về tư tưởng trong tập sách Giai Phẩm" (Ideological mistakes in the *Giai Phẩm* volume). *Văn Nghệ*, no. 118 (26 April–3 May 1956).

———. "Tim nghĩa hiện thực mới" (Seeking the meaning of the new realism). *Văn Nghệ*, no. 10 (March 1949), 2–10.

Nguyễn Hoành Khung. "Nhóm Thanh Nghị" (The Thanh Nghi group). In *Từ điển văn học* (Literary dictionary), edited by Đỗ Đức Hiểu et al. Vol. 2. Hanoi: NXB Khoa Học Xã Hội, 1984.

Nguyễn Hoành Khung et al., eds. *Văn xuôi lãng mạn Việt Nam (1930–1945)* (Vietnamese romantic prose [1930–1945]). 8 vols. Hanoi: NXB Khoa Học Xã Hội, 1989–90.

Nguyên Hồng. "Tuần báo Văn và một số bài cần được nhận định như thế nào?" (How should the weekly *Văn* and a number of articles be assessed?), *Văn*, 6 August 1957.

Nguyễn Hưng Quốc. *Văn học Việt Nam dưới chế độ Cộng Sản* (Vietnamese literature under the Communist regime). Stanton, Calif.: Van Nghe, 1991.

Nguyễn Hữu Đang. "Cần phải chính quy hơn nữa" (The need for more regularization). *Nhân Văn*, no. 4 (5 November 1956).

Nguyễn Hữu Đang and Nguyễn Đình Thi. *Một nền văn hóa mới* (A new culture). Hanoi: Hội Văn Hóa Cứu Quốc Việt Nam, 1945.

Nguyen Khac Vien. "Confucianism and Marxism." In *Tradition and Revolution in Vietnam*. Berkeley: Indochina Resource Center, 1974.

Nguyen Khanh Toan. *Twenty Years' Development of Education in the Democratic Republic of Vietnam*. Hanoi: Ministry of Education, 1965.

Nguyễn Mạnh Tường. "Concerning Mistakes Committed in Land Reform." In *The New Class in North Vietnam*, edited by Hoàng Văn Chí. Saigon: Cong Dan, 1958.

———. "Vừa khóc vừa cười" (Crying and laughing simultaneously), In *Giai Phẩm Mùa Thu, Tập III*. Hanoi: Minh Đức, 1956, 22–25.

Nguyen Minh Duong. "The System of Middle Technical Schools and Vocational Schools." In *Education in Vietnam, 1945–1991*, edited by Pham Minh Hac. Hanoi: Ministry of Education and Training, 1991.

Nguyên Ngọc, "Con đường đi của Phùng Quán, con đường sai lầm điển hình của một người viết văn trẻ" (Phùng Quán's path: The model of the incorrect path of a young writer). *Văn Nghệ Quân Đội* (April 1958).

Nguyễn Ngọc Thiện and Lữ Huy Nguyên, eds. *Tao Đàn, 1939*. Hanoi: NXB Văn Học, 1998.

Nguyễn Quang Thiều. "Nhà văn Vũ Bằng: Người tình báo mang bí số X10" (The writer Vũ Bằng: The secret agent X10). *Nhân Dân*, 21 April 2000.

Nguyễn Tế Mỹ, *Hai Bà Trưng khởi nghĩa* (The Trưng sisters' uprising). Hanoi: Hàn Thuyên, 1944?

Nguyễn Tuân. "Nhìn rõ sai lầm" (Seeing the errors clearly). *Văn Nghệ*, no. 41 (July 1953).

———. "Phê bình nhất định là khó" (Criticism is definitely difficult). *Văn*, 11 October 1957.

———. "Phở." *Văn*, 10–17 May 1957.

———. "Trò chuyện" (Conversation). In *Cách mạng, kháng chiến và đời sống văn học (1945–1954)* (Revolution, resistance, and the literary life [1945–1954]), edited by Viện Văn Học. Vol. 3. Hanoi: NXB Tác Phẩm Mới, 1985–93.

———. *Tùy bút* (Essays). Glendale, Calif.: Đại Nam, [1941, 1943] 1986?

———. *Vang bóng một thời* (Echoes and shadows of an era). Hanoi: Tân Dân, 1940.

Nguyễn Văn Bổng. "Nhận lại phương hướng qua việc phê bình tuần báo VĂN" (Reassess direction through the criticism of the weekly *VĂN*). *Văn*, 20 September 1957.

Nguyen Van Huyen. *Sixteen Years' Development of National Education in the Democratic Republic of Vietnam*. Hanoi: Foreign Languages Publishing House, 1961.

Nguyễn Vỹ. *Văn thi sĩ tiền chiến: Chứng dẫn của một thời đại* (Prewar writers and poets: Testimony to an era). Saigon: Khai Trí, 1970.

Nhà văn Việt Nam hiện đại: Nhân kỷ niệm 35 năm thành lập Hội Nhà Văn Việt Nam (Contemporary Vietnamese writers: On the occasion commemorating thirty-five years of the Vietnamese Writers' Association). Hanoi: Hội Nhà Văn Việt Nam, 1992.

Nhà Xuất Bản Văn Học. *35 năm văn học, 1948–1983* (Thirty-five years of literature, 1948–1983). Hanoi: NXB Van Hoc, 1983.

Nhóm Lê Quý Đôn. *Lược thảo lịch sử văn học Việt Nam* (A summary of Vietnamese literary history). Hanoi: Xây Dựng, 1957.

Như Phong, "Hoạt động của Hội Văn Hóa Cứu Quốc" (The activities of the Cultural Association for National Salvation). In *Một chặng đường văn hóa: Tập hồi ức và tư liệu về Đề Cương Văn Hóa của Đảng và đời sống tư tưởng văn nghệ, 1943–1948* (A cultural stage: A collection of memoirs and documents on the Party's "Theses on Culture" and on the ideological and intellectual life, 1943–1948). Hanoi: NXB Tác Phẩm Mới, 1985.

Nisbet, Robert A. *The Quest for Community*. London: Oxford University Press [1953] 1978.

Norbu, Dawa. *Culture and the Politics of Third World Nationalism*. London and New York: Routledge, 1992.

Phạm Duy. *Hồi ký thời cách mạng kháng chiến* (Memoir of the resistance period). Midway City, Calif.: PDC Musical Productions, 1989.

———. "Những bước đầu (trong nửa thế kỷ tân nhạc)" (The first steps [in the half century of modern music]). *Hợp Lưu* (Garden Grove, Calif.), no. 17 (June–July 1994), 23–41.

Pham Minh Hac, ed. *Education in Vietnam, 1945–1991.* Hanoi: Ministry of Education and Training, 1991.

Phạm Thế Ngũ. *Việt Nam văn học sử giản ước tân biên, Tập III: Văn học hiện đại, 1862–1945* (A new outline history of Vietnamese literature, volume 3: Contemporary literature, 1862–1945). Saigon: Anh Phương, 1965.

———. *Việt Nam văn học sử giản ước tân biên.* 3 vols. Reprint ed., with a preface by Trần Hữu Tá. [Sa Dec]: NXB Dong Thap, [1965] 1997.

Phan Cự Đệ. Introduction to *Tuyển tập truyện ngắn Việt Nam (1945–1954),* edited by Phan Cự Đệ and Hà Văn Đức (Hanoi: NXB Đại Học và Giáo Dục Chuyên Nghiệp, 1988).

Phan Cự Đệ and Hà Văn Đức, eds. *Tuyển tập truyện ngắn Việt Nam (1945–1954)* (Selected Vietnamese short stories [1945–1954]). Hanoi: NXB Đại Học và Giáo Dục Chuyên Nghiệp, 1988.

Phan Khôi. "Phê bình lãnh đạo văn nghệ" (Criticizing the leadership of art and literature), In *Giai Phẩm Mùa Thu, Tập I.* Hanoi: Minh Đức, 1956, 3–16.

Phan Ngọc. *Văn hóa Việt Nam và cách tiếp cận mới* (Vietnamese culture and the new approach). Hanoi: NXB Văn Hóa-Thông Tin, 1994.

Phong Lê, Vũ Tuấn Anh, and Vũ Đức Phúc. *Văn học Việt Nam kháng chiến chống Pháp (1945–1954)* (Vietnamese literature in the anti-French resistance [1945–1954]). Hanoi: NXB Khoa Học Xã Hội, 1986.

Phùng Quán. "Chống tham ô lãng phí" (Against corruption and waste). In *Giai Phẩm Mùa Thu, Tập II.* Hanoi: Minh Đức, 1956, 39–42.

———. "Thi sĩ và công nhân" (Poets and workers). In *Giai Phẩm Mùa Xuân, 1956.* Hanoi: Minh Đức, 1956, 27.

———. *Vượt Côn Đảo* (Escape from Côn Đảo). Hue: NXB Thuận Hóa, [1955] 1987.

Pike, Douglas. *PAVN: People's Army of Vietnam.* Novato, Calif.: Presidio, 1986.

Q. Ngọc and T. Hồng. "Phê bình lãnh đạo sinh viên (Criticism of the leadership of the university students). *Đất Mới,* 10 November 1956.

Remnick, David. *Lenin's Tomb: The Last Days of the Soviet Empire.* New York: Random House, 1993.

Rieff, Phillip, ed. *On Intellectuals: Theoretical Studies/Case Studies.* New York: Doubleday, 1970.

Rudman, Herbert C. *The School and the State in the USSR.* New York: Macmillan, 1967.

Schurmann, Franz. *Ideology and Organization in Communist China.* Berkeley: University of California Press, 1968.

Scott, James C. *Weapons of the Weak: Everyday Forms of Peasant Resistance.* New Haven: Yale University Press, 1985.

Selden, Mark. *The Yenan Way in Revolutionary China.* Cambridge: Harvard University Press, 1971.

Shils, Edward. *The Intellectual between Tradition and Modernity: The Indian Situation.* The Hague: Mouton, 1961.

————. *The Intellectuals and the Powers and other Essays.* Chicago: University of Chicago Press, 1972.

Smith, Anthony D. S. *Nationalism in the Twentieth Century.* New York: New York University Press, 1979.

Sơ thảo lịch sử văn học Việt Nam, 1930–1945 (An outline of Vietnamese literary history, 1930–1945). Hanoi: NXB Văn Học, 1964.

Sóng Hồng [Trường Chinh]. *Thơ* (Poetry). Hanoi: NXB Văn Học, 1983.

Spechler, Dina. *Permitted Dissent in the USSR: Novy Mir and the Soviet Regime.* New York: Praeger, 1982.

Swayze, Harold. *Political Control of Literature in the USSR, 1946–1959.* Cambridge: Harvard University Press, 1962.

Tai, Hue-Tam Ho. *Millenarianism and Peasant Politics in Vietnam.* Cambridge: Harvard University Press, 1983.

————. *Radicalism and the Origins of the Vietnamese Revolution.* Cambridge; Harvard University Press, 1992.

Tập văn cách mạng và kháng chiến (A collection of revolutionary and resistance literature). N.p.: Hội Văn Nghệ Việt Nam, 1949.

Taylor, Keith Weller. *The Birth of Vietnam.* Berkeley: University of California Press, 1983.

Tế Hanh. "Quan niệm siêu giai cấp của tôi về nhất tính và con người mới" (My above class view of humanity and the new person). *Nhân Dân,* 14 March 1958.

Thanh Lãng. *Phê bình văn học thế hệ 1932* (Literary criticism of the generation of 1932). 2 vols. Saigon: Phong Trào Văn Hóa, 1972–73.

Thayer, Carlyle A. "Political Reform in Vietnam: Doi Moi and the Emergence of Civil Society." In *The Developments of Civil Society in Communist Systems,* edited by Robert F. Miller. Sydney: Allen and Unwin, 1992.

Thế Lữ. "Những sợi dây trói buộc tôi trên đường phục vụ cách mạng" (The ties that bind me on the road in the service of the revolution). *Văn Nghệ,* no. 41 (July 1953).

Tô Hoài. *Cát bụi chân ai* (Dust upon whose feet). Hanoi: NXB Hội Nhà Văn, 1992.

————. *Chiều chiều* (Evening). Hanoi: NXB Hội Nhà Văn, 1999.

————. "Góp thêm vài ý kiến về con người thời đại" (To contribute a few thoughts on the people of the age). *Văn,* 4 October 1957.

————. "Nhận xét về tư tưởng của tôi" (Assessment of my thoughts). *Văn Nghệ,* no. 45, (November 1953).

————. "Nhìn lại một số sai lầm trong bài báo và công tác" (Reconsidering a number of mistakes in newspaper articles and work). *Nhân Dân,* 12 March 1958.

Tố Hữu. "Tổng kết cuộc đấu tranh chống nhóm Nhân Văn-Giai Phẩm" (Summarizing the struggle against the Nhan Van–Giai Pham clique). *Văn Học,* no. 3 (15 June 1958).

Tô Ngọc Vân. "Học hay không học?" (Study or not?). *Văn Nghệ,* no. 10 (March 1949), 54–58.

————. "Tâm sự một người bị đầu độc" (Confidences of one who has been poisoned). *Văn Nghệ,* no. 41 (July 1953).

———. "Vẫn tranh tuyên truyền và hội họa" (Still on propaganda paintings and art). *Văn Nghệ*, no. 2 (April–May 1948), 9–18.

Tôn Thất Tùng. *Đường vào khoa học của tôi* (My path to science). Hanoi: NXB Khoa Học Xã Hội, 1984.

Trần Công. "Về vấn đề lãnh đạo của Phòng Văn Nghệ Quân Đội" (On the leadership of the Army Office of Art and Literature). *Văn Nghệ*, no. 136 (30 August–5 September 1956).

Trần Dần. "Lão Rồng" (Old man Rồng). In *Giai Phẩm Mùa Xuân, 1956*. Hanoi: Minh Đức, 1956, 45–47.

———. "Nhất định thắng" (We must win). In *Giai Phẩm Mùa Xuân, 1956*. Hanoi: Minh Đức, 1956, 13–25.

Trần Dần, Trần Mai Châu, and Vũ Hoàng Địch. "Bản tuyên ngôn tượng trưng" (A declaration of symbolism). *Dạ Đài* (The netherworld), 6 November 1946.

Trần Độ. "Hai cuộc 'vận động văn hóa'" (Two "cultural campaigns"). In *Một chặng đường văn hóa: Tập hồi ức và tư liệu về Đề Cương Văn Hóa của Đảng và đời sống tư tưởng văn nghệ 1943–1948*. Hanoi: NXB Tác Phẩm Mới, 1985.

———. "Từ bản Đề Cương Văn Hóa Việt Nam năm 1943 nghĩ về văn hóa Việt Nam hiện nay" (From the 1943 "Theses on Vietnamese Culture" to thinking about contemporary Vietnamese culture). In *Bốn mươi năm Đề Cương Văn Hóa Việt Nam* (Forty years of the "Theses on Vietnamese culture"). Hanoi: NXB Sự Thật, 1985.

Trần Đức Thảo. "Nỗ lực phát triển tự do dân chủ" (The effort to foster democratic freedom). *Nhân Văn*, 15 October 1956.

Trần Hữu Tá. "Một công trình nghiên cứu đáng quí" (A respected research endeavor). In Phạm Thế Ngũ, *Việt Nam văn học sử giản ước tân biên*. Vol. 1. Sa Đéc: NXB Đồng Tháp, [1965] 1997.

Trần Huy Liệu. *Hồi ký Trần Huy Liệu* (Trần Huy Liệu's memoir). Hanoi: NXB Khoa Học Xã Hội, 1991.

Trần Thanh Mại. "Quan điểm và lập trường tư tưởng của một người tự xưng là Mác-Xít-Lê-Ni-Nít" (The views and ideological standpoint of a person who claimed to be Marxist-Leninist). *Nhân Dân*, 2–14 January 1957.

Trần Văn Giàu. *Sự phát triển tư tưởng ở Việt Nam từ thế kỷ XIX đến Cách mạng Tháng 8* (Intellectual development in Vietnam from the nineteenth century to the August Revolution). 2 vols. Hanoi: NXB Khoa Học Xã Hội, 1973–75.

Trinh Van Thao. *Vietnam du Confucianisme au Communisme*. Paris: L'Harmattan, 1990.

Trung Tâm Khoa Học Xã Hội và Nhân Văn Quốc Gia. *50 năm Đề Cương về Văn Hóa Việt Nam* (Fifty years of the "Theses on Vietnamese Culture"). Hanoi: NXB Khoa Học Xã Hội, 1995.

Trung Tâm Nghiên Cứu Quốc Học. *Luận về quốc học* (Debate on national culture). Danang: NXB Đà Nẵng và Trung Tâm Nghiên Cứu Quốc Học, 1999.

Truong Buu Lam, ed. *Borrowings and Adaptations in Vietnamese Culture*. Southeast Asia Papers, no. 25. Honolulu: Southeast Asian Studies, Center for Asian and Pacific Studies, University of Hawaii-Manoa, 1987.

———. *Patterns of Vietnamese Response to Foreign Intervention, 1858–1900.* New Haven: Council on Southeast Asian Studies, Yale University, 1967.

Trường Chinh. "Chủ nghĩa Mác và văn hóa Việt Nam" (Marxism and Vietnamese culture). In *Về văn hóa và nghệ thuật.* Vol. 1. Hanoi: NXB Văn Học, 1985.

———. "Đề Cương về Văn Hóa Việt Nam" (Theses on Vietnamese culture). In *Một chặng đường văn hóa: Tập hồi ức và tư liệu về Đề Cương Văn Hóa của Đảng và đời sống tư tưởng văn nghệ, 1943–1948.* Hanoi: NXB Tác Phẩm Mới, 1985.

———. "Mấy nguyên tắc lớn của cuộc vận động văn hóa mới Việt Nam lúc này" (Some major principles of the current movement of new Vietnamese culture). In *Về văn hóa và nghệ thuật.* Vol. 1. Hanoi: NXB Văn Học, 1985.

———. "Mấy vấn đề thắc mắc về văn nghệ" (Some issues of concern on literature and art). *Văn Nghệ,* no. 6 (October–November 1948), 1–8.

———. "Một con quỷ đội lốt Mác Xít" (A devil under the Marxist guise). In *Về văn hóa và nghệ thuật.* Vol. 1. Hanoi: NXB Văn Học, 1985.

———. *Về văn hóa và nghệ thuật* (On culture and the arts). 2 vols. Hanoi: NXB Văn Học, 1985.

Truong Chinh and Vo Nguyen Giap. *The Peasant Question (1937–1938).* Translated by Christine Pelzer White. Data Papers, no. 94. Ithaca: Southeast Asia Program, Cornell University, 1974.

Trương Tửu. "Bệnh sùng bái cá nhân trong giới lãnh đạo văn nghệ" (The sickness of the cult of personality within the leadership of art and literature). In *Giai Phẩm Mùa Thu, Tập II.* Hanoi: Minh Đức, 1956, 3–14.

———. "Tự do tư tưởng của văn nghệ sĩ và sự lãnh đạo của Đảng Cộng Sản Bôn-Sê-Vích" (Freedom of thought of intellectuals and the leadership of the Bolshevik Community Party). In *Giai Phẩm Mùa Đông, 1956, Tập I.* Hanoi: Minh Đức, 1956, 3–10, 63–72.

———. *Văn nghệ và chính trị* (Literature and art and politics). In *Giai Phẩm Mùa Thu 1956, Tập III.* Hanoi: Minh Đức, 1956, 3–18.

Tướng Nguyễn Sơn (General Nguyễn Sơn). Hanoi: NXB Lao Động, 1994.

Turley, William S., ed. *Vietnamese Communism in Comparative Perspective.* Boulder: Westview, 1980.

Tuyển tập Nguyễn Tuân (Selected works of Nguyễn Tuân). Selected and introduced by Nguyễn Đăng Mạnh. 2 vols. Hanoi: NXB Văn Học, 1991.

Văn nghệ vũ khí sắc bén (Art and literature: A sharp weapon). Hanoi: NXB Văn Học, 1962.

Văn Tâm. "'Vũ Như Tô' trong cuộc đời 'bát nháo'" ("Vũ Như Tô" in the "Chaotic" Life). Paper presented at a conference commemorating the life and works of the writer Nguyễn Huy Tưởng, Institute of Literature, Hanoi, 12 May 1992.

Vasavakul, Thaveeporn. "Schools and Politics in South and North Vietnam: A Comparative Study of State Apparatus, State Policy, and State Power (1945–1965)." Ph.D. diss., Cornell University, 1994.

Vella, Walter F., ed. *Aspects of Vietnamese History.* Asian Studies at Hawaii, no. 8. Honolulu: University Press of Hawaii, 1973.

Verdery, Katherine. *National Ideology under Socialism: Ideology and Cultural Politics in Ceaucescu's Romania.* Berkeley: University of California Press, 1991.

Viện Nghiên Cứu Hồ Chí Minh và các Lãnh Tụ của Đảng, ed. *Trường Chinh và*

Cách Mạng Việt Nam (Trường Chinh and the Vietnamese revolution). Hanoi: NXB Chính Trị Quốc Gia, 1997.

Viện Văn Học, ed. *Cách mạng, kháng chiến và đời sống văn học (1945–1954): Hồi ức-ký niệm* (Revolution, resistance, and the literary life [1945–1954]: Reminiscences-memories). 3 vols. Hanoi: NXB Tác Phẩm Mới, 1985–93.

Võ Nguyên Giáp, "Cách Mạng Tháng Tám, kháng chiến, đổi mới: Những cống hiến sáng tạo nổi bật của anh Trường Chinh" (The August Revolution, the resistance, renovation: Trường Chinh's notable creative contributions). In *Trường Chinh và Cách Mạng Việt Nam* (Trường Chinh and the Vietnamese revolution), edited by Viện Nghiên Cứu Hồ Chí Minh và các Lãnh Tụ của Đảng. Hanoi: NXB Chính Trị Quốc Gia, 1997.

Võ Thuần Nho, ed. *35 năm phát triển sự nghiệp giáo dục phổ thông* (Thirty-five years of the development of general education). Hanoi: NXB Giáo Dục, 1980.

Võ Văn Trực. *Chuyện làng ngày ấy* (Village stories in those days). Hanoi: NXB Lao Động, 1993.

Vũ Bằng. *40 năm "nói láo"* (Forty years of "lying"). Saigon: Phạm Quang Khải, 1969.

Vũ Cao, "Ý thức phá hoại và tư tưởng đồi trụy của Hoàng Cầm" (Hoàng Cầm's destructive tendency and depraved ideology). *Văn Nghệ Quân Đội* (April 1958).

Vũ Đức Phúc. *Bàn về những cuộc đấu tranh tư tưởng trong lịch sử văn học Việt Nam hiện đại (1930–1954)* (On discussing the ideological battles in modern Vietnamese literary history [1930–1945]). Hanoi: NXB Khoa Học Xã Hội, 1971.

———. *Trên mặt trận văn học: Phê bình-tiểu luận* (On the literary front: Criticism-essays). Hanoi: NXB Văn Học, 1972.

Vũ Ngọc Khanh. *Tìm hiểu nền giáo dục Việt Nam trước 1945* (Understanding the Vietnamese educational system prior to 1945). Hanoi: NXB Giáo Dục, 1985.

Vũ Ngọc Phan. *Những năm tháng ấy* (Those years). Hanoi: NXB Văn Học, 1987.

Vũ Tú Nam. "Sự thực về con người Trần Dần" (The truth about the person Trần Dần). *Văn Nghệ Quân Đội* (April 1958).

Vương Trí Nhàn. "Mặc cảm-tha hóa-phân thân trong tâm lý người cầm bút" (Complex-corruptiveness-self-division in the psychology of writers). *Cửa Việt* 15 (June 1992), p 65–71.

Werner, Jayne Susan. *Peasant Politics and Religious Sectarianism: Peasant and Priest in the Cao Dai in Viet Nam*. New Haven: Council on Southeast Asian Studies, Yale University, 1981.

Whitmore, John K. "Communism and History in Vietnam." In *Vietnamese Communism in Comparative Perspective*, edited by William S. Turley. Boulder: Westview, 1980.

———. *Vietnam, Ho Quy Ly, and the Ming (1371–1421)*. New Haven: Council on Southeast Asian Studies, Yale University, 1981.

Woodside, Alexander B. *Community and Revolution in Modern Vietnam*. Cambridge: Harvard University Press, 1976.

———. "The Struggle to Rethink the Vietnamese State in the Era of Market Economics." In *Culture and Economy: The Shaping of Capitalism in Eastern Asia,* edited by Timothy Brook and Hy V. Luong. Ann Arbor: University of Michigan Press, 1997.

———. "The Triumphs and Failures of Mass Education in Vietnam." *Pacific Affairs* 56, no. 3 (fall 1983).

———. *Vietnam and the Chinese Model: A Comparative Study of Vietnamese and Chinese Government in the First Half of the Nineteenth Century.* Cambridge: Council on East Asian Studies, Harvard University, 1988.

Xuân Diệu, "Dứt khoát" (Decisively). *Văn Nghệ,* no. 41 (July 1953).

Xuân Hoàng. *Âm vang thời chưa xa* (Echoes of a recent era). Hanoi: NXB Văn Học and Hội Văn Học Nghệ Thuật Quảng Bình, 1995.

Xuân Thu Nhã Tập. Reprint ed., with articles on *Xuân Thu Nhã Tập* selected by Nguyễn Bảo. Hanoi: NXB Văn Học, [1942] 1991.

Xuân Trường. "Cần xác định tự do của văn nghệ sĩ" (The need to assess the freedom of creative intellectuals). *Nhân Dân,* 6–8 January 1957.

Zahar, Renate. *Frantz Fanon: Colonialism and Alienation, Concerning Frantz Fanon's Political Theory.* New York: Monthly Review, 1974.

Zajda, Joseph I. *Education in the USSR.* Oxford: Pergamon, 1980.

Zinoman, Peter B. "The Colonial Bastille: A Social History of Imprisonment in Colonial Viet Nam, 1982–1940." Ph.D. diss., Cornell University, 1995.

Index

533 C9 FM 2565
07/13/06 32550   SELE